CLASSICS OF
SCIENCE FICTION AND FANTASY
LITERATURE

MAGILL'S CHOICE

CLASSICS OF
SCIENCE FICTION AND FANTASY
LITERATURE

Volume 1
Aegypt — Make Room! Make Room!
1 – 342

edited by
Fiona Kelleghan
University of Miami

SALEM PRESS, INC.
Pasadena, California   Hackensack, New Jersey

Library of Congress Cataloging-in-Publication Data
Classics of science fiction and fantasy literature / edited by Fiona Kelleghan.
    p. cm. — (Magill's choice)
"Plot summaries and analyses of 180 major books and series in the fields of science fiction and fantasy . . . all but eight of the essays in these volumes are taken directly from Salem Press's four-volume Magill's guide to science fiction and fantasy literature, which was published in 1996"—Publisher's note.
    Includes bibliographical references (p.) and index.
    ISBN 1-58765-050-9 (set : alk. paper) — ISBN 1-58765-051-7 (v. 1 : alk. paper) — ISBN 1-58765-052-5 (v. 2 : alk. paper)
    1. Science fiction—Stories, plots, etc. 2. Fantasy fiction—Stories, plots, etc. I. Kelleghan, Fiona, 1965-   II. Magill's guide to science fiction and fantasy literature. III. Series.

PN3433.4 .C565 2002
809.3'876—dc21

                                                                    2002001113

Contents

Contents

Publisher's Note

Classics of Science Fiction and Fantasy Literature is a two-volume set offering plot summaries and analyses of 180 major books and series in the fields of science fiction and fantasy. The titles it covers have been selected because they rank among the most frequently taught books in their fields in high school and undergraduate literature and cultural history courses. Articles are alphabetically arranged by titles and range from such childhood fantasy classics as Lewis Carroll's *Alice's Adventures in Wonderland* (1865) and L. Frank Baum's *The Wonderful Wizard of Oz* (1900) to such pioneering science-fiction works as H. G. Wells's *The War of the Worlds* (1898) and modern science-fiction and fantasy classics as Robert Heinlein's *The Moon Is a Harsh Mistress* (1966) and J. R. R. Tolkien's *Lord of the Rings* trilogy (1954-1955). Among other prominent writers whose books are covered here are science-fiction masters Isaac Asimov, Arthur C. Clarke, and Frank Herbert and writers John Crowley, Ellen Kushner, and C. S. Lewis. Immediately preceding the essays is noted scholar T. A. Shippey's broad survey of developments in the science-fiction and fantasy fields.

All but eight of the essays in these volumes are taken directly from Salem Press's four-volume *Magill's Guide to Science Fiction and Fantasy Literature*, which was published in 1996. The rest are entirely new articles on recently published works commissioned especially for this set. Each article discusses an individual book or series and often comments on other works by the same author. Individual articles open with basic reference information in a ready-reference format: author's name, his or her birth and death dates, identification of the work as either science fiction or fantasy, subgenre, type of work (such as drama, novel, novella, series, or story), time and location of plot, and date of first publication.

The main body of each essay contains two sections of nearly equal length. The first section is entitled "The Story" and the second "Analysis." The first section offers a brief summary of the work's plot and identifies major characters. The "Analysis" section offers a critical interpretation of the title. This section also identifies the literary devices and themes used in the work.

Readers will find several reference tools at the end of volume 2. These include an annotated bibliography and up-to-date lists of major science-fiction and fantasy award winners. Entirely new reference tools in this set include an annotated Web site list, a time line of book titles, and a general index. Author, title, and genre indexes are also provided to help readers find individual articles.

All essays are signed by their contributors, who include academicians, freelance writers, and independent scholars. A list of their names and affiliations appears at the beginning of the first volume. Salem's editors wish to thank them for their contributions. We wish especially to thank the set's Editor, Fiona Kelleghan of the University of Miami, who selected the works to be covered, provided a new introduction, and made numerous contributions to the set.

Contributors

Steve Anderson
University of Arkansas at Little Rock

Ronnie Apter
Central Michigan University

Gerald S. Argetsinger
Rochester Institute of Technology

Bryan Aubrey
Independent Scholar

Neal Baker
Dickinson College

Martha A. Bartter
Northeast Missouri State University

Karen S. Bellinfante
Independent Scholar

Nicholas Birns
New School University

Tim Blackmore
University of Western Ontario

Franz G. Blaha
University of Nebraska—Lincoln

Edra C. Bogle
University of North Texas

Janice M. Bogstad
University of Wisconsin—Eau Claire

Bernadette Lynn Bosky
Independent Scholar

Wendy Bousfield
Syracuse University

C. K. Breckenridge
Independent Scholar

John P. Brennan
*Indiana University—Purdue University
  at Fort Wayne*

Peter Brigg
University of Guelph

David Bromige
Sonoma State University

Edmund J. Campion
University of Tennessee

Shawn Carruth
Concordia College

Jeffrey Cass
Texas A&M International University

Christine R. Catron
St. Mary's University

Karen Rose Cercone
Indiana University of Pennsylvania

Daryl R. Coats
*Northwestern State University of
  Louisiana*

David W. Cole
University of Wisconsin—Baraboo

Peter Crawford
Independent Scholar

Shira Daemon
Independent Scholar

Radford B. Davis
Independent Scholar

Bill Delaney
Independent Scholar

Paul Dellinger
Independent Scholar

Francine Dempsey
College of St. Rose

Frank Dietz
University of Texas at Austin

Catherine Doyle
Christopher Newport University

Joyce Duncan
East Tennessee State University

Bernard J. Farber
Illinois Institute of Technology

James Feast
*Baruch College, City University of New
  York*

David Marc Fischer
Independent Scholar

Ronald Foust
Loyola University in New Orleans

D. Douglas Fratz
Independent Scholar

Jean C. Fulton
Landmark College

Charles Gannon
Fordham University

Tanya Gardiner-Scott
Mount Ida College

C. A. Gardner
Independent Scholar

Gayle Gaskill
College of St. Catherine

Marjorie Ginsberg
William Paterson College

Marc Goldstein
Independent Scholar

John L. Grigsby
Independent Scholar

Peter C. Hall
Independent Scholar

Betsy P. Harfst
Kishwaukee College

June Harris
University of Arizona

Darren Harris-Fain
Shawnee State University

Donald M. Hassler
Kent State University

Len Hatfield
*Virginia Polytechnic Institute and State
    University*

John C. Hawley
Santa Clara University

Robert W. Haynes
Texas A&M International University

Karen Hellekson
University of Kansas

David Hinckley
University of California, Riverside

John R. Holmes
Franciscan University of Steubenville

Susan Hwang
Independent Scholar

Earl G. Ingersoll
*State University of New York College,
    Brockport*

Alex Irvine
Independent Scholar

Archibald E. Irwin
Indiana University Southeast

John Jacob
Northwestern University

Daven M. Kari
California Baptist College

Cynthia Lee Katona
Ohlone College

U. Milo Kaufmann
*University of Illinois at Urbana—
    Champaign*

Kara K. Keeling
Christopher Newport University

Fiona Kelleghan
University of Miami

Richard Kelly
University of Tennessee

Howard A. Kerner
Polk Community College

Paul Kincaid
Independent Scholar

Jeff King
University of North Texas

Katharine Kittredge
Ithaca College

David C. Kopaska-Merkel
Dreams & Nightmares Magazine

Dennis M. Kratz
University of Texas at Dallas

Eugene Larson
Pierce College

William Laskowski
Jamestown College

Dianna Laurent
Southeastern Louisiana University

Steven Lehman
John Abbott College

Rania Lisas
Virginia Polytechnic Institute and State University

Janet Alice Long
Independent Scholar

Steven R. Luebke
University of Wisconsin—River Falls

R. C. Lutz
University of the Pacific

Robert McClenaghan
Independent Scholar

Andrew Macdonald
Loyola University, New Orleans

Edythe M. McGovern
West Los Angeles College

Edgar V. McKnight, Jr.
Gardner-Webb University

Kevin McNeilly
University of British Columbia

Willis E. McNelly
California State University, Fullerton

Daryl F. Mallett
Independent Scholar

Lawrence K. Mansour
University of Maryland

Joseph J. Marchesani
Pennsylvania State University— McKeesport

Wayne Martindale
Wheaton College

Charles E. May
California State University, Long Beach

Marvin E. Mengeling
University of Wisconsin—Oshkosh

Carole F. Meyers
Georgia Institute of Technology

Julia Meyers
Duquesne University

Joseph Milicia
University of Wisconsin—Sheboygan

Debra G. Miller
Eastern New Mexico University

Joseph Minne
Independent Scholar

Catherine Mintz
Independent Scholar

Trevor J. Morgan
Independent Scholar

Robert E. Morsberger
California State Polytechnic University, Pomona

Kevin P. Mulcahy
Rutgers University

Joseph M. Nassar
Rochester Institute of Technology

Keith Neilson
California State University, Fullerton

Jörg C. Neumann
University of Texas, Austin

George E. Nicholas
Benedictine College

John Nizalowski
Mesa State College

George T. Novotny
University of South Florida

Bruce Olsen
Alabama State University

D. Barrowman Park
Western Washington University

David Peck
California State University, Long Beach

Lawrence Person
Nova Express

Jefferson M. Peters
Kagoshima University

Thomas D. Petitjean, Jr.
Louisiana State University—Eunice

John R. Pfeiffer
Central Michigan University

Allene Phy-Olsen
Austin Peay State University

Clifton W. Potter, Jr.
Lynchburg College

Victoria Price
Lamar University

R. Kent Rasmussen
Independent Scholar

Alan I. Rea, Jr.
Bowling Green State University

Robert Reginald
California State University, San Bernadino

Mark Rich
Independent Scholar

Janine Rider
Mesa State College

Claire Robinson
Independent Scholar

Carl Rollyson
Baruch College, City University of New York

Michael-Anne Rubenstien
Independent Scholar

Nicholas Ruddick
University of Regina

Todd H. Sammons
University of Hawaii at Manoa

W. A. Senior
Broward Community College

Bill Sheehan
Independent Scholar

T. A. Shippey
St. Louis University

Charles L. P. Silet
Iowa State University

Amy Sisson
Independent Scholar

Ira Smolensky
Monmouth College

Maureen Speller
Independent Scholar

William C. Spruiell
Western Carolina University

Andrew Sprung
D'Youville College

Brian Stableford
King Alfred's College

Michael Stuprich
Ithaca College

Roy Arthur Swanson
University of Wisconsin—Milwaukee

Raymond H. Thompson
Acadia University

John H. Timmerman
Calvin College

Jeff VanderMeer
Independent Scholar

Mary E. Virginia
Independent Scholar

Janeen Webb
Australian Catholic University

Quinn Weller
University of Indianapolis

James M. Welsh
Salisbury State University

Donna Glee Williams
North Carolina Center for the Advancement of Teaching

Philip F. Williams
Arizona State University

John Wilson
Independent Scholar

Michael Witkoski
University of South Carolina

Carl B. Yoke
Kent State University

Marc Zaldivar
Virginia Polytechnic Institute and State University

List of Genres

The ready-reference top matter in each article identifies a primary genre—science fiction or fantasy—and a secondary classification of a narrower genre. Definitions of the latter classifications are provided below. Terms in SMALL-CAP type are subjects of their own entries.

Alien civilization: Centers on an attempt to present an alien (nonhuman, nonartificial) intelligence or civilization.

Apocalypse: Deals with the end of the world as known, often but not always through nuclear holocaust. This is a more dramatic form of the CATASTROPHE story. POST-HOLOCAUST fiction, in contrast, discusses the aftermath of the apocalyptic event more than the event itself.

Artificial intelligence: Plots deal with human-created forms of intelligence such as "thinking" computers, robots, androids, and cyborgs.

Catastrophe: Usually set on Earth, involving various natural disasters and attempts to deal with them.

Cautionary: Attempts to warn of some current or extrapolated danger, seriously and without amusement. May overlap with APOCALYPSE fiction.

Closed universe: Protagonists are in some type of closed environment that they perceive as natural and complete; they discover the "outside" during the plot action.

Cosmic voyage: Begins with early "voyage to the moon" stories and continues through longer space travels.

Cultural exploration: Works affected by anthropological theory. Cultures are different because of different cultural decisions, not different physical characteristics.

Cyberpunk: Characterized by extensive use of computers or artificial intelligences, often with a state of streetwise anarchy among the protagonists.

Dystopia: The opposite of UTOPIA; an imagined world that is horrific rather than ideal. Differs from CAUTIONARY works through an element of relish or deliberate exaggeration.

Evolutionary fantasy: Concerns attempts to demonstrate, disprove, or modify evolutionary theory. Some works deal with mutations. Overlaps to some extent with SUPERBEING stories.

Extrapolatory: Takes a feature of contemporary society and projects it into the future as increasingly dominant. May overlap with the CAU-TIONARY story.

Extrasensory powers: Characters possess some form of ESP. The society may be based on control and development of such powers. Overlaps with SUPERBEING stories.

Feminist: Characterized by a concern for altered female roles or by future gender war.

Future history: Extensive histories of the future, often in series form and often cyclic.

Future war: Central interest is on the nature of war rather than war as a threat or as part of the background.

Galactic empire: The plot is interstellar. A FUTURE HISTORY may contain a galactic empire; the galactic empire story will not be as encompassing in its span of time.

Heroic fantasy: Set in a fantasy world in which characters approach the scale of epic or romance; encompasses "sword and sorcery" plots.

High fantasy: Little or no connection with the current world, set "else-where." Many works of HEROIC FANTASY are also high fantasy, but not all high fantasy is HEROIC FANTASY.

Inner space: Stresses internal alterations of consciousness rather than external technological control.

Invasion story: Alien beings attack a planet.

Magical Realism: A relatively realistic plot is disturbed by figures of myth or fantasy.

Magical world: A type of HEROIC FANTASY with emphasis not on characters' quests but instead on social organization based on a technology that does not conform to current science.

Medieval future: A future era reverts to medieval social structures, which then are exposed to change. These works often are set on an alien planet with civilizations of some medieval type.

Mythological: Depends on the characters and settings of some established system of mythology.

New Wave: Imagistic and highly metaphoric, inclined toward psychology and the soft sciences, and often similar to works of DYSTOPIA. The

New Wave, largely contained in works of the 1960's, attempted to turn science fiction more toward mainstream literature. New Wave overlaps to a large extent with INNER SPACE fiction, and CYBERPUNK can be seen as a resurgence of the New Wave.

Occult: A mode of fantasy characterized by interest in the practices of magic and the supernatural, often with an element of the macabre.

Planetary romance: A type of HEROIC FANTASY but with scientific trappings, often set on Venus or Mars.

Post-holocaust: Set in a world recovering from a (usually nuclear) holocaust, often characterized by anarchy, mutations, and an attempt to struggle toward some form of civilization. Differs from APOCALYPSE stories in dealing with the aftermath of the holocaust rather than the holocaust itself.

Superbeing: Conjectures on the next stage of evolution, usually rejecting the idea of greater intelligence in favor of some exaggerated physical characteristic or a new form of mental power; the latter type overlaps with EXTRASENSORY POWER stories.

Theological romance: Often involves a divinely ruled universe within the framework of a postscientific society. Such works are seen as "antiscience" fiction.

Time travel: Characters are able to move forward or backward in time and often attempt to use this power to create or maintain an acceptable stream of history.

Utopia: Describes an ideal society.

Introduction

The trail of the fantastic has no beginning or end. Its stories have illuminated the path of the human imagination since recorded history began.

Hundreds upon hundreds of studies testify to the power of fantasy and science fiction. They are akin in some ways. The readers of one genre tend also to read in the other, and both genres are famously noted for arousing "the sense of wonder." Fantasy—to use the term both broadly and as a caption for "high" or "epic fantasy," which features such archetypes as wizards, royal youths of great destiny, talking animals, and eerie guides—is far older than science fiction, its progenitors stretching back to ghost civilizations: stories of the gods, folklore, mystical writings, riddles and rhymes, fairy tales of hauntings and revenge, of eldritch creatures seen in the twilight and heard in the wind. From the tunneled underworld of these ancestral roots stem the fantastic and its offshoots of fantasy, science fiction, and horror, the three having evolved with separate identifying characteristics.

These volumes in the Magill's Choice series contribute to a greater understanding of why special kinds of writing are important in excavating antiques and vestiges of the human heritage. Fantasy and science fiction shine light on the origins of our psychological and social development and throw a glow both on the obscure fragments of literatures of the past and on the course that future literatures may take.

The contributors to *Classics of Science Fiction and Fantasy Literature* celebrate two centuries of imaginations that blur fact and fiction in creating weird perspectives and fantastic geographies, symbols neither altogether Christian nor altogether innocent—animal motifs, cosmological aspirations, the syncretistic juxtapositions between the only world we have and the worlds we wish could be.

There are those who would ban the genres of science fiction and fantasy. Some concerned parents and religious leaders believe that young readers may be corrupted by tales of demons, witchcraft, and aliens. Others wish to eliminate or reinvent the terms; thus progressive authors who write within the genres want to "tear down the walls," believing that these genres should be subsumed by a single large category, known simply as "fiction," and so revalidated—when, in fact, hiding or eliminating them would devalue their essence. No novel of fantasy or science fiction deserves to become invisible by trivialization of the particular and peculiar excitements it has to offer.

Nobody doubts the greatness of the early works of the fantastic. Homer's *Iliad* and *Odyssey* (c. 800 B.C.E.) contributed prominent elements to fantasy today, such as the journey to exotic lands, the theme of transformation, an ecology of magic, and motifs of illusions and delusions. The Babylonian *Gilgamesh* epic (c. 2000 B.C.E.) is our earliest example of the quest story whose hero journeys to the land of the dead, an undertaking so courageous that it still finds champions today in works as diverse as Ursula K. Le Guin's *The Farthest Shore* (1972) in her Earthsea series and *The Hyperion Cantos* by Dan Simmons (1989-1997). The Old English *Beowulf* (c. 1000) and the German *Nibelungenlied* (c. 1200) depict great human heroism in the face of horrific monsters. Their battle sequences, songs, descriptions of feasts and contests, dragons, treasures, and other plot-dilating feats and quests often appear in modern fantasy, from Robert E. Howard's tales of Conan the Barbarian and the reveries of Zothique (1970) by Clark Ashton Smith (also a grandfather of science fiction) to the works of Lord Dunsany, George MacDonald, C. S. Lewis and, especially, J. R. R. Tolkien, whose *The Lord of the Rings* trilogy (1954-1955) stands as perhaps the greatest literary effort of the twentieth century to spring from one mind.

Science fiction is a creation of the nineteenth century, with Mark Twain's *A Connecticut Yankee in King Arthur's Court* (1889) towering as the first time-travel novel—a comic invention that heralded the contemporaneous, more serious works of H. G. Wells and Jules Verne. Its ancestors include the dreamlike, deliquescent voyage to another planet in Lucian of Samosata's *True History* (c. 150), the theme of man assaulting powers beyond his comprehension or control in Christopher Marlowe's *Dr. Faustus* (c. 1588), the utopian experiment of Francis Bacon's *The New Atlantis* (1627), and the scientific curiosity interwoven with the satire of Jonathan Swift's *Gulliver's Travels* (1726).

It was a work of nonfiction that gave science fiction its central thematic thrust: Charles Darwin's *The Origin of Species by Means of Natural Selection* (1859). The explorations of evolution that fueled Wells's *The Time Machine* (1895) and *The Island of Doctor Moreau* (1896) and Olaf Stapledon's stunning *Last and First Men* (1930) and *Star Maker* (1937) continued to build the sense of wonder soaring through all great science fiction, including works such as *Childhood's End* (1953) by Arthur C. Clarke, *Stranger in a Strange Land* (1961) by Robert A. Heinlein, *Planet of the Apes* (1963) by Pierre Boulle, the Patternist series (1976-1984) by Octavia Butler, *The Gate to Women's Country* (1988) by Sheri Tepper, and *Islands in the Net* (1988) by Bruce Sterling, to list only a few of the titles covered in these volumes. Science-fiction authors return again and again to the theme of evolution because of their great joy in playing with ideas, the sheer pleasure of turning the questioning spirit loose to ask *What if?* and *What might we become?*, in allowing an uncontrolled imagination to forge into uncharted territory, both outer space and inner space. The spray of phenomena we encounter in science fiction sets the brain aflame with revelation, offers nearly inexpressible insights into immense possibilities, evokes the beauty and anguish and exquisite pangs of one state of being glimpsing another. Mind and emotion reel in wonder at the center, yet there is no place or time that science fiction dares not rove.

Classics of Science Fiction and Fantasy Literature surveys 180 of the writers who have made the most lasting contributions to these genres. Many essays and the annotated bibliographies, selected from Salem Press's *Magill's Guide to Science Fiction and Fantasy Literature* (1996), have been updated for this two-volume set. The explosive vitality of both science fiction and fantasy in bookstores and all sorts of media, from television to comic books to computer games, makes an updated version most useful to the casual reader, the library patron, or the researching scholar.

Furthermore, science fiction and fantasy are found increasingly in the reading curricula of high school and college literature courses. These essays, with their easily readable format combining plot summaries with insightful analyses, are helpful to both the teacher and the student.

Each author selected here fits at least one of three categories. First are those authors who made essential contributions to the development of the genres. The brilliant and prolific Brian Aldiss, British author of the multiple-award-winning *Helliconia* series (1982-1985), is not the first to have called Mary Shelley the mother of science fiction with her *Frankenstein* (1818), though Wells and Verne between them would invent nearly every plot still used a century later: alien invasion, invisibility, bioengineered sentient animals, the time-travel machine, travel to other worlds, discovery of secret spaces and lost civilizations. Verne's glorification of technology still glows on the pages of most science fiction. Without L. Frank Baum, Lewis Carroll, Lord Dunsany, Edith Nesbit, and the "triumvirate" of the pulp *Weird Tales* magazine—Robert E. Howard, H. P. Lovecraft, and Clark Ashton Smith—science fiction and fantasy would not look as they do today.

Second are those authors who have devoted decades to one or both of these genres, such as Clarke, Heinlein, Le Guin, Isaac Asimov, Ray Bradbury, and Andre Norton, and who both participated in and ruled the golden age of science fiction and the ongoing golden years of fantasy. Their prolificity has won them as much renown as the high quality of their work.

Third are the authors who contributed works whose vision was so revolutionary or sublime that they rank among the most influential writers of the twentieth century; these include Philip K. Dick, who wrote dozens of mind- and genre-altering fictions, as well as many who wrote only one or two major works which are considered of lasting influence: Stapledon, Tolkien, Douglas Adams, Lloyd Alexander, and Alfred Bester.

Additions and updates include works written after the original set's publication and those whose popularity and critical acclaim demanded their inclusion. Now the reader will find Jonathan Lethem's *Amnesia Moon* (1995), Sean Stewart's *Mockingbird* (1998), Tim Powers's Fisher King Trilogy (1992-1997), Patrick O'Leary's *Door Number Three* (1995), John Crowley's still incomplete *Aegypt* series (1987-2000), Anne Rice's Vampire books (1976-2001), Dick's *VALIS* (1980), Karen Joy Fowler's *Sarah Canary* (1991), and James Morrow's *Only Begotten Daughter* (1990) and Godhead Trilogy (1994-1999).

—*Fiona Kelleghan*
University of Miami

Classics of
Science Fiction and Fantasy
Literature

Science Fiction and Fantasy

The urge to tell tales of wonder is at least as old as any records human beings possess, and almost certainly older. Although modern literary criticism tends to downplay that urge, or to assign it a lower seniority than other narrative forms, one could properly claim that there are in essence three different provinces of the realm of story, all of equal value and all of equal age. Most obvious is the urge to record what actually happened, or what people believe actually happened. This is called not story but "history." Next is the urge to make up stories about events that did not actually happen, and about people who may be complete inventions of the storyteller. This is called "fiction," a genre that extends from the anecdotes people still tell about things that (allegedly) happened to their (perhaps imaginary) friends all the way through to the great and developed complexity of the written novel.

Third and last in this progression is the urge to tell stories not only about invented events and invented people but also about invented creatures, such as werewolves and vampires, or invented worlds, such as Middle-earth or Atlantis or the Earthly Paradise, or to tell any kind of tale that invents not only the people who exist in it but also the conditions under which they exist. Perhaps it is significant that there is no generally accepted label in our culture for this final category of story. One might suggest the word "fantasy," a word related to both "phantom" and "fancy" and having a root meaning of "making (something) visible," specifically imagining or making images of something that is not actually there. Fantasy, however, has an established meaning in the parlance of modern literary marketing. Part of that meaning is "not the same as science fiction," a difference further discussed below.

The International Association for the Fantastic in the Arts has proposed "the fantastic" as a broader label to set against the very large categories of "history" and "fiction." This label covers both modern fantasy and modern science fiction, taking in as well the ancestor genres of fairy tale, romance, myth, legend, ghost story, and many others. Stories of "the fantastic" may be defined as including any set in a world different from our own or that include elements recognized as alien to our own, things that are not true or not yet true. The dominant modern branches of the fantastic are fantasy and science fiction, but the fantastic includes genres older than either of them.

These three very broadly defined types of story—history, fiction, and the fantastic—did not, as far as is known, develop out of one another. All three were present at the dawn of European literature more than two thousand years ago and no doubt existed earlier on other continents. As an example of history, one can point to Herodotus's *The History of the Persian Wars* (c. 430 B.C.E.), an account of the Greek and Persian wars and all that led up to them in the fifth and sixth centuries B.C.E. For fiction, one could cite Homer's epic poem *The Iliad* (c. 800 B.C.E.), an account of an even older war between Greeks and Trojans, possibly with a historical basis but clearly composed to tell a story of adultery and revenge, not to list dates and events. Finally, Homer's *The Odyssey* (c. 800 B.C.E.) is in many ways a classic example of the fantastic, with its much loved and still much imitated tales of one-eyed, man-eating giants and witches who can turn people into beasts.

These three cases should provide a salutary reminder that there is no seniority in literary modes and that the fantastic, far from being a junior partner to history and fiction, is as old as either of them. The examples also show how difficult it is to keep the basic distinctions between story types absolutely clear. Many historians, Herodotus included, have been called liars and writers of fiction. By contrast, much fiction has been, and sometimes still is, thought by many people to be literally true. To switch from early Greek to early British literature, Geoffrey of Monmouth, the author of *History of the Kings of Britain* (1718; first published as *Historia regum Britanniae*, c. 1136), was dismissed as a total fabricator by some of his contemporaries, and most modern scholars have agreed with that assessment. Geoffrey's retelling of the legend of King Arthur, however, was accepted as absolute fact by many readers from the twelfth century to the early sixteenth, when the first historian to cast serious doubt on Arthur's reality was dismissed by English patriots as a crazy and jealous Italian.

At present, books about King Arthur may be produced by professional historians, by writers of historical fiction, and by writers of the fantastic such as T. H. White, author of *The Once and Future King* (1958). One of the earliest references to the Arthur story is an incident that crept into real history when, in 1113, a Frenchman visiting Cornwall told a local resident that his belief that King Arthur was not dead but would return again was utter nonsense, or as one might now say, "completely fantastic." A fracas began when the Cornishman defended the truth of his belief, and it was the fracas, not the legend, that found its way into recorded history.

Arguments about literary genres usually are not taken as far as that, but the incident serves to demonstrate that one person's fantasy may be another person's history. Just the same, although figures such as King Arthur, Odysseus, and Beowulf may be very hard or even impossible to categorize, the basic idea of the three modes, with their different relationships to literal truth, remains valid. It also can be said that as time has gone by, the differences generally have become more marked and the distinctions have become clearer. One of C. S. Lewis's characters, the scholarly Dr. Dimble in *That Hideous Strength* (1945), the last work of Lewis's Space Trilogy, says at one point:

> if you dip into any college, or school, or parish—anything you like—at a given point in its history, you always find that there was a time before that point when there was more elbow-room and contrasts weren't so sharp; and that there's going to be a point after that time when there is even less room for indecision and choices are more momentous. . . . The whole thing is sorting itself out all the time, coming to a point, getting sharper and harder.

Dimble says this only to excuse his own side's resurrection of Merlin from the past and its use of a kind of magic that would now be unlawful but in the old days was not yet categorized, not yet ruled out. What he says has a kind of force, however, for literary genres as well. Even the well-publicized efforts of modern avant-garde writers to mix literary genres depend for their effect on awareness of what the genres are. When it comes to fiction and the fantastic especially, and beyond them to the modern division of the fantastic into fantasy and science fiction, the tendency of present-day readers to draw sharp lines of distinction has become very strong.

This is a result of the major social and psychological development that marks off modern times from all previous eras and that (however much one may complain about it) most people see as a process of continuous acceleration: The rise of science. It entirely confirms Dr. Dimble's theory to note that although "science" is a word of great age— *scientia* is only the Latin word for "knowledge"—the highly specialized meaning now given to the word has been traced by the *Oxford English Dictionary* no further than 1725, and then not very convincingly. As late as 1834, that dictionary recorded objections to the use of the newly invented word "scientist." Only in the later nineteenth century does one find the words "science," "scientist," and "scientific" being given their modern meaning. From then on, however, one can see the ideas of science and the scientific method taking hold in more and more minds, with ever increasing power, as tools for establishing human control over nature and as particularly reliable guides for systematizing some kinds of knowledge. This immense physical, mental, and semantic change has had its effect on literature, in particular on the whole realm of the fantastic and on its two major modern divisions of fantasy and science fiction.

To consider first the history of science fiction alone, one may say in brief that as human beings began to do things in sober reality that no human being had ever done before, storytellers began to wonder what limits on novelty there were and what in the world might happen next. This impulse intersected with the ancient urge toward telling tales of wonder but also tended radically to alter it. For example, stories had been told for countless generations about raising the dead. In Homer's *The Odyssey*, Odysseus calls up the ghost of Achilles to give him advice. In the Bible, one reads of Jesus' raising of Lazarus. The first is a matter of magic, the second of religion. In *Frankenstein* (1818), however, Mary Wollstonecraft Shelley imagines the creation of new life from the dead by scientific method, by means of a kind of electricity. The speculation nowadays would be classified as fantasy, because scientists are fairly sure that her method would not work. In Mary Shelley's time, this cannot have been so obvious. Scientists had made the legs of dead frogs react by stimulating them electrically. Who was to say that the method could not be extended and perfected?

In exactly the same way, but eighty years later, H. G. Wells in *The Island of Dr. Moreau* (1896) put forward the idea that human beings could create not life but intelligence, by taking animals and altering them surgically through "vivisection." After his book was published, Wells carried on an indignant correspondence designed to show that his idea was not impossible but had a basis in scientific fact. Although nowadays it appears certain that he was wrong, as with Mary Shelley this was not so obvious at the time. Michael Crichton's *Jurassic Park* (1990), with its dinosaurs revived from blood samples, probably will pass into the same area of "disproved theses" in even less time than Mary Shelley's or Wells's speculations, but for the moment at least a few of his conjectures appear plausible. The point is that science fiction in particular, whether *Frankenstein* or *The Island of Dr. Moreau* or *Jurassic Park*, tends to follow the frontier of scientific possibility. This frontier, effectively static for hundreds if not thousands of years, expanded with growing acceleration all through the nineteenth and twentieth centuries. Its expansion has created an ever increasing area of speculation and possibility in which science fiction can flourish.

Most modern definitions of science fiction accordingly make some reference both to the need for novelty and the use of the imagination (an ancient requirement of all forms of the fantastic) and to the need for logic, rigor, and control by the strict requirements of science (a distinctively modern demand). Robert Heinlein thus declared, in an essay printed in *The Science Fiction Novel* (1969), edited by Basil Davenport, that science fiction is:

> a realistic speculation about possible future events, based solidly on ade-
> quate knowledge of the real world, past and present, and on a thorough
> understanding of the nature and significance of the scientific method.

One notes, on one hand, words such as "speculation" and "possible," but on the other, the words "realistic," "adequate," "thorough," and "scientific." Kingsley Amis, another distinguished practitioner in the field, asserted in his *New Maps of Hell* (1961) that:

> Science Fiction is that class of prose narrative treating of a situation that
> could not arise in the world that we know, but which is hypothesized on
> the basis of some innovation in science or technology, or pseudo-science
> or pseudo-technology, whether human or extraterrestrial in origin.

There is a sense in this definition that Amis is rather "hedging his bet" by careful use of the term "pseudo," and one can see why. Who is to say that the science of *Jurassic Park* is not as unreal as that of *Frankenstein*? Never-theless, one sees once again the element of "not-truth" ("could *not* arise in the world that we know," emphasis added), qualified and even op-posed by "science," "technology," "innovation," and "hypothesized." One can sum up both Heinlein and Amis, and most other definitions of the genre, by saying that science fiction takes place in a world or setting that its contemporary readers know for certain is not true but that they are also prepared to accept as not impossible.

It may seem that this last requirement acts as a kind of restraint on the imagination, but to think that is to ignore the deep and powerful effect that real scientific innovation has had on the lives and attitudes of many modern readers. It is, after all, still possible for living memory to reach back to a time when it was generally accepted that human beings would never be able to fly. Many old people of the late twentieth century, as well as most of the early writers of American science fiction, grew up in a world that swept with unbelievable speed from the Wright brothers' flight in 1903 to dueling fighter planes in 1915, to transatlantic flights in 1919 and thousand-bomber raids in 1943, and then on to the *Enola Gay*—which dropped the atomic bomb on Hiroshima in 1945—the Strategic Air Command, everyday commercial traffic, and supersonic passenger jets. In the same way, the very idea of "wireless" transmission seemed in its beginnings eerie, almost ghostly, in the way that radio waves could be transmitted invisibly, impalpably, and apparently with nothing for them to transmit through. Technological advance led in quick succession to the radio becoming a normal household appliance, followed in turn by television and satellite links, accompanied by all the innovations of film technology from the first "cinema" to modern video.

It has been remarked often by science-fiction writers themselves that although many of them had imagined the first flight to the moon, none of them had ever thought that the first flight would be watched live on television by a mass world audience. In such cases, the progress of science outstripped even the range of imagination. One result has been the creation of a mass audience sensitized to the idea of unpredictable but nevertheless possible, or plausible, technological change. The modern subgenre of "cyberpunk" could not exist without an audience aware of the progress from vacuum tube to transistor to silicon chip, and from the giant computers of older science fiction, such as John Brunner's *Stand on Zanzibar* (1968), to the personal computers of today, the Internet, and the "hacker culture" that technology instantly if inadvertently created.

Science fiction thus differs from its ancestor forms of the past, such as the "utopia" or the "imaginary voyage," in containing within itself an element of belief, or at any rate something stronger than the "suspended disbelief" of older theories of ordinary fiction. Many, if not most, science-fiction readers firmly believe that there are alien intelligent races, simply because of what astronomy seems to say about the number of stars and planets in the real universe. It does not follow that one needs to believe that any of these races has contacted humans, and many popular stories of UFOs would be met with some scorn as scientifically implausible.

One might note the way in which intelligent Martians have drifted slowly out of the area of plausibility, or possible belief, as astronomy and space probes have increased knowledge of the planet Mars. Wells's *The War of the Worlds* (1898) drew on the theories of his own time, which saw Mars as an Earth-like but ancient and hence further-evolved planet. Edgar Rice Burroughs's Barsoom series, beginning in 1917 with *A Princess of Mars*, added to that the idea of reduced gravity and hence greater strength and speed for his Earth-born human hero. By the time of Kim Stanley Robinson's Mars trilogy (1992-1996), both these scenarios had become untenable, and the Mars of Robinson's imagination (which is also that of contemporary knowledge) is a different, less populated, but not less fascinating place. Scientific progress once again has ruled out some speculations and at the same time created completely different ones. Although these too may one day be ruled out in their turn, the Mars trilogy, like *The War of the Worlds* or *A Princess of Mars*, will remain science fiction as originally conceived, drawing on a deep well of belief and real knowledge, though such knowledge is always known and admitted to be incomplete.

Science fiction's modern companion genre, fantasy, has been less obviously but no less deeply affected by the triumph of rationalism and the accelerating awareness of science. It might seem that stories about dragons could be much the same in modern times as in the tenth century. Indeed, Smaug, in J. R. R. Tolkien's *The Hobbit* (1937), has an ancestry that stretches back to the Norse Fafnir and the nameless dragon that is the bane of Beowulf in the epic that carries his name, dating from about the eleventh century. Even if the creatures are the same, however, the context of belief in which they are embedded cannot help being different. To put it simply, although people find it much easier now to believe in voyages to Mars, they find it much less easy to believe in the existence of dragons on Earth.

To the audiences of Old Norse or Old English poems, it might not seem at all impossible that dragons existed, perhaps somewhere outside the rather small patch of territory they had explored. The *Anglo-Saxon Chronicle*, a work every bit as historical in its intentions as Herodotus's, and one that remains highly respected by modern historians, nevertheless records the appearance of flying dragons in Northumbria in the year 793 and shows no sign of intending to be "fantastic." The case is quite different now. It is reasonably certain that there are no canals on Mars, but it is 100 percent certain that there are no dragons (as traditionally described) on Earth. The world is too well explored to leave a place for them. In any case, the sheer mechanics of imagining a beast that could breathe fire, somehow insulate its own internal organs, and also find a means of ignition appears impossible. This has not prevented author after author from trying to create a situation in which the impossible dragon of tradition could become possible, whether through Tolkien's device of distancing the creature into a far-past world where all kinds of things appear to be different or Ursula Le Guin's method of creating "a world where magic works," governed, it seems, by a different set of physical laws.

Both Tolkien and Le Guin were well aware that they could not simply bring a dragon into the story and expect the skeptical and well-informed modern reader to accept it as a fact. If one wishes to continue to use the creatures of humanity's oldest fears and imaginings—such as dragons, elves, werewolves, and vampires—these creatures have to be given some kind of explanation, some kind of apparently rational setting. At the very least, the challenge of rationality has to be faced, not ignored.

One can say, then, that if science fiction deals with what is known not to be true, but not known to be beyond possibility, fantasy in its modern sense deals with what is known or very generally thought to be impossible. A common method of doing this is to set the tale in a different universe or an alternative reality, as is done in Stephen Donaldson's Chronicles of Thomas Covenant (1977-1983). One should note that this is not the same as setting it on an alien planet within this universe, for in that case the laws of physical causation as understood would still apply. In a different universe, the world and the characters may be ruled by magic, not science, and the problem (as, for example, in L. Sprague de Camp and Fletcher Pratt's Incomplete Enchanter series, 1941-1954) may be for the characters to understand the different logic of magic. Despite the appearance of Norse gods, giants, enchanters, werewolves, and other such beings, de Camp and Pratt's universe does run on logic: It is only the premises of the logic that have changed. Works of this nature demonstrate at once both the urge to escape from the confines of the real and accepted and an inability to let go of the cause-and-effect beliefs so thoroughly part of modern everyday life.

Modern definitions of fantasy accordingly often find difficulty in being both broad enough to take in what is an extremely prolific genre and narrow enough to say anything useful. It is hard to improve on Kathryn Hume's statement, in her book *Fantasy and Mimesis* (1984), that *"Fantasy is any departure from consensus reality*, an impulse native to literature and manifested in innumerable variations." This definition, however, needs to be filled out by a long discussion of the "variations" and leaves open the distinction between ancient examples of the fantastic such as *The Odyssey* and its modern mutations.

To understand the latter point, one needs only to look at some fantasy works. The fantastic is an ancient mode; fantasy (at least as defined by bookstores) is a modern genre. As a result, one often can find pairs or comparisons, with a traditional work of a kind that goes back to antiquity on one hand, and on the other a self-conscious modern version of the same thing. Thus, ghost stories are as old as literature, and no doubt older, but in the nineteenth century M. R. James (a famous classical scholar) still was capable of exploiting the ancient fears from his great depth of learning. Kingsley Amis's *The Green Man* (1969) also is very clearly a ghost story, but one that cannot rely on old assumptions about the afterlife and one whose agnostic hero finds it hard to have any belief in the afterlife at all. Argument about the very nature of ghosts and of religious belief becomes, accordingly, a vital part of Amis's tale.

In a similar way, *Baron Münchausen's Narrative* (1785) represents the old "traveler's tale" or "tall story." These are re-created in Sterling

Lanier's Brigadier Ffellowes stories (collected in 1972 and 1986), made plausible not only by their far-off settings but also by the cool and matter-of-fact narrative of the brigadier himself. Both *Dracula* (1897) and *Frankenstein* are rewritten by Brian Aldiss; Kenneth Grahame's animal fable of *The Wind in the Willows* (1908) is reshaped by modern knowledge of ecology and animal behavior in Richard Adams's *Watership Down* (1972); Angela Carter, Tanith Lee, and Jane Yolen have created among them a new genre of modern (and often both feminist and Freudian) fairy tale, related but also ideologically opposed to old tales like those of the Brothers Grimm; the almost contextless romance narratives of William Morris and E. R. Eddison are pulled firmly into shape with maps, calendars, languages, and appendices by Tolkien; traditional ballad is made into realistic narrative by Ellen Kushner's *Thomas the Rhymer* (1990) and Diana Wynne Jones's *Fire and Hemlock* (1985).

In all these cases, one can see a sense of argument, of explanation, one might almost say of discipline, falling on the old genres that once had no need to justify themselves. That sense of discipline parallels the growth of science fiction, as *Unknown* was for a while the partner fantasy magazine to science fiction's *Astounding* (note the implications of the two adjectives), and as joint audience interest created twin-track publications such as *The Magazine of Fantasy and Science Fiction* (still in existence) and *Science Fantasy* (unfortunately extinct).

Modern fantasy authors in particular are often eager to model their work on, to rewrite, or to reply to works of the past in which they see some element of the fantastic. John Gardner's *Grendel* (1971) is a retelling of the Old English epic of Beowulf from the point of view of the monster, not the hero; T. H. White's *The Once and Future King* passionately rehandles the story of Sir Thomas Malory's Middle English romance *Le Morte d'Arthur* (c. 1469); the medieval Welsh anthology of wonder-tales known as *The Mabinogion* provides the basis for Alan Garner's *The Owl Service* (1967) and for several other modern works; and the de Camp and Pratt Incomplete Enchanter series works its way through settings as diverse as the Icelandic *Prose Edda*, the Finnish *Kalevala*, Irish mythology, and English and Italian romantic epic.

The existence of horror stories indirectly raises an interesting question. Why are so many people prepared to write and to read pure fantasy in the modern day, when "consensus reality" is so strong and readers in a way have to be coaxed outside it? The answer, in the case of horror stories, is clear. These stories have an obvious motivation, which is to frighten their readers, duplicating in literary form the controlled fear of, for example, a fairground ride. Science fiction also can justify itself easily, as an "early warning system" or education in possibility. But fantasy? Is it not a kind of nostalgia, a reluctance to let go of old images, perhaps learned and loved in childhood, before the defenses of skepticism were raised?

Arguments against this "escapist" accusation are common and powerful. It has been pointed out that authors as different as J. R. R. Tolkien and C. S. Lewis, Kurt Vonnegut and Ursula Le Guin, and Stephen Donaldson and Gene Wolfe are all clearly addressing through their fantasies (just as much as through their works of science fiction) such grim and vital issues for the twentieth century and beyond as the origins of evil, the nature of war, and the future of the planet—topics that seem to be outside the scope of realistic fiction. It is also possible that "heroic fantasy" in particular—a mode that seemed dead until revived by Tolkien but now perhaps is among the most commercially successful and popular form of writing to be found in America—draws its impetus from deliberate rejection of the prevailingly unheroic, ironic, self-doubting attitudes of much realistic fiction: It is not an escape so much as a defiance.

What cannot be denied is the present competitiveness, one might almost say dominance, of the current fantasy/science-fiction field. Hundreds or thousands of titles are published each year in each genre. Some authors—among them Greg Bear, Gregory Benford, David Eddings, and Terry Brooks—figure consistently in best-seller lists. Both science fiction and fantasy have made the transition to film and television, with series as popular as *Star Trek* and *Star Wars*. In a more academic mode, authors such as Angela Carter are recognized subjects of study in universities across the world. Science fiction especially has been an immensely influential vehicle for feminist thought, through authors such as Joanna Russ, Suzy McKee Charnas, Marge Piercy, and James Tiptree, Jr. (the pen name of Alice Sheldon).

Experimental writing is represented by such tours de force as Russell Hoban's *Riddley Walker* (1980). Furthermore, in this situation of commercial success and commercial exploitation, although the line between fantasy and science fiction remains in most cases clear, there is a sense of continuous probing of the boundaries of both forms by several authors, prominent among them Tim Powers, Michael Swanwick, and Gene Wolfe. At the same time, if there is a shift of weight discernible, it is on the whole from science fiction toward fantasy. A number of established "hard science fiction" authors, among them Gordon R. Dickson, Orson Scott Card, and Piers Anthony, have shown themselves ready to move sideways into the writing of fantasy. Commercial considerations likely play a part in this move, but one may well believe that in the same way that science fiction earned public respect and won its way to literary favor through the middle of the twentieth century, so practitioners of fantasy have shown the world what can be done within that genre toward the end of the century, making their case not by argument but by example.

There is a further and final point that may be made about the nature of both modern genres, fantasy and science fiction, and about their joint relationship to the dominating principle of science. This is that there are many disciplines that aspire to the dignity of being scientific. The core disciplines remain, no doubt, physics, chemistry, biology, and mathematics: No one doubts that these, and their modern offshoots or specializations such as genetics and astronomy, are sciences in every sense of the term. At the other extreme, traditional humanities subjects such as history and literary study have ceased, after a sometimes brief flirtation with "scientificity," to make any claims of this nature. There remain what are often described as the "soft sciences," which include sociology, political science, economics, anthropology, and others. It is not often realized how fertile some of these fields have been for creative writers, nor how radically new they may be, developing over much the same relatively short period as the "hard sciences."

Just as one could see an "epistemic break" or major transformation between, say, medieval alchemy and modern chemistry, or medieval astrology and modern astronomy, so there are clear developments from the ancient habits of treasure hunting and grave robbing to systematic archaeology; from dilettante ethnography to modern anthropology; from belletristic philology to the nineteenth century science of comparative philology and through it to computational linguistics; from the antiquarian sketching of stones and monuments to the recovery of hieroglyphs, cuneiform, and the code-breaking ability to read totally lost and forgotten scripts such as Cretan "Linear B." All these "soft sciences" have provided major inspiration for creative writers.

The dream of inventing the mathematical hard science of "psychohistory" is at the heart of Isaac Asimov's famous Foundation series. Ursula K. (for Kroeber) Le Guin is herself the daughter of two of the most prominent American anthropologists of the twentieth century, Alfred and Theodora Kroeber. Tolkien has a fair claim to being one of the most influential ancient philologists of the twentieth century, even disregarding the effect of his fantasies. The power and lure of archaeology (a subject that filled the nineteenth and twentieth centuries with glittering discoveries from Mycenae to Babylon to Ur and Egypt's Valley of the Tombs) have given inspiration to authors as different as H. P. Lovecraft, Gregory Benford, and Larry Niven.

Perhaps the most dramatic development of recent years has been the sudden interest taken in the idea of alternative (or alternate) history, an idea that goes back at least as far as 1931, when the American novelist Winston Churchill wrote his provocatively titled essay "If Lee Had Not Won the Battle of Gettysburg," and that has led to such complex works as Philip K. Dick's *The Man in the High Castle* (1962), Ward Moore's *Bring the Jubilee* (1953), and Kingsley Amis's *The Alteration* (1976). In the late 1990's, more than a dozen well-known authors were working busily in the field, including at least one prominent American politician (Newt Gingrich) and the prolific Harry Turtledove, once a professional historian. Is this particular subgenre fantasy or science fiction?

If one looks at Mark Twain's *A Connecticut Yankee in King Arthur's Court* (1889) or L. Sprague de Camp's *Lest Darkness Fall* (1941), one would probably decide for fantasy: Neither work makes any serious effort to explain how the modern-day heroes find themselves suddenly "back in the past." Both of them, however, and Turtledove's stories as well, show a keen interest in the history of technology that gives them a claim to "not impossible" status. In cases such as these, the distinctions between fantasy and science fiction, between hard and soft sciences, lose their usual force. One may add that such works also are a powerful argument against a kind of ethnocentrism that could be called "chronocentrism," the belief that the way history did happen is the only way it could have happened, that the arrow of time points unerringly and inevitably to the world as it stands.

Both science fiction and fantasy functioned during the twentieth century, and continue to function during the twenty-first, as major explanatory tools that have provided meaning and insight to millions of readers, often about vital issues such as the origins of war and the nature of humanity, and often to readers who have been failed by all older and more traditional forms of writing (such as history and mainstream fiction). They also can be seen as the main indicators of radical shifts of attitude and understanding in the population at large. In the process, they have acted as powerful if unrecognized forces against prejudice and ethnocentrism, and they have served as guides to and recruiters for both hard and soft sciences. It has been acknowledged many times that there would have been no ventures into space, no moon landings or planetary flybys, without the stimulus of decades of space fiction. Both fantasy and science fiction have opened unexplored territories of the imagination.

—*T. A. Shippey*

Aegypt, Love and Sleep, and Daemonomania

Pierce Moffett abandons his academic career to write a quasi-historical book on a kind of magic practiced in the Renaissance

Author: John Crowley (1942-   )
Genre: Fantasy—Magical Realism
Type of work: Novels
Time of plot: The twentieth century and late sixteenth century
Location: The eastern United States and Europe
First published: *Aegypt* (1987), *Love and Sleep* (1994), and *Daemonomania* (2000)

The Story

Aegypt (also published as *The Solitudes*), *Love and Sleep*, and *Daemonomania* are the first three installments of Crowley's projected four-volume novel (collectively entitled *Aegypt*) that concerns myth, history, Gnostic religious philosophy, and Renaissance magic. Its governing theme—which is exhaustively explored and restated throughout the text—is that there is more than one history of the world.

Aegypt chronicles Pierce Moffett's escape to a rural life in the Catskills from his life in New York City and an unsatisfying academic career. *Love and Sleep* takes the reader forward to the next stage in Pierce's various types of research, both into historical accounts and into himself, to understand the "time when the world worked differently." It begins by chronicling Pierce's personal history as a boy growing up in the Cumberland Mountains of eastern Tennessee in the early 1950's. Stories are included about historical figures of the late sixteenth century, including Giordano Bruno, who is credited with discovering the concept of infinity, and the scientist/philosopher/magician Doctor John Dee. *Daemonomania* follows Pierce, Dee, and Bruno through their respective "passage times," periods of infinite possibility in which the world moves from what it has been to what it will eventually become.

Aegypt mentions Pierce's childhood and Doctor Dee's research with two short prologues. Primarily, however, it narrates the quest begun in Pierce's thirties. He sets out in the first section to interview for a teaching position at a small college in upstate New York. The bus he has taken breaks down, and he skips the interview to stay with Spofford, a former student who is now a shepherd in the small town of Blackbury Jambs. Pierce decides that he wants to stay, then briefly returns to the city to sell a book proposal to a former girlfriend. He can then settle in Blackbury Jambs to write a popular account of the epistemological break between the medieval and the modern periods, times of religious, magical, and scientific fervor. He meets Spofford's girlfriend, Rosie, and another woman, Rose, both of whom will help him in his quest. *Aegypt* focuses on Rosie; her husband Mike, whom she is in the process of divorcing; their small daughter, Sam; and their uncle, Boney Rasmussen. Rosie hires Pierce to work for Boney's foundation and put in order the papers of a deceased novelist, Fellowes Kraft (an allusion to Fellowescraft, the second level of masonry), who also worked for the foundation. Among Kraft's papers, Pierce discovers an unfinished work that matches his proposed book. *Aegypt* ends with his having created his project for the foundation but trying to decide what to do about his own book.

Love and Sleep continues the story of Pierce's book by documenting his motivations. The first thirteen chapters of part 1 narrate two years of Pierce's boyhood in the early 1950's, when he lived with his mother in the Cumberland Mountains. The focus is on his experiences with his cousins, mountain people alternately endowed and devastated by mining operations, and on his relationship to books and to Roman Catholic doctrine, all equally fantastic to him. The second section introduces the sixteenth century through texts of Fellowes Kraft read by Rosie Rasmussen and Pierce himself in the late 1970's. As Rosie and Pierce read, Pierce attempts to use the magical forces of Doctor Dee and his medium, Kelley, for his own purposes. Pierce appears to be a disturbed individual who uses his research for the foundation, which is simultaneously research for his own book, to satisfy lusts of spiritual and physical kinds. His discovery that a lost land of Aegypt may be responsible for the survival of magic in the modern world is confirmed for him (if not for the reader) by his analysis of accumulated personal occurrences. He notes that he "accidentally" ended up in Blackbury Jambs, home of Fellowes Kraft, whose novels he read as a child; that he was once sexually involved with a crazy gypsy (he takes "gypsy" as derived from the magical Aegypt); and that he finds himself editing the manuscript of a book by Kraft corresponding to the book he plans to write.

A third story, of Giordano Bruno, Doctor Dee, Rudolph II, and other historical figures from the sixteenth century, carries the reader into Pierce's and Fellowes Kraft's research in an immediate sense. Pierce learns enough of Dee's magic, he believes, to use the sexual energy of "coldly performed love" with the "other" Rose (Ryder) to create for himself a barely corporeal son and an incestuous (if imaginary) relationship, slipping further into his parallel world of magic. This novel ends with a section titled "Valetudo," which can be translated as ill health or health. Both Pierce and his friends fear for his mental health. His only solution is to wait for the next big change in "the way the world works" so that his self-created succubus will leave him.

In *Daemonomania*, the tone of the narrative grows progressively darker, as the characters struggle to find their way through an increasingly chaotic world. John Dee, deserted by the angels who promised him divine revelation, travels from London to Prague and then back, where he dies—alone and largely forgotten—at his English country home of Mortlake. Giordano Bruno continues to develop his heretical philosophies, gradually moving toward an enigmatic encounter with the Office of the Inquisition in Rome. In the twentieth century sections, Pierce and Rosie Rasmussen find themselves in conflict with an overbearing faith-healing cult called the Powerhouse. Pierce loses his lover, Rose Ryder, to the blandishments of the cult, while Rosie—whose former husband, Mike Mucho, is a fanatical convert—nearly loses her daughter Sam in a hotly contested custody fight. The effort to free Sam from the controlling forces of the Powerhouse—an effort in which Pierce plays a pivotal role—provides *Daemonomania* with its dramatic and symbolic climax, as Crowley reveals in typically oblique fashion that Sam's fate and the fate of the world are inextricably linked. As the novel ends, that wildly unstable world stands poised on the edge of irreversible change.

Analysis

These novels amply reward reading and rereading. Their structural details magnificently contribute to the experience of a story that is never completely told, only implied. The narrative is in third person, shifting among several characters and always unreliable, leaving much to delight a careful reader. Upon rereading, one discovers that seemingly unrelated episodes are, in fact, closely intertwined. This is apparent in the juxtaposition of narratives about the early 1580's and later 1970's and those concerning the lives of Giordano Bruno and Pierce Moffett.

There are many reviews of John Crowley's books but few critical articles about Crowley himself, although he has been many times nominated for the Hugo, Nebula, and World Fantasy Awards (which he won for *Little, Big* in 1981) and the American Book Award (for which he was nominated for *Engine Summer* in 1979 and which he won for *Little, Big* in 1981).

His later novels are different in tone from *Little, Big* but share ideas with that book. *Little, Big* also plays off the city of New York and the Catskills, but where that novel validates a magical dimension to the universe, grounded in Rosicrucians and Theosophists, the *Aegypt* novels sidestep the question while maintaining the tension. These three novels offer a more sobering and intellectual reading experience that amply repays a reader's attention but also demands much more of it.

Each of the *Aegypt* books is divided into three sections, each of which is given the title of a house of the zodiac: Vita, Lucrum, and Fratres in *Aegypt*; Genitor, Nati, and Valetudo in *Love and Sleep*; and Uxor, Mors, and Pietas in *Daemonomania*. The houses of the zodiac are explained by both the local astrologer, Val, and a writer from the 1620's, Fludd.

The discussion of the zodiac typifies the elaborate game the reader must play if the secrets of these books are to be unlocked. These secrets are revealed as Pierce himself searches for some confirmation of his book's theme, that once the world worked differently and that the last time a change occurred was at the cusp of the sixteenth and seventeenth centuries. He believes that the world is again in the midst of such a radical change. He also searches for magical powers that were available to historical figures so that he can put them to personal use, but his misuse of these magical powers leads him to the brink of psychological collapse.

The historical chapters provide a surprising amount of genuine historical detail. Each gives a nonscientific interpretation of events of the time and is linked to contemporary events. For example, England's defeat of the Spanish Armada in 1588 is known to have been aided by an unexpected wind, but the narration insists that there are no firsthand accounts of this wind. One of Kraft's books suggests that the wind was caused by demons conjured up by Doctor Dee. This historical occurrence is then mirrored in the cold and winds of 1977-1978 in the Catskills. The sum of these illusions re-creates an experience of Pierce's journey.

Both *Love and Sleep* and *Daemonomania* were written long after *Aegypt* and provide sufficient background to be accessible on their own. Still, the books are best read together and in sequence, for *Aegypt* is a single, hugely ambitious novel. Although many of its secrets are still concealed and its final shape still hidden from view—this grand, allusive work is clearly one of the most intricate, erudite, stylistically assured novels in the field of modern fantasy literature.

—*Janice M. Bogstad*
—*Updated by Bill Sheehan*

Alice's Adventures in Wonderland and Through the Looking-Glass

A young girl explores a bizarre world that lies underground and an equally strange land that lies on the other side of the looking-glass

Author: Lewis Carroll (Charles Lutwidge Dodgson, 1832-1898)
Genre: Fantasy—alien civilization
Type of work: Novels
Time of plot: Undefined, in dreamlands
Location: Wonderland and Looking-Glass Land
First published: *Alice's Adventures in Wonderland* (1865) and *Through the Looking-Glass* (1871 but dated 1872)

The Story

Alice's Adventures in Wonderland is an outgrowth of Lewis Carroll's earlier and shorter tale titled *Alice's Adventures Under Ground*, which he based on a story he told to Alice Liddell and her two sisters during a boat trip they took in 1862. Carroll completed this story, written in longhand and illustrated with his own drawings, in 1863. In 1864, he gave the manuscript to Alice as a gift. Revised and expanded by Carroll and newly illustrated by John Tenniel, this work evolved into *Alice's Adventures in Wonderland* the following year.

While listening to her older sister reading aloud, Alice drifts off to sleep and begins her dream adventures. She follows a white rabbit and falls down his hole into Wonderland. Alice is constantly at odds with the creatures who inhabit this alien world and also with her own body, which shrinks when she drinks from a mysterious bottle, then grows to enormous size when she eats a small cake.

She encounters many creatures endowed with wit and cleverness, who confuse her at every turn. She meets the ugly Duchess, whose baby turns into a pig in Alice's arms. Things are not what they seem. It is at the Duchess's house that she first sees the unsettling Cheshire Cat, who sits in the corner grinning, with his eyes fixed on Alice. Later, the Cheshire Cat reappears on a tree branch, from which he demonstrates his ability to vanish, leaving only his eerie smile lingering in the air.

At the Mad Tea-Party, Alice must exchange witty remarks and insults

Lewis Carroll. (Library of Congress)

with the Hatter and March Hare, an experience that further challenges her sense of time and logic. It is always six o'clock, always teatime, at this table.

The threatening nature of Wonderland is reinforced in the garden scene, dominated by the raucous Queen of Hearts, who continually shouts "Off with her head!" The threat becomes problematic, however, when the executioner is summoned to cut off the disembodied head of the Cheshire Cat.

Alice's last adventure is at the trial of the Knave of Hearts, who is accused of stealing the Queen's tarts. The Queen calls for the defendant to be sentenced before the jury submits its verdict, and it soon becomes clear that the law itself is on trial. Outraged at the absurd form of justice she witnesses, Alice asserts, "You're nothing but a pack of cards!" With that exclamation, she annihilates Wonderland as if by magic, and she emerges from her strange dream.

In *Through the Looking-Glass* (which carries the subtitle *And What Alice Found There*), Carroll again frames his story as a dreamlike experience, but this time he presents a world that is controlled by the rules of a chess game. Alice enters the geometrical landscape, which is laid out like a chessboard, as a pawn. During her movement across the board en route to becoming a queen, she may converse only with the chess figures on adjacent squares. Among the many memorable characters she engages are the White Queen, from whom she learns the advantages of living backward in time; the battling Lion and Unicorn; the pompous Humpty Dumpty; the bullying Tweedledee and Tweedledum, who tell Alice that she is merely an object in the Red King's dream; and the eccentric White Knight.

After Alice bids farewell to the White Knight, in a scene that may represent Carroll's adieu to Alice Liddell as she reached puberty, Alice goes on to become queen. In terms of the chess game, the pawn has become a queen, and in human terms, Alice's final move suggests her coming of age. It is at this point that she wakes from her dream and is left wondering who dreamed it all, herself or the Red King.

Analysis

Alice's Adventures in Wonderland presents a world in which everything, including Alice's own body size, is in a state of flux. She is treated rudely, bullied, asked questions that have no answers, and denied answers to her own questions. Her recitations of poems turn into parodies, a baby turns into a pig, and a cat turns into a grin. The essence of time and space is called into question, and her romantic notion of an idyllic garden of life turns out to be a paper wasteland. In order to escape that oppressive and disorienting vision, she finally denies it with her outcry, "You're nothing but a pack of cards!" and happily reenters the morally intelligible and emotionally comfortable world of her sister, who sits next to her on the green banks of a river in a civilized Victorian countryside.

The assaults on Alice's senses of order, stability, and proper manners wrought by such characters as the Hatter, the Cheshire Cat, and the March Hare make it clear that Wonderland is not the promised land, a place of sleepy fulfillment. Rather, Wonderland stimulates the senses and the mind. It is a *monde fatale*, one that seduces Alice (and the reader) to seek new sights, new conversations, and new ideas, but it never satisfies her. Conventional meaning, understanding, and the fulfillment that comes with illumination are constantly denied her. That is the secret of Wonderland: Its disorienting and compelling attractions make it a Wanderland and Alice herself an addicted, unfulfilled wanderer.

Significantly, she is presented with a stimulating, alluring vision early in her adventures. Alice finds a tiny golden key that opens a door that leads to a small passage. As she kneels and looks along the passage, she sees a beautiful garden with bright flowers and cool fountains. She is too large, however, to fit through the door and enter the attractive garden. Alice's dream garden suggests an adult's longing for lost innocence and youth, and her desire to enter it invests the place with imagined significance. Later, when she goes into the garden, it loses its romantic aspect. In fact, it turns out to be a parodic Garden of Life, for the roses are painted, the people are playing cards, and the death-cry "Off with her head!" echoes throughout the croquet grounds.

Alice's dream garden is an excellent example of Carroll's paradoxical duality. Like Alice, he is possessed by a romantic vision of an edenic

The Mad Hatter's tea party. John Tenniel's illustrations for the first edition set the "look" for most future illustrated books and film adaptations.

childhood more desirable than his own fallen world, but it is a vision that he knows is corrupted inevitably by adult sin and sexuality. He thus allows Alice's romantic dream of the garden to fill her with hope and joy for a time, but he later tramples that pastoral vision with the fury of the beheading Queen and the artificiality of the flowers and inhabitants.

Through the Looking-Glass abandons the fluidity and chaos of *Alice's Adventures in Wonderland* for artifice and strict determinism. In the first book, the emphasis is on Alice's adventures and what happens to her on the experiential level. In the sequel, Alice's movements are controlled strictly by the precise rules of a chess game. The giddy freedom she enjoyed in Wonderland is exchanged for a ruthless determinism, as she and the other chess pieces are manipulated by some unseen hand.

Whereas *Alice's Adventures in Wonderland* undermines Alice's sense of time, space, and commonsensical logic, *Through the Looking-Glass* questions her very reality. Tweedledum and Tweedledee express the Berkeleian view that all material objects, including Alice herself, are only "sorts of things" in the mind of the sleeping Red King (God). If the Red King were to wake from his dreaming, they warn Alice, she would disappear. Alice, it would seem, is a mere fiction shaped by a dreaming mind that threatens her with annihilation.

The ultimate question of what is real and what is dream, however, is never resolved in the book. In fact, the story ends with the perplexing question of who dreamed it all—Alice or the Red King? Presumably, Alice dreamed of the King, who is dreaming of Alice, who is dreaming of the King, and so on. The question of dream versus reality is appropriately set forth in terms of an infinite regression through mirror facing mirror. The apprehension of reality is indefinitely deferred, and the only reality may be one's thoughts and their well-ordered expression.

In the final chapter, Alice, having become Queen, asserts her human authority against the controlling powers of the chessboard and brings both the intricate game and the story to an end. In chess terms, Alice has captured the Red Queen and checkmates the sleeping Red King. In human terms, she has grown up and entered that fated condition of puberty, at which point Carroll dismisses his dream child once and for all from his remarkable fiction.

—Richard Kelly

The Amber Series

In Amber, a world of magic that can be reached from Earth by "traveling through shadows," members of the royal family fight among themselves for control of the kingdom and the worlds it controls

Author: Roger Zelazny (1937-1995)
Genre: Fantasy—heroic fantasy
Type of work: Novels
Time of plot: Contemporary on Earth and undefined but resembling medieval Earth on a variety of alternative worlds
Location: Earth, Amber, and the lands in between
First published: *The Chronicles of Amber* (1979; two-volume set including *Nine Princes in Amber*, 1970; *The Guns of Avalon*, 1972; *Sign of the Unicorn*, 1975; *The Hand of Oberon*, 1976; and *The Courts of Chaos*, 1978), *Trumps of Doom* (1985), *Blood of Amber* (1986), *Sign of Chaos* (1987), *Knight of Shadows* (1989), and *Prince of Chaos* (1991)

The Story

The story of Amber is told in two cycles, consisting of ten novels. The tale is extremely complex, written over a span of twenty years, and involves dozens of principal characters who are related in various ways. Amber is depicted as the "real world"; all other worlds, including contemporary Earth, are shadows cast by that reality. It is a world of magic and swordplay ruled by members of a bickering royal family who form temporary alliances and then regularly betray one another.

Outside Amber, the characters "travel through shadows" by creating differences in reality as they walk, ride horses, and occasionally even drive cars. Physical laws are different in the various worlds; a motor vehicle, for example, would be useless in Amber.

The first cycle, contained in *The Chronicles of Amber*, tells the story of Corwin, Prince of Amber. He is the son of King Oberon, who has disappeared. Corwin finds himself in a hospital in New York State, apparently injured in a car accident. He thinks of himself as Carl Corey and has little memory of his past. Gradually, he learns that there is more to his past than an ordinary earthly existence. His first clue is the discovery of a pack of tarot cards that includes trumps with the pictures of

Corwin and his brothers and sisters. Eventually, he is contacted by his brother Random and brought back to Amber, where he learns about the Pattern.

The Pattern is a mazelike series of twisting trails that can be walked safely only by a member of the royal family. Corwin learns that he is in great danger. His brother Eric is trying to claim the throne of Amber and has placed Corwin on the Shadow Earth (contemporary Earth) to get him out of the way. Corwin therefore walks the pattern in Rebma, a mirror image of Amber under the sea, as a means of regaining his memory. He then faces Eric, who for a brief period has managed to seize the throne.

The rest of the first cycle is concerned mainly with various intrigues in the Court of Amber and the opposition of the Courts of Chaos, which stand at the opposite end of the shadows from Amber. Along the way, Corwin meets Dworkin, a mad but powerful wizard. It becomes apparent that Dworkin is the oldest member of the House of Amber and creator of the Pattern. The Pattern has been damaged, and Dworkin's madness is a direct reflection of that damage.

The final showdown occurs at the Courts of Chaos, where Brand, the evil prince who has been responsible for much of the bloodshed within the royal family, is killed after wresting the Jewel of Judgment, a powerful charm that Dworkin used to create the original Pattern, from Corwin. Brand falls into a deep abyss still carrying the Jewel. The Unicorn, a mythical symbol of Amber, appears with the Jewel around his horn and presents it to Random, indicating that he, not Corwin, is to be King of Amber.

The second cycle, beginning with *Trumps of Doom*, follows the adventures of Merlin, the son of Corwin of Amber, and Dara, a princess of Chaos. He is one of few who have walked both the Pattern of Amber and the Logrus, its equivalent at the Courts of Chaos. He is a computer programmer in San Francisco on the Shadow Earth and has built a new computer, called the Ghost Wheel, that will not work. Merlin is content in contemporary Earth but is forced back to Amber when repeated attempts are made on his life.

The second series ends with another visit to the Courts of Chaos, which is seen from the inside. There, Merlin finds the answer to his many questions, and the Ghost Wheel finally is put into operation. The story is left open-ended. Because of the nature of the worlds involved and the differing time schemes in the various shadows, the series could continue indefinitely.

Analysis

The concept of parallel worlds is common in fantastic literature. Isaac Asimov used this idea in *The End of Eternity* (1955), though his method was science fictional rather than magical. C. S. Lewis created an alternative world in *The Chronicles of Narnia* (1950-1956), a series of children's fantasies with an overt Christian message. More recently, Stephen King embarked on an alternative world epic, the Dark Tower series, begun in 1982 and incorporating elements of horror.

Perhaps the most unusual concept in the Amber series is the ability of some of the characters not only to travel freely among the alternative worlds but also to create new ones in the process. When a prince of Amber travels through shadows, he does so by changing reality bit by bit. The characters speak various languages and have various identities in the worlds they choose to inhabit.

It is also possible for a shadow walker to bring materials from one world into another. In Amber, gunpowder is useless. Corwin, however, discovers that in the shadow world of Avalon, there is a type of jeweler's rouge that is benign in that world (and contemporary Earth) but highly explosive in Amber. He travels to a shadow world much like Earth except that South Africa has not been colonized by Europeans. There, he easily collects uncut diamonds, which he uses in the Europe of contemporary Earth to buy automatic weapons. He then has these weapons loaded with bullets propelled by the material from Avalon. With these weapons, he saves Castle Amber from invaders.

Unlike most fantasies, the Amber series is not a conflict between good and evil; rather, the fight is between order, represented by Amber, and chaos, represented by the Courts of Chaos. Underlying this theme is a strong suggestion that both Amber and Chaos are projections of something deeper and that one cannot exist without the other. Certainly, there are many characters who owe allegiance to both places. The most obvious is Merlin, who is searching for his father, Corwin of Amber, but was reared in the Courts of Chaos.

The ultimate reality of the situation remains elusive. At several points, various characters have glimpses of the "True Amber," of which Amber itself seems to be a shadow. There is a mythological assumption that the Houses of Amber and Chaos both spring from Dworkin and the Unicorn. The fate of Amber literally dictates the fate of the universe. All other worlds are shadows of Amber; therefore, if Amber is destroyed, all other places will be destroyed as well.

A final point concerns religious undertones. Although there are no references to gods as such, the Unicorn is more than an ordinary animal, and the princes of Amber themselves appear to be effectively immortal. Like the ancient Greek gods, they can be killed violently, but they do not appear to age as ordinary humans do, and they have amazing powers of regeneration. Corwin was first exiled to Earth during the Middle Ages, where he survived an outbreak of bubonic plague. In modern New York, he is still, to all appearances, a young man.

Amber owes many of its parts to sources from ancient legends and mythology to modern science fiction. The Amber books, for example, incorporate elements of time travel and use fantastic weapons. Sir Lancelot makes a brief appearance in *The Guns of Avalon*, and both Oberon and Merlin have names stemming from ancient legends.

Roger Zelazny has written many stories, varying from "sword and sorcery" tales to hard science fiction involving spaceships and alien worlds. In most cases, the distinctions between reality and fantasy, and between science and legend, are blurred. In the ten books that make up the Amber series, this is especially evident.

—*Marc Goldstein*

Amnesia Moon

A character named Chaos wrestles with the disintegration of reality and the possibility that he may have the power to help end it

Author: Jonathan Lethem (1964-   )
Genre: Science fiction—post-holocaust
Type of work: Novel
Time of plot: Near future
Location: Western United States
First published: 1995

The Story

Chaos lives in Hatfork, a Wyoming town struggling to survive in the aftermath of a nuclear war. Hatfork exists under the sway of a tyrant named Kellogg, whose dreams infiltrate the sleep of everyone who lives there. Impatient with the stagnation of the town, Chaos leaves with a young mutant girl named Melinda. Chaos and Melinda encounter several pockets of society, each with different reactions to and explanations of what happened after the nuclear war, and each with different receptivity to the dreams of Chaos and others.

In the mountains, they meet a group of people living in an opaque fog who call Chaos "Moon," thereby reminding him of an earlier identity. Here Chaos/Moon begins to recover fragments of his life before the changes, which are no longer attributed to a nuclear war. The people in the fog pour their energy into researching ways to see through the fog, and they grow hostile when Chaos begins transmitting Kellogg's dreams into their territory. Moon and Melinda then move on, only to discover the McDonaldians, who make hamburgers in an abandoned town and strictly adhere to long-irrelevant policies. Their next encounter occurs in the desert, when a strange machine drops a paint bomb on their solar-powered car, which consequently dies near Vacaville, California.

Vacaville is controlled by a Luck Board, which hands out jobs and houses in a system based on individual scores on a "luck test." The government of Vacaville also generates television programming starring only government officials. Moon and Melinda stay with Edie and her children Ray and Dave. Their arrival sparks the unwelcome interest of Cooley, a Government Star. Meanwhile, Moon's powerful dreams, apparently capable of broadcasting over long distances, attract an old friend to Vacaville. Moon then heads to San Francisco hoping to find Gwen, a past love, about whom he has been dreaming. There he becomes the focus of a plot to use his dreaming power to reclaim a single, unified reality. Many theories are exchanged about the causes of the reality breakdown, among them the idea that an alien invasion explains the strange machine that bombed Moon's car in the California desert. Moon flees San Francisco and heads back into the desert, and the puzzle of the reality breakdown is never solved.

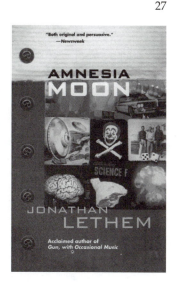

Analysis

This journey of discovery is part American road novel, part ironic Americana, and part homage to Philip K. Dick. Lethem takes tremendous pleasure in overturning American obsessions to discover what lies beneath, often only to discover yet something else to overturn. At the beginning of *Amnesia Moon*, Chaos is merely a flunky in a town full of flunkies controlled by Kellogg's dreams. By the end, he may be the sole hope of recovering a lost unified American culture. However, the novel suggests that even if he could dream a new America, the overriding story that his dreams would provide might not be better than the patchwork tyrannies of Hatfork, Vacaville, and San Francisco.

The science-fictional aspects of the book are in some ways grafted on, in the same way that Philip K. Dick often hid deeply serious speculations about reality behind cartoonish rockets-and-rayguns storylines. No irrefutable evidence exists in Lethem's narrative that there has actually been either a nuclear war or an alien invasion, and most of the characters do not care what has caused society's breakdown. The explanations invented by those characters who do care provide the science-fictional aspects of *Amnesia Moon*.

On some levels, the book is an absurdist fable, continually peeling away layers of reality with no real end or real answers in sight. At the close of the book, when Moon sees one of the strange machines that earlier paint-bombed his car, it may be human guerrillas warring with aliens—or it may be a local manifestation of someone's dream—or it may be an aspect of Moon's own dreams, dreams which remain mysterious to Moon throughout the story. Is Moon creating all of what he sees? Where are the boundaries between dreamer and dream, and between Moon's dreams and the dreams of others? Lethem's novel avoids providing concrete answers, while taking readers on a ride through a bizarre yet oddly familiar America.

—Alex Irvine

Animal Farm

> The animals of Manor Farm drive off the farmer who owns it and establish a community in which all animals are supposed to be equal, but their ideal state is corrupted when some animals prove to be "more equal than others"

Author: George Orwell (Eric Arthur Blair, 1903-1950)
Genre: Fantasy—animal fantasy
Type of work: Novel
Time of plot: The mid-twentieth century
Location: England
First published: 1945

The Story

A prizewinning boar named Major has a dream that he shares with the other animals of Manor Farm one night after the drunken farmer who owns the farm, Mr. Jones, has fallen asleep. Major advises the animals to reject misery and slavery and to rebel against Man, "the only real enemy we have." The rebellion, on Midsummer's Eve, drives Mr. Jones and his men off the farm.

Major draws up Seven Commandments of Animalism to govern the newly named Animal Farm, stipulating that "whoever goes on two legs is our enemy," that "all animals are equal," and that they shall not wear clothes, sleep in beds, drink alcohol, or kill any other animal. The pigs quickly assume a supervisory position to run the farm, and two of them, Snowball and Napoleon, become leaders after the death of old Major. Factions develop, and Napoleon conspires against Snowball after the animals defeat an attempt by Mr. Jones and the neighboring farmers to recover the farm at the Battle of the Cowshed.

Snowball is a brilliant debater and a visionary who wants to modernize the farm by building a windmill that will provide electrification. Two parties are formed, supporting "Snowball and the three-day week" and "Napoleon and the full manger." Meanwhile, the pigs reserve special privileges for themselves, such as consuming milk and apples that are not shared with the others.

Napoleon raises nine pups to become his guard dogs. After they have grown, his "palace guard" drives Snowball into exile, clearing the way

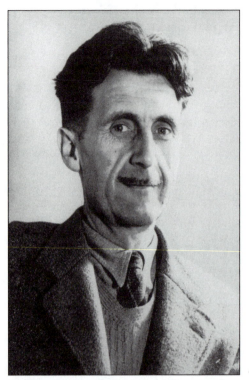

George Orwell. (Library of Congress)

for Napoleon's dictatorship. Napoleon simplifies the Seven Commandments into one slogan: "Four legs good, two legs bad." With the help of Squealer, his propagandist, Napoleon discredits Snowball's bravery and leadership in the Battle of the Cowshed and claims as his own the scheme to build a windmill. Every subsequent misfortune is then blamed on Snowball.

Thereafter, the animals work like slaves, with Napoleon as the tyrant in charge. Gradually the pigs take on more human traits and move into the farmhouse. Before long, they begin sleeping in beds and consuming alcohol. Napoleon organizes a purge, sets his dogs on four dissenting pigs who question his command, and has them bear false witness against the absent Snowball. He then has the dogs kill them, violating one of the Seven Commandments, which are slyly emended to cover the contingencies of Napoleon's rule and his desires for creature comforts.

Eventually, Napoleon enters into a political pact with one neighboring farmer, Pilkington, against the other, Frederick, whose men invade Animal Farm with guns and blow up the windmill. Working to rebuild the windmill, the brave workhorse Boxer collapses. He is sent heartlessly to the glue factory by Napoleon, who could have allowed Boxer simply to retire. All the principles of the rebellion eventually are corrupted and overturned. Finally, the pigs begin to walk on their hind legs, and all the Seven Commandments ultimately are reduced to a single one: "All Animals Are Equal, but Some Animals Are More Equal Than Others." The pigs become indistinguishable from the men who own the neighboring farms, and the animals are no better off than they were under human control.

Analysis

Of George Orwell's six novels, the two most famous, *Animal Farm* and *Nineteen Eighty-Four* (1949), were both written during the decade preceding his death. This animal fable is a political allegory of the Russian Revolution. The allegory, as various critics have demonstrated, has exact counterparts to the events and leaders of the Bolshevik Revolution, the October Revolution, and the development of the Soviet Union into a dictatorship under the control of Joseph Stalin.

The animals are led by the teachings of old Major, whose historical counterpart is Karl Marx. Snowball, the theoretician, represents Leon Trotsky, and it is Snowball who organizes the rebellion against Farmer Jones, who represents capitalism. Another swine, Napoleon, representing Joseph Stalin, discredits Snowball with the help of his propagandist, Squealer. Napoleon organizes a counterrevolution with the help of his guard dogs (the state police or palace guards, in terms of the allegory) and drives Snowball into exile (as happened with Trotsky), then plays one neighbor, Frederick (Adolf Hitler), against the other, Pilkington (a Churchillian Tory), paralleling the events of World War II.

Orwell explained his motive for writing the book in a special preface he wrote for the Ukrainian edition. He intended to expose the transformation of the Soviet Union from socialism "into a hierarchical state, in which the rulers have no more reason to give up their power than any other ruling class." Ultimately, the democratic principles of Animalism as defined by old Major are redefined as the totalitarian principles of Napoleon, and the Seven Commandments are changed to accommodate Napoleon's reign of terror, particularly the two words added at the end of one central commandment to make it read, "No animal shall kill another animal without cause."

This barnyard fantasy demonstrates how an ideal state founded on humane principles easily can be corrupted by the real world. Brutal tyrants driven by greed and ambition may lie and cheat to achieve their own selfish ends. The novel is distinguished by its clarity of style and the apparent simplicity of its narration, which has made it a classic that can be read on one level by younger readers for its story content and on other, more sophisticated levels by those interested in its political thesis. It has become a model of political allegory, a small masterpiece that speaks eloquently to the turmoil of the twentieth century.

—*James M. Welsh*

The Anubis Gates

Brendan Doyle, a poet and historian, joins a jaunt back to the eighteenth century that turns deadly and permanent

Author: Tim Powers (1952-   )
Genre: Fantasy—time travel
Type of work: Novel
Time of plot: 1684, 1802, 1810-1811, 1846, and 1983
Location: London, England, and Cairo, Egypt
First published: 1983

The Story

In *The Anubis Gates*, Professor Brendan Doyle is hired to give a lecture on Samuel Taylor Coleridge and then attend an 1810 lecture by Coleridge. The book's title refers to a set of holes in spacetime, created by worshipers of Anubis. Doyle and his party, led by millionaire J. Cochran Darrow, use one of these gates to travel to 1810. As they are leaving, Doyle is kidnapped by Dr. Romany, one of two sorcerers who created the gates. Romany takes Doyle to his camp to be tortured, but Doyle escapes.

Penniless and hungry, Doyle discovers that begging is the only employment for which he is fit. Romany has enlisted the beggar and thief guilds, led by Horrabin the Clown, to look for Doyle, but the beggars with whom Doyle falls in hate Horrabin and hide Doyle. Romany nevertheless finds him, and Doyle is forced to flee, escaping with the assistance of a young beggar named Jacky Snapp (actually a woman, Jacqueline Elizabeth Tichy, in disguise).

Doyle hopes to meet William Ashbless, a nineteenth century poet Doyle studied back in the twentieth century, and get some assistance. Ashbless never shows up where his biography claimed he wrote his first published poem, so Doyle angrily writes the poem himself from memory.

Doyle meets Dog-Face Joe, Romany's former partner, who is possessed by Anubis and cursed with ever-growing fur. Joe uses magic to trade bodies when the fur gets ahead of the razor, and he poisons his old bodies so they cannot tell tales. Joe switches bodies with Doyle, but Doyle survives. He realizes that his new body fits the description of William Ashbless, who apparently never existed, so Doyle becomes Ashbless. Doyle goes after Romany but is accidentally carried with the sorcerer through a gate to 1684. Doyle severely injures Romany and returns to 1810 alone.

Meanwhile, Darrow finally finds Dog-Face Joe, which is why he traveled to 1810: He wants to live forever. Joe will transfer Darrow into a succession of bodies, and Darrow figures to secretly own the entire world by 1983. Joe swaps bodies with Darrow, however, killing him. Joe is then killed by Jacky, who has been tracking him to avenge the murder of her fiancé.

Dr. Romany turns out to be a ka, a magical clone. The original, Dr. Romanelli, arrives in England, kidnaps Doyle, and takes him to Cairo. Doyle escapes and flees to England, but Romanelli recaptures him, along with Jacky and Coleridge. Romanelli tortures Doyle but is interrupted by a revolt of Horrabin's "Mistakes," the offspring of magically enhanced vivisection experiments. Romanelli flees with the dying Doyle to the underground river on which Ra sails the Sektet boat each night. Romanelli plans to ride the boat until dawn, when the Sun God is reborn, along with any passengers deemed worthy. Romanelli's soul fails the test, however, and it is Doyle who rides the boat through the healing dawn. He meets Jacky sitting by the Thames and discovers that she is his future bride: Jacqueline Tichy married William Ashbless.

They live happily together for many years, and the book ends when Doyle is attacked by the ka drawn many years before. Doyle kills the ka (which history has assumed was Ashbless) and begins a life that, for the first time in many years, will be a surprise to him.

Analysis

One of Tim Powers's finest novels, this book won the 1984 Philip K. Dick Award. Its fast pacing, one of Powers's hallmarks, never lets up from beginning to end. Highlights include further insights into the nature of a magical paradigm that was first outlined in *The Drawing of the Dark* (1979) and was used in *On Stranger Tides* (1987). Powers's theory of magic includes some engaging twists on old myths. For example, the power of a mage's real name presumably derives from its reflection of the mage's inner being. Thus, when a sorcerer undergoes a major personality change, his or her true name changes as well.

An important theme in this book is the gradual fading of magic. In Powers's schema, magic fades before the light of Christianity. As the last strongholds of magic-working religions are overwhelmed during the nineteenth century, magic gradually vanishes. As part of this process, the universe is transformed from a magical world to a scientific one. For example, until 1810, the sun actually was carried by Ra underground in a fabulous boat. By the end of the story, however, the underground channel has vanished, and the sun has become the ball of burning gas it is today. This is a delightful way to work the paradigm shift. In Powers's sixth novel, *Last Call* (1992), he uses a different paradigm involving the tarot and nonfading magic.

Powers brought the grotesque simile, another of his trademarks, to fantastic heights in this book. In one example, he describes a character's "blank smile returning to his face like something dead floating to the surface of a pond."

The plot of *The Anubis Gates* is similar to those of some of Powers's other novels. The protagonist encounters a problem, struggles against it, and gives himself up to drugs and denial but pulls himself together in the end. In this book, the "problem" that Doyle cannot face is the death of his first wife, and he is well on the way to becoming an alcoholic wreck in the first chapter. Being dumped into the nineteenth century in the midst of a struggle for mastery of the world seems to be what Doyle needs to take his mind off his misery.

An interesting facet of this book is the treatment of immortality. The Egyptian Master is more than forty-three hundred years old and is senile. His two servants, Romanelli and Amenophis Fikee, millennia old themselves, trudge through the same ruts they seem to have occupied since they reached adulthood. Extended life does not bring enhanced wisdom, and one is compelled to pity the doomed sorcerers even while loathing them. J. Cochran Darrow, the wealthy sponsor of the time trip, has personal immortality as his ultimate goal. This obsession destroys him and leads the reader to pity him. Powers's treatment of immortality strongly resembles that of Barry Hughart in the Master Li series.

—*David C. Kopaska-Merkel*

At the Back of the North Wind

A little boy named Diamond is befriended by the North Wind and finds in her an escape from poverty and disease into a world beyond pain and suffering

Author: George MacDonald (1824-1905)
Genre: Fantasy—high fantasy
Type of work: Novel
Time of plot: The nineteenth century
Location: London and Kent, England
First published: 1871 (serial form; *Good Words for the Young*, 1868-1870)

The Story

At the Back of the North Wind was first published in installments, with the first appearing in November, 1868, and others from November, 1869, to October, 1870. This work, George MacDonald's first full-length children's story, has been reasonably popular.

The story begins with a little boy named Diamond who is growing up in poverty. He is the son of a gracious coachman named Joseph, who is married to a kindly woman named Martha. Joseph works for the Colemans, who are kind enough in manners but not very generous in paying their employees, who live meagerly in the weatherbeaten room above the coach house. Mr. Coleman's speculation in questionable business matters eventually leads to his ruin and descent into near poverty. This state of hardship improves Mr. Coleman's character but makes life even more difficult for Diamond and his family.

Diamond's family goes through many trials as he is befriended by the North Wind and goes on adventures with her. She first meets him while he is sleeping in his bed in the hayloft. She coaxes him to join her for flights into the night. Diamond is often uncertain whether he has actually been outside during the night or has only been dreaming. On these trips with the North Wind, he meets a little girl named Nanny whom he befriends and later helps.

Diamond learns that the North Wind destroys ships and chimneys as well as rescuing people. He is troubled by her seeming dual nature but learns to accept both sides of her. Diamond's own health is uncertain at times, and he is sent to his aunt's home in Sandwich on the seaside. From

George MacDonald. (Hulton Archive)

this home he takes an adventure all the way to the back of the North Wind, or at least to a picture of it, as he later learns. For seven days, he lingers near death before returning to consciousness.

Some time after Diamond has recovered, he returns with his mother and her new baby to a home in the mews near London. Joseph is working for himself now and using his favorite horse from Mr. Coleman's estate, the horse for whom Diamond had been named. Diamond proves to be a helpful child, even taking over the family business when his father falls ill. While working, he meets Mr. Raymond, a man who loves children and stories and encourages Diamond to learn how to read. With Mr. Raymond's help, Diamond rescues Nanny from sickness and seemingly certain death. Mr. Raymond later gives Joseph the task of watching Ruby, a lazy horse who needs exercising, while Mr. Raymond spends three months on the Continent. When Mr. Raymond returns from vacation, he has a new bride with him and invites Joseph and his family to move to the country in Kent and serve as the Raymonds' hired help. There the family enjoys great comfort and some prosperity. Diamond seems lonely, however, in spite of friends such as Nanny and her friend Jim. Diamond takes a few more trips with the North Wind and finally makes a last journey to the back of the North Wind. He dies in peace.

Analysis

Like many of MacDonald's fantasy works, *At the Back of the North Wind* evolves organically, with many loose ends and an unexplained conclusion. As his first full-length story specifically written for children, this work embodies many small messages for the young, much like his earlier work *Phantastes* (1858), supposedly written for adults. If a distinction between his writings for children and those for adults is difficult to draw, this is so because, as MacDonald declared, he did "not write for children, but for the childlike, whether of five, or fifty, or seventy-five."

Two of MacDonald's later fantasy works for children, *The Princess and the Goblin* (1871) and *The Princess and Curdie* (1882), also proved to be popular for a time. MacDonald's fantasy work bears some resemblance to *Alice's Adventures in Wonderland* (1865) by Lewis Carroll (C. L. Dodgson), an author with whom MacDonald often corresponded.

Throughout *At the Back of the North Wind*, MacDonald introduces themes such as the value of kindness, cheerfulness in spite of poverty, and helping one's parents. The North Wind introduces the little boy Diamond to the harsh realities of life and leads him to understand that a positive attitude and selfless pattern of living will help everyone to endure the hardships of life more easily. Although they are not mentioned directly, much of this book emphasizes Christian values and Victorian ideals. The values of hard work, honesty, selflessness, and loving patience are all abundantly evident in the life of Diamond. He is sometimes teasingly called "God's baby" because his line of thinking is so different from that of other people. His good conduct makes the other coachmen feel ashamed of their cussing and mean ways.

These qualities of goodness in Diamond are prompted by his trip to the back of the North Wind, where he learns to be gracious and kind. Even Nanny, Diamond's spiteful friend, learns to be kinder by her dream trips guided by the North Wind while she recovers from a serious illness.

The strength of this novel lies in its imaginative presentation of difficult theological problems, such as providence or the hand of God as represented by the North Wind. The trials of daily life are seen as being potentially useful if people are selfless. What is less strong in this novel is the repeated use of lyrics, which are more chatty than interesting and purposeful. These verses do little to convey the beauty of the back of the North Wind, with which Diamond has fallen in love. Another weakness is the use of a lead character, Diamond, who seems too good for life. Like many of MacDonald's works, this one feels overly long, yet it is full of intriguing perspectives and imaginative treatments of the commonplace.

—*Daven M. Kari*

At the Mountains of Madness and Other Novels

In the primary novella, an expedition to Antarctica discovers the remains of a great alien civilization; other works describe various horrors

Author: H(oward) P(hillips) Lovecraft (1890-1937)
Genre: Science fiction—occult
Type of work: Collected works
Time of plot: The 1920's and 1930's
Location: New England and Antarctica
First published: 1964 (corrected edition, 1985; contains *At the Mountains of Madness*, 1936; *The Case of Charles Dexter Ward*, 1941; "The Statement of Randolph Carter," 1920; "The Shunned House," 1937; "The Dreams in the Witch-House," 1933; "The Dream-Quest of Unknown Kadath," 1948; "The Silver Key," 1939; and "Through the Gates of the Silver Key," 1934, written with E. Hoffman Price)

The Story

At the Mountains of Madness and Other Novels, which contains the title novella and several of H. P. Lovecraft's longer tales, was first published in 1964 by Arkham House, the Sauk City, Wisconsin, publishing house created in 1939 by Donald Wandrei and August Derleth for the primary purpose of making Lovecraft's work generally available to the American public. Until then, Lovecraft's tales had appeared only in the pages of such "pulp fiction" magazines as *Weird Tales* and were known to relatively few readers. By the 1950's, however, thanks to the efforts of Wandrei, Derleth, and other loyal members of the Lovecraft "circle," Lovecraft generally was recognized as one of the finest twentieth century American writers of horror fiction.

Although Lovecraft tried his hand at many kinds of horror story, he is best remembered for his tales of cosmic horror based on the so-called Cthulhu Mythos. These dozen or so tales, which include both *At the Mountains of Madness* and *The Case of Charles Dexter Ward*, employ a common background: the idea that Earth was inhabited for eons before the appearance of humans by a race of extraterrestrial/other-dimensional beings whose tremendous powers dwarf those of humankind. These beings, which Lovecraft calls the Old Ones, continue to exist both outside the earthly dimensions inhabited by humans and, more threateningly, in crypts hidden deep within the planet's surface or below the oceans' waters. Under the right circumstances, with the aid of forbidden knowledge gained from such books as the dreaded (but wholly fictitious) *Necronomicon*, they can be called back.

Although Lovecraft's linguistic style—with its excessive use of adjectives and arcane spellings—might well be termed idiosyncratic, it is difficult, even among those tales employing the Cthulhu Mythos, to identify any "typical" Lovecraft plot. *At the Mountains of Madness* tells of a scientific expedition sent by Lovecraft's fictional Miskatonic University to explore Antarctica, whereas "The Dreams in the Witch-House" is the story of a college student's macabre dreams while rooming in a reputedly haunted house. *The Case of Charles Dexter Ward* concerns a student in Lovecraft's hometown of Providence, Rhode Island, who is possessed by the malevolent spirit of his ancestor, a seventeenth century wizard.

Certain threads do seem to run through most of Lovecraft's fiction. There is, for example, the nature of the "cosmic" horror on which he so often depends. Rather than being actively evil, Lovecraft's Old Ones are more frequently indifferent, oblivious to such insignificant creatures as humans and completely uncaring. The creatures in *At the Mountains of Madness*, for example, are certainly repulsive—in fact, they very nearly defy description—but what makes them truly horrifying is their seeming disdain for human life. This aspect of his creations sets Lovecraft apart from other writers of horror fiction. The Old Ones' behavior toward humans usually lacks either calculation or ill will. They behave exactly as humans might toward ants: Those that get in their way are crushed, without explanation or apology. Traditional religious symbols offer no protection, nor do prayers or more conventional weapons.

The characters in Lovecraft's tales seem, for the most part, to be cut from similar fabric. With very few exceptions, they are decidedly ordinary and nonheroic. By profession, they are often scientists and antiquarians, who often are stereotyped as cold and emotionless. Whatever victories they achieve seem at best equivocal and temporary. Lovecraft's universe, in which humanity's role is so minor as to be irrelevant, allows for little more.

Analysis

Since Lovecraft's death in 1937, his fiction has gained steadily in popularity and critical prestige. This is hardly surprising, for his work, taken as a whole, possesses a strange but undeniable power, in large part because he avoids the standard horror fare of vampires, ghouls, and werewolves. He concentrates instead on creating a sense of horror that is as much intellectual and spiritual as visceral. There are few "chase" scenes in Lovecraft's work and few of the battles to the death between heroes and monsters that readers have come to expect from modern writers of horror fiction such as Stephen King. What readers experience instead is a gradually increasing sense of horror grounded in the awareness that the universe is not at all as people traditionally have conceived it. Humans are not the center of this or any other universe; they are mere specks of sentient matter protected only by their own ignorance and relative insignificance. All that knowledge finally can provide, as several of Lovecraft's narrators explain, is horror too great to bear.

A further strategy Lovecraft employs involves denying his characters the conventional props of religion and science. Lovecraft himself was a professed atheist, and his stories usually are set within a larger framework that might be called existential. The God of Judeo-Christian tradition is wholly absent, rendering moot the question of divine assistance in combating the monstrous creatures of Lovecraft's imagination. His characters neither seek God's help nor seem to expect it. In "The Dunwich Horror" (1929), perhaps Lovecraft's best-known story, several Miskatonic professors turn not to the Bible for help in foiling an evil plan to open the gates between dimensions, but to the *Necronomicon*. Science, constructed as it is from a mistaken view of the universe, is likewise of no real use. In fact, as the scientist-narrator tells readers at the beginning of *At the Mountains of Madness*, science's wisest course might be "to deter the exploring world in general" from uncovering more evidence of humankind's true place in the universe.

—*Michael Stuprich*

The Barsoom Series

John Carter, a Civil War veteran, journeys to Mars in a series of out-of-body experiences and establishes himself as one of the most respected warriors on the red planet

Author: Edgar Rice Burroughs (1875-1950)
Genre: Science fiction—planetary romance
Type of work: Novels
Time of plot: The late nineteenth and early twentieth centuries
Location: Earth and Mars
First published: *A Princess of Mars* (1917; serial form, as by Norman Bean, "Under the Moons of Mars," *All-Story Magazine*, 1912), *The Gods of Mars* (1918; serial form, *All-Story Magazine*, 1913), *The Warlord of Mars* (1919; serial form, *All-Story Magazine*, 1913-1914), *Thuvia, Maid of Mars* (1920; serial form, *All-Story Weekly*, 1916), *The Chessmen of Mars* (1922), *The Master Mind of Mars* (1928), *A Fighting Man of Mars* (1931), *Swords of Mars* (1936), *Synthetic Men of Mars* (1940), *Llana of Gathol* (1948; serial form, *Amazing Stories*, 1941), and *John Carter of Mars* (1964; serial form, *Amazing Stories*, 1941-1943)

The Story

Although the Barsoom series was written over a long period of time and spans a long time in its internal chronology, Edgar Rice Burroughs sustained his narrative by creating a plot line that chronicled the adventures of a family, not one individual. Through eleven novels, originally serialized in popular science-fiction magazines, the history of Mars is traced from ancient times to the present.

Seeking to recoup his fortunes after the defeat of the Confederacy, John Carter leaves Virginia to prospect for gold in Arizona. While trying to rescue his partner, who has been ambushed by Apaches, Carter is trapped in a cave by the same warriors, undergoes an out-of-body experience, and awakes on Mars.

A Princess of Mars initiates a series of amazing adventures. After being captured by a band of Tharks, the four-armed green men of Barsoom, the native name of Mars, Carter wins their admiration by strength of arms. Accepted into this warrior culture, he masters their language and encounters another captive, Dejah Thoris, Princess of Helium, a beautiful woman of the red Martian race. Carter falls in love with the princess, whom he rescues. They marry, and for nine years their happiness is complete. Then, while trying to save the system that stabilizes the atmospherem of Mars, Carter collapses. When he awakes, he is again in the cave.

After willing himself to return to Barsoom, Carter begins his adventures anew in *The Gods of Mars*. As he reveals the hypocrisy in the Martian religion, Carter encounters carnivorous plant-men, vicious white apes, the white race, and finally the black race of Mars. After an absence of a decade, Carter is surprised and delighted to find his son, Carthoris, who is almost grown. They escape death only to discover Dejah Thoris trapped in an impregnable prison.

Having delivered the Martians from the religion that had duped uncounted generations, Carter rescues his beloved in *The Warlord of Mars*. While seeking Dejah Thoris, he encounters the yellow race of Mars, overthrows a tyranny more pernicious than any he had yet encountered, and is proclaimed Warlord of Barsoom.

Thuvia, Maid of Mars is a love story that relates the adventures of Carthoris. Thuvia, princess of Ptarth, is kidnapped by a rejected suitor who frames Carthoris with the crime, but Carthoris proves his innocence and wins his bride after a series of harrowing adventures.

Tara of Helium, the daughter of Carter and Dejah Thoris, is the heroine of *The Chessmen of Mars*. After she lands her damaged aircraft in a violent windstorm, Tara begins a series of adventures that include her capture by the inhabitants of the city of Manator, who play jetan, the Martian version of chess, to the death with living beings. Through the same tenacity shown by the other members of her family, Tara overcomes all difficulties.

Inspired by Carter's example, Ulysses Paxton escapes from the trenches of World War I and awakes in the clinic of Ras Thavas, the title character of *The Master*

Edgar Rice Burroughs. (Library of Congress)

Mind of Mars, who has perfected a technique for transplanting organs—including the brain—from one human to another. When an evil ruler purchases the body of the woman whom Paxton loves, the Earthman embarks on a successful quest to rescue his beloved.

A Fighting Man of Mars relates the quest of Tan Hadron, who saves Mars while trying to rescue the woman he loves from a power-crazed warlord. Absent from this narrative are the philosophical speculations that form an important part of *The Gods of Mars* and *The Master Mind of Mars*. This tale is pure adventure.

Swords of Mars is fascinating not merely for the swashbuckling exploits found in all the Barsoom novels but also for the introduction of an artificial brain capable of guiding a Martian airborne vessel. After Dejah Thoris is injured in an accident, Carter seeks Ras Thavas, the mastermind of Mars, who is unfortunately the prisoner of his own creations, a group of artificial humans. Following a series of harrowing escapades, *Synthetic Men of Mars* concludes with the treatment and recovery of Dejah Thoris.

In *Llana of Gathol*, Carter encounters a race of white men who have lived in secret for ages in one of the ruined cities of Mars. His discovery of this race sets in motion a number of exploits that lead him across the face of the planet. He ends his adventure by delivering the city of Gathol from Hin Abtol, a would-be conqueror from the frozen wastes of Barsoom.

In the final volume, *John Carter of Mars*, the red planet is threatened by a gigantic white ape that is the creation of a scientist gone mad. The Warlord of Mars once again delivers his adopted home from destruction.

Analysis

With the publication of *A Princess of Mars*, his first novel, Burroughs began a series that would have a profound effect on the development of the genre of science fiction. Each volume originally was serialized in a popular journal, and Burroughs did not alter the episodic quality of his Barsoom stories when they were published as separate works.

The record of the deeds of John Carter and his family have endured partly because the reader encounters ideas and concepts that are usually the purview of philosophers and theologians. Many of the carefully crafted details in the stories might initially shock, but as a whole they become essential ingredients in the creation of a vision of another world that still captures the imagination. Burroughs is as successful as Jules Verne in predicting the shape of things to come, and his vision of the moral dilemmas that haunt his own century is both extraordinary and frightening.

Having deposited his hero on the surface of Mars, Burroughs casually mentions that Carter is naked—in fact, all Martians, male and female, prefer that state. The only accessories they wear are decorative harnesses and belts that provide protection and denote their status and accomplishments. By discarding the external adornments that occupy significant attention in other works of science fiction, Burroughs is able to concentrate on the internal habiliments of his characters. He is more concerned with the psychological than the fashionable. Because Carter accepts nudity as normal, the reader also tolerates this altered state of being. Burroughs also deals with Martian sexuality by revealing the fact that the women of Barsoom do not bear their young alive but instead lay eggs that take years to mature. Sex for the average Martian takes a poor second to the favorite preoccupation of violence.

Peace and tranquillity are almost unknown to the inhabitants of Barsoom. The moment they fight their way out of their shells, they are ready for conflict. It is impossible to exaggerate the importance of brutality in each and every story. Slavery is an accepted part of life. It is nonracial and is the potential fate of both sexes and all ranks, from rulers to commoners.

Carter embraces the life of the warrior and revels in it from the first page to the last; however, gratuitous violence and unwarranted cruelty are punished by Martian hubris because they are not part of the code of the warrior. In his sometimes stirring prose, Burroughs captures a rather unflattering reflection of his own world and its obsession with honor, duty, and war.

The discussion of race and religion is subtle and masterful. Each group of Martians boasts superiority only to be superseded by another. The green race is dismissed by the red as inferior, only to be labeled by the white with a similar epithet. Blacks dismiss whites only to be regarded as mediocre by the yellow inhabitants of Mars. Each racial division is equally deceived by the ancient religion of Barsoom, which is but a cult of death. The triumph of Carter over the superstition embraced by the inhabitants of his adopted world may well reflect the feelings of Burroughs himself toward the religious establishment of his own time. Carter often seems near to death, but he never surrenders control of his own fate to any power; he is ever the master of his soul. Carter is Everyman, and therein lies the enduring quality of the Barsoom series.

—*Clifton W. Potter, Jr.*

The Best of C. M. Kornbluth

> Out of contemporary conditions arise tomorrow's problems, which can be solved or understood only with the perspective of history

Author: Cyril M. Kornbluth (1923-1958)
Genre: Science fiction—extrapolatory
Type of work: Stories
Time of plot: The 1950's to the distant future
Location: Various sites, especially cities, on Earth and other planets
First published: 1976

The Story

Two of Cyril M. Kornbluth's most famous stories, the novelettes "The Little Black Bag" (1950) and "The Marching Morons" (1951), posit the same future. Twenty generations from now, prolific, low-IQ groups vastly outnumber intelligent people on Earth because of the latter's low birthrates. The moronic majority thrives only through the labors of the intellectuals.

The earlier story introduces elderly Bayard Full, a ruined, slum-dwelling, dipsomaniacal medical doctor. An accident sends a doctor's black bag from the future into his possession. Designed for use by idiots, the bag yields its secrets readily to Dr. Full and his accidentally acquired assistant, Angie. Reinvigorated and reformed, Dr. Full begins performing miraculous operations and nurturing a new self-image as benefactor of humanity. Angie, however, has less humanitarian goals and succeeds in destroying the hopes of both herself and Dr. Full.

"The Marching Morons" more fully explores the future world dominated by idiots. The intelligent minority faces one central problem: what to do about the ever-worsening population disparity between idiots and geniuses. The minority receives a windfall in the form of real estate salesman Honest John Barlow, revived from a state of suspended animation accidentally achieved in the twentieth century. Barlow agrees to solve the problem if he is given dictatorial power, a request that is granted readily. Barlow then suckers the general populace, through advertising and sly references during television sitcoms, into taking rockets to Venus, an unreachable promised land. They fall for the ruse and die in great numbers. In the end, Barlow suffers the same fate he inflicted on others.

Two late novelettes, "Shark Ship" (originally "Reap the Dark Tide," 1958) and "Two Dooms" (1958; Kornbluth's preferred title was "The Doomsman"), probe other grim futures. "Shark Ship" details life aboard a convoy of ships divorced from all contact with land. The lives of those on board depend on the spring swarming of plankton. When a storm destroys his ship's irreplaceable fishing net, Captain Thomas Salter finds himself, his ship, and his crew expelled from the convoy. An idea previously thought heretical now appears to be his only option: He must steer for land. The landing party discovers an America depopulated by death cults whose influence became pervasive in previous centuries. Surviving cult members give the landing party a taste of the violence that purged the once-overpopulated mainland.

"Two Dooms" follows atomic physicist Edward Royland on his accidental journey into an alternative universe where the Nazis and Japanese rule a divided United States. In his own world, Royland debated whether to delay progress at the Los Alamos nuclear research site or to help the atomic bomb achieve its terrifying result. Encountering both a slave village and a concentration camp in the alternative America, he comes to grips with the idea of life under bondage.

Other notable works in this volume include "The Words of Guru" (1941), an early but striking fantasy about a genius child acquiring supernatural power; "The Last Man Left in the Bar" (1957), a confrontation between aliens and a magnetron technician, written with an audacious literary command that anticipates the stylistic revolution of the 1960's; "The Altar at Midnight" (1952), a portrayal of the costs of spaceflight; and the influential "The Mindworm" (1950), detailing the rise and fall of a psychic vampire.

Analysis

Although Kornbluth received acclaim as a novelist, his reputation rests largely on his shorter works, which are recognized for their intelligence, incisive wit, and readability.

"The Marching Morons," one of the most famous novelettes in science fiction, has prompted many critics to examine its future scenario of an intelligent but overwhelmed minority. Those focusing on its genetics, however, have tended to overlook, and inadvertently belittle, the social criticism explicit in the story. When the intellectuals turn to Barlow to solve their problem, they find themselves employing a veritable Adolf Hitler. Kornbluth takes a global view, however: He juxtaposes Nazi gas chambers and American bombings of Japanese civilians by having Barlow's rockets lift off from Los Alamos. The intelligentsia appear as culpable as Honest John.

Kornbluth's concern with the ethics of theoretical science underlies both "Two Dooms," with its indecisive Royland, and "Gomez" (1954), whose protagonist, Julio Gomez, sits on a similar fence with regard to unified field theory, the implications of which terrify him. Both stories explore moral quandaries of the atomic age, as do such other works as "The Altar at Midnight," Kornbluth's fascinating first solo novel *Takeoff* (1952), and "The Remorseful" (1954).

Kornbluth's concern with the impact of theoretical knowledge parallels his concern with history. Historical insight appears as a redemptive if sometimes dangerous force throughout Kornbluth's works, notably here in "Shark Ship," "The Luckiest Man in Denv" (1952), "The Mindworm," and "The Adventurer" (1953).

Many of these stories shed light on other works. "The Rocket of 1955," a vignette that first appeared in a 1939 fanzine, and "The Marching Morons" anticipate *The Space Merchants* (with Frederik Pohl, 1953), whereas "The Little Black Bag" and "The Marching Morons" anticipate *Search the Sky* (with Pohl, 1954). "Two Dooms" bears comparison to Kornbluth's *Not This August* (1955), depicting an America beneath communist subjugation, and Philip K. Dick's *The Man in the High Castle* (1962). "With These Hands" bears comparison to Walter M. Miller, Jr.'s "The Darfstellar" (1955).

Critics judging Kornbluth by this anthology, edited by Pohl, have seen a growing bitterness in his later stories. This reflects editorial choice more than reality, because Kornbluth also wrote delightful humor in his last years, in stories not collected here. These tales demonstrate Kornbluth's effective use of everyday individuals from a variety of ethnic backgrounds as well as his well-tuned ear for dialect.

—*Mark Rich*

The Best Short Stories of J. G. Ballard

Stories focusing on protagonists' mental and physiological relationships with drastically altered environments

Author: J(ames) G(raham) Ballard (1930-   )
Genre: Science fiction—New Wave
Type of work: Stories
Time of plot: Primarily the near future
Location: Imaginary locales on Earth
First published: 1978

The Story

The Best Short Stories of J. G. Ballard contains nineteen impressive works published between 1957 and 1978 in such British and American magazines as *New Worlds*, *The Magazine of Fantasy and Science Fiction*, and *Amazing Stories*. Together, these stories show the extraordinary imagination and range of Ballard's storytelling. There are tales of spaceflight, urban isolation, psychological manipulation, and the outbreak of strange, imaginary diseases. The stories take place in the overcrowded cities of the future, on abandoned South Sea islands, and within view of the quiet but suddenly terrifying lawns of suburbia.

Ballard's stories show his preoccupation with the internal landscapes of the mind. They also contain unusual responses to the challenges his characters face. Harry Faulkner, in "The Overloaded Man," suddenly loses touch with his suburban neighborhood. He begins to perceive the world as an abstract painting and decides to drown himself to extinguish this new sensory overload. Contrary to expectations, the short story views Faulkner's action as a relative success.

Far from confining himself to realistic places, disasters, or injuries, Ballard invents new ones for most of his stories. He creates vivid cities of the future, such as an imaginary subtropical community, where "The Cloud-Sculptors of Coral D" reside and create their imaginary art, and the refuse-littered, abandoned launchpads of Cape Canaveral in "The Cage of Sand," where two men and a woman have gathered to watch the nightly appearance of as many as seven dead astronauts who orbit Earth in their functionless capsules.

Ballard's protagonists, though thrust into strange new worlds and alien landscapes, generally accept these with little questioning, as does Count Axel in "The Garden of Time." His flowers are able to stop time outside his mansion, where barbarian hordes ready themselves for a final assault. They will succeed when his last flower has been plucked.

Like Count Axel and Louisa Woodwind, whose husband is one of the dead astronauts, Ballard's protagonists typically are well-educated, articulate, and emotionally controlled men and women. As Harry Faulkner shows, however, beneath this tranquil facade of reason, control, and clinical detachment is a deeper layer of strange obsessions and aberrant needs.

This defiance of the normal and fictional probing of the radically new are crucial aspects of many of the stories. "The Terminal Beach" successfully experiments with style and language. It focuses on Traven's mindframe, which has guided him to maroon himself on the Pacific island of Eniwetok, the historical site of American nuclear tests. There, Traven tries to make his body a part of the natural landscape and to construct a complex system that integrates the living, the dead, and inanimate objects.

Analysis

Ballard's short stories were instrumental in the success of science fiction's New Wave movement. Many of the developments associated with it, such as a move toward inner space, a more critical attitude toward technology, and the redefinition of some of the conventions of science fiction (for example, time travel), are essential ingredients of Ballard's stories.

"Manhole 69" shows readers what an imaginative writer can do within the genre of science fiction. The story of three men whom a medical experiment has left with the inability to sleep turns to the unexpected when all three, rather than enjoy prolonged hours of productivity, withdraw into a form of autism.

The literary quality of such stories as "The Drowned Giant," which tells of the gradual dismemberment of the washed-up corpse of a gigantic man, also exemplifies how well New Wave science fiction brings literary respectability to a literature formerly dismissed by most critics. The stylistic experimentation visible in tales such as "The Terminal Beach" makes these pieces unique.

Although Ballard's stories have been compared with the works of mainstream American authors Donald Barthelme and William S. Burroughs, their focus on the inner cosmos echoes significant works of other science-fiction writers. For example, Alfred Bester's haunting tale of a murderer on the run from telepathic policemen, *The Demolished Man*

(1953), displays an intensity similar to Ballard's. Brian Aldiss also shares some of Ballard's concerns; in *Cryptozoic!* (1968; published in Great Britain as *An Age*, 1967), Aldiss takes the idea of time travel and accomplishes it with mind-altering drugs that allow his characters to leave the confines of the present.

With their uncomfortable dissection of Western cultural icons, stories such as "The Atrocity Exhibition" have been hailed as the fictional equivalent of the literary and cultural criticism of scholars such as Roland Barthes. Taking its cue from occupational therapy, "The Atrocity Exhibition" offers a series of violent pictures painted by imaginary inmates of an insane asylum. Its central, unsettling idea is that the products of human culture, taken from the fields of warfare, technology, art, and popular entertainment, not only are intrinsically violent but also correspond to the biological features of the human body.

From the stories in this collection, Ballard has moved on to write more experimental short fiction. He has also produced works whose content takes a more conventional form. He has even worked in the area of autobiography with his book *Empire of the Sun* (1984).

Ballard occasionally has been attacked by critics who have failed to grasp the premises of his fiction. Like the reviewer-turned-psychiatrist who perceived a psychopathic mind behind his work, they mistakenly have read his stories as straight advocacy of criminal insanity. Ballard's exploration of a new, purely fictional reality has met with increasing critical acclaim. His stories are often haunting and occasionally terrifying, but never conventional or dull.

—*R. C. Lutz*

Blood Music

Vergil Ulam injects himself with thinking cells that push his body and, eventually, the rest of Earth into the next stage in evolution

Author: Greg Bear (1951-   )
Genre: Fantasy—evolutionary fantasy
Type of work: Novel
Time of plot: The late twentieth century
Location: California, New York, Germany, and Great Britain
First published: 1985

The Story

Thirty-two-year-old Vergil Ulam is a brilliant but undisciplined bio-engineer at the Genetron laboratories in La Jolla, California. This area is known as Enzyme Valley, the biochip equivalent of Silicon Valley. His pet project is what he calls "biologic," the development of "thinking" lymphocytes that he describes as autonomous organic computers. When his employer learns that Ulam has been conducting this research for the past two years on mammalian cells, Ulam is fired. Before he leaves the building, he injects himself with the cells and destroys the records of his research.

Ulam had hoped to retrieve the lymphocytes from his system and continue his research. Two weeks later, though, he still has not found access to a lab, and he knows that it is too late to remove the altered cells. The first changes to his system that he notices are a craving for sweets, better eyesight, and a better sex life. When he realizes that there is no turning back, he visits his clairvoyant mother. She immediately discerns that his experiment has gotten beyond her son's control but that it is his life's work.

Ulam concludes that the lymphocytes have developed the capacity to spread their biologic traits to other types of cells and that they could migrate outside his body. He visits Edward Milligan, a school friend, and explains his theory that human DNA has spent millions of years building to a climax that is now expressing itself in Ulam's experiment, which offers the doorway for the lymphocytes to escape the human species. Listening to their activity inside his body, which he calls "blood music," he wonders when the cells will become cognizant of Ulam himself as an entity enclosing them. The answer comes soon, when he begins hearing words spoken within his brain by the other entities.

Milligan quickly understands the dangerous implications, confirmed when he walks in on Ulam and his girlfriend and discovers them changing into strange shapeless masses of flesh. To stop a possible epidemic, Milligan kills Ulam. Michael Bernard, head of Genetron, realizes that a mere handshake could spread the altered genes from one individual to another and that it is too late to stop it from spreading throughout the United States. Recognizing that he is infected, he flies to Wiesbaden, Germany, and secures himself in an isolation laboratory for observation.

Heinz Paulsen-Fuchs, the biologist who observed Bernard gradually showing signs of the transforming genes, knows he cannot hold off the terrified protesters who want to kill Bernard before Europe becomes infected. Meanwhile, the United States itself changes shape as the self-aware genes form a massive thinking community. Bernard communes with the cells inside himself and, with the help of a visiting British physicist, theorizes that thought, in sufficient quantity, could physically alter the universe. With all these cells suddenly conscious, the potential for change has become exponentially greater.

Bernard willingly allows his own transformation and "enters" the world inside himself. Viewed by the cells as one of their creators, he is treated with respect and moved into Thought Universe, where he recognizes that no one really dies; instead, there is endless replication within cells in the blood. Various humans resist transformation, and the cells respect their decision. Ultimately, the number of thinking cells becomes so large that their community of cooperation enters into a realm beyond physical matter.

Analysis

Greg Bear's topics range from fantasy to pure science fiction, and they generally demand that his protagonist come to a new understanding of the universe. During the 1980's, Bear won the Nebula Award twice, for the novella "Hard Fought" (1983) and for the short story "Tangents" (1986), and the Hugo Award (1984) for the short story "Blood Music," published in *Analog*. He has stated that *Blood Music*, his seventh novel, was influenced by his study of information theory and information mechanics. Upon the suggestion of David Brin and John F. Carr, Bear decided to expand "Blood Music," adding complexity with chapters devoted to new characters.

Much in the manner that James Blish's *A Case of Conscience* (1958) uses a fictional Jesuit astrophysicist to raise ethical questions regarding the individual moral systems of other galaxies, Bear builds his story on the writings of the actual Jesuit paleontologist Pierre Teilhard de Chardin, who combined Christian theology and evolutionary theory to posit Jesus Christ both as temporal and as a timeless symbol for the final step of evolution, which he described as a "noosphere." Bear is not directly theological, though he works with the idea of a creator; his basic debt to Teilhard is the notion of a critical mass of thinkers somehow transcending space and time and bringing into existence what amounts to a new heaven and a new Earth.

Bear's novel has been called a *Childhood's End* (Arthur C. Clarke, 1953) for the 1980's, and the comparison seems apt. Theodore Sturgeon's *More than Human* (1953) also comes immediately to mind as a source for comparison. *Blood Music* follows in the tradition of science-fiction writing that ponders the possibility that *Homo sapiens* may not be the final word in nature's self-expression. Bear's novel shows a greater scientific sophistication than Clarke's earlier work, focusing in convincing detail on the actual biological mechanisms used in laboratories of the 1980's and 1990's. It suggests that the human need to see humanity as the center of the biological universe is as egotistical as humanity's earlier notion that Earth was the center of the galaxy. As threatening as the notion of absorption into a larger community is to Bear's characters, he does his best to convince them, and his readers, that individual subjectivity may go the way of nation-states. In its place will come a cooperative assertion of racial memory.

—*John C. Hawley*

The Blue Sword and
The Hero and the Crown

Two women of Damar carry the same sword in two different eras and must learn to use both magic and swordplay to save the kingdom from the forces of evil

Author: Robin McKinley (1952-   )
Genre: Fantasy—heroic fantasy
Type of work: Novels
Time of plot: Undefined
Location: Primarily the land of Damar
First published: *The Blue Sword* (1982) and *The Hero and the Crown* (1984)

The Story

The Blue Sword and *The Hero and the Crown* are the first two books of a promised trilogy about the land of Damar. *The Blue Sword* takes place in the present, when Outlanders rule much of Damar. *The Hero and the Crown*, a "prequel," tells the story of an earlier Damar before the Outlanders arrived. Harry and Aerin, the two female heroes, each must learn to master her psychic powers. In addition, both endure extensive training in swordplay to prepare them for battle with Damar's longstanding enemy, the inhuman demon race of the North.

In *The Blue Sword*, Harry Crewe leaves her Homeland after her father's death and goes to live at the outpost where her brother Richard is stationed. Harry is restless and oddly drawn to the hills beyond her new home. Corlath, the king of the last remaining Free Hillfolk not under Homelander rule, comes to plead with the Outlander superiors to unite with him against a common enemy. A psychic hunch tells Corlath that Harry is destined to be important to the Free Hillfolk, and he kidnaps her. Harry is discovered to possess an abundance of the psychic powers needed to defeat the Northerners. Mathin, one of the King's elite Riders, puts Harry through a rigorous training period. Harry learns to ride Sungold, her new Hill horse, and to fight with a sword. She also learns to love her new home, and she makes many friends among both human and animal followers of Corlath. Harry eventually is given the sword that belonged to Lady Aerin, Dragon-Killer, a legendary female warrior who led Damar to victory against the North in an earlier era.

As the Free Hillfolk prepare for war, Harry must deal with the conflicting emotions of loyalty to her Homeland and of her growing love for Corlath and his people. Standing between two worlds, Harry must risk her connections to the Homeland and the Hillfolk in order to save them both. To accomplish this, she must draw on her untrained psychic powers to bury the enemy under a mountain. She succeeds in leading the Damarians to victory and in cementing her relationship with Corlath. As an Outlander queen of the Free Hillfolk, she will lead her newfound people into an era in which they hope to establish better relations with the Outlanders.

The Hero and the Crown tells the story of Aerin, the warrior who appears as a legendary figure in *The Blue Sword*. Aerin is the only child of King Arlbeth of Damar. Aerin's mother, who died when Aerin was born, was rumored to be a witch from the North. Her people do not trust Aerin enough to accept her as the heir to the throne, especially now that the demons of the North are threatening Damar once again. Tor, Aerin's cousin, has been designated as heir. To make matters worse, Aerin seemingly has none of the psychic powers that Damar's royalty should possess.

Feeling useless and unwanted at court, Aerin begins teaching herself how to kill dragons. She befriends her father's old warhorse, Talat, and discovers how to make a fireproof salve. She also coaxes Tor, who is already falling in love with her, to teach her the rudiments of sword fighting. Aerin becomes an expert dragon slayer and destroys Maur, the Black Dragon.

Aerin then begins training with the wizard Luthe, who teaches her to use the latent psychic abilities she has always possessed. He also gives her the fabled blue sword. Aerin must give up some of her humanity when Luthe is forced to grant her the power of partial immortality so that she can defeat her uncle Agsded, the evil wizard who is behind Damar's problems with the North. Aerin wins back the Hero's Crown, an amulet with protective powers, and returns to Tor and her people in time to lead them into victorious battle against the Northerners. Aerin's heroics earn her a place of honor in the hearts of her people; in addition, King Arlbeth has fallen in battle, so Aerin agrees to become Tor's queen. She must reconcile her love for Tor and Luthe, realizing that the immortal part of her will be able to rejoin Luthe someday.

Analysis
The Blue Sword and *The Hero and the Crown* were published after Robin McKinley's *Beauty: A Retelling of the Story of Beauty and the Beast* (1978), the

award-winning and critically acclaimed novel that established McKinley as an outstanding fantasy writer for young adults. The Damar novels also were well received, garnering McKinley several awards including a Best Young Adult Books citation from the American Library Association in 1982 and a Newbery Honor citation in 1983 for *The Blue Sword*, and a *Horn Book* honor list citation in 1985 and the Newbery Medal in 1985 for *The Hero and the Crown*. Although some of the themes in *The Hero and the Crown* are more mature than those of *The Blue Sword*, both books are classified by booksellers and librarians as young adult novels.

The setting of the novels—especially the Damar of Harry's time—is based partly on Rudyard Kipling's depictions of the British Empire. The Homelanders (or Outlanders, depending on which side one is on) display an obviously paternalistic attitude toward the native Damarians they govern. In the Damar of Aerin's time, the Outlanders are absent and the geography is somewhat different, but the magical psychic abilities of the heroine prove beyond a doubt that Harry's Damar has indeed evolved from Aerin's Damar. The origins of many of the customs, traditions, and rituals present in *The Blue Sword* are explained in *The Hero and the Crown* as well.

The heroines Harry and Aerin were born partly from McKinley's love of fairy tales and partly from her desire to create strong female characters who are able to do more than wait for male heroes to rescue them. Harry and Aerin are successful at many activities that, in fiction, traditionally have been assigned to men. Aerin slays dragons, and Harry triumphs over all the other novices, both male and female, to win a contest of horse riding skills and swordplay. Harry and Aerin don their armor and ride into combat with Gonturan, the fabled blue sword that each woman carries in her own time.

McKinley gives her female warriors more than simply courage to slay their enemies; Aerin and Harry retain their femininity throughout their adventures. Both women are rather reluctant heroes, and both must grapple with mixed emotions concerning duty and honor. Aerin, considered an outsider in her own land, must risk her life several times before she is able to prove her worth to herself and to her people. Likewise, Harry, born and reared as an Outlander despite her Damarian ancestor, must win a place in her new world without betraying her roots. Both women are at first hampered by ignorance and inexperience, and both succeed at last by dint of their honor, pride, and stubborn refusal to accept defeat.

The novels also have romantic themes in common. In *The Blue Sword*, the familiar motif of the abducted maiden falling in love with her captor is mitigated by the strength of the character of Harry. Far from being a meekly subservient prisoner, Harry fights her way up from the status of respected guest to become the savior of the land. In order to defeat the enemy, she must even defy Corlath's orders and seek her own allies. She earns Corlath's respect and will rule beside him as an equal.

In *The Hero and the Crown*, Aerin is at first too involved with her own misery to take much notice of Tor's affection for her. It is Luthe, the wizard, who initiates Aerin into the joys of romance. Aerin must make the difficult choice to return to Tor, her childhood sweetheart, to be queen beside him. This painful choice is made only slightly easier by Aerin's realization that the immortal Luthe will wait for the part of Aerin that is "no longer quite mortal."

Reviewers of both Damar novels have commended McKinley's well-rounded characters, creative settings, and suspenseful storytelling. The characters' emotional responses are often understated but never unbelievable or difficult to decipher. Romance, vivid action sequences, and captivating characters all contribute to the novels' popularity. Most critics believe that McKinley successfully blended the traditional fairy-tale form with some nontraditional heroines.

—*Quinn Weller*

The Book of the New Sun

The Earth of a distant future finds a hero to replace its dying sun

Author: Gene Wolfe (1931-   )
Genre: Science fiction—theological romance
Type of work: Novels
Time of plot: Millennia in the future
Location: Urth
First published: *The Shadow of the Torturer* (1980), *The Claw of the Conciliator* (1981; collected with *The Shadow of the Torturer* as *The Book of the New Sun, Volumes I and II*, 1983), *The Sword of the Lictor* (1982), *The Citadel of the Autarch* (1983; collected with *The Sword of the Lictor* as *The Book of the New Sun, Volumes III and IV*, 1985), and *The Urth of the New Sun* (1987)

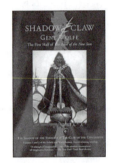

The Story

In an Earth (now called Urth) of the distant future, the Sun is slowly dying. Humanity is divided into the Commonwealth, centered roughly in what is now South America, and the Ascians, or those without shadow, who dominate the Northern Hemisphere. The society resembles medieval cultures such as that of the Byzantine Empire.

Severian is born into the hereditary Guild of Torturers in the city of Nessus. The Torturers are assigned to torment the enemies of the city's ruler. Severian, along with several other apprentices, is trained by the dour Master Gurloes. One of the few exceptions to their grim regimen is the annual celebration of their patroness, Holy Katherine. Severian meets a prisoner named Thecla, on whom he takes pity, eventually bringing her books and trying to console her. Severian gives Thecla a knife, and from the pools of blood he sees outside her prison door the next time he comes to visit her, he concludes that she has committed suicide. Severian informs Master Palaemon, one of his superiors in the Guild, of what he has done. Palaemon advises Severian to go into exile and gives him a resplendent sword named *Terminus Est* to aid him during his adventures and ordeals.

Severian ranges far and wide, eventually meeting an abandoned blond woman named Dorcas as well as the mysterious Dr. Talos and his sidekick, the giant Baldanders. Severian's network of acquaintances begins to solidify, forming a circle of personal loyalties around which his destiny will unfold. Eventually, some of these people's memories become fused with Severian's when he comes to be the representative of his entire planet.

Severian journeys to the north, toward the Windowless City of Thrax. He manages to get hold of the Claw of the Conciliator, which despite its name is not a weapon but a glowing, beautiful, and redemptive jewel that holds the promise of future peace for the warring and injured peoples of Urth. Along with Dorcas, he encounters the cannibalistic Alzabo and helps the people of the region surrounding Thrax win their freedom.

Severian finds out that Thecla has not in fact died but used the knife to escape. He also finds out that Baldanders and Dr. Talos are not what they seem. Dr. Talos is a mechanical man who, despite his air of authority, is Baldanders's servant. Baldanders, for his part, is in communication with extraterrestrial spirits called hierodules. These hierodules, Ossipago, Barbatus, and Famulimus, reveal to Severian the calamity that is overtaking Urth and inform him that he has been appointed to journey into space and find a new sun for the planet.

First, though, Severian has to attain full authority on Urth. With the backing of the power he has accumulated in Thrax and elsewhere, he returns to Nessus and is declared Autarch. He marries Valeria, an aristocratic lady of the city who is a suitable partner for him, although parts of his love will always be directed toward Dorcas and Thecla. As Autarch, Severian brings more justice to Urth than most of his predecessors had managed.

The hierodules arrange for a huge starship to transport Severian into space. Aboard the giant ship, Severian is attacked by "jibers," crewmen from other worlds who have been in the ship so long that they have become permanent residents of its underclass. He is saved from them by a pretty but strangely world-weary woman named Gunnie and an engaging sprite named Zak. Severian learns that he is going to the planet Yesod for a trial in which he will represent Urth. His task is to convince the Hierogrammate Tzadkiel to give Urth a new sun. Upon arrival at Yesod, Severian encounters a woman (actually an embodied, angelic larva) named Apheta who reveals the utter insignificance of Urth in the cosmic order but hints at implications in his mission that Severian himself has not realized.

Severian meets the great Tzadkiel only to find that it is the apparently harmless Zak, in vastly transmuted form. Tzadkiel informs Severian that he is Urth's new sun and that he will be returned amid great cataclysm for the planet's rebirth. Tzadkiel also indicates that, in some other dimension of time, he and all of his sort had been made by humans from Urth. Severian returns to Urth, this time accompanied by Gunnie's younger incarnation, Burgundofara. Much of Urth is destroyed, but Severian survives to see the planet renewed and renamed Ushas, signifying its new state of being.

Analysis

The Book of the New Sun is one of the most ambitious works of science fantasy to be published in the last quarter of the twentieth century, recognized with a World Fantasy Award for *The Shadow of the Torturer* and a Nebula Award for *The Claw of the Conciliator*. Science fantasy is an odd hybrid. Gene Wolfe's books combine the linguistic inventiveness and spiritual depth of the fiction of J. R. R. Tolkien with the scientific believability and historical sweep of the work of Isaac Asimov. Wolfe's writing, though, has a voice and a pulse utterly its own.

On one level, the Book of the New Sun is filled with conventional adventure of the "sword and sorcery" variety. Severian fights his way through challenges in Nessus and Thrax to emerge victorious as lord over all. This surface physical action, however, serves primarily to mask the true inner complexity of the series, swathed in Wolfe's complicated plotting and exotic vocabulary (all of which is derived from existing, though obscure, words in English, Latin, and Hebrew). Most readers will be deep into the series before coming close to guessing the ultimate significance of Urth's clearly decrepit state or what the New Sun will be.

Severian is typical of post-1960 science fiction in that he is an antihero as much as a hero. Although his narrative perspective governs readers' view of the story throughout, it is difficult to identify with him: He is too involved in torture, deception, and various other despicable acts. Wolfe presents Severian as able to come to terms with the evil he has done and integrate it with the far more dominant principles of altruism that largely govern his conduct. Severian goes into exile from Nessus only to provide cover for what he supposes is Thecla's suicide, and he takes on the self-sacrificing mission of leaving Urth and his Autarchy to go to Yesod in search of the New Sun. Because Wolfe lets Severian speak in his own voice, readers are privy to Severian's own ruthless self-examination and his own awareness of the complexity of his course in life.

Thecla is one of the most affecting of the supporting characters. Her disappearance and unlooked-for return add to her generally mysterious personality, giving her an air of sacredness (the name Thecla comes from an early Christian martyr) that makes her something of a spiritual reference point for Severian. Other characters deepen the strangeness and texture of Severian's journey and simultaneously exemplify Wolfe's literary allusiveness. The giant Baldanders testifies to the higher qualities of the human race that are latent in the weary and hard-pressed denizens of Urth. The name Baldanders is a reference to the work of Argentine writer Jorge Luis Borges. Dr. Talos, the mechanical man, is a portal to the strange, superhuman yet half-human, world of the hierodules; "Talos" was originally the name of a mechanical man in English poet Edmund Spenser's poem *The Faerie Queene* (1590, 1596).

The three hierodules, and even more the Hierogrammate Tzadkiel, emblematize the texture and philosophy of the book. Both words have a meaning, although in Greek: "hierodule" is "sacred slave," and "Hierogrammate" is "product of sacred writing." Tzadkiel reveals to Severian when he is on Yesod that the hierodules, superhuman though they may seem, were in fact themselves created by the human race long ago. Desiring to give their descendants a kind of sacred security, they had created the Hierogrammates to give their descendants succor when they need it.

Wolfe portrays a set of all-powerful deities created by humans who in turn help humanity of far-future Urth re-create itself. This paradox fits with all the displacements and foreshadowings in time that occur throughout the series. There also is a hope that there is an order outside time in the universe. "The Conciliator" clearly is analogous to Jesus Christ, and the characters of Thecla and Holy Katherine evoke the Virgin Mary.

At the end of the series, Severian returns to renewed Ushas and encounters simple fishermen who indicate that they revere Severian and two of his companions as gods. Severian, though, points out that only something called "the Increate" is truly worthy of worship. Wolfe makes it clear that this Increate is none other than the God of the Judeo-Christian tradition.

—*Nicholas Birns*

The Boys from Brazil

Notorious Nazi doctor Josef Mengele, alive and living in Brazil, dispatches young clones of Adolf Hitler, and only Yakov Liebermann can stop his plans

Author: Ira Levin (1929-   )
Genre: Science fiction—cautionary
Type of work: Novel
Time of plot: 1974-1975
Location: Various cities around the world
First published: 1976

The Story

Ira Levin presents an intricate plot involving Dr. Josef Mengele (the "Angel of Death" from the Nazi concentration camps), who has set up a laboratory in Brazil. Yakov Liebermann is a Nazi hunter, based on the legendary Simon Wiesenthal. The two enemies finally confront each other in the United States, where the plot is resolved.

Only far into the book do readers learn the nature of Mengele's plan, but there are intimations throughout. At a meeting of old Nazis, Mengele gives out the names and locations of ninety-four men who will have to be murdered within the next year. None holds an important position; most are civil servants or minor functionaries in government. They are spread all over the world. The Nazis are given new identity papers, passports, and money.

Unknown to Mengele, a young Jewish man interested in capturing Nazis has recognized Mengele and persuaded a waitress in the restaurant where the meeting is held to plant a tape recorder and to retrieve it for him. Mengele becomes suspicious, finds the waitress, and through her tracks down the young man, who is found in his hotel room playing parts of the tape to Liebermann. The young man is killed, but Liebermann has heard enough to pique his curiosity. He asks a friend at the Reuters news agency to note unusual deaths, and he travels to Germany to interview a woman who worked for Mengele during the war. She tells him enough to send him to a German scientist, who reveals that research is pointing toward the possibility of cloning a person from his or her cells.

Liebermann guesses that Mengele somehow has cloned Adolf Hitler and arranged for the ninety-four clones to be adopted. Each has the exact genetic code of Hitler, and each adoptive mother is married to someone unimportant, just as Hitler's mother was. Liebermann begins to track down these families. All the boys look alike, with pale skin and dark hair, and all are impolite. Liebermann travels to the United States, where he expects the next assassination to take place.

Meanwhile, Mengele's operation has been shut down by higher Nazi command, and the assassins have been called home. Mengele destroys his laboratory but intends to continue with the assassinations of the adoptive fathers. He also plans to kill Liebermann because of his interference. They meet at the home of one of the boys, whose father Mengele kills and tosses into the basement. When the boy comes home from school, Mengele and Liebermann are in a life-and-death struggle. The boy sends his dogs after Mengele because he has a gun. The boy figures out who has killed his father and orders the dogs to kill him.

Liebermann recuperates and makes one more stop in America. In New York City, he meets with radical Jews who know about the list of children that Liebermann carries. While they talk, Liebermann tears up the list and flushes it down a toilet, telling the leader that it is wrong to kill children, any children, and that simply because they have Hitler's genes does not mean they will turn out like him.

Analysis

This book raises many interesting ethical issues. Mengele is presented as completely evil, as one might assume he was. Levin's Mengele says that he asked Hitler in the middle of the war for a vial of his blood and some scrapings from his arm. He did not have the technology then to do anything with this material, but he developed the science in Brazil. He procured women to be implanted with embryos with Hitler's genetic code and to have the babies that would then be adopted by appropriate couples. The couples would match Hitler's parents in major respects, and Mengele planned for the adoptive fathers' assassinations to match Hitler's loss of his father.

Liebermann represents the forces of good. He is a crotchety older man who at first does not believe that Mengele's plan is being put into effect. Liebermann is portrayed as being almost a pauper, living in inadequate quarters, and having almost no help in his work of tracking down Nazis. He says that people had forgotten the days he had helped track down the infamous Nazi leader Adolf Eichmann.

Levin suggests that there always will be people like Mengele and like the militant Jews who wish to find the ninety-four Hitler clones and kill them. Liebermann is supposed to represent the moderate view of those who learn from history. He takes a chance that none of these children will become like Hitler, but he is steadfast that no one should do what the Nazis did in World War II, including killing children.

This novel was filmed in 1978, with Laurence Olivier and Gregory Peck playing Liebermann and Mengele. There are minor differences, but the film is true to the book.

Levin is proficient at developing twists and turns in the novel. At one point, one of the assassins notices someone he knew during the war, and he tells him his orders and asks about the postman of the town. Then, with no warning, he kills the man, saying that the target was not the postman but the old friend to whom he was talking.

This novel is science fiction, although cloning of cells and certain life-forms has been achieved. In the years after Levin wrote this book, much was done to produce changes in fetuses and to develop certain characteristics within them. It is conceivable that the sort of cloning represented in this novel will become scientific fact. Levin takes no moral stand on the ethics of such a scientific feat. He allows the reader to decide, based on who is manipulating the borrowed genetic material.

—*John Jacob*

Brave New World

Three misfits illustrate the flaws of a future world-state in which technology permits complete control of people and the government claims to provide happiness to everyone

Author: Aldous Huxley (1894-1963)
Genre: Science fiction—dystopia
Type of work: Novel
Time of plot: Half a millennium in the future
Location: What are now the United Kingdom and the United States
First published: 1932

The Story

In the totalitarian state of *Brave New World*, people are socially conditioned from conception; they are hatched from test tubes rather than born. Something, however, is wrong with Bernard Marx. Although he ought to be, in keeping with everyone else in this engineered society, an absolute conformist, he evinces certain quirks that his fellows find disturbing. They theorize that something must have gone wrong chemically during his incubation. Bernard dates Lenina Crowne, but he wants her all to himself. This is against the mores of their society, which prescribes communal sexual relations and proscribes monogamous pairing. Lenina is outraged by his request for monogamy. Any contravention of the societal motto of "Community, Identity, Stability" is regarded as a heinous offense.

Happiness is not an individual quest; it is a daily, community guarantee. Through early conditioning, people are educated to be happy for what they are allotted, with allotments made according to class, which is determined at conception. A drug called soma provides a haven from any temporary unhappiness.

Lenina and Bernard, on vacation, visit an Indian reservation in New Mexico that is a mixture of living museum and circus. There they find John, who was reared on the reservation by his mother, Linda, a woman from Western Europe. John later is revealed to be the illegitimate son of the director of the Bloomsbury Hatchery. As someone outside mainstream society, he is able to find flaws in it. He has escaped the universal conditioning and has steeped himself in the works of a forbidden au-

Aldous Huxley.
(Library of Congress)

thor, William Shakespeare. A collection of Shakespeare's works is the only book he has ever read. He is imbued with the spirit of drama and finds the utter placidity of the present world an affront to the human spirit: riskless, monotonous, and amoral. When Lenina, who fancies him, disrobes in preparation for a guiltless sexual episode, he rejects her for her whorishness even though he is in love with her.

After his mother's death from an overdose of soma, John attempts to subvert some workers who are about to receive their allocation of the drug. This causes a riot, which results in the banishment to Iceland of Bernard and Helmholtz Watson, another "flawed" person. Mustapha Mond, controller of Western Europe, refuses to extend this sentence to John, wanting to keep him nearby so that he can study him.

John retreats from the world into a lighthouse, where he flagellates himself for his sins. He is recorded doing so by a reporter with a sound camera, and this footage is made into a "feelie," a film with sensations added, that receives widespread attention. Tourists arrive in helicopters to gawk at this curious creature who cultivates his own pain. Among them is Lenina. John lashes her and, as she writhes on the ground, himself. This drives the onlookers into an orgiastic frenzy, which catches John up in its license. The next day, when he realizes to what degrading ends his self-mortification has been put, he hangs himself.

Analysis

Brave New World sold more than fifteen thousand copies in its first year and has been in print ever since. It has joined the ranks of utopian/dystopian satires such as Jonathan Swift's *Gulliver's Travels* (1726) and George Orwell's *Animal Farm* (1945). The author himself has said that he wanted to warn against the conditioning of human beings by a manager class with the latest technology at its fingertips. Humanity could lose its soul through such a process, Aldous Huxley feared, trading in its unique qualities in exchange for security and for drugged and directed "happiness."

There cannot have been a year since its publication in which this novel has not been compared to the present condition of humanity and found to be a perspicacious guess at the shape of things to come. Huxley, for example, did not exactly predict television, but he foresaw other means of mass hypnosis.

An ingenious and persuasive writer, Huxley renders his analogue quite credibly, although requirements of his genre necessitated more conflict than would be plausible in a state as well managed as the one the novel presents. The characters for the most part think too much like Huxley and too little like people who have been brainwashed into conformity.

Huxley's vision of sexuality in this futuristic society anticipates the repressive desublimation of a world in which the social obligation to be sexual defuses passion. This vision runs into trouble because the only choices permitted to his protagonist are a sulky celibacy and a foreordained and regulated promiscuity. The liberating powers of a passionate sexuality are left out of Huxley's equation even though, when he includes a few nonconformists, he allows that there can be exceptions in this totalitarian society. It becomes a question, then, of why some exceptions exist and not others; there is no reason for the lack of a female equivalent to Bernard or Helmholtz.

Huxley in essence equates happiness with barbarism and unhappiness with culture. The happiness, however, is shown to be false. Characters all evince signs of deep disturbance. True happiness must be what they are missing. One can ask why Huxley did not portray a more efficient society, one that was able to erase this distinction between the true and the false. It may be precisely this flaw in the novel that explains its continuing popularity.

—*David Bromige*

Bring the Jubilee

In a world in which the South won the American Civil War, historian Hodge Backmaker travels back in time to study a battle site and accidentally alters the course of history

Author: (Joseph) Ward Moore (1903-1978)
Genre: Science fiction—alternative history
Type of work: Novel
Time of plot: 1938-1952 and 1863
Location: An alternative United States of America
First published: 1953 (serial form, *The Magazine of Fantasy and Science Fiction*, 1952)

The Story

Bring the Jubilee has become a classic in the alternative-history subgenre of science fiction. The bulk of the novel is set in an alternative world years after the South won the American Civil War. This first-person memoir begins with young Hodge Backmaker leaving his backwater hometown for New York City in 1938. Life in the twenty-six United States is hard. The War of Southron Independence, as the Civil War is known, has financially and spiritually crushed the North. Backmaker outlines an unfamiliar world in which the telegraph and gaslight are the norm, the wealthy own steam-driven "minibles" instead of automobiles, and the lower classes sell themselves into indentured servitude. The strong Confederate States stretch south from the Mason-Dixon Line into Mexico. Even the European landscape differs. Napoleon VI rules France, and Germany is known as the German Union.

After losing everything he owns to muggers on his first night in New York, Backmaker meets Roger Tyss, a bookseller and anti-Confederate revolutionary. Tyss gives Backmaker a job in his bookstore. Backmaker spends several years there, reading as much as he can and learning to think and study. He befriends René Enfandin, consul for the Republic of Haiti, who is an oddity in New York because he is black. Backmaker is crushed when Enfandin is shot and seriously wounded, forcing his return to Haiti.

At the age of twenty-three, Backmaker accepts an invitation to go to Haggershaven, an intellectual community in York, Pennsylvania. There,

Backmaker becomes a well-regarded historian specializing in the War of Southron Independence. He marries and settles down, but he calls his own scholarship into question after receiving a letter from a colleague asking him to reconsider some of his ideas. In crisis, he allows physicist Barbara Haggerwells to talk him into trying out her new invention, the HX-1, a time machine. She suggests that he use it to visit Gettysburg, the site of an important Confederate victory, and settle his doubts once and for all.

Without telling his wife, Catty, Backmaker allows himself to be transported to June 30, 1863. He walks the thirty miles to the battle site and positions himself. Unfortunately, Confederate troops spot him and question him. Because Backmaker promised Haggerwells that he would not interfere lest he change history, he says nothing. The nervous Confederates convince themselves that Yankees are up ahead and retreat, but during the altercation, a man is shot and killed. Backmaker realizes that the man looks familiar to him.

The Confederate withdrawal from the area means that history as Backmaker knows it changes. Backmaker watches the battle, and, sickened, realizes that the North, rather than the South, will hold the Round Tops. When he returns to the pick-up site and fails to return to his own time, he realizes something far worse: The dead Confederate was Barbara Haggerwells's grandfather. His death means that there is no hope of return to his world. He has changed the course of history and wiped out his own world, along with all the people he loves. Ironically, the world he has brought into being is the world of the reader.

Analysis

Two important themes in *Bring the Jubilee* are the nature of time and the importance of the individual in history. Both are important concerns of alternative history in general. Like Philip K. Dick's alternative history *The Man in the High Castle* (1962), *Bring the Jubilee* questions the role of chance in determining events. Does an individual have the power to change events, or are all events predestined?

Ward Moore explores these themes through Backmaker's discussions with Tyss and Enfandin. Tyss argues that all actions result from stimuli, not thought, and that free will is an illusion. He also argues that time loops endlessly, with people repeating the same events. Moore contrasts Tyss's point of view with that of Enfandin, who believes that everything is an illusion and that only God is real. Backmaker, however, argues that "there must have been a beginning. . . . And if there was a beginning, choice existed if only for that split second. And if choice exists once it can exist again."

Backmaker, dreamy by nature, is not inclined to action but instead to let his life go as it may. Haggerwells must convince him to use her invention to go back in time; he uses her persuasion as an excuse to go, absolving himself of responsibility. He comes to realize that even his refusal to speak to the Confederates at the battle site is a choice. His remark that "if choice exists once it can exist again," coupled with the fact that he changes history, leads Backmaker to believe that free choice exists. He is haunted by the fear that he has wiped out Catty, Haggerwells, and his world, and that he is doomed to wipe them out repeatedly as time loops around again. Still, by allowing Backmaker to change history, Moore refutes Tyss's model of the world and implies that individuals are capable of free choice and action. Backmaker grows from a boy who cannot make decisions into an adult who realizes that not making a choice is a kind of choice.

Bring the Jubilee is Moore's second science-fiction novel, following *Greener than You Think* (1947). None of his other works, mainstream or science fiction, deals with time and history as explicitly as this famous work. Moore's depth of characterization, emotion, and detail make this an enduring classic.

—*Karen Hellekson*

Camp Concentration

In a situation resembling the Vietnam War, Louis Sacchetti, a poet and conscientious objector, is moved to a secret underground facility, where experiments are undertaken to radically accelerate intelligence using lethal syphilis

Author: Thomas M. Disch (1940-   )
Genre: Science fiction—inner space
Type of work: Novel
Time of plot: The near future
Location: A disused gold mine in Colorado
First published: 1968

The Story

Louis Sacchetti is told by General Haast, the camp commandant, that he has been moved to Camp Archimedes to record what he sees. Dr. Aimée Busk, the camp psychiatrist, further explains that as those around him are dying of syphilis induced by the strain Pallidine (which kills in about nine months), they undergo stunning increases in intelligence, which the military hopes to employ.

In his diary, which forms the bulk of the narrative, Sacchetti reports meeting the other men at the camp. Among them is George Wagner, the first prisoner Sacchetti meets and the first he sees entombed. The prisoners' leader is Mordecai Washington, who knew Sacchetti in his school days. Washington is deeply immersed in alchemical studies and has become a magnificent polymath in only a few months. The prisoners prepare a brilliant production of Christopher Marlowe's *Doctor Faustus*, but Wagner dies before he can play the lead. Then Washington and Haast take part in an alchemical attempt to obtain immortality, but it goes wrong, and Washington dies horribly. The following night, Sacchetti dreams the truth, that he is infected and dying. The balance of his journal is in scraps, heavy with literary allusion, showing that he gets sicker and more brilliant each day.

Busk leaves the camp, and a new group of subjects arrives, centered on Skilliman, a failed but nasty and ambitious scientist who chooses the Pallidine treatment in order to develop weapons. Sacchetti sets up a museum of artifacts that add up to the fact that Busk, as a result of sexual intercourse with Washington, has spread the syphilis rapidly across the United States. Skilliman's conflicts with Sacchetti, the only survivor of the original group, begin as Sacchetti starts to draw off Skilliman's followers. A confrontation ensues in which Skilliman demands that Sacchetti, now blind, be executed. Instead, Haast kills Skilliman and reveals that the alchemical experiment was a disguised brain pattern exchange in which Washington's mind came to occupy Haast's body. The simultaneous reverse action of the "mind reciprocator" so horrified Haast that it was he who died in Washington's body.

The novel closes on a challenge to the changed prisoners, who look forward to a future of both genius and eternal life, although that prolonged life would be at the repeated cost of the lives of others, until a vaccine is found for the Pallidine infection.

Analysis

Camp Concentration is a vital meeting of several forces. Thomas M. Disch, though living in the United States, was much influenced by the British New Wave writers who were exploring the inner space of human consciousness through literary experimentation. *Camp Concentration* is a conscious variation on Thomas Mann's monumental *Doctor Faustus* (1947), in that it deals with the price of genius and is set against a background of wartime tyranny, which sharpens the novel's moral aspect. The novel is set during a war in the future, but it is a very near future (attested by the presence of President McNamara, presumably the 1960's secretary of defense). This is clearly a novel about the illegitimacy of the war in Vietnam and the methods of the military research establishment.

The novel's most important aspect is its experimentation with literary style. Sacchetti is a poet and litterateur from the start (he cites Fyodor Dostoevski's *The House of the Dead* [1915] on the first page of the text), but his literary allusions become far more pronounced as his intelligence and reading accelerate as a result of the syphilis. Others, like Washington, bring in Arthur Koestler's definitions of genius, and there are extensive references to the alchemical masters and great writers who have had syphilis. As Sacchetti's illness advances, his journal disintegrates into a literate, allusive stream of consciousness in which he quotes or mentions such diverse figures as Heinrich Himmler, Saint Augustine, Hans Yost, André-Georges Malreux, and John Milton, along with citing the Bible. The texture gives a rich, complex speculation on disease, genius, and death.

The text has an overriding tone of moral confrontation. Sacchetti, an intellectual Roman Catholic, has become a conscientious objector to the war and is aware of the issues surrounding what is happening to him and the other subjects. Skilliman, who seems at first to be injected into the latter part of the text only to fill the void created by the deaths of the earlier group of subjects, is the immoral practitioner of science—the man willing to use his increased intelligence for personal fame and to create weapons of destruction. Sacchetti engages in a series of dialogues with him and his young assistants and emerges victorious in moral fact (and in winning over the assistants), although it appears that he has lost in physical and practical terms. Washington-Haast's murder of Skilliman and Sacchetti's escape into a healthy body reestablish the balance, but it is arguably a *deus ex machina* ending.

The idea of a plague spreading from the evil machinations of military research, of the moral sickness of the society becoming a physical sickness unto death, is a marker of the conscience of the text. Even the surprise ending has moral implications: Several of the infected prisoners choose physical death over the act of sentencing to death whomever they could have exchanged bodies with. *Camp Concentration* is a brilliant, tough book, bringing broad issues and complex literary continuity into science fiction.

—Peter Brigg

A Canticle for Leibowitz

A monastic order struggles through many centuries of war and barbarism to maintain its commitment to God

---

Author: Walter M. Miller, Jr. (1923-1996)
Genre: Science fiction—future history
Type of work: Novel
Time of plot: About 2600 to 3781
Location: The southwestern United States
First published: 1960 (serial form, *The Magazine of Fantasy and Science Fiction*, 1955-1957)

The Story

The novel has three sections, with narratives separated by about six hundred years between sections. From the perspective of the Abbey of Saint Leibowitz, church history is recapitulated in a future "Dark Age," a "Renaissance," and an apocalyptic "Modern Age."

The first section, "Fiat Homo" ("let there be man"), begins about 2600 C.E. A twentieth century atomic war and a repressive Age of Simplification have almost wiped out the past. Brother Francis, a simple monk fasting in the desert, uncovers an underground chamber with "Fallout Survival Shelter" written over it. He believes that Fallout is the name of a demon and has no conception of the war that destroyed civilization. The shelter contains documents written by Leibowitz, an engineer who stayed on at the abbey after the war and devoted himself to the preservation of knowledge.

In the timeless life of the abbey, the Blessed Leibowitz finally is declared a saint. Brother Francis devotes fifteen years to illuminating a wholly meaningless blueprint. On the way to New Rome to present his illumination to the pope, he is robbed by mutants. The pope gives the monk enough gold to buy back the illumination. In the second encounter, however, the mutants steal the gold and cannibalize him, casting him as a martyr.

In the second section, "Fiat Lux" (let there be light), set in 3174 C.E., the church is challenged by new ideas and powerful princes. Dom Paulo, the current abbot, struggles to preserve the abbey against outside influence. Thon Taddeo, a brilliant but arrogant scientist, reveals more about the Leibowitz memorabilia in a few minutes than the monks have been able to in centuries. In a symbolic scene, a crucifix is taken down so that an arc lamp can be installed for the thon. The abbot, arguing that the pursuit of knowledge, though not evil in itself, cannot be the purpose of humankind, orders the crucifix to be returned to the wall. Thereafter, all will read *ad Lumina Christi,* or "in the light of Christ."

The third section, "Fiat Voluntas Tua" ("let there be your will"), is directed against humanism, a view that argues that humanity is the proper focus of human attention. In 3781 C.E., atomic war breaks out, and millions are poisoned with radioactivity. The government sets up mercy camps, offering euthanasia to those dying in agony. Two characters frame the issues significant to Dom Zerchi, the latest abbot. Dr. Cors, a mercy camp administrator, argues that suffering is evil and should be alleviated. The abbot, in contrast, rejects euthanasia as a violation of God's will. The other significant person in this section is Mrs. Grales, a mutant who wants Rachel, the dormant extra head on her shoulder, to be baptized. Dom Zerchi, fearful of the implications, puts off her request. A bomb hits the abbey, killing Mrs. Grales and mortally wounding the abbot. At this moment, however, Rachel unexpectedly comes alive. As his last act, Dom Zerchi struggles through the wreckage to baptize her. Thereafter, the Vatican sends three bishops into space in an emergency plan to preserve the apostolic succession.

Analysis

In a brief writing career that extended from 1949 to 1957, Walter M. Miller, Jr., produced the justly praised novel *A Canticle for Leibowitz* and forty-one shorter pieces of science fiction. All of them, including the original serialized version of the novel, appeared in such popular publications as *Galaxy* and *The Magazine of Fantasy and Science Fiction.*

Miller's work shows the usual characteristics of genre writing: action plots, ready characterizations, and a bright but brittle acquaintance with technology and ideas. Miller's commitment to Roman Catholicism, however, immediately set his work apart. With a skillful play on the willing suspension of disbelief, he used the science-fiction story as a what-if instrument to make religious doctrine real by asserting it as the fictional given and then testing it with intellectual challenges.

A Canticle for Leibowitz addresses, directly or indirectly, various theological concerns. If there is another species possessing free will, is it then subject to the same pattern of divine history, with a fall from grace and a hope for redemption? Would a degenerate race lose its soul? At what point in human evolution is found *homo inspiratus,* the creation of the soul? Logically, must this not occur at one precise moment? How could it be developmental? Given the perceived scale of astronomical time, how long will it take the Second Coming to occur? Will it be a universal event, occurring everywhere at once, or in only one place at a time? (Miller's answer appears to be the latter.) If all are not on the same schedule, then what of those races that exist before the Fall? As humanity continues to evolve, what happens to its relationship to God? What happens if disaster breaks the apostolic succession of God's divinely ordained church?

Although his concerns may seem musty and medieval, Miller turns them into a compelling drama. He joins the argument that began in the Renaissance between science and religion, paradoxically using the naturalistic tone of "hard" science fiction to suggest that matters ordinarily resting on faith are literally true. A central artistic strategy of the novel, for example, is to make real the sense of historical development implicit in Christianity. As does Judaism, Christianity asserts a time line that includes creation, the Fall of Man, God's identification with a national people, the coming of a messiah, his death and resurrection, and ultimately the Second Coming, in which the meaning of history vanishes. From a Christian perspective, all steps but the last have been completed. From the perspective of modern astronomy, this may seem to be vainglorious mythmaking on an insignificant planet. Miller's precise purpose is to square these perspectives in the framework of the scientifically understood cosmos. If and when the space-traveling delegates of New Rome ever return to Earth, Bishop Zerchi declares, "you might meet the Archangel at the east end of Earth, guarding her passes with a sword of flame."

—*Bruce Olsen*

A Case of Conscience

Convinced that the planet he is investigating has been created by Satan to delude humanity, a priest-biologist welcomes the experiment that destroys the planet and its intelligent inhabitants

Author: James Blish (1921-1975)
Genre: Science fiction—apocalypse
Type of work: Novel
Time of plot: 2049-2050
Location: Lithia, a planet 50 light-years from Earth; New York City; and Vatican City
First published: 1958 (book 1 abridged as "A Case of Conscience" in *If*, 1953)

The Story

Ramon Ruiz-Sanchez is a Jesuit priest as well as a biologist with the United Nations (U.N.) survey team on the recently discovered planet of Lithia. Lithia, dominated by a species of intelligent reptilians, is an apparent utopia. The Lithians have no crime, no politics, and no religion, and their ethical code (otherwise identical to that of Christianity) is based on pure reason. Despite their planet's iron-poor crust, the Lithians have developed advanced technologies, including a planetary communications web based on pulses emitted by the gigantic Message Tree, the roots of which reach into the planet's bedrock.

When the survey team meets to make its recommendations before departing from Lithia, Ruiz is in surprising near-agreement with physicist Paul Cleaver. Cleaver advises closing the planet publicly while secretly turning it into a nuclear weapons laboratory. Ruiz also votes to close the planet, with a permanent quarantine, because he has become convinced that Satan created Lithia as a convincing demonstration that virtue is possible without God's grace. The other two team members recommend that Lithia be opened. The tie vote means that the planet will remain at least temporarily off limits. As the terrestrials leave, Ruiz's Lithian friend Chtexa gives him a farewell gift, a sealed vase containing the fertilized embryo of Chtexa's child. The embryo, as it develops outside the body, will replicate the evolutionary history of its species.

Book 2 opens in a U.N. laboratory back in New York, where Ruiz and lab director Liu Meid are observing the movements of the tiny Lithian, whose name (inscribed in his genetic code) is Egtverchi. When Lithia team member Mike Michelis arrives to request his help writing a non-classified version of the Lithia report, Ruiz casually announces that he expects to be tried in Rome for teaching the heresy of diabolical creation.

As Egtverchi develops, it is clear to Ruiz that he will prove to be a sentient being eligible to become a naturalized U.N. citizen. Events rapidly prove Ruiz correct. Egtverchi, who reaches adulthood within months, becomes a television celebrity and a satirical commentator on terrestrial society. His large following seems to be composed primarily of psychopaths created by the unnatural living conditions of Earth's "shelter economy."

Meanwhile, the pope advises Ruiz to consider whether Lithia might be possessed rather than created by Satan. The distinction would allow Ruiz to abandon his heresy while literally exorcising the Lithian menace. As a last resort, Ruiz takes Egtverchi to the Canadian retreat of solid-state physicist Count d'Averoigne, who has devised an apparatus allowing simultaneous communication with the Message Tree. Egtverchi proves unresponsive to the remonstrances of his Lithian father, and Ruiz learns that Cleaver, back on Lithia in charge of the weapons project he proposed, is cutting down the Message Tree.

When Egtverchi's last broadcast touches off widespread rioting, the United Nations attempts to arrest him, but he stows away on a starship bound for Lithia. Ruiz, Liu, and Michelis join Count d'Averoigne at his lunar observatory, where he has set up a telescope that allows simultaneous viewing of interstellar objects. Communicating through the starship, the count has warned Cleaver that his experiment might destroy the planet, but he fears that Cleaver may stubbornly persist. Ruiz pronounces his exorcism shortly before the image of Lithia explodes, taking the monitor screen with it.

Analysis

A Case of Conscience compares favorably with other novels of apocalyptic science fiction, such as Arthur C. Clarke's *Childhood's End* (1953), and with other novels treating conflict between science and religion, such as Walter M. Miller, Jr.'s *A Canticle for Leibowitz* (1960). For the most part it avoids the sentimental, stilted narrative voice that often blemishes science fiction with a cosmic reach, and the machinery of its tight plot does not dissipate the "double truth" of its theme.

It is much to the credit of James Blish's novel that it does not attempt to downplay the very real conflict between the scientific and religious worldviews. Instead, it thematizes that conflict in the attractively human-scale figure of Ruiz. Ruiz underlines the novel's title by constantly being attuned to the promptings of conscience, no matter how inconvenient, and constantly aware of his mental life, whether it is driven by reason or by emotion. He is mortified when the pope shows him that his lapse into heresy was the result of an unscientific failure to consider alternative hypotheses. He is annoyed by his chronic sinusitis. He is bemused when he finds himself, a professed celibate, having vaguely lustful thoughts about the nubile and modest Liu Meid. He is aware of his own worldly satisfaction when he proves to be correct in his predictions. At once a minister of religion and a practicing scientist, Ruiz knows that apparently contrary propositions can be said to be true—the sick child is saved by prayer, *and* she is saved by an antibiotic. Lithia is destroyed by an exorcist, *and* the planet is destroyed in a massive industrial accident.

A blemish on the novel is the caricature of the amoral scientist in the form of Paul Cleaver, who comes across as a pasteboard villain, cursing, angry, and violent for no particular reason. His assertion of scientific and technological arrogance is too much like the vulgarity of the real estate developer who wants to build a shopping center in the last piece of wetland. He is thus in stark contrast to the complex and tormented Ruiz. The severe contrast can make the novel seem less ambiguous than it is. Few writers, however, can resist the urge to indulge in the luxury of a comical villain, and despite this fault Blish's novel improves with each reading.

—*John P. Brennan*

The Caves of Steel and The Naked Sun

Police detective Elijah Baley, with the aid of the robot R. Daneel Olivaw, solves murders in an enclosed New York City of the future and on the planet Solaria

Author: Isaac Asimov (1920-1992)
Genre: Science fiction—artificial intelligence
Type of work: Novels
Time of plot: About 5000 C.E.
Location: New York City and the planet Solaria
First published: *The Caves of Steel* (1954; serial form, *Galaxy*, October-December, 1953) and *The Naked Sun* (1957; serial form, *Astounding Science-Fiction*, October-December, 1956)

The Story

Isaac Asimov wrote *The Caves of Steel,* under the persuasion of Horace Gold of *Galaxy* magazine, as a follow-up to his popular robot short stories. Following its success, Asimov wrote a sequel, *The Naked Sun,* for rival magazine publisher John W. Campbell, Jr., and for Doubleday Books.

The novels envision a future humanity split into two antagonistic groups. Those remaining on Earth have developed a fear of open spaces. They live in covered megacities, the "caves of steel" of the title, resigned to extreme overcrowding and rationing of virtually all amenities. The Spacers, descendants of the colonizers of fifty "Outer Worlds," have much longer life spans and superior technology on their sparsely populated planets, and they forbid "disease-ridden" earthlings from immigrating to their worlds.

Spacers make extensive use of robots. The more primitive models permitted on Earth are violently hated by most City dwellers, especially "Medievalists," who yearn sentimentally for pre-City days. The only contact between Spacers and Earthmen is through Spacetown, a diplomatic/military base at the western edge of New York City.

As *The Caves of Steel* opens, police detective Elijah "Lije" Baley is summoned by his Medievalist boss, Commissioner Julius Enderby, to investigate a murder. A Spacer robot-scientist named Sarton has been shot in Spacetown, presumably by an Earthman. Baley must accept as a partner a Spacer robot created by Sarton. The robot, named R. Daneel Olivaw, looks human enough to "pass" among hostile Earthmen.

In the course of the investigation, Lije makes a number of embarrassing wrong guesses. He first supposes that Daneel is really Sarton in disguise but is convinced when Daneel exposes the machinery beneath his skin. Later, he guesses that Daneel is the killer. An expert convinces the Earthman that the Three Laws of Robotics built into a robot's positronic brain absolutely prevent it from intentionally harming a human. Lije is dismayed to find that his wife works for a secret Medievalist society, though she appears innocent of the crime. Finally, Lije proves that Enderby is the killer. Daneel reveals that the Spacers' ultimate goal on Earth is to convince Earthmen to break out of their stagnant cities to colonize uninhabited planets, with the help of robots.

Isaac Asimov. (Library of Congress)

The Naked Sun shifts the setting to the planet Solaria, where Lije and Daneel attempt to solve another murder. Lije is extremely reluctant to accept the assignment because of his Earthman's agoraphobia, but his boss orders him to do so because his observations can be invaluable to Earth intelligence. Dr. Rikaine Delmarre has been clubbed to death with a blunt object, which is now missing. His wife, Gladia, was found in a faint near the body, and a robot-witness's positronic brain has gone haywire. Solarian security chief Hannis Gruer believes that Gladia is connected to a plot against the human race that Delmarre was uncovering. Gruer himself is the victim of a nearly fatal poisoning.

Lije is pleased to be reunited with Daneel and startled to learn that Solarians have a phobia of their own: Living alone on large estates, communicating via holographic projections, they have a horror of physical human contact or even presence. Marriage and procreation are seen as distasteful necessities, fetuses are removed for incubation, and children are raised on "baby farms."

In the course of the novel, Lije feels drawn to Gladia, who seems to have a repressed interest in close contact with a fellow human. Lije seeks to overcome his fear of open spaces under a "naked sun." Escaping from Daneel, who wishes to keep him "from harm" (as the Three Laws of Robotics direct) by not letting him travel out of doors, Lije contacts five suspects—a family doctor, a sociologist, the acting security chief, a supervisor at the baby farm, and a roboticist. He brings them and Gladia into one room (holographically), in classic detective fashion, for the denouement. The villain turns out to be the roboticist, Jothan Leebig, who has found ways of circumventing the Three Laws of Robotics and tricking robots into becoming agents of crime. He also has manipulated Gladia. Gladia moves to the planet Aurora so that she can obtain human company, and Lije makes a plea to his supervisor concerning the need for Earthmen to overcome their own fears and colonize the stars.

Analysis

Although Asimov's name is strongly connected to science fiction concerning robots, he did not invent the word "robot"; the haunting title of his first story collection, *I, Robot* (1950), was taken from another writer; and the idea of writing a robot detective novel set on an overpopulated Earth came from Horace Gold of *Galaxy*. Asimov did coin the word "robotics," as he often noted with pride, and much more important, he created a body of work that has deeply influenced almost all science fiction involving robots that goes beyond simple views of robots as killing machines.

Asimov's influence extended beyond literature to visual media. Famous examples include the amusing Robbie of the film *Forbidden Planet* (1956); the Vulcan Spock of the *Star Trek* (1966-1969) television series and later films, who although flesh and blood is a close cousin to Daneel in his devotion to logic and his utterly impassive tone; the android Data of *Star Trek: The Next Generation* (1987-1993), whose "positronic brain" is the writers' direct homage to Asimov; and the Replicants of the film *Blade Runner* (1982). The Replicants, unlike Asimov's robots, had no qualms about harming the humans they perfectly resembled. Like Asimov's robots, however, they could be detected as nonhuman via a questionnaire, much like the one administered to Daneel in *The Caves of Steel*.

Asimov saw fit to describe the two novels as "a perfect fusion of the murder mystery and the science-fiction novel." Even if critics have found flaws in both the mystery writing and the science fiction, one could hardly disagree about the fusion. In each novel, the solution depends on a human psychology determined by the technological environment of Earth or Solaria. Moreover, the robot detective is the ultimate embodiment of the mythic sleuth of the Sherlock Holmes variety: a creature of pure logic. Daneel is such a vivid creation that readers often forget that in both novels he is really only a sidekick to Lije Baley, who brilliantly solves both murders. In *The Naked Sun*, Lije frequently reminds himself that robots are "logical but not reasonable," though this distinction is never made clear.

Of the two novels, *The Naked Sun* is much more in the classic mystery tradition, with practically a "locked room" murder and all the suspects brought together for the denouement. It seamlessly weaves social concerns of Asimov's own era into the plot, such as worries about technological advances that may lead to extreme social isolation. *The Caves of Steel* is much less concerned with crime solving in some of its chapters. Its goal is to provide an in-depth study of a future City, its spectacle and its social problems. Written at a time when the United States reveled in its postwar prosperity and international power, *The Caves of Steel* is about the dangers of the coming megalopolis, including overcrowding and overreliance on a technological infrastructure. It also seems to foreshadow U.S. fears of losing status as an economic and technological superpower; perhaps Asimov was thinking more of the losses of the British Empire or the shift in local power from inner cities to the "outer worlds" of the suburbs.

Readers of the late twentieth century and beyond may smile at a few of the novels' lapses in predicting the future. For example, no one seems to have thought of shatterproof lenses for eyeglasses. The same reader may feel some dismay at the author's indulgence in certain social stereotypes of his era. For example, Lije's wife, Jessie, the only female character in *The Caves of Steel*, is constantly underlined as a "typical woman," which is to say that she is pathetically hysterical and dependent, whether in her role as a housewife or indulging in secret meetings. Gladia, in the second novel, falls into the category of the femme fatale, but she literally knows not what she does. She is, at least, conceived as a more complex character. Future critics will doubtless explore Asimov's views of imperial expansion and his analogies of robots to human slaves.

Asimov began another novel soon after the success of *The Naked Sun*, aiming for a trilogy, but he abandoned it. Only after the popularity of a sequel to his Foundation series, years later, did he decide to write *The Robots of Dawn* (1983), set on Aurora and featuring Gladia as well as the detectives, followed by *Robots and Empire* (1985), which linked the Robot series to the Foundation series.

—Joseph Milicia

The Childe Cycle

Prompted by various near-supermen, the human race splinters into the Men of War, Men of Faith, and Men of Philosophy, and then begins the laborious process of reintegration

Author: Gordon R. Dickson (1923-2001)
Genre: Science fiction—future history
Type of work: Novels
Time of plot: The late twenty-first century to the late twenty-fourth century
Location: Sixteen human-inhabited planets in eight star systems
First published: *The Genetic General* (1960; serial form, "Dorsai!," *Astounding Science-Fiction*, May-July, 1959), *Necromancer* (1962; also titled *No Room for Man*, 1963), *Soldier, Ask Not* (1967; serial form, *Galaxy*, 1964), *The Tactics of Mistake* (1971), *Three to Dorsai!* (1975; contains *Necromancer*, *The Tactics of Mistake*, and *The Genetic General*), *Dorsai!* (1976; contains *The Genetic General* with restored text), *The Spirit of Dorsai* (1979; includes "Amanda Morgan," "Brothers," and three bridge sections; "Brothers" first appeared in *Astounding: John W. Campbell Memorial Anthology*, 1973), *Lost Dorsai* (1980; includes "Lost Dorsai," "Warrior," a critical essay, and an excerpt from *The Final Encyclopedia*; serial form of "Lost Dorsai," *Destinies*, February-March, 1980; serial form of "Warrior," *Analog*, December, 1965), *The Dorsai Companion* (1986; contains most of *The Spirit of Dorsai* and *Lost Dorsai*; adds new material), *The Final Encyclopedia* (1984), *The Chantry Guild* (1988), *Young Bleys* (1991), *Lost Dorsai: The New Dorsai Companion* (1993; contains most of the fiction from *Lost Dorsai* and excerpts from "A Childe Cycle Concordance"), and *Other* (1994)

The Story

The Childe Cycle (also known as the Dorsai Cycle) of novels and stories actually begins with *Necromancer*, in the later part of the twenty-first century, on an Earth ruled cautiously by the computers of the World Complex. Paul Formain, a one-armed mining engineer, resolves a stalemate between Kirk Tyne, head engineer of the World Complex, and Walter Blunt, head of the Chantry Guild. The Guild seeks the violent overthrow of the technocracy headed by Tyne. Formain manages to wrest control of

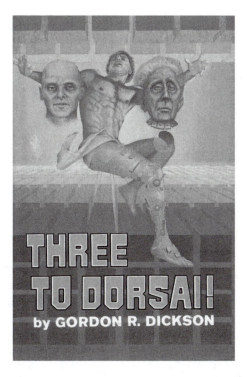

the Guild from Blunt and send the human race out to the stars, something neither Tyne nor Blunt wanted.

The Tactics of Mistake takes place a century later, after the human race has settled Mars and Venus as well as thirteen other planets—called the Younger Worlds—orbiting seven other star systems. Cletus Grahame, a military genius from the planet Dorsai, pits himself against one of the most powerful men on Earth, Dow deCastries. Grahame wins the conflict, thus gaining independence from Earth for the Younger Worlds.

By the time of *Soldier, Ask Not*, in the late twenty-third century, the human race has fragmented into specialized types, called Splinter Cultures. The three main types are the Men of War (Dorsai), who live on Dorsai; the Men of Faith (Friendlies), who live on Harmony and Association; and the Men of Philosophy (Exotics), who live on Kultis and Mara. Helping to link all the Younger Worlds together are the members of the Interstellar News Services, including Tam Olyn. After seeing his brother-in-law killed in cold blood by a Friendly mercenary, Olyn embarks on a vendetta against Harmony and Association. When he is thwarted, Olyn returns to Earth, eventually to take over the directorship of the Final Encyclopedia, a gigantic information storage system orbiting the Mother Planet.

Dorsai! also takes place during the late twenty-third century. It is the story of Donal Grahame, great-great-grandson of Cletus Grahame, who uses his Dorsai military training and what he calls "intuitional logic" to overcome William of Ceta, a merchant who nearly succeeds in controlling the complicated transactions that tie the Younger Worlds together economically. Donal, like his ancestor Cletus, frees the Younger Worlds from a threat to their independence.

The last four novels in the series are all set around the middle of the twenty-fourth century, and they all concern two powerful antagonists: Hal Mayne and Bleys Ahrens. They are antagonists because each is the human embodiment of a different historical response of the "racial animal"—Gordon Dickson's name for the consciousness of the human race as a whole—to the crisis of the Splinter Cultures' failure. Bleys wishes the human race to stop changing; Hal wishes the race to keep changing, for the specialized types of the Splinter Cultures to become reintegrated, and for the reemergence of an improved "full spectrum" humanity.

Young Bleys details Bleys Ahrens's childhood, adolescence, and young manhood, ending in his taking control from his older brother, Dahno, of an organization called the Others. *Other* records the initial moves in Bleys Ahrens's quest to rule most of the Younger Worlds.

The Final Encyclopedia begins where *Young Bleys* ends, with the death of Hal Mayne's three tutors at the hands of Bleys's bodyguards. It traces a similar period in Hal's life, ending with Hal blockading himself, the Final Encyclopedia, Old Earth, and nearly everyone from the Dorsai behind an impenetrable shield. Outside are Bleys's minions, with time, power, and technology on their side.

Three years later, at the beginning of *The Chantry Guild*, Hal is despondent at not being able to find a way of using the Final Encyclopedia to gain entrance to what he calls the Creative Universe. Eventually, Hal works his way out of the impasse after journeying to a new Chantry Guild hidden on Kultis, one of the two Exotic planets, now under occupation by soldiers controlled by the Others.

In addition to these novels, Dickson wrote four shorter Childe Cycle pieces. He called these shorter pieces "illuminations" because they shed light on events only briefly mentioned in, or completely outside, the novels. "Amanda Morgan" shows how the women, children, and old men of Dorsai defeat Dow deCastries's elite invasion troops. "Warrior" tells how Ian Grahame, Donal's uncle, renders justice for the unnecessary death of one of Ian's officers. "Lost Dorsai" is the story of Michael de Sandoval, a Dorsai who uncharacteristically refuses to use weapons but who manages to conquer an entire army. In "Brothers," Ian Grahame ensures both that the men who assassinated his beloved twin brother Kensie are found and executed and that the Dorsai troops do not run amok in their grief over losing Kensie.

Analysis

Even in its own terms, the Childe Cycle is one of the most ambitious projects in the history of science fiction. The series consists of more than a million words, thus being comparable in scope to Isaac Asimov's Foundation series and Robert A. Heinlein's Future History stories. The Childe Cycle is part of an even larger project, a set of interlocking novels—originally conceived of as three historical, three contemporary, and three science-fiction novels—each standing on its own but all eventually forming part of one gigantic "consciously thematic story," a term Dickson used for the work.

Dickson's themes are almost all pairs of opposites. Evolution is crucial, and stasis is death; freedom is necessary, and too much control is fatal; duty to a cause above self is good, and selfishness is bad; and empathy liberates, and isolation confines. The exception to this series is the paradoxical mantra of the new Chantry Guild on Kultis, which is a key to the cycle's overall structure: "the transient and the eternal are the same." What Dickson seems to say is that during the thousand-year period his consciously thematic story will cover, patterns repeat.

The individual novels differ in some respects. The earlier novels are shorter and less easily understood than the later novels. The basic structure, however, is the same throughout the cycle: A young but incredibly confident and talented man overcomes an older and seemingly invincible opponent, each victory supposedly bringing the human race a step closer to a time when everyone has the abilities of the gifted. Dickson's heroes are not really supermen, for Dickson honestly believes that the traits they exhibit are available to all human beings, either in the past as models, in the present with a little training, or in the near future with some trailblazing by the gifted.

Dickson is philosophically a "hard-headed" romantic, and the Childe Cycle reminds readers of the work of another hard-headed romantic science-fiction author, Poul Anderson. Both authors intermingle the conventions of hard science fiction—plausible extrapolations of current scientific knowledge—with ideas stemming from their study of various romantic authors and mythologies.

Even more than Anderson, Dickson wishes to blur the line between fact and fiction. In Hal Mayne's Creative Universe, one has only, in true romantic fashion, to wish for a thing to be true, and it will become true in actuality. English romantic poet William Wordsworth (1770-1850) said, "The Child is Father of the Man." Dickson says, with the idea resonating from *Necromancer* to *Other*, that "The Wish is Father of the Deed." Ever the optimist, Dickson wanted the human race to improve, and spent most of his long writing career nobly mapping out a blueprint to follow.

Critics have given Dickson comparatively little attention, probably because his work may seem dated, as if he stopped developing as a science-fiction writer about 1960. He may also seem derivative to some, for a typical Childe Cycle novel often reads like a combination of breakneck (but overly long and overly detailed) space-opera action, in the style of E. E. "Doc" Smith, and clumsy, obviously symbolic interior monologues reminiscent of the work of A. E. van Vogt, laced with too many heavily melodramatic confrontation scenes. Despite this critical indifference, Dickson won one Nebula and three Hugo Awards, all for shorter fiction and two for Cycle pieces—a 1965 Hugo for "Soldier, Ask Not" and a 1981 Hugo for "Lost Dorsai."

—*Todd H. Sammons*

Childhood's End

The Satan-like Overlords attempt to guide a reluctant human race
to its apocalyptic transformation and union with the Overmind

Author: Arthur C. Clarke (1917-   )
Genre: Science fiction—evolutionary fantasy
Type of work: Novel
Time of plot: About 1985-2085
Location: Earth and NGS 549672, the planet of the Overlords
First published: 1953

The Story

Childhood's End is an account of the final one hundred years of human
life on Earth, from the time of the Overlords' arrival in their huge spaceship to the time of the dramatic, rapid evolution of all human children
into a nonhuman form that achieves unity with the Overmind. A series
of human characters—most notably George Greggson, Jean Morrel, and
their two children—encounter the technologically advanced Overlords,
whose Stardrive-based spaceships, truth-in-history machines, and pan-
oramic viewers (which allow observation of every detail in an area many
miles away) provide the science-fiction aspects of Arthur C. Clarke's
novel. The evolutionary fantasy element appears in human children as
they transform into nonhuman entities that destroy Earth in the power
of their fusion into the Overmind that controls, and perhaps is, the universe.

Childhood's End begins with an event often anticipated and described
in science fiction: the arrival of an alien species on Earth. This species is
unusual, however, both in its refusal to allow itself to be seen for fifty
years and in its benevolence, as it prohibits cruelty to animals and otherwise guides humanity beyond the barbarity of war and destruction into
an era of peace and economic prosperity. The negative results of the arrival and assumption of control by the Overlords are powerful as well,
though less dramatic. A consequence of the end of energizing conflict
and struggle is the decline in creative achievement in art. Likewise, religious belief is terminated by the Overlords' technology, which allows direct visual access to most events in human history, thus exposing the
myths and half-truths that had been accepted as truth over the ages.

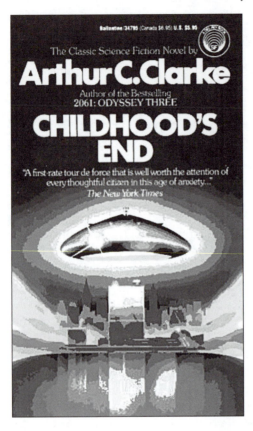

When this latter debunking is fully achieved, the Overlords reveal themselves. Gigantic, barb-tailed, winged, horned, Satan-like creatures, they disembark from their spaceship and generate only a brief reaction of terror. Reason then conquers the remnants of Christian memory, and the Overlords are accepted as intriguingly intelligent and benevolent masters.

To some creative artists and philosophers, however, life without ambition and original human achievement is insufficient. Thus, some fifty thousand join to form a colony dedicated to artistic and intellectual life, the kind of human psychological development that had been stalled by the Overlords' control. Among those joining the island colony are George Greggson, Jean Morrel, and their two young children. Unknowingly, Jean has attracted the attention of the Overlords because of her prescience in correctly identifying their home planet, NGS 549672, even though they never revealed their place of origin to any human. It is this psychological insight that the Overlords secretly have come to inhibit, or at least supervise, as it develops from the mental power implicit in extrasensory perception phenomena throughout human history into the mind-over-matter power that constitutes unity with the Overmind.

The psychological power latent in Jean becomes fully realized in her children; they control objects telekinetically and experience visions of planets even the Overlords have never visited. Soon all human children develop this power. They quickly become nonhuman and oblivious to their parents, who then annihilate themselves because they cannot retrieve their children or even become like them. Only Jan Rodricks remains, having stowed away on an Overlord ship, visited NGS 549672, and returned to a desolate Earth eighty years later. He describes the apocalypse for the Overlords, who have retreated, their supervisory task completed. Even Jan himself fades into nothingness as the children consume the substance of the Earth in their transformation into pure light energy and depart with the Overmind into the stars.

Analysis

The creative complexity of Clarke's novel has made it a classic of modern science fiction. The work is difficult to categorize or synthesize. On one level, it operates as a reasonably believable extrapolation from modern scientific and technological progress into a material utopia. The novel has its dystopian psychological dimension as well. *Childhood's End* also reflects the aspect of Clarke's writing most fully realized in *2001: A Space Odyssey* (1968), his creation of brilliantly evocative, colorful, fantastic descriptions of nonexistent other worlds as an exercise in human imaginative expression. The description of the metamorphosis of the mountain on NGS 549672 in *Childhood's End* is an excellent example. Closely allied with this fantastic physical description is the imaginative leap made by Clarke in his depiction of the fantasy transformation of human children into psychic superpowers and spiritual essences.

Also intimately connected to this imaginatively mystical element in Clarke's writing is his recurring theme of religion—particularly Christianity—as an imperfect embodiment of powerful but misunderstood psychic and spiritual forces. For example, in the 1956 Hugo Award-winning story "The Star," Clarke ironically presents the star of Bethlehem as the supernova stage of another planet's sun. Billions of people die on that planet as the supernova guides the shepherds to the place of birth of one child on Earth. The same reversal of Christian belief, or enlargement of the context surrounding it, is obvious in *Childhood's End*, with the Overlords as an ironically benevolent reversal of the human image of Satan.

Also fundamental to *Childhood's End* is Clarke's recurring theme of the existence of, and inevitable human contact with, other life-forms in the universe. With an intensity akin to religious conversion, Clarke presents this theme in his famous 1951 story "The Sentinel," the progenitor of *2001: A Space Odyssey*. On a moon expedition, the narrator of "The Sentinel" finds a crystal pyramid left by an alien species and accepts the fact of that species' existence; similarly, the Overlords' arrival in *Childhood's End* is represented as an inevitable progression in human encounters with the life-forms "out there."

In its complexity and multifacetedness, *Childhood's End* represents the great artistic power of Clarke in all three of his writing styles, which, according to James Gunn in *The Road to Science Fiction: From Heinlein to Here* (1979), are extrapolative, ingenious, and mystical. What the novel lacks in formal unity and harmony it more than compensates for in pure energy, originality, and profundity.

—*John L. Grigsby*

The Chronicles of Narnia

The creation, salvation, and apocalyptic remaking of the land of Narnia and the adventures of children there

Author: C(live) S(taples) Lewis (1898-1963)
Genre: Fantasy—theological romance
Type of work: Novels
Time of plot: 1900-1949 in Earth time, during which 2,555 years pass in Narnia
Location: England, Narnia, and magical lands surrounding Narnia
First published: *The Lion, the Witch and the Wardrobe* (1950), *Prince Caspian* (1951), *The Voyage of the "Dawn Treader"* (1952), *The Silver Chair* (1953), *The Horse and His Boy* (1954), *The Magician's Nephew* (1955), and *The Last Battle* (1956)

The Story

The seven books constituting the Chronicles of Narnia tell how Aslan the Lion, son of the Emperor-beyond-the-Sea, sings Narnia into being from nothing and later saves it from evil by sacrificing himself and rising again. He spares nothing to make others good if they are open to change. The fictional history of the adventures does not correspond to the order of either composition or publication, but author C. S. Lewis provided a suggested order for reading the stories that is adhered to in the following plot summaries.

In book 1, *The Magician's Nephew*, the adult Andrew Ketterley, who dabbles in magic, discovers rings that can transport their wearers into other worlds and back (he thinks). He tricks his nephew Digory Kirke and Digory's friend, Polly Plummer, into trying the rings. The two children discover that yellow rings transport them to the Wood between the Worlds. Once there, green rings can plunge them into pools magically leading to other worlds.

In the dead world of Charn, Digory's unbridled curiosity leads him to release an evil witch, Jadis, from a deathlike enchantment. Jadis forces her way back to Earth, where she works her destructive evil. The children use the rings to get her out of Earth, but instead of getting her back to Charn, they go to Narnia, a new world the lion Aslan is singing into existence. Because Digory and Polly brought evil into Narnia, Aslan gives them a role in containing it. They ride a winged horse to a far garden, bringing back an apple to plant in Narnia as temporary protection against Jadis. Aslan gives Digory an apple to take back to Earth and use to cure his dying mother. Digory plants the apple's core, and from the tree that grows he has a wardrobe made.

In book 2, *The Lion, the Witch and the Wardrobe*, Digory is the mature Professor Kirke. Peter, Susan, Edmund, and Lucy Pevensie come to his home to escape the London air raids of World War II. While playing hide and seek, they enter the enchanted wardrobe and pass into Narnia. Edmund betrays his siblings and all of Narnia for the White Witch Jadis's offer of Turkish Delight candy and power.

The Witch has created a never-ending winter with no Christmas, but she fears an ancient prophecy that when two boys and two girls take the thrones at Cair Paravel, her reign will end, and Aslan will return and claim his rightful rule. According to the magic built into Narnia at its creation, Jadis has rights to all traitors, but by a deeper magic, an innocent person may die in place of the guilty, which Aslan does. The Witch thinks Aslan a fool and herself the conqueror when she kills Aslan on the Stone Table. By a deeper magic that she does not know, Aslan rises from the dead, frees Edmund and all the Witch's captives, and leads a victorious conquest. Aslan destroys the Witch and places the children on the four thrones of Narnia. After many years, while hunting the White Stag, the children unintentionally stumble back through the enchanted wardrobe to the professor's house, with no lapse of Earth time.

The action in book 3, *The Horse and His Boy*, takes place entirely in Narnia and surrounding countries. A talking horse, Bree, born a free Narnian but stolen young and used as an ordinary riding horse by an evil Calormene master, rescues a boy named Shasta. Shasta actually is Prince Cor, the older twin son of King Lune, ruler of Archenland, a friendly neighboring country of Narnia. Shasta was stolen because of a prophecy that he would one day save Archenland. Bree and Shasta escape with two others. Through many adventures, they save Archenland and Narnia from surprise invasion.

The four Pevensie children, earlier kings and queens of Narnia, return in the fourth book, *Prince Caspian*. While waiting for the train back to boarding school, they vanish into Narnia at the blast of a magic horn Susan had left in Narnia. The Pevensies help Prince Caspian wrest Narnia from the Telmarines and his evil and usurping Uncle Miraz, who has tried to erase every memory of Narnia. Peter Pevensie, former High King himself, faces Miraz in single combat and is about to defeat him when the evil forces attack. Aslan calls the trees to life, and the

Telmarines are routed. All who wish, even Telmarines who will accept forgiveness, may enter Narnia through a magic door, but the Pevensies must return to the railway station and school.

Edmund and Lucy return to Narnia in book 5, *The Voyage of the "Dawn Treader."* They are accompanied by their selfish and obnoxious cousin Eustace Scrubb. They enter Narnia by falling through a Narnian seascape hanging on a wall, and they are rescued from the sea by their old friend King Caspian, who is fulfilling a vow to search for seven Narnian lords. One of the faithful seven helps Caspian save the Lone Islands from slave trade. Eustace becomes a dragon because of his greed but is painfully "undragoned" by Aslan. Reepicheep the Mouse, the most fearless of the Narnians, fulfills his quest to find Aslan's true country.

In book 6, *The Silver Chair*, Eustace Scrubb and Jill Pole escape school bullies through a courtyard door and enter Narnia. They are met by Aslan and given four signs to aid in rescuing Prince Rilian from the evil queen of Underland. Underland is deep underground and is peopled by Earthmen, whom the queen rules by terror and plans to use in overthrowing Narnia. The wise Marsh-wiggle Puddleglum helps the children release Rilian from an enchanted silver chair and return him to Narnia.

Book 7, *The Last Battle,* is a complex account of the end of Narnia and its re-creation into a permanent paradise by Aslan the Lion, creator and rightful ruler of Narnia. Various children have been called, by various means, from Earth into a Narnia in crisis. This time, a train crash sends all the earthly friends to newly created, everlastingly good Narnia, but they must first fight in the old Narnia's last battle. A clever ape named Shift forces his donkey companion Puzzle to wear a lion's skin so that he can masquerade as Aslan. By this deception, they rule Narnia. When the deception is broken, the Calormenes, under Rishda, launch an attack on the Narnians. Rishda calls on the evil god Tash, who destroys Rishda himself in the end.

Tirian, the present king of Narnia, and the friends from Earth all die in the battle, but as they see Narnia destroyed by a cataclysmic flood, then swallowed by a dying sun, death becomes for them the doorway to a new and better Narnia. They are invited "farther up and farther in." The "Great Story" begins, "in which every chapter is better than the one before."

Analysis

This series combines the elements of youth and childhood that Lewis loved and employed in many of his works: enchantment, magic, talking animals and trees, Arthurian legend, other worlds and journeys among them, time travel, and myth. The series contains elements of many genres: utopias, fairy stories, children's stories, medieval chivalric romances, fables, folktales, and novels. Its ideas pull from a deep well of learning in history, literature, philosophy, and religion. Although they never obtrude, St. Paul and the Gospel writers, Saint Augustine, Dante, John Milton, and Edmund Spenser are always visible in the subtext. Lewis acknowledges many specific authors, especially Edith Nesbit, George MacDonald, Beatrix Potter, H. G. Wells, and (preeminently) the biblical writers. The Bible provides the structure, patterns, and values of the Chronicles. The marvel of these books is in the convincing mix of all these elements and the ease of reading. Simplicity and profundity dance together.

In the Chronicles of Narnia, ordinary people such as cab drivers and schoolchildren are chosen to perform extraordinary feats and fulfill extraordinary destinies. They battle evil from within, in the form of laziness, greed, pride, selfishness, and disbelief, as well as evil from without, in the form of soldiers, traitors, witches, enchantments, and an assortment of evil mythological creatures. All these challenges are met with the richer resources of good, flowing out of its source in Aslan, who is to the world of Narnia what Christ is to Earth according to the biblical account. Aslan creates Narnia, populates it, providentially watches over it, and guides it to its end and new beginning.

As is usual in Lewis's books, evil is portrayed as the drying up of human potential, as restriction and imprisonment. The dwarfs who reject Aslan in *The Last Battle* cannot see him, and Eustace embodies greed in the form of a dragon. Goodness is expansive and liberating. Those Jadis turned to stone are restored to life by Aslan's breath, and Eustace is "undragoned" to become a hero and liberator of others in turn. The stable that Aslan occupies at the end of *The Last Battle* is bigger on the inside than the outside and opens into the new Narnia. The grand achievement of this series is its awakening of a longing for the good, for justice, purity, truth, courage, charity, patience, and perseverance.

The influence of the series is vast. When J. R. R. Tolkien's *The Lord of the Rings* trilogy and Lewis's work appeared during the 1950's, they revived fantasy literature from its doldrums. The Narnia books have been the subject of conferences, scholarly work, artworks, and television and video performances. An estimated twenty million or more readers have enjoyed the Chronicles. Perhaps no other work has done more to rehabilitate the reputation, multiply the readership, and broaden the creative potential of fantasy literature in the twentieth century.

—*Wayne Martindale*

Cities in Flight

Earth's culture, represented by the flying city of New York, spreads through the galaxy and decays as the universe comes to an end

Author: James Blish (1921-1975)
Genre: Science fiction—future history
Type of work: Novels
Time of plot: 2012-4004
Location: Earth, Jupiter, various star systems in and beyond the galaxy, and the center of the universe
First published: *Cities in Flight* (1970, as tetralogy); previously published as *Earthman, Come Home* (1955), *They Shall Have Stars* (1956; also published as *Year 2018*), *The Triumph of Time* (1958; also published as *A Clash of Cymbals*), and *A Life for the Stars* (1962)

The Story

Much of the material making up *Cities in Flight* was published in other forms between 1950 and 1962 and in a different order from that presented in the completed tetralogy. The core of the story idea was published in a series of novelettes—"Okie" (1950), "Bindlestiff" (1950), "Sargasso of Lost Cities" (1953), and "Earthman Come Home" (1953)—which were revised and combined into *Earthman, Come Home*, the third novel in the chronological sequence. *They Shall Have Stars*, the first novel in the sequence, was formed by combining the novelettes "Bridge" (1952) and "At Death's End" (1954). The second novel in the sequence, *A Life for the Stars*, was published as juvenile science fiction fours years after the fourth, *The Triumph of Time*.

The overarching conception melding these disparately written pieces into a single volume is James Blish's elaboration of a complete future history that begins in the early twenty-first century, as the United States and the Soviet Union are about to merge into a single bureaucratic state. Blish conceives of a new galactic Earthmanist culture—a version of Western culture—formed on the basis of antigravity screens (spindizzies) that allow entire cities to take flight and anti-agathics (antideath drugs) that allow the long lifetimes required for interstellar flight.

Earth dominates the galaxy after the defeat of the previous hegemony, the Vegan tyranny, a vaguely defined humanoid/alien civilization. The galaxy is "pollinated" by Earth cities, which function as itinerant industrial bases (Okies) and are policed by the Earth "cops," who exist in creative tension with the Okies. A basic plot idea throughout the series is that some cities are good citizens, such as New York City, the "protagonist" city of the series. Others have become rogues, or "bindlestiffs." The worst of these, the legendary Interstellar Master Traders (IMT), have slaughtered an entire planet. As background to the narrative, Earth culture decays as Earth's growing bureaucracy and fear of the Okies destroys the galactic economy. As time itself draws to an end, in the fortieth century, a new alien civilization, the Web of Hercules, rises to power.

They Shall Have Stars tells, in alternating narratives, of the development of the two technologies on which the rest of the series depends. Bliss Wagoner, a U.S. senator, secretly sponsors both projects in an effort to create an escape route for Western culture. In the first of the two narratives, a space pilot, Paige Russell, falls in love with Anne Abbott, the daughter of the president of the drug company where immortality drugs are being developed. The second narrative is told from the point of view of Robert Helmuth, a construction supervisor of the giant "bridge" being built on Jupiter by remote control to test the theories that will make antigravity possible. At the end, Wagoner arranges for Russell and Abbott to become the nucleus of a colonizing diaspora from Earth. Wagoner is executed for treason by the paranoid head of the Federal Bureau of Investigation.

A Life for the Stars, set in the thirty-second century, tells of the departure of Earth's cities. Crispin DeFord, a youth, is impressed by the city of Scranton, Pennsylvania, as it departs from an Earth whose economy has collapsed. The novel is essentially a coming-of-age story in which the young DeFord, thrust into perilous circumstances, manages by virtue of his wits and the help of older mentors to survive and, at the end, to become city manager of New York, which Scranton encounters in space. Much of the narrative deals with DeFord's education, after he is transferred to New York, in the culture and technology of the Okie city. DeFord demonstrates his abilities in a series of daring escapades that help save New York from a bindlestiff.

Earthman, Come Home, set in the last half of the fourth millennium, tells of New York under the guidance of Mayor John Amalfi and the new city manager, Mark Hazelton. A series of escapades, including equipping the entire planet of He with spindizzies (told in *A Life for the Stars*), brings the city into constant conflict with the Earth police. New York is forced to join a "hobo jungle" of unemployed Okie cities. Amalfi, through his understanding of the principles of cultural development, is able to manipulate the cities to march on Earth and, through their flight across the galaxy, to lure out of hiding the Vegan Fort, the last lurking vestige of the Vegan tyranny. Amalfi destroys the Fort by "flying" a planet at intergalactic speed across the path of the Fort as it enters the solar system. New York ends up grounded on a planet in the Greater Magellanic Cloud, where it must defeat the IMT, which has hidden there, in order to begin a new culture in the wake of the collapse of the old.

The Triumph of Time is set in the first years of the forty-first century. The scientists of New York and the planet He, now returned from intergalactic space, discover that in the repeating cycles of time itself a twin antimatter universe will collide with the known universe to begin a new big bang. The only chance for "survival"—which amounts to the right to determine the physical composition of a new universe—is to fly to the center of the universe. To do this, Amalfi must fight off a rebellion against New York's hegemony in the Greater Magellanic Cloud, dispel the apathy of a culture grown old, and race the rising galactic civilization, the Web of Hercules, to the center. At the end, at the moment of his death, Amalfi chooses to make a new universe completely different from the old one.

Analysis

Cities in Flight as a whole is more than the sum of its parts, which are pastiches of the science-fiction tradition. The bold image of flying cities and the theme of immortality come directly from part 3 of Jonathan Swift's *Gulliver's Travels* (1726), although Blish borrows none of Swift's satire. Most of the narrative is typical "space opera" on a grand scale. Devices of science are manufactured as the plot demands, within a context of flashing space battles and an entire galaxy improbably turned into a human landscape that looks and behaves like a somewhat comic map of nineteenth century Europe, complete with squabbling governments and officious military. Blish's imagined future, sweeping to the end of time itself, is in the high science-fiction tradition reaching back to H. G. Wells and Olaf Stapledon, although Blish compresses his future into a few thousand years. The mapping of the detailed future history that Blish added as *Cities in Flight* developed is much like the work of Robert A. Heinlein in his Future History and Isaac Asimov in the Foundation series. Blish's imaginary history reflects directly the ideological concerns of America in the Cold War period.

Cities in Flight derives a distinctive quality and sense of wholeness from the claim, woven into and around the narrative, that the series reflects a serious philosophy of history. This claim is supported by the excerpted fictional study *The Milky Way: Five Cultural Portraits*, which Blish adds as prologue to some of the novels. Critics have discussed Blish's reliance on Oswald Spengler's *The Decline of the West* (1918-1922), a work that presents a theory of evolution of cultures and civilizations as an organic, cyclic process. Richard D. Mullen discusses this idea in "Blish, van Vogt and the Rise of Spengler" in the *Riverside Quarterly* (1968).

This tetralogy cannot be taken seriously as philosophical fiction. Some of Blish's later fiction, most notably *A Case of Conscience* (1959), stakes a more serious claim. *Cities in Flight*, however, is held together imaginatively by a consistent tension between two ideas. The first is that history and cultures rise and fall in repeated patterns. This process is inexorable and shapes and transcends the will of the individuals in those cultures. The second is that rare and perceptive individuals, such as Bliss Wagoner and John Amalfi, can see those patterns and act as agents of creative change, to some extent transcending them. The thousand-year life span of Amalfi represents this transcendence.

Blish reproduces images of the typical American hero, a self-reliant, institution-defying individual. The weight of historical destiny—the triumph of time—hangs heavily over the narrative and informs the characterization of Amalfi, who is a well-developed, self-conscious figure. This realistic characterization gives *Cities in Flight* and its ambivalent end real poignancy.

—*D. Barrowman Park*

City

The history of the Webster family and its robot, Jenkins, as human-kind abandons its cities and eventually its planet

Author: Clifford D. Simak (1904-1988)
Genre: Science fiction—future history
Type of work: Stories
Time of plot: From the 1990's until thousands of years in the future
Location: Earth, Jupiter, and another dimension
First published: 1952

The Story

Winner of the 1953 International Fantasy Award for best fiction, *City* is assembled primarily from eight stories published between 1944 and 1951. Framed by an "Editor's Preface" and "Notes," these tales are presented as a future ethnographer's collection of "the stories that the Dogs tell." After the death of John W. Campbell, Jr., in 1971, Clifford D. Simak wrote a ninth story for editor Harry Harrison's *Astounding: John W. Campbell Memorial Anthology* (1973); in 1980 this last story was added to a revised version of *City*, along with an "Author's Note."

The first three tales in *City* chronicle humankind's abandonment of its cities for a pastoral existence made possible by advanced technology. In the first story, "City," set in the 1990's, John W. Webster flees to the country and builds a house. Much of the rest of *City* focuses on that house and Webster's descendants.

"Huddling Place," the second story, is set in 2117. Jerome A. Webster has written the first reference work on Martian physiology. He is needed to save the life of the Martian philosopher Juwain. Jerome's robot, Jenkins, fails to notify Jerome that a spaceship has arrived to take Jerome to Mars; the robot believes that its agoraphobic owner would not leave the house. Juwain therefore dies before he can reveal a secret mental concept that supposedly would solve many of humankind's problems. More than sixty years later, in "Census," Jerome's son Thomas perfects the technology needed to take humankind to the stars. Thomas's son Allen pilots the first spaceship to Alpha Centauri, and another son, Bruce, has given dogs the ability to speak through a genetic engineering technology called "boosting."

The next two stories, "Desertion" and "Paradise," depict humanity's abandonment of its native planet. More than a century has passed when astronaut Kent Fowler and his dog Towser are genetically transformed into "lopers," the native life-form of Jupiter. As lopers, they discover that Jupiter is a veritable paradise that they are loath to leave. Only after five years does Fowler return to his base to report his findings. On Earth, president Tyler Webster, afraid that it would mean the end of humankind, tries unsuccessfully to suppress Fowler's information. His fears are warranted: Once Fowler's report becomes known, most of humankind leaves Earth to live on Jupiter as lopers.

The remaining stories illustrate the fate of Earth after humankind's exodus. Almost two millennia later, in "Hobbies," a few humans still live in Geneva, "wild robots" have gathered in the countryside, and dogs have begun efforts to "civilize" wolves and have discovered the existence of other dimensions. To allow the dogs to develop unhindered by humans, Jon Webster seals off Geneva before putting himself into suspended animation. Another five thousand years pass before the events in "Aesop." Most of the world's animals can talk and live in harmony; unfortunately, killing is reintroduced to the world by an other-dimensional being and descendants of humans who were not sealed in Geneva. After the other-dimensional being is stopped, Jenkins the robot takes the unsealed humans to another dimension, where he remains for five thousand years.

Returning to Earth in "The Simple Way" (originally published as "The Trouble with Ants"), Jenkins discovers that ants, "boosted" thousands of years earlier, are erecting an enormous, continuously expanding building. As available living space becomes scarcer, the wild robots travel to the stars and the animals leave Earth to live in other dimensions. "Epilog" takes place untold millennia after Jenkins's return. He is the only robot on Earth, pondering the mystery of the ants as a spaceship lands near Webster House. Some of the wild robots who had left Earth millennia earlier have returned to invite Jenkins to assist in the work to be done on other planets.

Analysis

Important for many reasons, *City* remains Simak's most famous work. Its first two stories are generally recognized as the first works representative of Simak's fully developed style. All the tales contain elements and motifs found frequently in his stories and novels. The fourth tale in the work, "Desertion," is one of science fiction's most frequently anthologized stories. This collection is also notable for being recognized as an important work at a time when science fiction and fantasy were only beginning to receive serious notice within the literary community. The International Fantasy Award, which *City* won in 1953, predates both the Hugo and the Nebula awards. *City* received its award the same year that Alfred Bester's *The Demolished Man* (1953) became the first winner of the Hugo as best novel.

City is representative of two publishing trends in science fiction: a 1940's trend in which writers produced several stories linked by recurring characters, settings, or themes (for example, Robert A. Heinlein's Future History stories) and a 1950's trend in which writers produced "fixups," assembling previously published short stories, often with new framing or cementing material, into "novels." Other noted examples of such "fixups" include Ray Bradbury's *The Martian Chronicles* (1950), Theodore Sturgeon's *More than Human* (1953), and A. E. van Vogt's *The War Against the Rull* (1959).

Since its earliest days, science fiction has probed for what constitutes the nature of humanity. Few works explore human nature as well as *City*. Simak uses mutants, extraterrestrials, boosted animals and insects, humans transformed into extraterrestrials, extradimensional beings, and robots to highlight, contrast, re-create, and even warn against such human qualities as aspiration, doubt, love, homesickness, aggression, passivity, and curiosity.

The conclusion of "Desertion," in which a man and his dog literally become equals, is one of science fiction's most brilliant expressions of the possibility that humanity is not the highest form of existence in the universe. This possibility is likewise evident in the fact that Joe the mutant and Juwain the Martian both possess mental capabilities beyond those of mere humans, and the animals of Earth (with minor mechanical assistance) achieve a universal peace, something humans were able only to dream of. Ironically, the most "human" character in *City* is Jenkins, one of science fiction's most fully developed robots. Simak was guilty of understatement when, in his author's note to "Epilog," he explained that the collection's last tale "had to be Jenkins's story"; because Jenkins is humanity's last representative, his story offers the final comment on humanity's fate.

—*Daryl R. Coats*

The Conan Series

Conan the Barbarian battles men, magic, and monsters in the mythical Hyborian Age, rising from penniless wanderer to king of Aquilonia, the mightiest of the Hyborian nations

Author: Robert E. Howard (1906-1936)
Genre: Fantasy—heroic fantasy
Type of work: Stories
Time of plot: About 15,000 B.C.E.
Location: A fictional Earth
First published: *The Coming of Conan* (1953), *Conan the Barbarian* (1954), *The Sword of Conan* (1952), *King Conan* (1953), *Conan the Conqueror* (1950; previously published as "The Hour of the Dragon," *Weird Tales*, 1935), and *Tales of Conan* (1955)

The Story

Robert E. Howard wrote the Conan stories (arranged above in order of internal chronology) as episodes from the life of the invincible barbarian hero. The Gnome Press collection includes all of Howard's Conan stories, commentary regarding Conan and his world, and two tales of King Kull, another ancient barbarian king. Most of the stories were originally published in *Weird Tales* between 1929 and 1936, except those in the last book, *Tales of Conan*, which was compiled from previously unpublished manuscripts. L. Sprague de Camp edited the entire collection.

The Kull tales begin with *The Coming of Conan*. With his Pictish friend Brule, Kull battles the uncanny serpent men. Kull is a mighty barbarian warrior from Atlantis who has usurped the throne of the kingdom of Valusia, and Brule is a guerrilla fighter and fantastically skilled hunter. Conan is a fusion of these two characters. He is the greatest swordsman of his age, with the strength, speed, and ferocity of a beast of prey and senses so acute that he surpasses wild men and animals in tracking and stalking.

After the Kull stories begin the adventures of Conan, set in the prehistoric Hyborian Age. Although little is known of Conan's early years, it is established that he was born in the midst of a battle, literally bred to war. At the sack of Venarium, an Aquilonian outpost in Cimmeria destroyed by the barbarians, he acquired a curiosity about the Hyborian civilizations. When he was about seventeen years old, he began the wanderings that would make him legendary throughout the world as a thief, mercenary, bandit chieftain, pirate captain, general, and ultimately barbarian king of Aquilonia itself.

The most basic plot element is Conan's heroic character. He embodies "natural" virtues such as independence, courage, indomitability, and a simple honesty about himself and his desires. He rejects the "civilized hypocrisy" of legal abstractions, so he is often at odds with the law. Although not given to wanton cruelty, he is vengeful and merciless in his anger. This is counterbalanced by an unswerving loyalty to deserving comrades and a loathing for bullies and other cowardly types. Naturally curious and almost fearless, Conan enjoys the adventurous life and will brave any danger to help a woman in distress. These personality traits—and his mighty sword arm—impel him from adventure to adventure. His restless need for action will not allow him to enjoy times of peace, even that for which he battles as king of Aquilonia.

Conan inevitably faces situations with impossible odds against his success, but with heroic fortitude and tremendous luck he invariably succeeds. Although he frequently begins an adventure out of selfish motives, his actions always help defeat some monstrous evil. One good example is the earliest Conan story, "The Tower of the Elephant." Setting out to steal a fabulous gem, "The Heart of the Elephant," rumored to be kept in a mysterious tower, he braves natural and supernatural obstacles to attain his goal, only to voluntarily free a mysterious being from another planet, Yag-Kosha, who wreaks awful magical vengeance on the tower's builder, the evil magician Yara. The jewel that Conan sought is absorbed into the spell, and he flees while the tower crashes to ruin behind him.

In what many regard as the greatest Conan story, "The Queen of the Black Coast," the encounter with supernatural evil is again central. Fleeing the agents of civilized law, Conan forces passage aboard an Argossean merchant ship bound for the northern coast of what is now Africa. There all but Conan are massacred by black pirates, whose leader is a legendary white beauty, Belit. She falls in love with Conan, and they roam the coast, pillaging and destroying, until Belit elects to search for a prehuman ruin rumored to hold great treasure.

One member of the elder race that built the city remains, now devolved into a diabolical, bat-winged ape creature. The thing craftily separates Conan and some spearmen from Belit and the rest. Conan's men are killed when the fumes of the black lotus put Conan into an enchanted slumber. He awakes from the spell to find Belit hanged from the yardarm of her ship by a golden necklace from the horde she had intended to steal. As night falls, Conan awaits the demoniac being and his were-hyena servants atop a pyramid at the center of the city. In a terrific battle, he is saved at the last moment by the ghost of Belit, returning as she promised to save her lover. At dawn, Conan places the treasure and her body in her ship, which he makes a funeral pyre. As the flames blend with the rising sun, he vanishes into the jungle.

The hero's encounter with the "unnatural" (evil) and his incredible triumph is the archetypal pattern of all the Conan stories. Nearly infinite variations are possible within this simple matrix, as illustrated by the above examples as well as the abundance of heroic "sword and sorcery" fantasy written since the Conan stories. Conan is the first true "sword and sorcery" hero.

Analysis

Howard's Conan stories constitute a new subgenre of heroic fantasy. Fritz Leiber coined the term "sword and sorcery" to describe this hybrid, which merged the naturalistic epic—of which the tales of Tarzan are perhaps the best example—with elements of the fairy tale and the horror story. Sword and sorcery assumes that the intimate connection of pretechnological peoples with their own mythic consciousness makes them susceptible to dark supernatural influences, yet also attunes them to their own heroic potential. Monsters are the genre's embodiment of the darkness within the human soul, but they are also symbols of what lies outside the narrow confines of modern rationality. The world is presented in terms of a struggle between great forces, not of Judeo-Christian good and evil but of natural law and unnatural chaos, and the hero's victories imply a larger order from which overcivilized (decadent) people have become estranged.

Another way to view this is that people's lives lose the potential for mythical significance through the sterile logic of technological advancement. This romantic affirmation of the natural primitive, however, is qualified by a darker undertone: Naturalistic fantasies treat aggression as more basic than communal behavior, more fundamental even than maternal bonding. Socialized behavior is superimposed on an instinctive survival/reproductive urge that is both competitive and selfish. This is why Howard believed in the inevitable collapse of civilization: The purely animal is more natural and therefore stronger than the civilized superego. It is natural to struggle and slay for survival, and unnatural to live in peace and to prosper as a community. As a nameless forester puts it at the end of "Beyond the Black River" (*Weird Tales*, 1936),

"Civilization is unnatural; it is a whim of circumstance. And barbarism will always triumph."

Because of its fantastic removal from the constraints of everyday reality, sword and sorcery became an effective medium for writers who wished to test ultimate questions about the relationship of values to ideas of natural order, of dreams to reality, of nature to the supernatural, and of law to chaos. Howard's own answers were equivocal: He opposed reason to instinct, the latter of which he saw as more natural, yet he respected artistic achievement, which he viewed as unattainable without civilization and the use of higher reason. He opposed the "unnatural" repressive qualities of civilization by linking them with degeneration and diabolism, while attributing similar qualities to primitive shamans. Although he clearly admired the heroic exploits of his barbaric protagonist, he had Conan himself observe that he was unable to create and was able only to destroy.

Sword and sorcery has provided a rich vein of popular fantasy literature. Important authors in the genre include Lin Carter, L. Sprague de Camp, John Jakes, Fritz Leiber, Michael Moorcock, Andrew J. Offutt, Manly Wade Wellman, Karl Edward Wagner, and even female authors such as Andre Norton and Marion Zimmer Bradley, who adapted the anachronistic devices of the genre to their own ends. De Camp turned unpublished stories by Howard into finished works as well as writing some new Conan stories. Carter, Offutt, Robert Jordan, Steve Perry, and Bjorn Nyberg also have written Conan stories. Howard's original fusion of naturalistic and supernatural mythic themes in the Conan stories played the definitive role in establishing a popular subgenre of heroic fantasy.

—*David Hinckley*

A Connecticut Yankee in King Arthur's Court

A nineteenth century American is transported to sixth century England, where he tries to implant modern technology and political ideas

Author: Mark Twain (Samuel L. Clemens, 1835-1910)
Genre: Science fiction—time travel
Type of work: Novel
Time of plot: The late nineteenth and early sixth centuries
Location: England
First published: 1889

The Story

The novel is told within a frame set around 1889. During a day tour of England's Warwick Castle, the anonymous frame-narrator meets an American—later identified as Hank Morgan—who relates how he was transported back to the sixth century. When he was a foreman in a Connecticut arms factory in 1879, an employee knocked him unconscious; he awakened in England in 528 C.E. That night, Morgan leaves a manuscript containing his story with the narrator, who stays up reading it. Morgan's own first-person account forms the novel's main narrative.

Morgan's narrative spans roughly ten years. After awakening in England, he is captured and taken to Camelot, where he is denounced as a monster and sentenced to be burned. He knows that a solar eclipse occurred at the very hour when he is scheduled to die, so he threatens to blot out the sun. When the eclipse begins, people conclude that he is a powerful magician. King Arthur not only frees him but also agrees to make him his prime minister. Morgan then enhances his reputation by blowing up the tower of Merlin the magician. Soon dubbed the "Boss," Morgan reorganizes the kingdom's administration and gradually introduces modern inventions and innovations, such as matches, factories, newspapers, the telegraph, and training schools. Although he is eager to introduce democracy and civil liberties, he proceeds cautiously to avoid offending the powerful Church.

After seven years, Morgan's administration is so firmly established

The frontispiece to the first edition of Mark Twain's A Connecticut Yankee in King Arthur's Court, *illustrated by Dan Beard.* (Arkent Archives)

that he leaves Camelot. Wearing armor, he goes on a quest with a woman named Sandy to rescue princesses—who turn out to be hogs. During his return, he stops at a holy shrine, where King Arthur joins him. They disguise themselves as freemen in order to travel among commoners. A nobleman treacherously sells them to a slave caravan that takes them to London, where Morgan kills the slave driver while escaping. Before being recaptured, Morgan telegraphs Camelot asking for help. As he and the king are to be hanged, Sir Launcelot arrives with five hundred knights mounted on bicycles to rescue them.

Back in Camelot, Morgan wins many jousts using his lasso and kills a knight with a pistol. He then challenges all the knights at once. Five hundred knights attack, only to scatter after he starts shooting them. This triumph leaves him England's unchallenged master, so he unveils his secret schools, mines, and factories. Finally ready to take on the Church, he has slavery abolished, taxation equalized, and all men made legally equal. Steam and electrical power proliferate, trains begin running, and Morgan prepares to send an expedition to discover America.

When Morgan visits France, the legendary tragedy of Arthur's breach with Launcelot unfolds, plunging England into civil war. Morgan returns to find that the Church has put him and his modern civilization under its Interdict. With only fifty-three trustworthy followers left, he retreats to a fortified cave that is attacked by twenty-five thousand knights. His modern weapons annihilate the knights, but the enemy corpses trap him in the cave. Merlin casts a spell to make him sleep thirteen hundred years.

A postscript to the final chapter returns the story to the present. The frame-narrator finishes reading Morgan's manuscript and visits him in time to see him die.

Analysis

A Connecticut Yankee in King Arthur's Court was the first book that Mark Twain finished after publishing *Adventures of Huckleberry Finn* (1884). Because of its setting, it often is classified as one of his historical novels, along with *The Prince and the Pauper* (1882) and *Joan of Arc* (1896), but it has little in common with either. The novel more closely resembles his 1879 short story "The Great Revolution in Pitcairn," also about an American trying to modernize an archaic society.

The germ of *A Connecticut Yankee in King Arthur's Court* goes back to Twain's 1866 visit to Hawaii, which made him want to write a novel exploring the islanders' feudalistic characteristics. He started this book in 1884 but soon abandoned it and turned instead to a parody of medieval England. His new target was Arthurian romances, whose popularity Alfred, Lord Tennyson's *Idylls of the King* (1859-1885) had helped to revive. Twain's novel incorporated some elements that he had intended for his Hawaiian novel; for example, he modeled King Arthur partly on Hawaii's King Kamehameha V.

A Connecticut Yankee in King Arthur's Court is the first novel-length treatment of travel into the past. Twain's use of time travel as a plot device may have been influenced by Edward Bellamy's future-travel story *Looking Backward: 2000-1887* (1888). He also was probably influenced by a novella that Max Adeler (Charles Heber Clark) published as "Professor Baffin's Adventures" (1881; later retitled "The Fortunate Island"). Adeler's story lacks time travel but resembles Twain's novel in having an inventive American drop into an Arthurian world (on an uncharted island) that he tries to modernize. Similarities between the stories were such that Clark accused Twain of plagiarism.

A Connecticut Yankee in King Arthur's Court mixes satire, burlesque, sociological diatribe, and violence too thoroughly to permit the novel's easy classification. Even its designation as a time-travel story is problematic. Aside from the prologue's vague allusion to "transmigration of souls" and "transposition of epochs," it makes no attempt to explain how Morgan reaches the sixth century, beyond stating that he is knocked on the head. His return to the nineteenth century is less mysterious: Merlin puts him to sleep for thirteen centuries. Back in the nineteenth century, the only tangible evidence of Morgan's sixth century industrial civilization is a bullet hole in a suit of armor hanging in Warwick Castle. If his experience was merely a dream, it would explain his story's ahistorical elements, such as making sixth century England resemble the High Middle Ages and using a solar eclipse that never occurred.

Although the novel's time-travel elements might be regarded as fantasy, Morgan's actions in the sixth century definitely constitute science fiction. Immediately after reaching Camelot, he pledges to "boss the whole country inside of three months," using his modern education and know-how. Once he sets out to revolutionize England, the story becomes sociological science fiction. Ultimately, he fails in his battle against the Church, and all of his impressive achievements are crushed. If the novel is viewed according to modern conventions of time-travel stories, one might conclude that the reason for Morgan's failure is the impossibility of altering the space-time continuum. What interested Twain, however, is the resistance of human beings to change, a profoundly pessimistic theme that he explored in many of his late writings.

—*R. Kent Rasmussen*

The Cyberiad

The adventures of two constructors in their travels across space

---

Author: Stanisław Lem (1921-   )
Genre: Science fiction—dystopia
Type of work: Stories
Time of plot: The distant future
Location: Various planets and space between them
First published: *Cyberiada* (1965; English translation, 1974)

The Story

The Cyberiad, subtitled *Fables for the Cybernetic Age*, is a collection of related short stories set in a time after robots have escaped slavery at the hands of humanity; they live free throughout the galaxy. They have developed a feudal society, complete with kings, princesses, evil pirates, paupers, and serfs, and they seem to be much more like humans than unlike them. Most planets have one or two kingdoms, and the denizens of a particular kingdom tend not to travel much. Interstellar travel, like international travel during the Middle Ages, is reserved primarily for those who do not belong to the feudal hierarchy.

The principal characters are two such travelers, Trurl and Klapaucius, who have just received their "Diplomas of Perpetual Omnipotence" as constructors. The title is roughly equivalent to that of the medieval magician or sorcerer. They are friends and rivals, and the stories center on their adventures together as they build machines to improve the collective condition, or at least make some money.

Trurl and Klapaucius serve as advisers, matchmakers, storytellers, and judges as they travel among the stars. In a typical story, the constructors create a (usually sentient) machine for some educational or contractual purpose, and it either works but with unexpected results or fails to perform. In another common plot, the constructors build a machine to repair an individual, social, or political problem on a planet they are visiting. The remedy seldom succeeds, but if it does, the success is incidental. There are several stories in which Trurl and Klapaucius figure peripherally and one in which they are absent but are mentioned.

The most common English-language edition of this collection contains fifteen stories. The first three set the scene and tone for the nine that follow; the final three sum up the themes previously presented. There is no overlying plot, and each story has a multitude of pitfalls and plot twists.

There were several editions of the book published in the original Polish, of which the third is definitive. The most common English edition omits roughly a third of the stories in the third Polish edition. All but one of these stories are available in English translation as *Mortal Engines* (1977).

Analysis

The prose of the stories in *The Cyberiad* is a peculiar mix of current usage, archaic medieval language, and jargon from various technical disciplines, particularly cybernetic theory, electronics, and quantum mechanics. The hard sciences around which modern technology is based gain the semblance of medieval magic and make the principal characters resemble Terry Pratchett's wizards.

An interesting feature of the language in the work is its literalness: changing the description changes the described. In one case, the lack of a dragon was changed into the back of a dragon, producing a dragon with two backs. This literalness is familiar to anyone who has dealt with a computer, and it adds an additional humorous element.

Stanisław Lem. (Franz Rottensteiner)

Various themes appear in the stories, among them the blindness of love, the follies of greed and pride, the insidiousness of bureaucracy, and the folly of blind suspicion. In all, the stories are reminiscent of Aesop's fables, as the title suggests. The stories as a whole equate the condition of all conscious things, machine and flesh, and suggest that a conscious effort to improve the existence of others creates more grief than doing nothing.

Stanisław Lem's characters are all tools he uses to illustrate some point. Kings are inevitably poor rulers, through either cruelty or lack of interest. When political systems other than monarchies are described, however, they are shown to be worse because they were intended to work a greater good. Cruelty is usually associated with stupidity in these stories. Lem suggests that the cruelest of all are those who would rearrange a culture to improve the lot of its people. A cybernetic Karl Marx is put to death with the approval of Trurl not because he tried to improve the lot of his people with revolutionary sociopolitical ideas but because he did not desist after his initial failure. The implication is that only individual, not societal, happiness can be increased through one's actions.

One would be mistaken to state, however, that the collection appears either philosophical or gloomy. The fable format and clever humorous devices ensure that, depending on personal tastes, the reader will find the stories either humorous and whimsical or ponderous and belabored. The philosophical issues appear only after consideration, a necessity for any Polish author who hoped to avoid political entanglements in the 1960's.

Translator Michael Kandel was nominated for an award for translating *The Cyberiad*. Lem has said that Kandel is probably the best translator his work will ever have. Because Polish shares few linguistic or cultural roots with English, Kandel resorted to using an analogous form of translation in which an untranslatable feature (for example, a pun) is replaced with a compensatory feature of a similar sense in English at a different, but logical, insertion place in the text. This approach has great dangers associated with it. It demands that the translator be nearly as skillful, or even more so, than the author and have as good a literary sense as the author. Because Lem has been accused by some Polish critics of having created his own language from Polish in *The Cyberiad*, and because it is in a format that is easily deadened by translation, the demands on a translator of this work are exceptional. Fortunately, Kandel was up to the task, and his translation carries both the meaning and the sense of Lem's prose and poetry.

—*Radford B. Davis*

Cyteen

Reseune labs uses advanced psychogenetics to replicate its brilliant leader, Ariane Emory, after she is killed

---

Author: C. J. Cherryh (Carolyn Janice Cherry, 1942-   )
Genre: Science fiction—future history
Type of work: Novel
Time of plot: The twenty-fourth century
Location: The planet Cyteen
First published: 1988

The Story

Fifty years after the Treaty of Pell established an uneasy peace between Earth and its former colonies in the Merchanter's Alliance and in Union, an aging Ariane Emory is the most powerful figure in Union politics. She is the virtual owner of its most advanced research laboratory, Reseune; councillor for science to the Council of Nine in Union's government; and, within the council, leader of its majority faction, the Expansionists.

Through Reseune labs, she developed the "azi," androids whose expanding population enabled Union to secede from Earth. Now researching how to replicate Union's most gifted citizens psychosocially as well as biologically, Emory seduces and co-opts Justin Warrick, a teenager who is an inexact replicant of her brilliant colleague and rival, Jordan Warrick.

When Emory's frozen corpse is discovered at Reseune, her successor at the lab and on the council, Giraud Nye, extorts a confession from Jordan Warrick and exiles him to a remote laboratory on the far side of Cyteen, meanwhile keeping Justin and Justin's azi lover, Grant, as virtual hostages at Reseune. With his brother Denys, Giraud immediately begins an attempt to replicate Ariane Emory and recover her much-needed abilities amid the fractious and conspiratorial politics of Union.

Using extensive notes left by Emory and by her mother, one of Reseune's founders, the Nyes' project succeeds in producing a second Ariane, whose abilities compare favorably with those of the original. With the advantage of a computerized tutorial left by Emory, however, the second Ariane proves herself not only a precocious researcher and skilled politician but also a more decent human being than her predecessor.

Despite the psychological damage to Justin Warrick wrought by Emory's sexual manipulation of him, his father's implication in her murder, and the Nyes' continuing hostility, the second Ariane recognizes his innate decency and potential brilliance. She sets out to win him over, first as his teacher and then as an essential supporter in the political turmoil that threatens to envelop Reseune as the military faction in Union turns ugly and threatens the Expansionists' majority on the council.

When the aged Giraud Nye dies abruptly, the eighteen-year-old Ariane is able to counter the threatening politics from Union. A nearly successful attempt to assassinate her, however, seems to imply that Giraud and Denys, rather than the Warricks, have been the more serious threat to Ariane Emory's hegemony.

Analysis

Cyteen is one of the central texts in C. J. Cherryh's sprawling future history, in which the former colonies of Earth become the political rivals of Alliance and Union. At 680 pages, it is also one of the longest. It lays out the foundations of that rivalry on Union's home planet. Other works that are central to this future history include *Serpent's Reach* (1980), *Downbelow Station* (1981), *Merchanter's Luck* (1982), and *Rimrunners* (1989). Like *Downbelow Station*, *Cyteen* was voted a Hugo Award for best novel of the year, and in 1989, it was republished as three volumes: *The Betrayal*, *The Rebirth*, and *The Vindication*.

As John Clute has noted in *The Encyclopedia of Science Fiction* (1993), the Alliance-Union rivalry gives Cherryh a flexible but powerful structural focus for her future history. Such a focus offers a much-needed center for a writer whose plots are dense with tangled political machinations and conflicting motivations. Paradoxically, even a novel with the heft of *Cyteen* can seem too cramped for the psychological, social, and political action that Cherryh pours into its pages.

At the heart of *Cyteen* is an intersecting double plot: the project to replicate Ariane Emory and the effort to restore Justin Warrick's disrupted research potential. Through the former, Cherryh invokes fundamental questions about the formation of an individual's identity and the potential of biological engineering to alter people's assumptions about the genetic roots for such identity and the subsequent socialization of the individual. The focus of these questions in Ariane Emory is framed by the book's emphasis on her psychological and social engineering of the azi, the androids who provide bulk and ballast for Union's population. Together, Emory and the azi give *Cyteen* an awareness of human reason entangled in complex emotions that extends the boundaries delineated by Isaac Asimov in his Foundation series, begun in 1942, with later volumes that converge with his robot stories.

In the other strand of this double plot, Cherryh explores the ambiguous zone between human psychology in Justin Warrick and azi psychology in his companion, Grant. Both embody an admixture of logic and emotion, but for Grant, logic is fundamental, engineered into the deepest levels of awareness, and emotion is a "flux" state that disturbs mental equilibrium. For Justin, however, logic is an imperfectly exercised control over the more fundamental emotional flux. The sexual compatibility and mutual respect that characterize Justin and Grant provide a marked contrast to the more disturbed relationships among most of the human characters who populate *Cyteen*. In the end, the second Ariane is able to recover Justin's abilities by respecting the relationship that he and Grant have established.

The profusion of social and political disturbances that surround this double plot suggests that humanity's difficulty in reconciling logic and emotion remains profound. Even science, which offers a model for the appropriate exercise of reason in human endeavor, is compromised by the sheer complexity of human nature and the politics that intervene when science has to operate in the world. In *Cyteen*, the scientists themselves are all-too-imperfect human beings. That point, richly illustrated by the human characters' convoluted motivations, should resonate through the related volumes in Cherryh's future history.

—*Joseph J. Marchesani*

The Dark Is Rising Sequence

Young people help to collect various talismans of power that will aid the Light in its final, supernatural battle against the Dark

Author: Susan Cooper (1935-   )
Genre: Fantasy—high fantasy
Type of work: Novels
Time of plot: Primarily the 1960's, with journeys in time to earlier eras
Location: South Cornwall and Buckinghamshire in England; the vicinity of Aberdyfi in North Wales
First published: *Over Sea, Under Stone* (1965), *The Dark Is Rising* (1973), *Greenwitch* (1974), *The Grey King* (1975), and *Silver on the Tree* (1977)

The Story

Although she did not initially plan to write a sequence, Susan Cooper found, when she returned to provide a sequel to the first book, not only that she had four more books to write but also that the fantasy element, originally peripheral, had become central. The forces of good and evil, known as the Light and the Dark, are locked in a supernatural struggle for power over humankind. As the sequence title proclaims, the Dark is rising for a final major assault. The books describe how various talismans of power are collected to aid the Light in the impending crisis.

Over Sea, Under Stone begins as an exciting children's adventure story set on the southern coast of Cornwall during the summer holidays. The three Drew children, Simon, Jane, and Barney, hunt for the Grail and, despite the danger posed by some sinister villains, they eventually find it, although the accompanying manuscript is lost in the sea. Only at the end do they begin to suspect that their mysterious great-uncle Merry, as they call Professor Merriman Lyon, is none other than Merlin.

In *The Dark Is Rising*, the setting shifts to the twelve days of Christmas in a small village in Buckinghamshire. Will Stanton, the seventh son of a seventh son, discovers on his eleventh birthday that he is the last born of the Old Ones, an immortal race with supernatural powers dedicated to the struggle against the Dark. The Old Ones are led by the Lady and Merriman, here in the guise of the butler at the village Manor. Their foes are led by the Dark Rider. Despite fierce resistance from the Dark, wielding the weapons of fear and deceit as well as cold and flood, Will succeeds in his assigned task of gathering the six signs of power. At the novel's conclusion, he releases the Wild Hunt to disperse his enemies.

Greenwitch returns to Cornwall in the spring, bringing together the Drew children, Will Stanton, and Merriman to search once again for the Grail, which has been stolen by the Dark, and for the lost manuscript that will allow them to decipher the writing on the sides of the vessel. Eventually they succeed, but first they must propitiate the Greenwitch, a traditional image of leaves and branches cast into the sea each spring for good luck in fishing and harvest. Like the Wild Hunt, she is part of the Wild Magic, a force distinct from both the Light and the Dark. She gives the manuscript to Jane, who alone has shown her compassion.

In *The Grey King,* Will travels during the Halloween season to his aunt's farm near Aberdyfi in Wales. He wishes to recuperate from a serious illness that has robbed him of some of his memories. His task this time is to find a golden harp that is guarded in a secret cavern by the High Magic, yet another force in the author's magical equation, then to awaken the six Sleepers by playing to them. He is aided by Bran, a strange albino boy who turns out to be the son of King Arthur and Queen Guinevere, brought forward in time by Merriman/Merlin. He is opposed by the Grey King, one of the most powerful lords of the Dark. Working through the malice of petty-minded people as well as his own mighty power, the Grey King causes the death of Bran's dog Cafall and very nearly foils the plans of the Light.

The sequence concludes at Midsummer with *Silver on the Tree.* This novel opens in Buckinghamshire as Will collects the six signs of power from their place of safekeeping so that Merriman can take them back in time to aid King Arthur at the Battle of Badon. The story moves to Aberdyfi, where Will, Bran, and the Drews all meet to search for the Lady. She appears to Jane, to whom she imparts vital directions. Thanks to these and to help from the bard Taliesin, Will and Bran are able to travel back in time to the Lost Land of King Gwyddno, who gives Bran the Crystal Sword. With this, he is able to cut from the midsummer tree the silver blossoms, thereby gaining a final victory for the Light over the assembled powers of the Dark that have been opposing them bitterly at every turn. The Light and the Dark both withdraw, leaving humanity to work out its own fate without external intervention.

Analysis

Susan Cooper has written novels and plays for adults as well as for children, but none has achieved more success than the Dark Is Rising sequence, for younger readers, written early in her career. Three of the books have won awards. *Over Sea, Under Stone* won a competition for a family adventure story held by publisher Jonathan Cape, *The Dark Is Rising* was a 1974 Newbery Honor Book, and *The Grey King* was the 1976 Newbery Award winner.

Among the qualities for which the sequence has gained praise is the powerful sense of double reality of ordinary life, on one hand, and of the realm of High Magic, on the other. In part, this comes from the clearly realized setting, recalled from the author's own childhood, and from the skillful integration of regional legends, such as the stories of Arthur and the drowned lands of King Gwyddno.

The books also recognize the problems that young people must deal with every day, including misunderstandings and disagreements that disrupt even the closest families; hostility and bullying practiced by others of their own age; and impatience, unkindness, and even cruelty of adults too preoccupied with their own concerns to take account of the feelings of others. The results of such problems often are fear, loneliness, and a sense of betrayal that can embitter and destroy. This perpetuates a cycle of darkness that only love can break, a love so strong that it will forgive mistakes and injuries.

This situation finds a striking parallel in the supernatural world, where a struggle is taking place between the Light and the Dark. The latter seeks to gain control over humankind, using as its weapons fear and deceit. Those who give way to anger, prejudice, and self-centeredness, such as Caradog Prichard in *The Grey King* and Mr. Moore in *Silver on the Tree*, become vulnerable to its power, allowing the Dark to grow in strength. Opposed to it is the Light, which endeavors to protect humankind. Although generous and forgiving, the Light can be uncompromising in the sacrifices it requires of its followers. Virtue, after all, is never easy.

The Old Ones are charged with ensuring the preservation of the world from the Dark. At times the struggle may be so close that it leaves little room for acts of charity and mercy, or for protecting a wayward child. Acts of betrayal may have consequences too far-reaching to be overlooked.

Under these circumstances, the young protagonists are expected to assume responsibilities at an earlier age than usual. Their help is needed desperately, and they can be given only limited protection. This leads to a growth in maturity and understanding. Simon abandons his initial resentment of Will, Will comes into his power as an Old One, and Bran discovers his heritage as the Pendragon, heir to his father, King Arthur. These changes come at a price, for they bring not the freedom that young people expect but still heavier burdens. Thus, at the conclusion of the sequence, Bran is free to choose whether to join his father or to remain with his stepfather. Although torn, he decides to stay with the latter, recognizing that loving bonds are the strongest thing on Earth. As a result, he gives up his chance for immortality in the Otherworld beyond time, choosing instead to live and die like all humans. The choice is hard, and what is gained comes at a painfully high cost.

Part of that cost is the alienation as one grows away from the friends and family that surround one in childhood. Twice Will is obliged to erase the memories of beloved brothers who react badly to the discovery of his powers. Bran's special qualities mark him as different, attracting taunts and resentment.

Although the sequence encourages young people to strive to create a better world, it also warns that problems do not end with the end of childhood. Difference still attracts hostility, whatever one's age or station in life, and even the most deserving of aims exacts a price.

—*Raymond H. Thompson*

Dark Universe

Descendants of nuclear war survivors who moved underground must relearn their sense of sight and the nature of the world

Author: Daniel F. Galouye (1920-1976)
Genre: Science fiction—post-holocaust
Type of work: Novel
Time of plot: An indeterminate time in the future
Location: Below and on the surface of Earth
First published: 1961

The Story

Dark Universe was the first—and most popular novel—of New Orleans journalist Daniel F. Galouye, although he had been publishing magazine stories since 1952. It was nominated for a Hugo Award.

The story is seen—or, rather, heard—by young Jared Fenton, whose primitive people live in total darkness and think of Light as a dimly remembered religious deity. They are preyed on by zivvers, other underground humans whose eyes have adapted to provide limited sight in the infrared spectrum, and "monsters" that inspire fear because they cause people to disappear and because they use light, which is alien to Jared's people.

Jared is the son of his tribe's ruler, the Prime Survivor. He is pressured into an arranged marriage (or "unification") with Della, the niece of another tribe's leader, to unite the tribes against the zivvers. Della has developed the zivver ability and, because Jared is exceptionally gifted at sensing people or objects by vibrations from sound echoes, believes he is secretly a zivver also. She persuades him to flee with her to the zivver group, which Jared has been seeking for his own reasons: He believes that Light is a natural phenomenon and that he might learn its nature through the zivvers.

Eventually, the young couple become outcasts and fugitives from both groups. Jared's people also decide that he is a zivver and therefore an enemy. The zivvers test him and discover that he is not one of them. He and Della fall into the hands of the monsters, who are revealed to be descendants of survivors from underground shelters who are now re-inhabiting Earth's surface, which has purified itself. The two tribes and the zivvers from Jared's underground world have also sprung from a survival group, but something has gone wrong in their complex. They have lost their artificial light and, gradually, all knowledge of their origins. The monsters have been kidnapping them, a few at a time, and re-educating them.

Still not fully understanding or accepting the explanation, Jared escapes and makes his way to the surface. He realizes the truth of what he has been told and looks forward to a new life in a new world with Della.

Analysis

The paperback original employs a theme that would dominate Galouye's work: distorted perceptions of reality. In this case, without ever stating it overtly and keeping entirely to the point of view of his protagonist, Galouye is able to establish his nonvisual setting within the first two pages and show how Jared and other characters have adapted to it. He tells nearly the entire story without resorting to the visual sense—no small feat—but never loses the reader.

Nuclear war was a concept familiar to science-fiction readers even before the first atomic weapons were used in 1945, to the extent that editor Horace Gold announced in the January, 1952, issue of *Galaxy* that he would no longer buy "atomic doom" stories for his magazine. Such stories continued to be written, though, some of the best known being Walter M. Miller, Jr.'s *A Canticle for Leibowitz* (1960), Mordecai Roshwald's *Level 7* (1959), and Pat Frank's *Alas, Babylon* (1959), all showing the aftermath of nuclear destruction. Neville Shute's *On the Beach* (1957; filmed in 1959) familiarized the general public as well.

It becomes obvious to most readers how Jared's people came to be in their situation, especially when Strontium and Cobalt are deified as demons, Radiation is described as a kind of hell, and Hydrogen is named as the devil. One religious tenet holds that the presence of Light Almighty in Paradise made it possible for people to know what lay ahead without smelling or hearing it. Jared is accused of being blasphemous when he suggests that there may be natural explanations for these concepts and that Light is something attainable in this life.

It is fascinating to follow Jared's reasoning as he presses his inquiries, especially considering that most readers already know the answers. One breakthrough comes when he finds that the "roaring silence" that emanates from the monsters, which is how the survivors perceive their lights, is cut off when he closes his eyes and that it is not coming through his ears after all.

The book also includes the science-fictional concepts of extrasensory powers (one of the survivors has developed telepathy), genetic mutations from radiation (sou-bats are giant and marauding descendants of cave bats), and immortality (in the elderly Forever Man, who lived in the prewar surface world and understood Light but has suppressed those memories over generations and withdraws into himself when Jared tries to awaken them).

Galouye is thorough in showing how his underground people have adapted to their environment, sometimes with amusing results. The word "hear" is substituted routinely for "see." Reference is made to the "holy bulb" as a source of Light, which is likened to God. The words "Light!" and "Radiation!" are used as expletives. A courtesy between two strangers is the Ten Touches, which give each an idea of what the other is like. The worst offenses that can be committed are murder and "misplacement of bulky objects."

Dark Universe, although it has a more upbeat ending than most novels in the nuclear armageddon lineage, is very much a part of that heritage, which includes such works as Philip K. Dick's *Dr. Bloodmoney: Or, How We Got Along After the Bomb* (1965), Harlan Ellison's "A Boy and His Dog" (1969), and David Brin's *The Postman* (1985). Its well-realized underground world sets it apart from those that preceded and followed it.

—*Paul Dellinger*

Davy

Davy recounts his development from an ignorant boy into a free-thinking adult and his attempt to bring enlightenment to his post-holocaust civilization

Author: Edgar Pangborn (1909-1976)
Genre: Science fiction—post-holocaust
Type of work: Novel
Time of plot: The twenty-fourth or twenty-fifth century
Location: New England, the Atlantic Ocean, and the Azores
First published: 1964

The Story

Davy's coming-of-age story is not unique to science fiction, and Edgar Pangborn has no use for typical science-fictional devices such as spaceships and ray guns. Nevertheless, *Davy* is science fiction because of its vivid future world. In the late twentieth century—the "Old Time"—nuclear holocaust, plagues, and increases in world temperature and ocean levels destroyed human civilization. After about a hundred years, in the vast wilderness of what once was New England, a new civilization began to grow, a collection of small, bellicose countries dominated by the Holy Murcan Church, an organization forbidding books, free thought, gunpowder, and atoms. Because the Old Time people squandered the world's resources and the remnants of humanity have lost the Old Time science, the fragile civilization is ignorant and superstitious.

In the year 331 of this transformed world, Davy, at the age of twenty-eight, begins writing several intertwining stories: his growth to manhood, his relationship with his wife, their attempt to enlighten the benighted age, their founding of a colony, and the history of his era. The most compelling conflict in *Davy* next to that between enlightenment versus ignorance is Davy's struggle to tell his stories honestly and effectively.

Red-haired Davy was born in a whorehouse, reared in an orphanage, and bonded out as a yard-boy for a tavern. At the age of fourteen, he runs away, in the process accidentally committing his first homicide, having sex for the first time, and stealing an Old Time French horn. Thus begin Davy's picaresque adventures.

With help from the fascinating people he meets as he journeys through his wild world, Davy learns to play his horn, loses his religious superstitions, and becomes a free-thinking and loving person. Davy first joins company with Jed Sever, a sensitive and pious giant; Sam Loomis, a laconic loner; and Vilet, a sensual prostitute. After several adventures, including a comic scene with a "quackpot" medium and a tragic scene with a tiger, Davy and Sam join Rumley's Ramblers. The Ramblers are a communal troupe of independent entertainers who travel through the New England territories performing music and plays, selling home-made cure-alls, and passing along news.

When Davy leaves the Ramblers after several years, he meets and marries Nickie, a "sweet pepperpot" noblewoman who belongs to the Society of Heretics, an underground organization that promotes enlightenment and resists the church's dogma. Through Nickie, Davy meets her cousin Dion, Regent of Nuin. Nickie and Dion educate Davy in Old Time literature and ideas, and Davy and Nickie help Dion try to drag their country out of the dark ages. Their heretical ideas, such as abolishing slavery and promoting free education, meet with disapproval from the Holy Murcan Church, which foments a rebellion. The Heretics lose the war and flee Nuin on a ship into the unknown waters of the Atlantic. It is during this voyage and subsequent establishing of a colony in the Azores that Davy begins to write his book. The novel concludes with Davy setting sail to continue lovingly exploring the uncharted territories of world and mind.

Analysis

A plot summary of *Davy* neglects one of the novel's pleasures and important themes: the richness of the English language. Davy and Pangborn love language, from coarse prose to beautiful poetry, and the novel reflects that love. Davy often sets off on delightful Melvillean digressions on such topics as bedbugs. Additionally, a transformed language adds flavor to his narration. The transformed language appears in neologisms (mahooha), portmanteaus (prezactly), contracted forms (Febry), and distorted forms (sack-religion). Even cultural icons appear changed: Davy's world has a Saint George Washington. Pangborn uses such language to engage the intellect, make readers laugh, and show how fragments of civilization persist through time, transformed to suit new ages.

Pangborn returned to the world of *Davy* in *The Judgment of Eve* (1966), *The Company of Glory* (1975), and short stories such as those collected in *Still I Persist in Wondering* (1978). *Davy*, written in the middle of his career, is Pangborn's most defining and enduring work. *Davy* was runner-up for the 1965 Hugo Award for best science-fiction novel and placed on the 1972 *Locus* poll for best novel of all time. Critical opinion of *Davy* is favorable. George Zebrowski writes that *Davy* "is one of the lasting works of SF," and Spider Robinson says that "reading *Davy* has measurably and significantly, and for the better, changed my life."

Davy is part of the tradition of post-holocaust novels in which human civilization is portrayed as cyclic and, despite human folly, inextinguishable, from George R. Stewart's *Earth Abides* (1949) to Russell Hoban's *Riddley Walker* (1980). *Davy* also belongs to the tradition of science fiction that emphasizes humanistic concerns such as love, tolerance, inner growth, art, and psychology, rather than technological dreams. Pangborn's contributions to these traditions are his combination of loving humanism, rich language, an expansive view of life, self-reflexive narration, and playful humor. Describing a sunrise scene of ethereal beauty, for example, Davy shows a pair of monkeys copulating in a tree. If *Davy* can be summed up with one word, it would be the term of endearment between lovers in the novel: "spice."

In the above traits, *Davy*, like almost all of Pangborn's fiction, transcends its genre. It also recalls fiction such as Henry Fielding's *Tom Jones* (1749) and Mark Twain's *Adventures of Huckleberry Finn* (1884). The richly realized setting; the many vivid and unforgettable characters; the intertwined earthiness and sublimity, beauty and filth, and comedy and tragedy; and the powerful theme that people must light fires—both smaller and larger than the sun—in human minds and hearts all make *Davy* one of the best novels of any genre.

—*Jefferson M. Peters*

The Demolished Man

Lincoln Powell attempts to prove that Ben Reich has committed murder, an almost unheard of act in the year 2301

Author: Alfred Bester (1913-1987)
Genre: Science fiction—extrasensory powers
Type of work: Novel
Time of plot: 2301
Location: New York City
First published: 1953 (serial form, 1952)

The Story

On the surface, *The Demolished Man* is a slick, futuristic detective novel, but the book is much more complex than such a surface description implies. Ben Reich, a wealthy and powerful man, has planned a merger with the D'Courtney Cartel. When that merger is apparently thwarted by Craye D'Courtney, Reich plans to murder his rival. The difficulty confronting Reich is that in the year 2301, murder has been virtually eliminated because of the emergence of Espers, people gifted with and trained in the use of extrasensory perception. Espers are classified according to their levels of ability; an Esper 1 is the most gifted and best-trained of the Esper Guild members. Because Espers can "peep" accused suspects, or look into their thoughts, hiding guilt from them is virtually impossible. The Esper Guild, however, maintains strict rules for its members. Even though Lincoln Powell, a police prefect and an Esper 1, determines very early that Reich is guilty of D'Courtney's murder, he is unable to make use of the knowledge without supporting evidence. He must present enough evidence to the police computer, "Old Man Mose," to ensure a conviction; otherwise, Reich will go free.

Reich has powerful means of thwarting the police investigation. He can hire the best Espers to help him, he can afford massive bribes and incentives, and he has friends in high places in the police department. Powell, however, is not without resources of his own. He is a superb detective in addition to being an incredibly gifted Esper. He manages to locate a witness to the crime, Barbara D'Courtney, the daughter of the victim. She is so traumatized by the murder, however, that she must undergo considerable psychotherapy to counteract her state of shock. She must be regressed to a state of birthlike innocence and carefully brought through normal growth stages in order to preserve her mental functions. As she goes though these stages under Powell's observation, he comes to realize that he is in love with her.

Meanwhile, Old Man Mose has rejected Powell's plan for prosecution, and Powell has no idea why. He discovers that the motive for the murder is so complex and so deeply hidden in Reich's subconscious that he must combat Reich in ways that play upon his psychological makeup. Only in that way is he able to accomplish his objective of having Reich "demolished," or psychologically broken down and rebuilt into the man his better nature will allow. Powell also is able to find a satisfactory outcome for his love of Barbara D'Courtney.

Analysis

Alfred Bester won the first Hugo Award in 1953 for *The Demolished Man*. Bester had published numerous short stories prior to this book, his first novel and generally considered to be his best. The quality of the book is attested by the fact that it has held up for more than forty years as a fascinating study of the human mind, of psychic and psychological detective methods, and of the intricacies of human relationships. It is especially effective in its study of the ways in which the Espers relate to one another and to society.

Powell, for example, has a private house rather than the standard apartment. This is not because of his superior economic means. Esper 1's must have private residences because they are bombarded by the thoughts of others in small, poorly insulated apartments, and they must have privacy to maintain their sanity. Being an Esper is a decidedly mixed blessing. Insight into the thoughts of others is a gift, but that gift is received whether one chooses it or not, and Espers cannot avoid knowing things that they might rather not know. Early in the book, Bester describes the dialogue at a party. It is presented typographically to show that strains of the conversation intertwine because the Espers at the party can both hear spoken conversation and understand the unspoken thoughts behind it. They also play a game of creating word patterns, much like poems but with visual aspects, in their minds for others to perceive.

There are ways to protect one's thoughts from Espers. Reich adopts a mindless jingle that he keeps running through his mind at all times to try to block the Espers. This works with Espers of the lower grades; it fails with Espers of Powell's quality.

Use of a computer as a guide to the likely success of prosecution of a case is another interesting device. Readers of the 1990's and beyond would probably not question this plot device or find it unusual, but in 1953, when computers were in their infancy, it was a speculation into the future of a new and interesting machine. Technology in *The Demolished Man* takes a secondary position to psychology. Although most of the psychology seems at odds with present-day psychotherapy, that is not necessarily a flaw. Readers might assume that the psychotherapy described in the novel is more advanced, as it is from an imagined future; it is in fact dated.

A minor flaw in the book, one that might disturb feminist readers, is the love angle. Powell finds himself unable to love his longtime associate, Mary Noyes, who makes no secret of her love for him, yet he falls in love with Barbara D'Courtney, who has been regressed to an infant and who loves him in a childlike way as she "grows" back into an adult self. Despite such minor problems, this book is a classic of science fiction that should be included on every reading list of major works in the genre.

—*June Harris*

Dhalgren

Kid embarks on a quest of self-discovery in Bellona, a city transformed into an anarchist realm by its entrapment in a distorted space-time continuum

Author: Samuel R. Delany (1942-   )
Genre: Science fiction—New Wave
Type of work: Novel
Time of plot: The 1970's
Location: Bellona, an imaginary American city
First published: 1975

The Story

Written over a period of four years and spanning more than eight hundred pages, *Dhalgren* is Samuel R. Delany's magnum opus. *Dhalgren's* main character is the twenty-seven-year-old Kid, who suffers from selective amnesia and other mental disturbances. At the novel's start, Kid is hitchhiking to Bellona, a midwestern city trapped by a mysterious disaster in a shifting zone of reality where time runs in loops and occasionally a giant red sun or two moons appear in the heavens.

On his way into Bellona, Kid meets a strange Asian woman who, after they make love, turns into a tree. This surreal opening begins *Dhalgren's* conflicting realities: Are the novel's strange events real, or are they the result of Kid's delusional point of view?

Upon entering Bellona, Kid becomes the lover of a former electrical engineer named Tak, who introduces Kid to the cult of George Harrison, a powerful black man worshiped in Bellona's ghetto. Tak takes Kid to the city's hippie commune, and there Kid meets Lanya, who becomes Kid's next lover. Kid also finds a notebook containing the journal of an anonymous past owner. Because of *Dhalgren's* time loops and Kid's amnesia, Kid himself could have written the journal at an earlier or later time.

Kid begins to write poetry in this notebook. These poems become the basis for *Brass Orchids*, a book published by Roger Calkins, the eccentric owner of the city's newspaper, the *Bellona Times*.

Kid receives a severe beating from a trio of scorpions, the name given to Bellona's street gangs. On occasion, scorpions venture out from their nests, or home bases, terrorizing Bellona's residents. Gang members wear projectors that conceal their bodies in holographic images of griffins, spiders, dragons, and other mythical or fantastic creatures.

After this incident, Kid meets June Richards. The Richards family tries to lead an unchanged bourgeois existence in the midst of Bellona's chaos. George Harrison reportedly raped June during the riots that occurred during Bellona's mysterious catastrophe. Kid comes to realize that the so-called rape was an act of mutual desire filled with mythological portents.

Later, Kid is drawn unwittingly into a scorpion run on Emboriky's, a major department store that is the stronghold of a group of armed white racists. During the run, Kid displays the kind of crazy bravery the gang admires. As a result, Kid becomes the leader of a scorpion nest and acquires as a lover a gang member named Denny who becomes part of a three-way sexual relationship with Lanya.

The remainder of the novel concerns Kid's adventures as a scorpion and a poet. While prowling Bellona's shattered streets, Kid awaits the second meeting between George and June. Kid believes that when this meeting occurs, Bellona will plunge once more into an apocalyptic frenzy.

Inspired by metafictional technique (fiction that comments on itself as fiction), Delany wrote *Dhalgren*'s final chapters in columns, with one side following the story and the other commenting on the action, presenting alternative plot lines, or revealing passages from Kid's notebook. This method creates a dual ending. One possibility is that June and George meet, the mysterious apocalypse strikes Bellona again, and Kid flees the city. In a manner reminiscent of James Joyce's *Finnegans Wake* (1939), the last line of *Dhalgren* is a half sentence completed by the half sentence at the novel's start, creating a closed loop. Thus Kid is caught in Bellona's circular time pattern. The other possibility is that the ending is merely a fiction of Kid's notebook, and both the arrival and exit scenes are not real. Kid has always been in Bellona and will always remain there, its scorpion poet.

Analysis

Dhalgren is a pivotal work in Delany's career. Although it continues many of the themes of his earlier novels, *Dhalgren* has a dense, literary style and unflinching examination of drug use, deviant sexuality, and violence that also point toward future works such as *Tales of Nevèrÿon* (1979) and *Stars in My Pocket Like Grains of Sand* (1984).

Unlike *Babel-17* (1966), *The Einstein Intersection* (1967), and *Nova* (1968),

Dhalgren explores countercultural themes such as bisexuality, drug use, race relations, and the connection between artistic and criminal cultures, without far future or deep space settings to blunt the controversial nature of these subjects. The immediacy of *Dhalgren*'s 1970's setting, combined with its difficult literary style and explicit sex and violence, alienated much of Delany's previous readership, who had come to expect works like *Nova* and *Babel-17*, which essentially were stock space epics written with stylistic flare and a 1960's hip sensibility.

Also alienated were many science-fiction reviewers and critics, who regarded *Dhalgren* as at best incomprehensible and at worst a disgrace to the field. *Dhalgren* nevertheless sold well, more than a million copies in less than a decade. In his collection of essays *The Straits of Messina* (1989), Delany attributes these sales to interested readers and sympathetic reviewers outside the science-fiction field.

Dhalgren has its science-fiction defenders, most notably Theodore Sturgeon and Frederik Pohl, and the novel's critical support has increased over the years. What critics praise in *Dhalgren* are its literary experimentation, its highly charged language, and its depth of character. Few other works in any field have portrayed life on the fringes of society with such richness of detail and depth of understanding. *Dhalgren*, with its nonlinear structure, stream-of-consciousness passages, and self-commentary, evokes the brilliant literary innovations of James Joyce, Jorge Luis Borges, and Thomas Pynchon.

Dhalgren may well be the climax of science fiction's New Wave exploration of expanded themes and stylistic techniques. At the same time, its focus on the urban fringe foreshadows the arrival of science fiction's cyberpunk movement in the mid-1980's.

—*John Nizalowski*

The Dispossessed

Shevek, a physicist raised in an anarchist society, fulfills a lifelong quest to bridge two worlds, two theories of time, and two sets of obligations—to himself and to community

Author: Ursula K. Le Guin (1929-   )
Genre: Science fiction—utopia
Type of work: Novel
Time of plot: Several hundred years in the future
Location: Anarres and Urras, planets orbiting Tau Ceti
First published: 1974

The Story

The Dispossessed: An Ambiguous Utopia is one of several of Ursula Le Guin's works chronicling the evolution of a "League of all Worlds" governed by principles superior to those of known political and colonial systems. Although *The Dispossessed* takes place in the League's prehistory, the novel's loving portrait of a working anarchist society on one world develops in detail the principles of noncoercive social organization.

The novel chronicles the life of Shevek, a physicist reared on a world settled by the followers of an anarchist philosopher, Odo. The Odonians, "bought off" 170 years before Shevek's time with an offer to settle their mother planet's arid moon, Anarres, live without laws, according to the apparently irreconcilable principles of absolute individual freedom and absolute commitment to the good of the community. Anarresti social order is maintained primarily by education, which inculcates a horror of "egoizing." The Anarresti live in isolation from their mother planet, Urras, a lush world that Anarresti education demonizes as a place of injustice and evil.

Through a series of struggles, Shevek strives to balance loyalty to the society that formed him with rebellion against subtle conformist pressures that stifle his ambitious work in theoretical physics. The conflict climaxes after a long famine, during which Shevek accepts four years of separation from his wife and his work to perform manual labor in his planet's harshest desert. After this trial of physical, emotional, and intellectual self-denial, Shevek vows, "by damn, I will do my own work for a while now!"

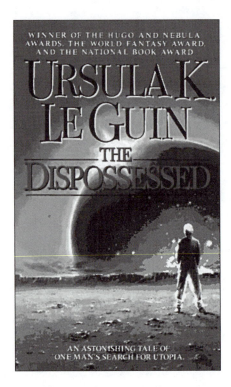

That work has been kept alive, ironically, through extended contact with the physicists of the mother planet, Urras—that is, with despised "propertarians." After his desert ordeal, Shevek accepts a standing invitation based on his groundbreaking physics and becomes the first Anarresti in 170 years to visit the mother planet. In the face of intense opposition, he vows to "go to Urras and break down walls."

On Urras, Shevek is treated as an honored but subtly controlled guest, kept from any genuine contact with the poor. His hosts are determined to "buy" him. They believe that his work, once completed, will bring them wealth, power, and prestige. Shevek moves from admiring awe and a kind of racial homesickness for the lush mother planet to revulsion against a social world dominated by competitive struggles for power and wealth. When a chance comes to lend support to the poor people of Ai-Io, the wealthy host-nation, Shevek seizes it, traveling secretly to the slums and leading a demonstration against an unjust war. This self-liberation from a luxurious "prison" comes in the wake of the fulfillment of Shevek's scientific work: completion of a General Temporal Theory that unites apparently irreconcilable theories about time.

The antiwar demonstration, climaxing with Shevek's speech urging renewed Odonian revolt, is broken up by a military crackdown. Shevek hides for three days in a basement with a mortally wounded demonstrator who dies in Shevek's care. Following this near-death descent, Shevek emerges suddenly in the Terran (Earth) Embassy, where he gains asylum and arranges for his theory to be broadcast to all worlds, thus eluding his hosts' desire to possess it and enabling instantaneous communication between the "nine known worlds." In a final wall-breaking action, Shevek agrees to let a young man from Hain, oldest of the known inhabited worlds, accompany him home to Anarres.

Analysis

Like most of Le Guin's heroes, Shevek embodies the author's imaginative quest to balance poles of paradox. In physics, his quest is to reconcile sequency, "the arrow of time," and simultaneity, "the circle of time"—that is, becoming and being. His General Temporal Theory, a restatement of Odo's dictum, "true voyage is return," asserts that "you *can* go home again . . . so long as you understand that home is a place where you have never been." A well-lived life comes full circle, linking past and future by fulfilling long-term promises, but also gets somewhere, effecting meaningful change.

The novel's structure embodies this gnomic principle. The odd-numbered chapters chronicle Shevek's sojourn on the mother planet Urras; even-numbered chapters bring his life on Anarres from infancy to the moment he decides that he must go to Urras. The two narratives merge in chapter 13, which anticipates Shevek's return home to an Anarres transformed by his rebellious journey—that is, to a place he has never been.

Le Guin has voiced the hope that science fiction can achieve the kind of idiosyncratic characterization championed by Virginia Woolf and widely considered integral to realistic fiction. *The Dispossessed*, however, reflects a different imaginative goal, indeed a passion, common to virtually all of Le Guin's work: to imagine an ideal person—in this case, as the embodiment of a nearly ideal society. "What is it like," asks the Terran ambassador Keng, "what can it be like, the society that made you? . . . you are not like other men."

Although Le Guin is not much interested in Christian paradigms, she is keenly conscious of archetypal formulations of the hero's journey, and she quite pointedly sends Shevek to hell and back on both worlds. His sojourn in "the dust" during the famine on Anarres is one hell. Out of the long separation comes renewed commitment—to marriage, to work, and to continuing the Anarresti revolution. On Urras, Shevek's quest to "break down walls" is consummated by his three-day basement ordeal, which he equates with hell. It is after rising from this depth that Shevek releases his theory, thus extending the blessings of communication and brotherhood that are "the Promise" of Anarres.

—Andrew Sprung

Do Androids Dream of Electric Sheep?

Rick Deckard must find and kill a group of androids who have escaped from a colony on Mars and come to Earth

Author: Philip K. Dick (1928-1982)
Genre: Science fiction—post-holocaust
Type of work: Novel
Time of plot: 1992
Location: The San Francisco Bay Area
First published: 1968

The Story

Do Androids Dream of Electric Sheep? recounts a day in the life of bounty hunter Rick Deckard. The action begins on the morning of January 3, 1992, as Deckard and his wife, Iran, wake up in their apartment; it concludes the following morning, as an exhausted Deckard returns to bed. In that twenty-four-hour period, Deckard faces the greatest challenge he has ever encountered: He must "retire" a rogue band of "organic androids" (or "andys," as they are called) of a design so advanced that they are almost indistinguishable from human beings. His task is complicated by his attraction for another android, Rachael Rosen, who tries to prevent him from carrying out his mission.

The story is set in a gray world devastated by "World War Terminus" and the resulting radioactive fallout, which is slowly depopulating the planet. Many people have left to settle in a colony on Mars, where androids are employed for hard labor, domestic service, and other purposes. In making their escape from Mars and servitude, the rogue andys that Deckard is to retire killed a number of humans. The people who remain on Earth have witnessed the extinction of many animal species. Possession of an animal—a horse, a sheep, or even a cat—confers status; for those who cannot afford the real thing, artificial animals are available. Deckard himself has an electric sheep but greatly desires to own a living creature. That is the primary motivation in his quest: The bounty he earns of $1,000 per andy will enable him to buy a genuine animal.

Like a knight in a medieval romance, Deckard undergoes a series of trials as he retires the andys one by one. Nothing is as it first appears to be. A Soviet policeman turns out to be one of the andys in disguise.

Another bounty hunter, Phil Resch, is falsely identified as an android by a San Francisco police inspector—himself an android—who hopes that Resch and Deckard will kill each other. Most mutable and devious of all is Rachael Rosen, who seduces Deckard, then calmly tells him that he will be unable to continue as a bounty hunter; no one ever has after being with her. Deckard, however, proves her wrong. Although he cannot bring himself to kill Rosen, he completes his task, retiring the last three fugitive andys after his tryst with her.

The novel ends on a note of reconciliation and domesticity. Deckard returns home to his wife. They had argued to start the day, but now Iran greets him warmly, fussing over him until he falls asleep. The last line in the book is a celebration of everyday human routine: Iran, "feeling better, fixed herself at last a cup of black, hot coffee."

Analysis

One of Philip K. Dick's recurring themes figures prominently in *Do Androids Dream of Electric Sheep?* This theme is identified in Dick's 1978 lecture, "How to Build a Universe That Doesn't Fall Apart Two Days Later," collected in *The Shifting Realities of Philip K. Dick: Selected Literary and Philosophical Writings* (1995), edited by Lawrence Sutin. In that lecture, Dick observes that throughout his career he has been preoccupied with the question, "What constitutes the authentic human being?" Dick often explores this question in novels and stories featuring androids or other constructs closely resembling human beings. These include the novels *The Simulacra* (1964) and *We Can Build You* (1972) and stories such as "The Electric Ant" (1969).

In *Do Androids Dream of Electric Sheep?*, Dick imagines a near future in which successive generations of androids become ever more sophisticated in their mimicry of humans. The model that Deckard must retire, the Nexus-6, is the most advanced yet. There remains one crucial difference between humans and androids: empathy. Androids can learn to mimic human concern, but they do not genuinely feel empathy for other creatures. Deckard employs a psychological/physiological test, the Voigt-Kampff Altered Scale, that detects the absence of empathy in the microseconds before it can be faked.

This emphasis on empathy as the defining human characteristic runs throughout the novel. It is poignantly embodied in the "chickenhead" John Isidore ("chickenhead" being a derogatory term for humans who, as a result of the fallout, lack normal intellectual capacities). Isidore innocently befriends three of the fugitive andys, then watches in horror as they gratuitously cut the legs off a spider. Empathy also is at the core of the quasi-religious movement known as Mercerism, in which both Deckard and Iran participate. So intense is the identification experienced by communicants in "fusion" with the archetypal figure of Wilbur Mercer that they sometimes emerge from a session with wounds inflicted by rocks thrown at Mercer, rather like Christian saints who receive the stigmata.

Dick's characters, however, are far from sainthood. The most important lesson Deckard learns in his long day is imparted to him in a revelation from Mercer. Deckard, appalled by the killing, wonders if he can finish the job. He explains later to Iran, "Mercer said it was wrong but I should do it anyhow." As a character recognizes in another Dick novel, *The Man in the High Castle* (1962), "There is evil! . . . It's an ingredient in us. In the world." Acknowledging that, one does the best one can.

Many people know the story of *Do Androids Dream of Electric Sheep?* not from the novel itself but from the film based on it, *Blade Runner* (1982). The film departs from the book in many ways, most conspicuously in its treatment of the protagonist. Dick's Deckard is a bounty hunter but also a husband. In the film, Deckard (played by Harrison Ford) is a loner, a futuristic private eye. Dick's final message is a modest affirmation of human virtues; the film's conclusion is both cynical and romanticized, showing Deckard with the beautiful android. As for empathy, that theme is turned upside down: Mercerism disappears from the story altogether, and Deckard survives only because the leader of the androids (or "replicants," as they are called in the film), his mortal foe, shows compassion for him.

—*John Wilson*

Doomsday Book

While a time-traveling historian is stranded in England during the Black Death, her twenty-first century colleagues battle their own epidemic and seek to rescue her

Author: Connie Willis (1945-   )
Genre: Science fiction—time travel
Type of work: Novel
Time of plot: December, 2054-January, 2055, and 1348
Location: Oxford, England, and Ashencote, a nearby village
First published: 1992

The Story

Kivrin Engle, a brilliant and determined young woman, is the first historian to journey back to the Middle Ages. She makes the trip despite the misgivings of her teacher and mentor, Mr. Dunworthy. His anxieties seem justified when the technician in charge of the time "net" mumbles that something is wrong and then collapses from a deadly new strain of influenza shortly after sending Kivrin to the past. What gradually becomes clear is that Kivrin has been infected with that same flu and sent not to 1320, as intended, but to 1348, the year the Black Death began to ravage England.

Unbeknown to her, Kivrin's arrival in the past is witnessed by an illiterate but saintly priest, Father Roche, who brings the sick and delirious woman, whom he regards as a messenger from heaven, to the castle of his lord. Kivrin is nursed back to health by Lady Eliwys and her family, who were sent by her husband to hide from the plague in this remote village. While anxiously trying to relocate her rendezvous point—the exact location where the gateway in time will reopen—she quickly grows to love the people, especially Eliwys's two young daughters, Agnes and Rosemunde. Travelers fleeing a nearby city bring the plague, and Kivrin realizes for the first time that she is in the wrong year. With little hope of returning to her own time, she does her best, along with Father Roche, to battle the plague and save the people of the village.

In the twenty-first century, Kivrin's plight becomes an afterthought to all but Mr. Dunworthy as Oxford comes under a quarantine and doctors and scientists race to find a vaccine. Dunworthy does his best to mobilize the resources of the university to fight the epidemic and care for the sick, all the while trying to find some confirmation that Kivrin's time traveling has gone well and she at least is safe.

Connie Willis effectively uses the parallel plots of the novel, cutting back and forth between the time lines, to increase suspense, create ironic juxtapositions, and ultimately affirm the common humanity of people battling disaster. In twenty-first century England, the epidemic is finally halted, but in the fourteenth century, the progress of the Black Death is inexorable. One by one, Agnes, Rosemunde, Lady Eliwys, and all the people of the village die in agony, despite the heroic efforts of Kivrin and Father Roche. Roche eventually dies, but the utter bleakness of the catastrophe and Kivrin's grief are in some small measure relieved by his gratitude and love for Kivrin, who has indeed become the messenger from heaven of his simple faith, bringing comfort to the dying and surviving to bear witness. As Kivrin struggles to sound the death knell as a memorial for Roche, the sound of the bell brings Dunworthy, who, though still weak from his own near death from influenza, has come back through time to seek Kivrin and bring her home.

Analysis

Although Willis employs the common device of time travel, she is not interested in creating paradoxes or exploring alternative histories. Time travel is for her a means of juxtaposing two societies confronting similar crises, of exploring human nature in the presence of overpowering fear, and of celebrating human courage and generosity.

Following the success of *Lincoln's Dreams* (1987), the critical and popular acclaim for *Doomsday Book*, which won both the Hugo and Nebula awards for best science-fiction novel, established Willis as one of the top American science-fiction writers. *Doomsday Book* exhibits Willis's characteristic strengths: thorough scholarship, graceful prose, and a rare combination of profound compassion and keen intelligence. There is even a touch of the humor present in many of her short stories in Dunworthy's struggles with bureaucratic rigidity and the complaints of self-centered people who do not quite notice that there is an epidemic going on. Also evident is Willis's ability to realize a time and place and create vivid characters whose joys and sorrows will haunt the reader's memory.

Time travel is one of the classic plot devices of science fiction. *Doomsday Book* has antecedents dating back to Mark Twain's *A Connecticut Yankee in King Arthur's Court* (1889) and H. G. Wells's *The Time Machine* (1895). Much of twentieth century time-travel fiction has focused on the mutability of time: Characters travel back to the past and change it, either inadvertently or deliberately. Authors such as Poul Anderson have developed story sequences in which rival groups battle over time, seeking to change the past (and hence the future) or to preserve an immutable past. In *Doomsday Book*, the immutability of the past is a given. It is the combination of Kivrin's powerlessness, despite all of her modern knowledge, to do anything to stop the plague or to save even a single victim, and her heroic persistence in trying nevertheless, that gives the novel a tragic power rare in science fiction.

Willis's depiction of medieval England is compelling. She captures the sounds, sights, and smells with convincing verisimilitude. She neither patronizes the past nor sentimentalizes it. If she does not share Father Roche's simple yet profound faith in the ultimate goodness of God, she treats it and him with the utmost respect. The double plot, which allows her to contrast two periods so vividly, also enables her to portray an essential humanity. Despite the differences in language, culture, and knowledge, the people of both centuries are remarkably alike: Both centuries have their share of fools, bigots, and cowards, but most people in both are a blend of fear and courage, selfishness and nobility. In both periods, despite the prevalence of death and despair, there is a persistence of human love and caring, personified in Roche, Kivrin, and Dunworthy, that cannot be overcome.

—*Kevin P. Mulcahy*

A Door into Ocean

Inhabitants of an ocean world with an entirely female population resist takeover

Author: Joan Slonczewski (1956-   )
Genre: Science fiction—alien civilization
Type of work: Novel
Time of plot: The distant future
Location: The planets Valedon and Shora
First published: 1986

The Story

For forty years, traders from the planet Valedon have colonized the ocean planet Shora. The story concerns the increasing threat to the inhabitants of Shora and to the balance of life on their ocean home as the effects of colonization escalate and as they face the military invasion of their planet by the occupying forces of Valedon. The population of Shora—all females, who call themselves Sharers—resists the traders and soldiers by peaceful, nonviolent means. They also resist by trying to understand the Valans and by attempting to heal them both physically and spiritually. Although their advanced skills in life sciences might enable them to devise means of destroying the invaders, Sharers resist the temptation to destroy those who would destroy them. Influenced by their wordweaver, Merwen, they maintain the possibility that the Valans are human and that their healing will result in the survival of Sharers and Valans alike.

The story opens with the arrival of the Sharers Merwen and Usha in a port city on the planet Valedon. They have come to learn if the Valans are human in spite of their very different physical characteristics, actions, and values. They return to Shora accompanied by a young boy named Spinel and another Valan, the wealthy and noble Lady Berenice, called Nisi by the Sharers. These two Valans share the lives of Shorans who live on the raft Raia-el.

When Sharers boycott Valan traders, Spinel joins them. Although the boycott is successful in achieving the immediate demands of the Sharers, a worse threat takes the form of a plan to bring Shora under the control of Valedon. Realgar, the Valan to whom Nisi is engaged, arrives to head the military occupation of Shora. Pressures against the Sharers and their environment increase as a result of escalating Valan frustration with the Sharers' refusal to capitulate. Sharers struggle with the question of the humanity of the Valans but remain steadfast in their decision to resist without killing.

The ultimate action against the Sharers is precipitated by Nisi's attempt to destroy herself along with the Valan military headquarters. Some of the Valans have come to respect the Sharers, and their appreciation is intensified when Valans injured in the explosion are rescued and healed by Sharers. In a climactic series of conversations with the imprisoned Merwen, Realgar is forced to recognize his own fear and to face his endangered humanity. His defeat is complete when the High Protector of Valedon chastens him for the mutiny in his troops. Realgar resigns his position and, with all the trader and soldier Valans, withdraws from Shora. They leave the Sharers to the work of repairing their lives and their planet. Nisi remains to become healed of her double betrayal, and Spinel, drawn by his love for Merwen's daughter, Lystra, remains as hope for a transformed future.

Analysis

A Door into Ocean is the second science-fiction novel by professor of biology Joan Slonczewski, following *Still Forms on Foxfield* (1980). Like her other novels, it has been praised by critics for the accuracy of its science, the completeness of its alternative cultures, and its characterization. It won the John W. Campbell Memorial Award as best science-fiction novel of 1986.

As a work of science fiction, the novel offers the situation of the alien encounter. Shifting the scene from one planet to another, it explores the situation of alien encounter from the perspectives of both worlds, opening with the visit of the Sharers to Valedon. As in other science-fiction novels describing encounters with aliens, the story raises and examines the issue of the nature of humanity. When Valans turn purple like the Shorans, they fear the loss of their humanity. When Merwen considers the possibility that some of the Shorans are willing to hasten the death of the invaders, she worries that Sharers will lose their identity.

The two societies are not portrayed in monolithic and static terms, but the novel presents the encounter between Valedon and Shora as a juxtaposition of utopia and dystopia. The utopian society of Shora is not without difference, nor is the dystopian world of Valedon without its redeeming qualities. At the end of the novel, Spinel chooses to remain on the utopian Shora, but his choice carries the possibility of the transformation of Shora because he retains his Valan stonesign and knows that Lystra wishes to have daughters with him, daughters who will differ from both of them.

This novel has been discussed in the context of women as writers of science fiction and as a work of feminist science fiction. The portrayal of the world of Shora, with its highly advanced life-shaping science, its openness to all learning, and its egalitarian politics, values those matters that have been seen as feminist areas of concern. This emphasis critiques the patriarchal culture of Valedon as it also critiques the dominance of science itself, since the outcome of human action always remains unpredictable and uncontrollable. As Merwen knows in the final series of conversations with Realgar, it is wordweaving, the uncertain art of persuasive language, that will determine the final outcome.

Critic Robin Roberts, author of *A New Species: Gender and Science in Science Fiction* (1993), has highlighted *A Door into Ocean* as an example of postmodernist feminist science fiction because of its attention to the function of language. A deconstructive model is at play in revisions both of the convention of the alien encounter and of the static and monolithic utopia. The model carries through in the critique of the dominance of science and of patriarchy. It is mediated by the characterization of Merwen as a wordweaver and by a peculiarity of Sharer language: In every utterance, its opposite is present.

—*Shawn Carruth*

Door Number Three

A psychiatrist treating a woman claiming to have been left on Earth by aliens finds himself fighting the Holock, creatures from the future who devour human dreams

Author: Patrick O'Leary (1952-   )
Genre: Science fiction—time travel
Type of work: Novel
Time of plot: 1990, with parts set in the far future
Location: The United States
First published: 1995

The Story

Psychiatrist John Donelly is treating Laura, a woman who claims to have been left on Earth by the alien Holock. She claims that she has only one year to convince one person—anyone—that her story is true, or she will have to leave Earth. She says that the Holock take great interest in earthly affairs because entering human dreams is their primary form of entertainment. Donelly believes her story is an elaborate delusion, until strange events—and even stranger dreams—invade his mundane existence. His dreams become more vivid, each of them featuring the same ten-year-old boy. One of his colleagues is murdered the same night that Laura strikes him after he tells her he does not believe her. A detective investigating the murder tells Donelly that a Vietnamese soldier he killed during the Vietnam War has begun appearing in his dreams, asking him about Laura and the Holock.

Donelly meets Saul, Laura's former "guardian angel" and the unwitting progenitor of the Holock. Saul reveals that the Holock come not from space, but from Earth's own post-holocaust future, and that they devour dreams, preventing humanity's ethical evolution to ensure their own eventual creation. He also says that Donelly's child will be the savior of the human race. Donelly sleeps with Laura, who soon reveals her pregnancy and allegiance to the Holock, then disappears into the future.

To set things right, Donelly asks to use Saul's time machine. This device induces a form of mental time travel that not only causes users to "blip" back and forth throughout their own lifetimes, but generates changes that ripple out into both the past and the future. Donelly soon finds himself on the run from government agents, who have made a deal with the Holock. He eventually tracks down Laura in the future, only to find her living with an alternate version of himself, the self that really slept with Laura, the one he finally agrees to kill in order to save the world and usher in a new golden age, free of the Holock.

Analysis

Door Number Three is a clever, well-written, and intricately constructed debut novel. Despite spinning variations on many classic science-fiction themes, it is boldly original. It betrays few evidences of being a first novel, as O'Leary worked with editor David Hartwell for seven years to hone the novel through multiple drafts. Its prose is smooth and polished, its characters vivid and memorable, and its plot gripping.

O'Leary manages to juggle time travelers, alien abductions, government conspiracies, and dream-eating monsters without ever descending into clichés. He slowly and skillfully invests the Holock with a sense of menace far more frightening than the standard "alien grays" so often depicted in popular media. While the novel's themes of paranoia and loss of reality have earned O'Leary comparisons with Philip K. Dick, the analogy distorts as much as it reveals. While Dick's best work displays an organic paranoia that reflects the disorder in his hapless protagonists' minds, O'Leary's carefully crafted plot forces these experiences on his protagonist from without.

The intricate twists and turns deployed in the time travel portions of *Door Number Three* recall the equally ingenious plotting of Robert A. Heinlein's "By His Bootstraps." While the idea of "mental" time travel has been used before, the idea of changes in the future rippling back to effect the past may be original to O'Leary. The ambitious looping and nesting structure of the novel as a whole merits comparison with K. W. Jeter's *The Glass Hammer* (1985) and Geoff Ryman's *The Child Garden* (1989). As in those overlooked masterpieces, the story itself could not be told in a linear narrative with the same impact.

Door Number Three ranks alongside Mary Doria Russell's *The Sparrow* (1996), Ken MacLeod's *The Star Fraction* (1995), and Raphael Carter's *The Fortunate Fall* (1996) as one of the most impressive science fiction debuts of the 1990's. O'Leary afterward went on to publish *The Gift* (1997), a flawed but engrossing fantasy, and *Other Voices, Other Doors: A Collection of Stories, Meditations and Poems* (2000). O'Leary may yet prove to be one of science fiction's major talents.

—*Lawrence Person*

Dracula

Count Dracula, a vampire, moves to England from his native Transylvania in search of new blood

Author: Bram Stoker (1847-1912)
Genre: Fantasy—cautionary
Type of work: Novel
Time of plot: The end of the nineteenth century
Location: Transylvania and England
First published: 1897

The Story

Jonathan Harker, an English solicitor, visits Count Dracula in Transylvania. He finds death's aura and aroma surrounding Dracula. Harker is attacked by three female vampires, who are warded off by Dracula. Harker is his; they are given a baby to feed on. When Harker demands to be released, Dracula obliges, but a pack of wolves surrounds the castle entrance. The next day, Harker awakes, weak and sick, with a wound on his throat. Dracula leaves Harker at the castle as a prisoner.

In England, Harker's fiancé, Mina Murray, visits her friend, Lucy Westenra, a "New Woman" who plans to marry nobleman Arthur Holmwood. During Mina's visit, a ship runs aground in Whitby. The only living creature aboard is a gray wolf, which escapes into the countryside.

Lucy begins to sleepwalk. Mina follows her and sees a tall, thin man bending over Lucy in a churchyard. The man disappears when Mina approaches. Lucy grows so ill that Mina is forced to call Dr. Seward, Lucy's former suitor. While Lucy improves, Mina receives word that Harker, who had been reported missing, has been found near Budapest. Mina goes there and marries Harker.

Lucy's condition worsens, and Seward calls Dr. Van Helsing from Amsterdam. Van Helsing notices two puncture wounds on Lucy's throat. Lucy is given transfusions directly from the men, who guard her by night. Seward falls asleep while guarding Lucy and finds her more ill when he awakes. More transfusions ensue, and Van Helsing insists that Lucy wear a necklace of garlic every night.

One night, a wolf crashes through the window, the necklace slips off, and Lucy is further victimized. Van Helsing tells Holmwood that Lucy is near

An advertising poster for Tod Browning's 1931 film
production of Dracula, *starring Bela Lugosi.*

death. Holmwood kisses Lucy, who fastens her teeth to his neck. Lucy dies. Several neighborhood children are discovered far from home, alive but with their throats punctured. They say they followed a pretty lady in white.

Harker returns to England. Van Helsing suggests that Lucy is a vampire's victim. By night, Holmwood, Seward, Van Helsing, and Quincey P. Morris visit Lucy's tomb and find it empty. At daybreak, Lucy returns, and they drive a stake through her heart, cut off her head, and stuff garlic in her mouth.

Mina is vampirized by Dracula. The men track Dracula in London, but he escapes. By hypnotizing Mina, they learn that Dracula is at sea. They follow him to Castle Dracula. Wolves encircle the men and Mina, who gather safely within a "magic" circle Van Helsing traces. The men overtake the cart carrying Dracula's coffin. As the sun sets, Harker slashes Dracula's throat with his kukri knife and Morris gouges Dracula's heart with his bowie knife.

Analysis

Interest in vampires, like the creature itself, never dies. Bram Stoker's novel focuses on the victimization of women. Stoker's view is opposed to that of the "New Woman," a feminist construct of the late nineteenth century.

Stoker makes references to the New Woman in *Dracula* through Mina, characterizing her as a well-informed woman of the 1890's. Mina sets herself above the New Woman, rejecting the concept for its sexual openness. The overall structure of *Dracula* indicates that Stoker employs Mina to reject the concept of the New Woman, represented by the female vampire as energized and aggressive female sexuality.

The first half of the novel presents woman as vampire. Stoker focuses on the female vampire by introducing the three female vampires who live in Dracula's castle, then centering on Lucy, Dracula's first English victim. In the second half, the focus of the story is the fight to save Mina, shifting away from the presentation of woman as vampire. The focus becomes the fight against vampirism, and, metaphorically, against energized female sexuality or the New Woman.

Lucy, the primary female focus of the first half of the novel, is turned by Dracula into one of "those awful women." The New Woman exists in her personality, however latent, surfacing when Lucy is vampirized by Dracula. In her vampirized state, she no longer suppresses her desire. Van Helsing takes it upon himself to protect men from the evils of the vampire, and, hence, the evils of the New Woman. Lucy, confronted by the men in her crypt, takes on the full-blown characteristics of the New Woman, preying on a child and speaking of her wanton desire for Holmwood. By calling Holmwood to her side, Lucy suggests that he break with the patriarchy. This does not happen because Lucy is summarily destroyed by the men; the vampire/New Woman is destroyed by the patriarchy.

The scourge of vampirism/New Womanhood also calls at Mina's door. Mina represents traditional Victorian womanhood but also feels the effects of vampirism/ New Womanhood. Dracula seduces her, forcing her to drink his blood from his breast while her husband sleeps in the same bed. The patriarchy comes to Mina's rescue. As the vampire's, or New Woman's, influence over Mina grows, Dr. Seward metaphorically sees the New Woman overcoming the traditional woman. The role of Stoker's male characters is to prevent the acceptance of the New Woman by keeping women in their place, and, hence, the patriarchy in order. To do this, the men must destroy Dracula. Van Helsing chooses to fight the vampire to save the patriarchy.

At the novel's end, by destroying Dracula, Van Helsing and the men destroy vampirism and, metaphorically, the New Woman, preserving the sanctity of womanhood and the patriarchal order. Stoker's novel is therefore anti-New Woman and antifeminist. It came at a reactionary time when literary England was up in arms against the very idea of the New Woman.

—*Thomas D. Petitjean, Jr.*

Dreamsnake

A feminist quest in which young healer Snake searches for a dream-snake across the deserts and mountains of an Earth altered by a nuclear holocaust in its distant past

Author: Vonda N(eel) McIntyre (1948-   )
Genre: Science fiction—post-holocaust
Type of work: Novel
Time of plot: Indefinite future
Location: An unidentified desert, a mountain village, the healers' community, and a dome that shelters an alien ecosystem
First published: 1978

The Story

In "Of Mist, and Grass, and Sand" (1973), the Nebula Award-winning novelette that became the first section of *Dreamsnake*, Vonda McIntyre introduces her protagonist Snake, a young traveling healer who uses her knowledge and her genetically altered snakes to treat illness and suffering. Snake is called to help a family whose son is dying of a large tumor. To comfort him, she leaves Grass, her treasured dreamsnake, on the child's pillow while she prepares Mist, her cobra, to treat the child. When she returns from a strenuous night of altering Mist's venom into a medicine against the child's cancer, she finds that the parents have killed her dreamsnake out of their desert-bred terror of snakes.

Without her dreamsnake, whose bite eases death, Snake is handicapped as a healer. She becomes afraid when she is called to a patient's side: Will the patient be dying and ask Snake for the help she can no longer give? *Dreamsnake*, which won both Hugo and Nebula awards, expands the original novelette by tracing Snake's quest to obtain a new dreamsnake and continue her career as a healer.

Snake first directs her steps toward the healers' "station," the home community where she was trained. She intends to ask her elders to forgive her error in judgment and give her a new snake, knowing that the scarcity of dreamsnakes makes it unlikely that her request can be granted. Along the way, people call on her as a healer, not recognizing that she is impaired by the lack of one of the basic tools of her profession, the means to assist at death. While trying in vain to help a woman dying of radiation exposure, Snake decides that instead of returning in shame to her home, she will go to the Center, the underground city that preserved itself and its technology before the nuclear devastation of the planet. Because the Center communicates with offworlders and the dreamsnakes are believed to come from another planet, it is possible that the people of the Center can help her. The isolated and paranoid city refuses her.

As she travels and treats the ill, Snake becomes aware that she is being followed. Her stalker ransacks her possessions and later attacks her and tries to steal her snakes. She assumes that a "crazy" is following her. Eventually she turns the tables and becomes the follower, after she learns that her assailant is addicted to dreamsnake venom; she infers that someone, somewhere, has enough dreamsnakes to use them wastefully. The pathetic but sly addict leads her to "the broken dome," an alien habitat where a multitude of dreamsnakes are being exploited by a bitter, soul-twisted albino giant who hates the healers because they were not able to cure his genetic deformities. With the help of her adopted daughter and the man who loves her, Snake triumphs and comes away from the broken dome not only with dreamsnakes but also, and more important, with the knowledge of how to breed them successfully.

Analysis

In this early novel, published before the author's highly visible career producing novelizations of Star Trek films, McIntyre follows the well-established tradition of the masculine heroic quest story but modifies the form to suit a feminist worldview. As is typical of quest stories, in *Dreamsnake* a young protagonist sets out on a difficult journey to find something of great value and encounters trials and adventures along the way. Instead of a weapon, a woman, or a treasure, the thing of great value for which McIntyre's protagonist searches is a dreamsnake, a tool of nurturing.

In the traditional male-oriented trajectory of a heroic quest, the obstacles encountered by the hero are enemies with whom he must fight in order to prove himself. In *Dreamsnake*, the trials are challenges of healing and caring, not challenges of force; there are patients to be treated, not enemies to be bested. Snake is tested, strengthened, and softened by her encounters with a woman with a broken spine and radiation poisoning, an arrogant injured aristocrat who will not follow her advice, a young man who has failed to master control of his own fertility, and a scarred young victim of sexual abuse whom Snake finally adopts as her own daughter. The maturity Snake wins through her quest is not the hardness of a battle-seasoned warrior but the humanity of a woman who can deal honorably with her professional responsibilities and also accept responsibility for a child and for a mate.

McIntyre expresses her feminist vision not only by appropriating and modifying a traditionally masculine form; she also constructs a world of characters who are not bound by gender-role constraints. She frequently introduces characters by generic titles, such as "owner," "chemist," "innkeeper," "guard," and "herder," leaving their gender to readers' imaginations. When a gender-revealing pronoun, such as "him" or "her," finally appears, readers may be surprised to find their stereotypes challenged.

McIntyre conceives a society in which both men and women are free to develop to their full potentials. Snake herself supports that conception. She is able to give a good account of herself in a fight, bathe a newly crippled woman who has wet the bed, be tender and truthful with children, use her physical prowess and stamina to escape from her enemies, live fully even in the full knowledge of her coming diminishment with age, and experience the entire range of emotions available to a human being.

—*Donna Glee Williams*

The Dune Series

> The planet of Arrakis goes through several politico-environmental upheavals in a spacefaring yet feudal society dependent on the addictive spice melange

Author: Frank Herbert (1920-1986)
Genre: Science fiction—galactic empire
Type of work: Novels
Time of plot: The 57th year of the Padishah Emperor, Shaddam IV (102d century C.E.) through the following five thousand years
Location: Primarily Arrakis (the planet called Dune and later Rakis) and Chapterhouse
First published: *Dune* (1965; serial form, *Analog*, 1963-1965), *Dune Messiah* (1969), *Children of Dune* (1976), *God Emperor of Dune* (1981), *Heretics of Dune* (1984), and *Chapterhouse: Dune* (1985)

The Story

The Dune series can be seen as a set of three two-volume novels. The first involves the family of Paul Atreides, its battle for the planet Arrakis, and Paul's coming of age as the messianic Muad'Dib. The second concerns the life of Paul's son Leto II, from childhood to his ascendancy as God Emperor of Dune. The third deals with the ongoing machinations of the Bene Gesserit, an ancient society of women devoted to mind and body control and eugenics, in their attempt to control the sociopolitical environment of the Dune universe millennia later, as well as the ramifications of their betrayal by the Atreides family. *Dune* itself was rejected by twenty-two publishers before being accepted by Chilton of Philadelphia. It remained in print for at least the next thirty years.

In *Dune*, the Atreides family emigrates from their home world of Caladan to the desert world of Arrakis, pressured by the political dalliances of the Emperor Shaddam IV. Arrakis (Dune) had been controlled by the Baron Harkonnen, and it was there that he had gained his great wealth from trade in melange, an addictive spice. Melange is essential to the functioning of all elements of society, including the Spacing Guild, for which it ensures the ability to fold space.

The Harkonnens set a trap for the Atreides family in which Duke Leto Atreides and his weapons specialist, Duncan Idaho, are killed. His Bene

Gesserit consort, Jessica, and their son, Paul, flee to the domain of the Fremen, the desert people of Arrakis. Once there, Paul partakes of melange and begins to show signs that he is the Kwisatz Haderach, a messiah-like culmination of the Bene Gesserit's breeding program. Jessica was supposed to have had a girl, who would be married to the Harkonnen boy Feyd-Rautha, thus solidifying the aristocratic alliances and placing the Bene Gesserit fully in command of galactic political affairs. The Bene Gesserit time line is thrown off, and sociopolitical upheaval ensues. The rest of the novel involves the Atreideses' attempt to retake the planet of Arrakis from the deposed Harkonnens and the installation of Paul as its ruler.

Frank Herbert. (Andrew Unangst)

All of this occurs in the intricately realized ecology of the desert planet. The desert is essential to the complex life cycle of the sandworms, whose larval forms, the sandtrout, produce melange. A vast history unfolds, supplemented by chapter-heading epigraphs on the life of Paul Atreides, or Muad'Dib as he comes to be known by his Fremen followers, from the Princess Irulan, his legal wife and the daughter of Emperor Shaddam IV.

Dune Messiah takes up the story of Paul and Jessica in their life with the Fremen as they consolidate their power on Arrakis. Chani, Paul's Fremen concubine, has died in childbirth, and Paul must ultimately sacrifice himself in the defense of their children, his prescient sister Alia, and Arrakis.

Children of Dune continues the story of Paul's son, Leto II, and his daughter, Ghanima, when they are nine years old. Leto takes on the outer covering of the sandtrout—the larvae of the giant sandworms—and effectively becomes a superman, a worthy successor to his messianic father, and rightful emperor of the galactic empire. Neither of the two volumes following *Dune* has the scope of the original, and both lack the hagiographic epigrams of Princess Irulan, which give readers much information concerning the overall effect of the future history. The books do not suffer for this—in fact, the action intensifies to the point of absurdity (Leto's sandtrout symbiosis, for example)—but they are different in kind.

The fourth volume, *God Emperor of Dune*, returns to the form of the first volume and is set some 3,500 years in the future. Leto II, in his symbiotic state with the sandworm, has become immortal and rules the galactic empire from his throne on Arrakis with infallible foresight. One result of that foresight is the empire's stagnation. He comes to realize in his lengthy reflections that this cannot continue and so devises his own downfall. The plot here is thin, and the musings are long—features only too characteristic of the later volumes in the *Dune* series.

Heretics of Dune, the fifth volume, concerns the Bene Gesserit and the Tleilaxu in the eventual planned destruction of the planet Rakis, as it has come to be called. A third Kwisatz Haderach of sorts, the militant Sardaukar Bashar Miles Teg, sacrifices himself for the sisterhood as the several guilds fight for ascendancy in the shattered empire through control of Rakis, the worms, and melange. The Mentat warrior Duncan Idaho, cloned here for the twelfth time, provides a thread of continuity from *Dune*, as does the interminable talk of the millennia-old treachery of Lady Jessica and her illicit son Paul. All of this takes place 1,500 years after the self-destruction of Leto II, God Emperor, and the regathering of the lost tribes of the once-flourishing Rakis. This volume introduces the dark mirror version of the Reverend Mothers of the Bene Gesserit, the Honored Matres of Rakis. They play the role of archnemeses in the sixth and final volume, *Chapterhouse: Dune*.

After the willful destruction of the planet of sandworms, whose spice is essential to the operation of the galactic empire for all the guilds by this point, the Honored Matres vow revenge on the sisterhood. The Bene Gesserit reincarnate Teg, who, as the old myth went, could move faster than light, to fight the Honored Matres. They rely on Duncan Idaho's weapons abilities in their plan, but Duncan chooses to honor Bene Gesserit teachings of nonaggression and slips into a parallel space. The remnants of the Fremen and the guilds join him in his flight from the Honored Matres.

Analysis

Although *Dune* did not receive universal critical acclaim on its appearance, it won both the 1965 Nebula Award (the first Nebula) and tied for the 1966 Hugo Award. The success of *Dune* and its sequels stems in large part from the response on college campuses. Like J. R. R. Tolkien's *The*

Lord of the Rings trilogy (1954-1955), Frank Herbert's book presented a traditional epic with heroic characters in a well-realized environment, augmented by appendices and a map. The ecology movement had burgeoned, and *Dune* consciously used the environment of the desert as dire warning. As the drug culture flowered, the psychedelic melange, or spice, served as a handy symbol for lysergic acid diethylamide (LSD).

Dune came early in Herbert's career, preceded only by *The Dragon in the Sea* (1956; retitled *Under Pressure*, 1974), and fixed a benchmark for the rest of his career. It also made him one of science fiction's most financially successful authors. The novel was filmed in 1984.

The entire Dune series unfolds from the well-conceived original. Each later volume develops the ramifications of Jessica's decision—and that of her son Paul and grandson Leto II—to betray the Bene Gesserit guild and take the unfolding of sociopolitical events into their own hands. Paul is similar to Isaac Asimov's "Mule" in the Foundation series. After becoming the first male Bene Gesserit in history, he disrupts the plans of the Bene Gesserit to obtain control of the known universe. By the sixth volume, Atreides blood runs in the veins of almost everyone of any consequence in the Dune universe. This is a fine reversal on Baron Harkonnen's desire to see all Atreideses dead.

The long view of history, the vision of messiahs, and the unflinching critique of the myth of progress fit well into the epic-heroic structure. Herbert is able to include strong female characters, the Bene Gesserit, in a staunchly Middle Eastern milieu of *chaumurky* and *chaumas*—poison in the drink and poison in the food—and curved, poison-tipped blades. The characters are many and the plot intricate, but too much in the later volumes is lengthy narrative. The "heroes"—Paul, Leto II, and the twelfth Duncan Idaho—make antiheroic decisions, and the plots come off as anticlimactic despite epic events. The action is too often presented in the blink of an eye—literally in the case of Teg in *Heretics of Dune*—and the reader is privileged to learn about it after the fact through the ruminations of the characters.

—*U. Milo Kaufmann*

The Dying Earth Series

A gallery of sorcerers and rogues employ mischief and magic in their adventures during the final days of Earth

Author: Jack Vance (1916-   )
Genre: Fantasy—medieval future
Type of work: Novels
Time of plot: The twenty-first aeon, far in the future
Location: Primarily Ascolais and Almery
First published: *The Dying Earth* (1950), *The Eyes of the Overworld* (1966; serial form, *The Magazine of Fantasy and Science Fiction*, 1965-1966), *Cugel's Saga* (1983), and *Rhialto the Marvellous* (1984)

The Story

Jack Vance's stories of the dying Earth consist of three novels and one collection of stories that reads as a novel. The series is loosely linked by a shared setting and repeated characters. Each individual volume stands on its own, and within volumes the particular chapters form largely self-contained episodes.

The first volume, *The Dying Earth*, sets the stage and establishes the basic premises. The novel, more accurately a collection of stories, is set in the distant future. As Earth itself and human history near their end, rogues and charlatans abound, and science has been replaced by magic. The setting is more medieval than futuristic. Humankind is few and scattered, with small, isolated pockets of people spread across the wilderness. Travel is dangerous, because creatures such as deodands, flesh-eating ghouls, and pelgranes, winged ravagers of the air, wait for the unwary or the luckless.

The Dying Earth introduces these themes through the stories of such characters as Turjan of Miir, who wishes to create life in his castle laboratory. Lacking the proper knowledge of incantations, he turns to the powerful, mysterious Pandelume, who aids Turjan in return for a favor, the theft of a magical amulet. Aided by Pandelume's spells, Turjan succeeds, creating a beautiful woman, T'sain, who becomes his companion. In a following story, Turjan is captured by a rival, Mazirian the Magician, who tortures Turjan to gain his secret powers. T'sain saves her creator and lover.

Such is the pattern of stories in *The Dying Earth*. Characters appear only to be replaced by others, such as Ulan Dhor, who travels to the ancient city of Ampridatvir, where he wakes the sleeping god-king Rogol Domedonfors, unleashing devastation. Ulan Dhor's story is the only one in the series that departs from fantasy into more traditional science fiction, as Ulan Dhor escapes using a flying machine found in the ancient city.

The two novels that feature Cugel the Clever, *The Eyes of the Overworld* and *Cugel's Saga*, are picaresque tales in which a series of adventures befalling the protagonist are laid on a simple, sturdy framework. In the earlier work, Iucounu the Laughing Magician traps Cugel robbing him and casts a spell to send Cugel far beyond Almery, where he must secure the Eyes of the Overworld (special lenses with magical powers) and return them to Iucounu. To ensure Cugel's diligence, Iucounu clamps a barbed creature named Firx to Cugel's liver. Whenever Cugel delays, Firx's agitations painfully remind him of his duties.

Cugel acquires the Eyes of the Overworld through typical trickery and returns to Almery, along the way encountering numerous adventures in a variety of settings and managing to escape harm, and sometimes even death, by his wits. He rids himself of Firx as his first step in taking revenge on Iucounu, something he ponders at every step back to Almery. In the novel's final scene, however, Cugel is tricked by Iucounu and finds himself on the same desolate beach where he began his long journey home.

Cugel's Saga begins at this point. Like the preceding novel, it is a tale of Cugel's return, again progressing through territory filled with dangers presented by sorcerers, strange beasts, and stranger human beings. Early in the novel, Cugel escapes from the wizard Twango, carrying with him Spatterlight, a scale from the creature Sadlark, who long ago crashed to Earth from the higher realms. Twango has been painstakingly salvaging Sadlark's scales and selling them, through an intermediary, to an unknown sorcerer.

When Cugel returns to Almery, he is confronted by Iucounu, who demands Spatterlight, for it is the Laughing Magician who has been collecting the scales. Cugel surrenders the treasure but tricks Iucounu into destroying himself. Cugel claims the wizard's magnificent palace as his own.

The setting remains the same but the characters change for the fourth book in the series, *Rhialto the Marvellous*. Rhialto, a magician, joins a number of fellow wizards to form a loosely knit association to protect their interests. The association is guided by the Blue Principles, which are intended to protect these unscrupulous sorcerers from attacking one another.

Rhialto is accused and convicted of offenses against the Blue Principles, and then, through ever-increasing difficulties, must prove himself innocent and wreak vengeance on his enemies, most notably Hache-Moncour, who is motivated by envy of Rhialto's elegant style. Because Rhialto the Marvellous is a true Vance hero of the dying Earth, he is successful, and Hache-Moncour's punishment is suitably apt.

Analysis

Vance's stories of the dying Earth are most notable for the individuality of their characters, realism of their setting, and elegance of their literary style. Major characters such as Cugel the Clever, Rhialto the Marvellous, and Iucounu the Laughing Magician are presented in extended descriptions that reveal their individual personalities. Vance sketches even his relatively minor characters with deft, individualizing strokes that render them vividly and memorably. Often, he concentrates on the essential quality that sums up the basic character of the individual, often a typically human defect, such as pride, lust, or, most often, greed. Even in the fantastic land of the dying Earth, millennia in the future, human nature remains basically the same.

Remaining unchanged, human nature also remains essentially flawed. There are no larger-than-life heroes in the world of the dying Earth; even the best of them, Ildefonse the Preceptor, leader of the magicians in *Rhialto the Marvellous*, has a generous supply of faults and weaknesses, most notably his lack of firmness. That failing allows the plot against Rhialto (and, therefore, the plot of the novel) to develop. Both Rhialto and Cugel are picaresque characters, closer to rogues than to heroes.

The landscape in which these figures find themselves is presented with a deceptively careful accuracy. Vance takes considerable pains to give the geography of the dying Earth a precise set of place names, so that the reader gains an impression of a real, if not entirely realistic, world. Names such as Shanglestone Strand, the Tustvold Mud-Flats, and the River Scaum give weight and presence to the setting of the books, and cities such as Saskervoy, Port Perdusz, and Kaspara Vitatus, in addition to being named, have their odd buildings and odder customs described in quick, vivid detail.

At Gundar, for example, Cugel stumbles upon men tending a strange device, a stone fire pit ringed by five lamps, each with five wicks with an "intricate linkage of mirrors and lenses" above them. Puzzled at first, Cugel later learns that this is an instrument tended by members of the Order of Solar Emosynaries so that the dying sun will remain alive a bit longer. The incident is so clear in its description, yet casual in its presentation, that its air of reality is enhanced.

Vance employs this technique throughout the series, offering the strange, the bizarre, and the magical in a matter-of-fact fashion that, paradoxically, simultaneously emphasizes the unusual nature of being extraordinary yet very ordinary indeed. Although such places and things may not exist in the reader's world, they seem very plausible in the world of the dying Earth.

Finally, Vance's series is distinguished by its literary style, which has an ironic, even arch, tone. His sentences are varied in their syntax, and his vocabulary is extensive, frequently exotic but always precise. Vance's use of language in his fantasy world is less like the heroic prose of J. R. R. Tolkien than it is akin to James Branch Cabell's mocking, playful style in *Jurgen* (1919).

Characters such as Cugel and Rhialto are deft in their linguistic usage, as swift and cutting with their words as with their swords. In fact, words often are weapons on the dying Earth. Through this fact, Vance subtly emphasizes the importance of the spoken word. Curses and spells work their magic by being recited in the correct form and with the proper pronunciation. As Vance points out in the introduction to *Rhialto the Marvellous*, "magic is a practical science, or, more properly, a craft," and it works because "a spell in essence corresponds to a code, or set of instructions."

In the genre of science fiction and fantasy, Vance's tales of the dying Earth occupy a special niche as supremely crafted examples of stories set in a distant future that oddly resembles the medieval past. Although haunted by demons and monsters, it is peopled by characters such as Cugel the Clever and Rhialto the Marvellous, who are all too human to be alien to readers.

—*Michael Witkoski*

Dying Inside

A man with the ability to read minds confronts, in middle age, the gradual loss of his powers

Author: Robert Silverberg (1935-   )
Genre: Science fiction—extrasensory powers
Type of work: Novel
Time of plot: Primarily 1976, with flashbacks
Location: New York City
First published: 1972

The Story

David Selig is a forty-one-year-old man gifted from birth with the ability to read minds. The main conflict in the novel is his attempt to come to terms with the gradual loss of this ability. He has never known why he was born with his gift, nor does he understand why he is losing it.

Ironically, Selig's ability to know what others are thinking has caused him to feel alienated throughout his life. Instead of being able to forge closer bonds with other humans, such as his parents and his sister, Judith, he becomes isolated from them because he can see beyond the surface of everyday life. He understands the selfishness and pettiness beneath the facades of human behavior.

As the novel opens, Selig lives a hermetic existence, eking out a living by ghostwriting papers for college students. His story contains several flashbacks telling about formative incidents in his life. These include a visit as a child to a psychiatrist; his relationship with another telepath, Tom Nyquist; and his failed love relationships with two different women, Toni and Kitty.

His telepathic ability is responsible in part for the breakups of both relationships. As Toni experiences an LSD trip, Selig is unable to avoid entering her mind and consequently experiencing the drug's effects. Toni mistakenly thinks his strange behavior is a deliberate attempt to confuse and hurt her, and she leaves him for that reason. Kitty is a young student whose mind Selig is unable to enter. Fascinated by her and wanting to make her into the soulmate and confidante he has never had, he insists that they study and experiment with telepathy. Finally, his pressuring and manipulation drive her away.

At the end of the novel, Selig's powers have deserted him. Moreover, his career as a ghostwriter is ended when he is beaten by a dissatisfied customer and then discovered by campus security. The novel concludes with an open ending and a tentative affirmation: Selig must reevaluate not only his self-identity but also his relationships with others, especially the sister he has always disliked.

Analysis

Dying Inside appeared relatively late in Robert Silverberg's voluminous literary career. He has written and edited scores of books. In at least one way, *Dying Inside* typifies his writing. Unlike Isaac Asimov, who is more concerned with the technical science aspects of science fiction, Silverberg seems especially interested in character; he shows how human personalities are affected by scientific phenomena and reflects on the political and social implications of such phenomena. For example, there is little explanation of how and why Selig has his special powers: They simply exist. Silverberg attempts to establish some scientific plausibility by explaining that Selig's receptive ability is greater during a high pressure system when the humidity is low. Readers discover that he is losing his powers, but neither they nor Selig knows why.

These details seem secondary to Silverberg's main interest, which is to present an extraordinary fictional situation and explore its metaphorical possibilities. At one point in the text, for example, Selig's sister asks him whether his loss of his power is like a loss of sexual potency. This level is further developed by some of the diction and imagery Silverberg uses to describe Selig delving into others' consciousness: He "enters" and he "penetrates." This analogy underscores the theme of alienation, for Selig is unable to establish true intimacy in either a sexual or a platonic relationship. The point of view of the narrative, which alternates between first and third person, further suggests Selig's alienation, not only from others but also from himself.

One reviewer pointed out that the diminishing of the middle-aged Selig's powers resembles the waning of passion and intensity so often associated with middle age. In this way Selig's unusual situation may be somewhat universalized. This apparent strength of the novel has been viewed as a weakness by at least one reviewer, who wrote that the novel has more to do with growing older than it does with science fiction and that it is more about alienation than aliens.

Silverberg attempts to develop his hero's situation by associating it with those of many other alienated literary heroes of the twentieth century. There are allusions to T. S. Eliot's "The Love Song of J. Alfred

Prufrock" (1915), Samuel Beckett's *Malone Dies* (1956), James Joyce's "The Dead" (1914), and E. M. Forster's *A Passage to India* (1924). As part of his job as a ghostwriter, Selig writes an essay about Franz Kafka's *The Trial* (1937) and *The Castle* (1930). Finally, an essay called "Entropy as a Factor in Everyday Life" uses physics' second law of thermodynamics as an analogy to Selig's view of his own life and the world around him.

Despite being nominated for a Nebula Award in 1972, *Dying Inside* received some unfavorable reviews. Several critics thought that the main character was unlikable, full of spite and self-pity, and others generally found the novel depressing. The novel remains interesting for its descriptions of telepathic experience and, perhaps less important, for its relationship to other twentieth century works.

—*Steven R. Luebke*

E Pluribus Unicorn

Short stories by one of science fiction's most empathetic writers and a grand master of literary style

Author: Theodore Sturgeon (Edward Hamilton Waldo, 1918-1985)
Genre: Science fiction—cultural exploration
Type of work: Stories
Time of plot: Various
Location: Primarily on Earth and a spaceship
First published: 1953

The Story

The stories collected in *E Pluribus Unicorn*, originally published between 1947 and 1953, share an intense and compassionate examination of human behaviors of all kinds and descriptions, including the bizarre, the cruel, the abnormal, the tender, and the sexual. Theodore Sturgeon first broke into science fiction in 1937, rapidly becoming one of editor John Campbell's famous "Golden Age" writers. The early, groundbreaking (and rule-breaking) stories of *E Pluribus Unicorn*, his second story collection (following *Without Sorcery*, 1948), display his mastery in explorations of human emotions.

"The Silken-Swift" (1953), the lead story, is a marvelous reconstruction of the traditional unicorn-and-virgin story, vividly demonstrating that virginity does not necessarily denote an immaculate character and that internal beauty means more than external beauty. "Bianca's Hands," the next story, was first printed in Britain in 1947. Some American editors considered it so depraved that they not only refused to print it but also advised Sturgeon to destroy it. The hands belong to a congenital idiot, Bianca, and the plot deals with the fate of the young man who falls in love with her (or, more precisely, her hands). The story is explicit in its examination of fetishism, and it raises serious issues of tragedy.

"The World Well Lost" (1953) deals honestly and sympathetically with homosexuality. It caused quite a stir in the science-fiction community when it was published and still stands as a landmark in the evocation of love in a psychological sense. "The Professor's Teddy Bear" (1948), "The Music" (original in this collection), "Fluffy" (1947), "Die, Maestro, Die" (1949), "Cellmate" (1947), and "A Way of Thinking"

(1953) explore less positive emotions, including hate, jealousy, and vengeance, and show them as the opposites of love and loyalty. "The Sex Opposite" (1952) and "It Wasn't Syzygy" (originally published as "The Deadly Ratio" in *Weird Tales*, 1948) go far beyond the limits of the day in suggesting sexual combinations; at the time, even homosexuality was somewhat taboo as a topic. "A Saucer of Loneliness" (1953) and "Scars" (1949) describe and evoke the desperation of the lonely and the misunderstood. In each of these stories, Sturgeon sympathetically and non-judgmentally invests himself in the inner workings of his viewpoint characters.

In the introduction, well-known science-fiction editor and anthologist Groff Conklin notes that "you don't read these stories; they happen to you." He promises that the contents will "set you beside yourself, send you into jet-propelled shivers, and generally termite your placidity." This does not seem like an overstatement. In these stories, Sturgeon shows himself as working well above the limits often imposed on science fiction.

Analysis

The stories in this collection demonstrate not only the wide range of Sturgeon's psychologically oriented interests but also the range of his ability. Some of the stories included in *E Pluribus Unicorn* seem exploratory or allusive; all show his stylistic mastery. Sturgeon's greatest weakness lies in creating satisfactory conclusions to his stories, a problem more obvious in his novels than in his shorter works. Still, some of these tales seem either hastily written or truncated, and many of them give the impression of being postmodern, requiring the reader to complete the tale. On the other hand, "The Silken-Swift" is rightly construed as a masterpiece both of literary elegance and behavioral analysis, as is "Bianca's Hands," though with entirely the opposite emotional impact.

Sturgeon taught himself and wonderfully employs the literary technique of using poetic meter in prose passages for emotional effect. This shows up most clearly in the fully accomplished works—"The Silken-Swift," "Bianca's Hands," "A Saucer of Loneliness," "The World Well Lost," and "Die, Maestro, Die"—although it can be detected in virtually every story. It appears clear that Sturgeon derived the initial impetus from his observations of partial or inadequate responses to emotional and social problems. His observations inevitably led him to pose alternative, imaginative ways of dealing with (if not solving) these problems. The reader gets the feeling of looking over Sturgeon's shoulder as he develops his personal motto: "Ask the next question." In his later years,

Sturgeon wore a silver Q with an arrow through it as a symbol of this motto.

In all these stories, Sturgeon clearly, analytically, and sympathetically delineates characters with some strengths and many weaknesses, showing the difficulties they encounter with an unsympathetic world (one especially unsympathetic to weaknesses or differences). His treatments of underground cultures, particularly that of homosexuals, likely influenced such writers as Samuel Delany and Harlan Ellison. Even when Sturgeon's characters behave in desperate or unbalanced ways, they refuse either blame or rejection. Sturgeon's stories clarify the terror of being utterly "known," with nothing hidden. When he creates a deranged or desperate character, he tells the story from that character's own point of view, making the reader understand and, to an extent, sympathize. When he creates a character with warm, human sympathies, readers feel as though they have made a new friend. It is this characteristic of radical acceptance, of wise understanding couched in lyric prose, that readers gain—and appreciate—in Sturgeon's stories.

—*Martha A. Bartter*

Earthsea

A trilogy relating the adventures of Ged from his days as a young
goatherd to his rule as Archmage

Author: Ursula K. Le Guin (1929-   )
Genre: Fantasy—high fantasy
Type of work: Novels
Time of plot: Undefined, on another world
Location: A cluster of islands known as Earthsea
First published: *Earthsea* (1977, as trilogy; also published as *The Earthsea
   Trilogy*, 1979); previously published as *A Wizard of Earthsea* (1968), *The
   Tombs of Atuan* (1971), *The Farthest Shore* (1972), and *The Other Wind*
   (2001)

The Story

Earthsea begins on the island of Gont, a land famous for wizards. There, a
young goatherd named Ged, called Duny as a boy and called Sparrow-
hawk familiarly, overhears his aunt using a common, rustic spell on the
animals. Ged duplicates the words, but without any understanding of
them. The spell works, and the goats come running around Ged. He is
terrified, because he has no knowledge of how to undo the spell.

The event is revealing. Ged has powers, but as a teenage boy he is
naïve about those powers. He has no knowledge and thus no mastery,
and power without knowledge is a dangerous thing. At first, Ged is in
love with power itself. The island Mage, Ogion, recognizes the power
within Ged and attempts to nurture it with understanding.

Restless in his training, Ged eventually is sent to the island of Roke,
the spiritual locus for all Earthsea and training ground for mastery of
magical power. Ged learns it all too well. In his competition with an
older student, Jasper, Ged succumbs to the use of his arts for mere personal power. In an effort to summon the spirit of a dead woman, he unleashes a shadowlike creature into the world of Earthsea. The creature
comes to represent the dark uses of magical power as a shadow self of
Ged himself, lured to personal glorification. *A Wizard of Earthsea* concludes with Ged's defeat of the shadow. The defeat is only a temporary
abeyance of its threat, however, for Ged has neither fully understood its
significance nor mastered its nature.

The second novel, *The Tombs of Atuan*, shifts in point of view from Ged to a young priestess, Tenar. Renamed Arka, the Eaten One, Tenar serves the ancient powers of Earth among the desert tombs of Atuan. She traps Ged, on a quest to find the Ring of Erreth-Akbe, in the labyrinth beneath the temple. Ged tells her her true name and identity, and she decides to join him on his quest. They succeed, but at the cost of the temple's destruction. Tenar returns with Ged to Gont, where she will live with Ogion.

The second novel reveals Ged's growing mastery of magical arts and his increasing power through them. The power enables him to know the true things and hidden essences veiled within an outward nature. The increasingly complicated riddle is whether he truly knows his own essence, particularly in relation to the shadow.

In *The Farthest Shore*, Ged is now Archmage, the most powerful magician in Earthsea. His power has deepened with knowledge. He receives a message from a young prince named Arren, the narrator of the story, that increasingly people are rejecting the beliefs that grant their lives wholeness. Ged discovers that a wayward Mage has opened a hole in the earth, letting disharmony flood the land. Ged's quest is to close that gap, to confront the shadows of disharmony, and to use his power to restore Earth's balance. He must finally confront and master the shadow of his own nature. As is so often the case in fantasy literature, the ultimate quest is for self-understanding. Succeeding in his quest, Ged returns to the peace of Gont among the goats.

Analysis

The basic framework of *Earthsea* is the pattern of the initiation story. In such stories, a naïve and innocent young person acquires knowledge and experience. The pattern is familiar in high fantasy, a subgenre explicitly about magical powers and their harms and benefits. In this case, the young protagonist discovers knowledge about such magical powers and inevitably confronts some conflict about the mastery of the powers. Tempted to turn them to mere personal gain, the protagonist is caught between that desire and the urgent needs of others. A second constituent element of fantasy literature, the quest, operates powerfully in the trilogy and provides the high adventure of the plot. In addition, as in many works of fantasy, the quest parallels the protagonist's discovery of a hidden self.

Within this traditional framework, Ursula K. Le Guin exercises her own kind of literary magic. She is influenced by the teachings of the *Tao-te Ching* ("Classic of the Way and Its Virtue"), supposedly created by the sixth century B.C.E. Chinese philosopher Lao Tzu. Le Guin has orchestrated classical elements of Daoism, and its later developments with Buddhism beginning in the third century C.E. into her novels. Fundamental Daoist points influencing the development of the plots include the belief that life consists of a balance and that every human action affects that balance, the belief that through "weakness" or service to others lies one's strength, and the belief that bureaucratic or political power threatens the balance.

The idea of balance is key, particularly as fundamental Daoism affected the religion of Buddhism and acquired wide popular appeal. Balance harmonizes conflicting tensions. Every darkness contains a bit of light, every sorrow a bit of joy, and so forth. One must live life so as to provide an equilibrium between the tensions.

In *Earthsea*, that balance is terribly distorted when the naïve young Ged first exercises his magical power as an act of proud competition on the island of Roke. He violates orders and therefore violates harmony. He unleashes the shadow of disorder into Earthsea. Ged must come face to face with the shadow that lies within himself, the pride-humility, love-hatred dialectics in his own nature.

As he moves from naïveté to growing awareness of his magical gifts, Ged begins to comprehend the challenge to those gifts. As is so often the pattern in fantasy, he is abetted by the appearance of a special helper, in this case the Mage Ogion, who tutors Ged in the nature of the powers that constitute the balance. At his earliest stage, Ged hungers for power. Gradually, he comes to understand The Powers for their sake and for that of others. His unleashing of the shadow shapes the transition in this realization.

During his advanced training at Roke, Ged quickly outstrips even his masters in knowledge of magical power. One challenge remains: mastery of The Powers to restore harmony. As he restores harmony in the lives of others whom he has threatened by unleashing the shadow, he discovers that by serving others he restores himself. This is the discovery in *The Tombs of Atuan*.

In her illustration of discovery of a true self, Le Guin orchestrates another interesting variation on a traditional fantasy pattern. In the Western literary tradition, the task of the classical hero is twofold: to defeat some threat to the people and to lead the people into a perception of restorative order. To achieve these ends, the classical hero is divinely gifted, sometimes considered, in fact, part human and part god. With these gifts, the classical hero acts for the people, frequently in a superhuman way.

The fantasy hero lies in this tradition but with a difference. The fantasy hero has no pretensions to superhuman status; the hero's origins often are common, even lowly. Fantasy heroes often take on their quests with fear and quite often with a desperate loneliness. The heart of modern fantasy is the premise of a very ordinary character being tested beyond expectation or human hope for success. This hero, although often provided with supernatural helpers, ultimately must rely on little more than human intelligence and determination. The quest to aid others ultimately is a test of the hero's own nature and sufficiency.

The Farthest Shore brings the Archmage Ged to the final step in his quest for harmony. That step is not completed through knowledge, concern for others, or an apprehension of universal order in balance; it is completed in action that leads to internal restoration of balance. The final quest leads to Ged's confrontation with the shadow, which ultimately is his final reconciliation with his own nature and the subduing of his errors of pride. Ged's friend Esstarriol observes that Ged made himself whole. Knowing his true self, Ged cannot be used or possessed by any power other than himself, "never in the service of ruin, or pain, or hatred, or the dark."

—*John H. Timmerman*

The Einstein Intersection

Lobey, a musician, shepherd, warrior, lover, and telepath, embarks on a quest to retrieve Friza, his beloved, from the realm of death

Author: Samuel R. Delany (1942-   )
Genre: Science fiction—mythological
Type of work: Novel
Time of plot: The distant future
Location: A jungle village, a desert, and the city of Branning-at-Sea
First published: 1967

The Story

The surface story of this novel is a reliving of the Greek myth of Orpheus and Eurydice. Lobey and Friza fall in love, and after an all-too-brief period of happiness, she is killed. Still grieving for his lost love, Lobey embarks on a quest to confront Friza's murderer and retrieve her from death. Believing they know what killed Friza, the elders of Lobey's village send him to battle a mutation, a gigantic man-bull. He tracks it to its subterranean lair, and, like Theseus, slays the Minotaur in its Labyrinth. Lobey later finds that this creature was not, after all, Friza's killer.

The real culprit is another mutation named Kid Death, a desert-born, white-skinned redhead with gills and a mouth full of shark's teeth who kills whatever frightens him. He has the power to reanimate those he kills. He can control, but he cannot create and cannot make order from chaos.

Like the mythic Orpheus, Lobey is a musician, and as such, he understands order. By killing and then reanimating Friza, Kid Death impels Lobey to interact with him, hoping to gain his grasp of order. Childlike in appearance, his demeanor alternately craftily evil and poignantly naïve, Kid Death is an unusual antagonist. He is powerful yet vulnerable, a merciless killer yet, in the end, a pitiful victim who begs for his life. It may be argued that Kid Death's "villainy" stems from being different, having needs that are drastically opposed to those of the majority.

In this novel, difference is the essential concept. Lobey finds that it cannot be mentioned openly in polite society. He must discover for himself how he is different; it cannot be told to him. That difference must then be kept to himself. Throughout the novel, Samuel Delany emphasizes that every individual is unique; each is different from all others.

Upon his first visit to a city, Lobey sees a billboard displaying a picture of two identical women. The caption reads, "These identical twins are not the same." Lobey misses the point. Snickering, some young boys let him in on the unmentionable implication: "If they're not the same . . . they're *different!*" Uniqueness or difference is what all the characters have in common. The underlying assumption is so fundamental that it is kept subliminal. When Lobey announces to a sophisticated urbanite that he is different, he is baffled by the other's amused, and later hostile, reaction. He does not realize that he is belaboring the obvious and revealing himself as foolish.

Analysis

The title is explained in the final section of the novel. Lobey is told that Einstein, a human mathematician, defined the limits of perception by expressing mathematically how the condition of the observer influences the thing observed. Goedel, Einstein's contemporary, noted that there is an infinite number of true things in the world for which there is no way of ascertaining their truth. At the intersection of these two theories, humanity left the confines of Earth for "somewhere else . . . no world in this continuum." Then Lobey's ancestors, an alien civilization, came to Earth, taking human forms and souls. Their descendants strive to discern their own trajectory while confined to human form, thought, and mythology.

Delany blends an intoxicating brew of myths. The Orpheus/Eurydice story is only one ingredient. Lobey may also be read as Odysseus on a journey. Kid Death is an obvious Lucifer/Satan cognate, and Delany adds to the outlaw archetype's character a soupçon of Billy the Kid. Other archetypal, yet uniquely drawn, characters appear. Spider, a four-armed driver of a dragon herd, is identified also as the Betrayer, Judas Iscariot, Pat Garrett, and King Minos. Green-Eye, a prince working as a dragon herder, has only one eye. He may be read as a cyclops guarding a flock or as the son whose eye is "single," intent on its own perception and purpose. He is a Christlike savior and redeemer. Contrasting with Friza as the unique beloved is The Dove, the embodiment of all desire. She appears as Helen of Troy and film stars Jean Harlow and Maria Montez. She is the key image in an advertising campaign aimed at keeping people dissatisfied, working against the tendency to bond with only one other. The Dove is the fuel that powers the genetic engine, keeping genes mixing toward greater diversity, in the same way Delany keeps myths mixing in the novel. He suggests that the old myths may be mutable, that they do not have to have rigidly predictable outcomes.

Despite Delany's assertion that the old myths need not predict the outcome, Lobey's Orphic quest is unsuccessful. He momentarily regains Friza. While he marvels at this miracle, Friza covers his eyes with her hands. The Dove tells him to choose between reality and everything else. Surprised and off balance, Lobey states the obvious: "I can't see anything with your hands in front of my . . ." When he regains his sight, Friza is gone. Even at the novel's end, he is still not sure which he chose. This indeterminacy is as it should be. Lobey, the creator of order, must choose either to return to the old mythic paradigm in which reality is a closed system or to use myth as a vehicle to perceive/create a new reality. In some sense, Lobey has arrived at the Einstein Intersection, the point at which perceived reality meets infinite possibility.

The Einstein Intersection is among the earliest of Samuel R. Delany's mature works. With *Babel-17* (1966) and *Nova* (1968), it stands as one of several masterpieces of the early career of this prolific writer.

—*Karen S. Bellinfante*

The Elric Saga

Elric, last emperor of the decadent, prehuman Melniboneans, abandons his kingdom in a quest for freedom and identity that ironically destroys the world he seeks to preserve

Author: Michael Moorcock (1939-   )
Genre: Fantasy—heroic fantasy
Type of work: Novels
Time of plot: Undefined
Location: Earth and an alternative dimension
First published: *The Elric Saga* (parts 1 and 2, 1984), which includes *Elric of Melniboné* (1972; U.S. title, with cuts, *The Dreaming City*, 1972), *The Sailor on the Seas of Fate* (1973), *The Weird of the White Wolf* (1976), *The Vanishing Tower* (1971, also published as *The Sleeping Sorceress*), *The Bane of the Black Sword* (1977), and *Stormbringer* (1965, rev. 1977); *Elric at the End of Time* (1984); *The Fortress of the Pearl* (1989); and *The Revenge of the Rose: A Tale of the Albino in the Years of His Wandering* (1991)

The Story

Stormbringer, the first novel in the Elric Saga to be published, was actually the last of the series according to internal chronology. It was first published serially by the British magazine *Science Fantasy* (1963-1964). The single volume *Stealer of Souls* (1963) was expanded, with the addition of stories from the separately published collection *The Singing Citadel* (1970) and the return and revision of the omitted portions of *Stormbringer*, into the six-volume saga. *The Fortress of the Pearl* is an additional adventure that occurs between the events narrated in *Elric of Melniboné* and *The Sailor on the Seas of Fate*, and *The Revenge of the Rose* apparently occurs between the events of *The Vanishing Tower* and *The Bane of the Black Sword*.

The Elric Saga tells the story of Elric, last emperor of the Bright Empire of Melniboné, whose inhuman race has ruled their world for ten thousand years. It is, even in its decline, more than a match for the human upstarts of the Young Kingdoms. These strange people inhabit the

Dragon Isle, on which rests their only settlement, Imrryr, the Dreaming City of unearthly beauty and unimaginable horror.

Elric has the dual misfortune of being an albino, which causes him some physical weakness, and being so unusually intelligent and sensitive—for a Melnibonean—that he has a conscience and is capable of both pity and remorse, an anomaly that raises questions about his fitness to rule a people who create orchestras from the dying screams of tortured slaves. Loudest among Elric's critics is his greedy cousin Yyrkoon, who lusts after the throne and the power of bygone days. Elric has great inner strength and sorcerous powers, which Yyrkoon discovers when he attempts to usurp the Ruby Throne and is resoundingly defeated.

The battle ends triumphantly for Elric, but it is a victory that costs him dearly, because he must invoke the aid of the demon-god of Melniboné, Arioch of Chaos. This act sets in motion events that lead to his world's destruction in a final battle between the supernatural forces of Law and Chaos. Particularly important in this regard is his acquisition of the black runesword Stormbringer, in reality a demoniac entity of monstrous evil that devours the souls of people and gods alike, giving their strength to Elric and so creating an unholy addiction from which he never completely recovers.

Elric unwisely leaves his kingdom in the hands of Yyrkoon to quest for freedom and for answers to his people's identity, hoping to free them from their own degeneracy and from the whims of the Lords of Chaos. While he is abroad, Yyrkoon successfully usurps the throne and recovers the other black sword, Mournblade.

Meanwhile, Elric endures a series of adventures with the disturbing import that he is not and never will be master of his own destiny. Returning in secret to Melniboné, he discovers that his beloved cousin Cymoril has been placed in an enchanted sleep by Yyrkoon. Frustrated in his attempts to awaken her and rejected by his own people, Elric organizes the fleets of the Young Kingdoms to sail against Melniboné. He succeeds in sacking the city but fails miserably in his real purpose. Yyrkoon confronts him with Mournblade, and the two black swords possess their wielders. Cymoril awakes during the fight, and Yyrkoon flings her toward Elric. She dies horribly as Stormbringer drinks her soul. Elric kills Yyrkoon, but the damage is done.

After the sack of Imrryr, the raider fleet is attacked and destroyed by the vengeful Melniboneans. Only Elric's ship escapes, by sorcerous means, in an apparent betrayal of those men who had trusted him (though he really could not save them). The despairing Elric now wanders the world, still seeking the truth and freedom he is denied, though he continues to involuntarily fulfill his destiny. He makes a powerful and elusive enemy in Theleb Ka'arna, sorcerer of Pan Tang. His quest for vengeance occupies a considerable portion of the saga and ends with hard-won and somewhat equivocal success: The vampiric runesword takes Theleb Ka'arna's soul only after much destruction, including the death of Myshella, the Dark Lady of Castle Kaneloon, Elric's first new love after the death of his cousin.

During the saga, Elric falls in love with several women. His last and greatest love, his human wife Zarozinia, impales her Chaos-altered body on Stormbringer to give Elric the strength he needs to destroy the Lords of Chaos in the final battle. After the defeat of Chaos, Elric again flings away Stormbringer, only to have the black blade fly from the ground and impale him. The sword then transforms into a demoniac being, standing over the fallen albino and saying, "Farewell, friend! I was a thousand times more evil than thou!"

Analysis

Elric is a fascinating creation, not least because he is a considerable change from the brawny Neanderthal hero tradition in fantasy begun with Robert E. Howard's Conan the Barbarian. Cultured, brilliantly intelligent, and physically delicate though immensely psychologically powerful, Elric starkly contrasts with the brutal simplicity of Conan. Where Conan is a wild barbarian warrior, Elric is the highly cultured product of a dying civilization. Where Conan grows quickly bored and irritated with philosophical questions, Elric is forever seeking the answers to the mysteries of life. Where Conan is direct and simple in his desires, Elric is subtle and inwardly tortured by his conflicting emotions.

A mighty sorcerer, Elric dislikes invoking supernatural aid, though he resorts to it frequently. In his questing after truth instead of power or wealth, he again differs from the typical hero of "sword and sorcery" fantasies. When angered he can be horrifyingly merciless, but he is reluctant to use force, again in contrast to typical heroes of fantasy. He is capable of compassion and pity, but also of demoniac cruelty. Ironically, it is his compassion for his people that alienates him from them.

Irony is an abiding characteristic of Michael Moorcock's work, particularly the Elric Saga. It is ironic that Elric leaves the Bright Empire to seek freedom only to fulfill his destiny, that he seeks to free himself with a sword that only enslaves him, that in seeking to save his people he eventually destroys them, that he kills Cymoril when he wishes to free her, and that his own divided character will not let him find the peace he craves.

Indeed, Melniboneans cultivate a refined sense of irony, as Elric's own behavior continually illustrates.

Closely related to irony is paradox, in that both involve the juxtaposition of apparent opposites. The paradoxical beauty and horror of Imrryr are matched by the paradoxical character of its last ruler. Elric's plight is itself paradoxical, in that by acting according to the compassionate side of his nature and questing for truth, he brings about his own and his world's destruction. Time paradoxes abound, as Elric discovers that he is one incarnation of the Champion Eternal, a being of almost infinite power who exists simultaneously on all the million spheres of Earth. Several times Elric meets other versions of himself, from good Prince Corum of the Vadhagh to the terrible Prince Gaynor the Damned, doomed to serve Chaos for all eternity. Elric himself is seeking answers he is better off not knowing, the most exquisitely cruel paradox of all.

Moorcock blends British folklore, biblical sources, and other mythological motifs with original characterization and unusually profound philosophical insights, creating a world at once new and yet familiar, a world similar enough to reality to make satiric social commentary possible, yet different enough to evoke the sublime wonder engendered only by the very best fantastic literature. If there are minor stylistic flaws and inconsistencies in the earlier books of the original saga, they are still exceptional in their brilliant synthesis of the modern novel and the mythic. The more recent novels, *The Fortress of the Pearl* and *The Revenge of the Rose*, represent the work of a mature and extraordinarily gifted author. On the whole, the Elric Saga is one of the finest fantasy epics ever written.

—*David Hinckley*

The Ender Series

After annihilating the alien Buggers, Ender Wiggin justifies the lives of the dead and strives to prevent the destruction of three other sentient life-forms

Author: Orson Scott Card (1951-   )
Genre: Science fiction—future war
Type of work: Novels
Time of plot: The near future and three thousand years later
Location: Earth and the Hundred Worlds planets of Lusitania and Path
First published: *Ender's Game* (1985; largely expanded version of a novella in *Analog*, 1977), *Speaker for the Dead* (1986), *Ender's War* (1986, omnibus edition of *Ender's Game* and *Speaker for the Dead*), *Xenocide* (1991), and *Children of the Mind* (1996)

The Story

The novella version of *Ender's Game* (1977) was Orson Scott Card's first published science-fiction story. The tale of Ender Wiggin, a child being trained to lead Earth's space fleet in a war against the alien Buggers, quickly became one of the most popular *Analog* novellas of all time. Several years later, while Card was working on *Speaker for the Dead* (1986), he discovered that the novel's extensive background could best be established by revising *Ender's Game* as a novel and developing Ender's character as the adult "speaker." *Xenocide* (1991) continues the story, developing both the characters and the themes introduced in *Speaker for the Dead*. A fourth Ender novel, *Children of the Mind* (1996) concludes the series.

Ender's Game tells how Earth barely defeats a fleet of alien Bugger ships that attacks without warning or provocation. A generation later, Earth believes that the Buggers will return in strength, intent upon destroying humankind. Military intelligence frantically tries to identify a genius to lead a successful military defense. Ender Wiggin is bred to be that leader. As a child of six he is sent to a space Battle School where, for five years, he engages in a series of war and strategy games designed to prepare him for the anticipated war. Mazer Rackham, who orchestrated the first military victory against the Buggers and who has been kept alive via relative space travel, supervises the child's final training. To

Ender's surprise, he discovers that he was not playing games; he actually was directing Earth's offensive against the Buggers, resulting in their complete destruction. The story ends years later, when Ender discovers a message and a queen pupa left to him by the Bugger Hive Queen. Ender becomes the Buggers' interpreter and apologist. As a "speaker for the dead," he compassionately explains the Buggers' desire for reconciliation with humankind and their prayer for forgiveness. He departs to search the universe for a safe place where the queen pupa can hatch.

Speaker for the Dead is set three thousand Earth years later. Ender is still alive as a result of extensive travel at the speed of light. Another intelligent alien species has been discovered on the Hundred Worlds planet of Lusitania, and a human colony has been established to observe the alien Pequininos, or Piggies. When a Piggy brutally disembowels the xenobiologist Pipo Figueira, Ender travels to Lusitania to speak his death. He learns that a Piggy goes through three stages of life, first as a larva, then as a Pequinino, and finally as an intelligent tree. A drug is administered so the Piggy can be ceremoniously disemboweled to achieve the third, adult life phase. When the Piggies disemboweled Pipo, their intent was to honor him. Ender also discovers that the Piggies' life transformation is made possible by a highly contagious virus called the descolada, absolutely necessary to them but deadly to all other lifeforms. *Speaker for the Dead* ends with the Starways Congress sending a fleet to annihilate Lusitania, thereby ensuring that the deadly descolada will never be spread. This xenocide will destroy Piggies, humans, and, unbeknownst to everyone except Ender, the Buggers who have finally found a new home on Lusitania.

Xenocide begins on the Hundred Worlds planet of Path, a religious colony where the "god-spoken" pay the price of revelation through humiliating obsessive-compulsive behavior. Gloriously Bright, the youngest of the god-spoken, is given the impossible task of discovering how the entire star fleet, on its way to annihilate Lusitania, suddenly vanished. On Lusitania, Ender works with the colonists and Piggies, trying to discover a way to render the descolada harmless against humans but still effective in its life-transforming function for the Piggies. The story becomes complex as divisions occur among the Piggies, among the humans, and among the god-spoken of Path. Misunderstandings and misinterpretations of data lead to cataclysmic mistakes in judgment. It is discovered that both the obsessive-compulsive behavior on Path and the deadly properties of the descolada on Lusitania have been produced through intentional genetic engineering. Although cultural traditions and relationships are destroyed in the process, Lusitania successfully alters the descolada. Every sentient species is saved, and Ender is left to re-establish relationships among species, worlds, and, most important, his own family, all the while trying to stop the Starways fleet.

Analysis

Orson Scott Card is deeply concerned about the impact of his stories. He has written several essays and books explaining how he creates characters and how he addresses ethical, moral, and theological issues in his fiction. As he matured as a writer, he repeatedly returned to his early work in order to rewrite his stories to make them more "true." Card does not pretend that the incidents really happened; what he wants is for his readers to believe that his stories truthfully describe how people make ethical decisions and how they can improve the human condition.

Card believes that a story should be an end unto itself and consciously writes to the reader rather than to the critic. He reveals his characters' innermost beliefs and motives through their choices and actions. Card wants his readers to feel the choices his characters make and creates strong situations because he believes that a story's emotional impact is more important than its critical interpretation. Card believes that people have a hunger for stories that make sense of things.

Readers identify with Ender Wiggin's loss of innocence. Employment of a child as a hero has become one of Card's most successful and most used techniques. His stories typically focus on children endowed with remarkable gifts that must be developed and used to provide salvation for their communities. *Xenocide*'s god-spoken, Gloriously Bright, is one such child facing almost unbearable opposition. Ender is brilliant, but as a boy he must pay the price of loneliness that is demanded of children who value genius more than athletic ability and strength. Readers also respond to Card's creation of futuristic battle-training strategies. Each phase of Ender's training, each new game, rings true. Ender's training regimen, it is interesting to note, has been read as both a justification of and a denunciation of the military mind.

When Card rewrote *Ender's Game* as a novel, his increased skill as a speculative writer was manifest through the new dimensions brought to the story. Ender is led to discover the true nature of the alien Buggers and becomes their apologist. Because of his sympathetic explanation of their lives, Ender, who became the literal savior of humankind by defeating the Buggers, became despised as "Ender the Xenocide."

In *Speaker for the Dead*, the religious metaphor of Ender's life is extended when he arrives to speak for the dead of Lusitania and discovers the secret of the descolada. Ender evolves from the role of savior and prophet to that of martyr, knowing he will become infected with the virus and be quarantined on Lusitania for the rest of his life. *Speaker for the Dead* is typical of Card's intent to expand science fiction beyond its adolescent action characters with no ties to mothers, fathers, or children. His unique blend of storytelling and morality mature in this tale of adult family relationships.

Card creates his most complex ethical dilemma in *Xenocide*. The Starways Congress has sent a fleet to destroy Lusitania, including the descolada, Piggies, and humans. Card succeeds in weaving an intricate tale that threatens the existence of four sentient alien species, the human colony, and the god-spoken elite of Path. In each facet of the tale, ethical dilemmas are created as individuals try to do the right thing but, out of ignorance, make cataclysmic mistakes that can lead only to annihilation. Ender's character progresses from martyr to discoverer and creator as Card amplifies the themes of military might and obeisance to authority, adding an examination of religious obsessive-compulsive behavior and theorizing on the nature of eternal intelligences.

Card's Ender Wiggin stories established him at the cutting edge of character-based speculative science fiction. *Ender's Game* received the Nebula (1985), Hugo (1986), and Hamilton/Brackett Awards (1986). *Speaker for the Dead* earned an unprecedented second set of science fiction's highest honors, the Nebula (1986) and Hugo (1987), as well as the Locus Award (1987). *Xenocide* received several nominations and received the best novel (1992) award from the Association for Mormon Letters.

—*Gerald S. Argetsinger*

Engine Summer

In the aftermath of a holocaust, humankind survives in isolated settlements, each establishing its own perspective on advanced technology

Author: John Crowley (1942-   )
Genre: Science fiction—post-holocaust
Type of work: Novel
Time of plot: Several generations after a holocaust
Location: Earth
First published: 1979

The Story

Looming behind the narrative is a legendary story of humankind before the Storm. While those known as the angels vigorously pursued technological advancement, the Long League, led by its matriarchs, tried to counter the ill effects. Taking a third option, the people of Big Belaire avoided technological conflict by taking to the Road and finally building the Warren. When the Storm came (whether it was ecological disaster or warfare, or both, is unclear), the angels departed Earth in their flying city, their proudest achievement, leaving the rest of humankind behind in isolated pockets.

The story opens with Rush that Speaks, a disembodied voice, telling his story to the angels. The voice belongs to an imprint of the original Rush's memory, personality, and consciousness, recorded in one of the angels' miraculous machines. The actual Rush lived six hundred years earlier, in an era that was itself several generations after the Storm.

Rush's story is a detailed account of humankind's survival on Earth after the Storm. It begins in his birthplace, the Warren, a settlement that strives to live within human limits and in harmony with nature and whose chief virtue is telling the truth. Periodically, the people known as Dr. Boots's List, who claim to be descendants of the Long League, visit the Warren to trade, especially for St. Bea's bread, an organic substance that promotes a sense of well-being and unity with the environment.

Once a Day, Rush's adolescent love, leaves with Dr. Boots's List. He follows her a year later. Before searching for her, he spends a year with Blink, a hermit who has collected books and other artifacts from the angel ruins.

After virtually sleeping through winter in Blink's treehouse, Rush moves on, walking over the Road, the crumbling interstate highway system. When he finds Dr. Boots's List on the Road, Once a Day is with them. He accompanies the group to Service City, where they live with their giant cats in a ruined angel building.

Each member of Dr. Boots's List routinely receives a letter from Dr. Boots. When Rush asks for his letter, he is taken to a machine that allows him to enter into the mind of a recorded personality. The experience leaves him feeling a sweet simplicity that is beyond the need for words. Later he will learn that the mind recorded in the machine is a cat who was named Dr. Boots.

Once a Day, fearing that Rush's experience with Dr. Boots will change him in a way that she cannot accept, will not return to Service City until Rush leaves. He moves on, next encountering Teeplee, a scavenger living amid the ruins of the angels, aimlessly gathering objects that he does not understand. After a short time scavenging with Teeplee, Rush decides to return to the Warren.

Before reaching the Warren, Rush encounters a man parachuting from the sky. He is Mongolfier, an angel from the floating city, alerted to Rush's position by objects that Rush scavenged. He has a simple request: He wants to record Rush's mind, just as Dr. Boots's mind was recorded. Rush agrees, and at this point the story comes full circle. The living Rush goes on to the Warren, presumably to live out his life. The recording of his mind stays with the angels. To generations of angels living in the floating city, he tells his story up to the point of meeting Mongolfier. He knows nothing further, not even what happened in the remaining life of the person he was.

Analysis

In post-holocaust novels, humanity has been wiped out in many different ways—ecological calamity, nuclear warfare, extraterrestrial invasion, and so on. The special turn that *Engine Summer* takes on this subgenre is that it does not emphasize the process of destruction; instead, it focuses on the way of life of the survivors. Further, the world is not presented in a coherent form by an omniscient narrator. As in Russell Hoban's *Riddley Walker* (1980), another post-holocaust novel, readers themselves reconstruct the lost world from what the narrator reveals.

At the basic narrative level, *Engine Summer* reveals several forms of technological adaptation. The people of the Warren live largely unconcerned with the angels, as they had gone separate ways even before the

Storm. Pieces of angel technology are worth saving as curiosities, but the people of the Warren do not seek them out. They value knowledge, even angel knowledge, but only if it serves wisdom.

The people of Dr. Boots's List, on the other hand, gather and proudly use the artifacts, even those they barely understand. They treasure most the machine that stores the mind of Dr. Boots, though their encounter with it leaves them passive and accepting of a static way of life amid the angel ruins. Later, the depiction of Teeplee, whose entire existence is given over to scavenging angel artifacts, is a commentary on the pointlessness of Dr. Boots's List.

Finally, the angels themselves, heirs to technological perfection, can be seen only as selfish and inhumanly cruel. Although Mongolfier takes a heroic risk to record Rush's mind, he is not typical of his kind. The rest remain in their flying city, far above the dangers and ills of Earth, experiencing only through the mind of Rush what a real life might be like. They wake him century after century, unwilling to erase him from the machine and end his agony. He will live indefinitely in a kind of Indian summer, what his people mistakenly call engine summer.

An author of both science fiction and fantasy, John Crowley has one of the finest prose styles of his generation, and his closely textured fiction invites several levels of interpretation. Perhaps it is for these reasons that his output has been comparatively small—no more than a handful of novels and several story collections in a career that started in 1975 with his first science-fiction novel, *The Deep*.

—*Steve Anderson*

Eon and Eternity

The return of an asteroid through time and space remakes the history of the human race

Author: Greg Bear (1951-   )
Genre: Science fiction—future history
Type of work: Novels
Time of plot: 2000 C.E. and after, as well as various time metrics in alternative universes
Location: Earth and alternative Earths, the asteroid Thistledown, and the cosmic space known as "the Way"
First published: *Eon* (1985) and *Eternity* (1988)

The Story

Eon and *Eternity* are among the most ambitious science-fiction novels ever published. They chronicle a number of futures for the human race and perhaps the most sweeping, speculative, and awesome future history ever proposed.

On December 31, 1999, Earth's scientists are nervous. A mysterious asteroid called "the Stone" has suddenly come into orbit around Earth. When American space missions explore "the Stone," they find that it not only seems to have been inhabited by humans but to have been occupied more than a millennium ago.

The other side of this enigma is glimpsed when veteran Hexamon operative Olmy reports to his superior, the presiding minister of Axis City. Axis City is a settlement of humans, in the far future, who have explored a relativistic cosmic continuum called "the Way" and established themselves there in commerce and rivalry with various alien peoples. The leaders of the Hexamon, which is the political structure of the humans in the Way, are stunned to find out that Thistledown, the asteroid spaceship from which their ancestors had set out from Earth more than a thousand years before, had not only returned to its original orbit but gone back to a time three hundred years before it had been constructed. Olmy returns to Thistledown in order to explore further.

Meanwhile, the American expedition explores the asteroid's seven chambers and finds out much of the amazing truth for themselves. The expedition, led by the capable Garry Lanier, includes Karen Farley, a

British-born Chinese scientist with whom Lanier falls in love, and Patricia Vasquez, a brilliant young Hispanic American scientist who alone can understand the mathematical intricacies of the far future. For Earth people, the biggest secret of Thistledown is not the Way itself but the asteroid's library, which contains pictures of a nuclear conflagration that had taken place in Thistledown's "past" at a date in the near future of Earth. Russia has a spy within the expedition, and thus the secret gets out, bringing political tensions on Earth to the breaking point. Ironically, the pictures of the conflagration on the parallel world touch off, in the present world, the very events they depict. Much of Earth is destroyed, and all existing political systems are reduced to ruins.

Patricia's parents and fiancé are among those vaporized to death, and she becomes at once both inconsolably depressed and determined to find some way, in the topsy-turvy world of parallel universes made possible by the advanced mathematics of the Way, to reverse time and fate, thus bringing her loved ones back. In conducting this research, she threatens the fundamental equilibrium of the Way, so Olmy abducts her and takes her to Axis City. Olmy, though, has special plans for Patricia. He realizes that her mentality is similar to that of Konrad Korzenowski, the man who centuries "later" in time had designed the Way. Korzenowski has been assassinated, but Olmy, using the advanced technology of the Hexamon, can revive him if Patricia agrees to share her mentality.

Meanwhile, the desperate Russians attack Thistledown itself, though the danger is defused when their old-guard Communist leaders are outwitted by Pavel Mirsky, a visionary subordinate. Hexamon authorities take all humans from Thistledown to Axis City. The Earth people are awed by the technological progress the Hexamon people have made in their thousand-year odyssey, but the Hexamon is in itself split. The Way is filled with pernicious, alien enemies called the Jarts, against whom the Hexamon is barely holding its own. Part of the Hexamon wishes to destroy the Way and go into orbit around Earth, while the other wishes to accelerate the speed of the Way and thereby crush the Jarts. Because the two plans are not incompatible, it is decided that Axis City will split into two parts. Meanwhile, Korzenowski is reincarnated using Patricia's mentality. He decides to go with the Earthbound faction. Patricia gets her part of the bargain and is allowed to search for an alternative Earth where she can find her loved ones. She fails in this attempt, landing in an alternative universe where the Ptolemaic dynasty of Egypt in the Hellenistic Era was never conquered by Rome, and therefore all of subsequent history has been altered.

Lanier returns to Earth with the Korzenowski faction and marries Karen Farley. The Laniers participate for fifty years in the Hexamon-led reconstruction of Earth from its nuclear devastation. This peace is imperiled when Mirsky reappears, after having gone with the part of the Hexamon who had accelerated to infinity. Mirsky reveals that his group has literally traveled to the end of time, where an impersonal entity called the Final Mind, the culmination of all mental being, prevails. The Final Mind feels endangered by the existence of the Way, which has been closed but not destroyed, and therefore asks the Hexamon to reopen it. Olmy participates in this project, capturing a Jart who he thinks he can use for intelligence. The Jart deceives him and dominates him. It is revealed that the Jarts are in fact performing the Final Mind's mission in insisting on destroying the Way. The Way is successfully destroyed, and Korzenowski decides to join the Final Mind, where humanity's ultimate destiny lies. Lanier and Mirsky, though, are sent by the Final Mind back through history, for reasons and purposes unknown even to them. They will carry on the human quest for knowledge that the now-destroyed Thistledown exemplified.

Analysis

Greg Bear's novels are so massive and ambitious that even an extensive summary hardly does them justice. Bear's sweeping vistas show how successful a complex and visionary conception of the future can be. Although some of Bear's shorter-term predictions have been superseded by history, his long-term vision of the future is compelling.

For all the complexity of the *Eon-Eternity* diptych, the two books are dominated by several basic themes. Perhaps the most central of these is the opposition between going "home" and journeying "out," of seeking knowledge versus returning to deep and permanent loyalties. This dichotomy can be seen even within the councils of the advanced Hexamon itself, in which the "Geshel" faction, favoring technological progress, is opposed to the "Naderite" group, which opposes science and wishes to return to Earth. Bear implies that it is foolish to hope to suppress either of these tendencies in the human spirit. When the Naderites let the Geshels take half of the Hexamon into infinity and take their half to Earth, this does not prevent the eventual emergence of neo-Geshels within the Naderite group who wish to reopen the Way.

Bear threads this going home/voyaging forward dichotomy throughout the two books. Lanier and his wife Karen go home with the Naderites, even though it is to a devastated Earth they have never known. Patricia, on the other hand, attempts the absolute negation of all given reality. Her only purpose is to recover and rejoin her family. The Hexamon itself has made many almost inconceivable steps forward. It has made it possible to store souls in a kind of eternal afterlife, to traverse different dimensions of time and space, to preserve essential human identities even after the body has died, and to allow humans to assume any size, shape, or form that they wish. None of these achievements can eliminate human nature. The bickering between the Naderites and Geshels is as fierce as that between the much more "immature" Russian and American factions among the earthlings.

The figure caught most paradoxically between these two tendencies is Korzenowski. Born of Naderite parents, he nevertheless designed the Way, which made it possible for all the Geshel dreams of progress to come true. Even though he seems to have betrayed his heritage, he becomes the Naderite patron saint who is needed to lead the Hexamon back to Earth. With a name clearly alluding to the original Polish name of the twentieth century British novelist Joseph Conrad, Korzenowski exemplifies the contradictory bind brought into being by the engagement between scientific, intellectual curiosity and human yearning.

It is Bear's deep spiritual and psychological insight that makes the reader able to digest the huge panoply of concept and detail he portrays in these two books. Whatever complexities humans of the future may produce, Bear implies, they will always be involved in two central pursuits: the perennial quests to know and to love.

—*Nicholas Birns*

Fafhrd and the Gray Mouser

Fafhrd and the Gray Mouser are two friends of questionable ethics who become the most renowned rogues and swordsmen in the world of Nehwon

Author: Fritz Leiber (1910-1992)
Genre: Fantasy—magical world
Type of work: Stories
Time of plot: Slightly before 200 B.C.E. to about one thousand years later
Location: Nehwon, a universe in a bubble
First published: *Swords and Deviltry* (1970), *Swords Against Death* (1970; expanded from *Two Sought Adventure,* 1957), *Swords in the Mist* (1968), *Swords Against Wizardry* (1968), *The Swords of Lankhmar* (1968; part as "Scylla's Daughter" in *Fantastic,* 1961), *Swords and Ice Magic* (1977), and *The Knight and Knave of Swords* (1988)

The Story

The Fafhrd and the Gray Mouser series was written over a period of at least four decades as thirty-six short stories and one novel (*The Swords of Lankhmar*). The stories form a coherent whole: the adventures of two of the greatest swordsmen and greatest rogues any world has ever known. The first three books were collected as *The Three Swords* (1989) and the second three as *Swords' Masters* (1990).

Fafhrd is a tall northern barbarian, and the Mouser is a small, dark man of uncertain but urban origin. They share a common attitude toward life because they are the sundered halves of an even greater hero from ages past. They meet as youths in fabled Lankhmar, the most cosmopolitan of the many cities of Nehwon, and instantly become friends. (Actually, this is their second meeting but their first "on camera.") Their friendship appears destined to last a lifetime. Thirty-four of the thirty-seven stories in this series chronicle their joint adventures; the first two occur before the two meet, and the third is the tale of their meeting. These adventures cover much of Nehwon and even part of the ordinary world. Fafhrd and the Mouser save Lankhmar many times, and the world itself more than a few, but many of their adventures are the sort that would naturally befall a pair of reckless wanderers in a world full of magic, mystery, and danger.

The two rogues have two magical patrons, neither of whom is human. Ningauble of the Seven Eyes and Sheelba of the Eyeless Face appear to be self-appointed protectors of Nehwon, occasionally sending the cavalry (in the form of Fafhrd and the Gray Mouser) to avert some catastrophe.

Fafhrd and the Gray Mouser encounter many women romantically over the years and care about more than a few deeply, but their friendship for each other always comes first. This is clearly true even in the last two books, when they make long-term attachments to two ladies of fabled Rime Isle (Fafhrd's love is Afreyt; the Mouser's is Cif).

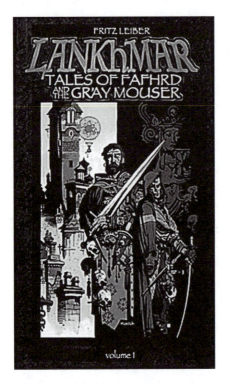

Most of these stories have the typical structure of an adventure story: Evil entities have designs that should be thwarted. Fafhrd and the Gray Mouser discover these designs, either by accident or otherwise, and oppose the villains. Not all the villains are killed, but their nefarious plans are rendered, at best, only partially successful. A few opponents come back to fight in subsequent stories, but there is no "evil mastermind" analogous to Fu Manchu or Professor Moriarty. Death, the Power of the Shadowlands, comes closest, with the sorcerer Quarmal, Lord of Quarmall, a distant second. At the end of the series, the two swordsmen, now middle-aged, are still firmly attached to each other and to their lady loves. It is clear that they were intended to have more adventures.

Analysis

Fafhrd and the Gray Mouser were actually created by Harry Otto Fischer, but, with the exception of ten thousand words of "The Lords of Quarmall," Fritz Leiber wrote all the stories. The author's presence is felt through the somewhat archaic device of a narrator, whose comments, in the hands of a lesser writer, might have prevented total immersion within the fictional world. Leiber's mastery of narrative, pacing, dialogue, and character grab the reader and force him or her headfirst into fog-shrouded Lankhmar, or wherever Fafhrd and the Gray Mouser's wanderings take them.

The early stories in the Fafhrd and Gray Mouser series helped spawn an entire genre of fantasy stories whose protagonists are likable antiheroes. Leiber's literary influence on fantasy in the twentieth century has been exceeded only by J. R. R. Tolkien. L. Sprague de Camp was a contemporary and mined the same vein. Fantasy writers who appear to have been influenced strongly by Leiber include P. C. Hodgell, Michael Moorcock, and Roger Zelazny. The Thieves' World series of anthologies, edited by Robert Asprin and Lynn Abbey, could never have existed had not Leiber helped invent the genre to which it belongs. Fantasy roleplaying games owe their existence in part to this genre and, therefore, indirectly to Leiber.

Fafhrd and the Gray Mouser were explicitly a reaction to improbable fantasy heroes such as Robert E. Howard's Conan; Leiber said as much in an author's note in *The Swords of Lankhmar*. Indeed, in some ways they are almost parodies. Leiber made a point in his introductions to most of the books of asserting that Fafhrd and the Gray Mouser were the best swordsmen in all the worlds. In what he called "Induction," at the beginning of the first book, *Swords and Deviltry*, Leiber even claimed that Fafhrd and the Gray Mouser were the two reincarnated halves of a greater hero. This cannot be taken seriously, and the idea was used in only one of the stories ("The Curse of the Smalls and the Stars," one of the latest). Even the name of the world is a joke: It is "Nowhen" backwards, a reference to the famous novel *Erewhon* (1872) by Samuel Butler, but one evidently used only to amuse those in the know. This is not the only such sly inversion; for example, in *The Swords of Lankhmar*, Kokgnab is named as a source of subtle massage techniques. Even the seamy-side attitude of the whole series was in part a reaction to J. R. R. Tolkien's approach to heroic fantasy. Leiber hints at this as well in *The Swords of Lankhmar*.

There is far more to these stories, however, than reaction to traditional fantasy literature. The novelty of the likable antihero probably contributed much to the early popularity of the series. In addition, the strongly developed protagonists gave the reader something easy to identify with. The continued success of these stories, however, does not result from novelty. Leiber's story ideas were original and intriguing. He gave free rein to his imagination in inventing villains, religions, cultures, natural laws, and more. Nehwon sports a truly preposterous mythology and magic (not to mention geography), which add to its charm. Talking skulls and killer jewels are but the tip of the iceberg. Leiber was a good enough writer to make even the most ridiculous notion acceptable. His combination of writing skill, excellent story ideas, a unique and enchanting setting, and good characterization made the Fafhrd and Gray Mouser series what it is and earned for it a place among the great works of fantasy literature.

Leiber also employed, though sparingly, a trick used by many fantasy writers, that of having his characters discover, or know, scientific principles not known on Earth before the scientific age. For example, in "Stardock," the Mouser intuits why water boils at a lower temperature at high altitudes. Leiber reversed the trick in "Trapped in the Sea of Stars," having Fafhrd guess at cosmological interpretations that would be correct on Earth but are subsequently proved wrong in Nehwon.

There is another reason for the popularity of the Fafhrd and the Gray Mouser stories. Leiber peppered many of them with references to the ordinary world, such as the mysterious interworld traveler Karl Treuherz. "Adept's Gambit" even takes place on Earth, in the eastern Mediterranean of more than two millennia ago. These references to things terrestrial seem incongruous and so disturb the suspension of disbelief, but at the same time they provide personal interest for the reader.

It is interesting that, in so many stories, written over a span of about forty years, there are so few inconsistencies. The most glaring is the unintended sex change Sheelba undergoes in "The Curse of the Smalls and the Stars." In this story he becomes and has ever been a she, yet in all earlier stories featuring Sheelba, he was definitely male.

The role of sex (as opposed to gender) is important in this series, and it looms both larger and more kinky in the later stories. This is probably because the earlier stories were published at a time when sex in fantasy fiction was hardly acceptable, at least to publishers. By the time the later stories were written, many restrictions had been lifted. Leiber received the World Fantasy Award for Life Achievement, in no small part because of his success with the Fafhrd and the Gray Mouser stories.

—*David C. Kopaska-Merkel*

Fahrenheit 451

A depiction of a futuristic society in which reading is forbidden and books are burned by firemen

Author: Ray Bradbury (1920-   )
Genre: Science fiction—dystopia
Type of work: Novel
Time of plot: An indeterminate time in the future
Location: Implicitly an anonymous location in the United States
First published: 1953 (expanded version of "The Fireman," *Galaxy Science Fiction*, 1951)

The Story

It is ironic that in 1953, an asbestos edition of the novel, which describes a terrifying, censorship-obsessed society that burns books, was published. Ironic too is that in the 1980's, Ray Bradbury found that the publisher had, through the years, silently censored from his original text seventy-five sections of *Fahrenheit 451*. Stories published in the 1953 edition are omitted from most later editions.

Fahrenheit 451, which takes its title from the temperature at which paper burns, takes place in a sterile, futuristic society in which firemen burn books because the State has decided that books make people unhappy. Suspected readers are arrested. Instead of reading, people listen to "seashells," tiny radios that fit in the ear, and watch insipid television shows projected on wall-to-wall screens. In school, students play sports and learn nothing. Fast driving is encouraged, and pedestrians are arrested. Indiscriminate drug use, suicide, overpopulation, and war are rampant.

In this world lives Guy Montag, the main character, who smilingly and unquestioningly accepts his job as a fireman. Guy's wife, Mildred, watches endless hours of television and overdoses on narcotics. Early in the novel, a young neighbor, Clarisse, shocks Guy by asking whether he ever reads the books he burns and whether he is happy. Although she is later killed by a hit-and-run driver, Clarisse is the catalyst through which Guy begins to evaluate his life and career, and finally the society he supports. Clarisse and Mildred are foils: Clarisse's thinking and questioning is a threat to the State, whereas Mildred's zombielike addiction to television and pills makes her the personification of this society.

Guy's reeducation continues when he is deeply moved by the self-immolation of an old woman who chooses to die with her books rather than be separated from them. It is at this point, early in the novel, that Guy secretly takes and reads one of the old woman's books to satisfy his curiosity.

Captain Beatty, Guy's supervisor and a master at brainwashing, rewrites history to say that firemen have always set fires and reading has always been forbidden. Beatty explains the State's philosophy that humans need only entertainment, not the insights, self-reflection, uncertainty, and occasional sadness provided by books. Beatty explains that in order to achieve societal equality and happiness, people should not be given two sides of an issue or books to debate, think about, or question. He insists that because some people dislike certain books, all books should be burned to ensure everyone's happiness.

Guy's increasing inner numbness draws him closer to reading books. It also draws him to Faber, a retired professor of English. Faber, a foil to Beatty, explains to Guy that what is contained in books gives life depth and meaning. Books can present a higher quality of information as well as the time to think about and then act on that information.

After Guy reads aloud to Mildred and her friends Matthew Arnold's "Dover Beach," a poem about the erosion of faith, they turn him in to the police for breaking the law. When Beatty and the firemen arrive at the Montags' house, Guy kills Beatty. He escapes to a remote colony of intellectuals, one of several such groups that live in the woods. Group members have memorized and therefore "become" books. They recite their books, thereby passing on their knowledge to their children, who will await the rebirth of a literate civilization. The novel ends with a quotation from the last chapter of the Bible and the guarded optimism that the antiliterate State will soon self-destruct and a new, cultured society will rise from the ashes.

Analysis

Fantasy and science fiction are closely intertwined, and *Fahrenheit 451* falls into both genres. No time machine carries the reader into this dark future, but Bradbury takes a seemingly unreal world and makes every element of it real and credible. From the technicians who apathetically pump the stomachs and transfuse the blood of the unhappy many who take daily drug overdoses to the blaring multiwalled televisions, Bradbury's attention to detail makes this nightmare seem plausible, vivid, and alive.

Fahrenheit 451 fits clearly into the utopia-dystopia motif that appeared in science fiction throughout the twentieth century. Whereas utopian fiction presents an idyllic world or society, dystopian fiction often portrays the individual's struggle against the implacable state in an ugly, depressing world. To illustrate two types of dystopias, Aldous Huxley's *Brave New World* (1932) is a frightening view of a technology-obsessed future, and George Orwell's *Nineteen Eighty-Four* (1949) is an appalling picture of an absolute dictatorship's effect on the human psyche. Bradbury's novel is a confluence of these dystopias. The brain-dead media and faster cars of the future (technology) add to the suffocation of individuals in a sterile State in which reading and thinking are outlawed (dictatorship).

Fahrenheit 451 falls in the middle period of Bradbury's literary career. Such short stories as "The Scythe" (1943) and "The Lake" (1944) belong to Bradbury's early period (1943-1945). These works are in the realm of fantasy and deal with the implications in life of choosing imagination over rationality. The practice in these works of having a hero who intuits some scary reality and tries to change things leads to the character of Guy Montag in *Fahrenheit 451*, which was written, along with *The Illustrated Man* (1951) and *The Martian Chronicles* (1950), during Bradbury's vintage period (1946-1955). All three books were adapted into screenplays. Science-fiction elements as well as dystopian landscapes enter his work during this time. Products of his later period, beginning in 1957, include *Dandelion Wine* (1957) and *I Sing the Body Electric* (1969). Many of his later works deal with magic, joy, and human eccentricity.

Critics believe that *The Martian Chronicles* is Bradbury's most successful work, exploring the tension between the needs of the individual and those of society. Although some debate whether Bradbury's work belongs to science fiction or fantasy and some consider his work simplistic, others feel strongly that it has been unfairly neglected and underrated and that his diverse and copious literary output is of astonishing quality and variety.

—*Howard A. Kerner*

The Falling Woman

The intense struggle of Elizabeth Butler, who is forced to choose between the overlapping demands of the present and the past

Author: Pat Murphy (1955-   )
Genre: Fantasy—Magical Realism
Type of work: Novel
Time of plot: The mid-1980's, with flashbacks to the 1940's
Location: Yucatan digs in Mexico, and Berkeley, California
First published: 1986

The Story

The Falling Woman concerns the efforts of Elizabeth Butler (Liz) to achieve self-understanding by choosing between the unknown past and present reality. Liz must decide whether to fulfill the wishes of a Mayan ghost, Zuhuy-kak, who believes the blood sacrifice of Liz's estranged daughter, Diane, will restore power to an ancient Mayan goddess. Her option is to deny this past world that she cherishes and accept the present world she loathes. Six chapters, interspersed with ones devoted to Liz and Diane, describe ancient Mayan customs and cyclic concepts that emphasize the key Mayan belief that people need to know and understand their past in order to understand their future. Two characters, Diane and Zuhuy-kak, exert emotional and psychological pressures on the central character, Liz, while Tony Baker provides comforting support.

Liz is an archaeologist, lecturer, and writer whose youthful efforts to secure freedom to develop her talents resulted in a nervous breakdown, attempted suicide, divorce, and loss of child custody. At the Dzibilchaltún dig, codirected with Tony, Liz exists on the psychic border between past and present. Seeing both sides, she simultaneously observes ancient ghosts and modern humans pursuing daily activities. In these ruins, Liz talks to herself, daydreams about the Mayan shadows who ignore her, and reflects that psychiatrists would suggest that these supernatural phantoms are hallucinations, parts of herself projected from her subconscious mind.

A wish fulfillment activates the fantasy plot. Although she laughs at students' visions of treasure, Liz expresses her own dream of locating a tomb at the excavation. Later, as Liz sits by the cenote, one ghost stops, stares, and questions her presence. Liz is equally astounded. She discovers that rules of reality are changing and barriers are down. Speech is possible between Zuhuy-kak, dead a thousand years, and Liz. After Liz passes a riddle test, Zuhuy-kak promises friendship and aid in revealing hidden secrets. That night, during her dreams, Liz relives the shadow's memories of falling in the waters of Chichén Itzá's sacred cenote. At dawn, she finds a partly raised stone, a clue that leads eventually to buried secrets in Zuhuy-kak's tomb.

Exploration of the past continues when Diane Butler arrives unexpectedly. She wants to learn why Liz abandoned her in childhood. As Liz and Diane share separate memories, Zuhuy-kak also tells Liz about her life and insists that Liz sacrifice Diane. To protect her daughter, Liz asks Diane to leave the Yucatan and offers herself as a sacrifice. When the girl refuses, Liz asks Tony, a father figure to Diane, to help guard the girl's safety.

The fantasy climaxes as Liz achieves self-understanding. She realizes that her sacrificial abandonment of Diane on her educational altar was just as unacceptable and futile as Zuhuy-kak's desired sacrifice. After Diane and Zuhuy-kak share this knowledge, all three free themselves of past mistakes. Diane lifts her unconscious mother, and the shadow shoulders her dead daughter; both trudge out of the cave. As Diane follows the light of Zuhuy-kak's flickering torch, she moves toward a future with Liz, one that begins on the bridge at Strawberry Creek in Berkeley.

Analysis

Pat Murphy began publishing in the 1970's, but her first awards came in the 1980's. She received a Nebula for *The Falling Woman* and another Nebula the same year, along with a Theodore Sturgeon Memorial Award, for "Rachel in Love" (*Isaac Asimov's Science Fiction Magazine*, 1987; chapbook, 1992). "Rachel in Love" was included in *Points of Departure* (1990), a short-story collection that won the Philip K. Dick Award.

Murphy's writings synthesize science-fiction and fantasy elements with universal human concerns and problems. Her themes include alien encounters/estrangement, parent/child or male/female relationships, and self-realization/development of talents. Her first novel, *The Shadow Hunter* (1982), uses time-travel technology to move a prehistoric man into an alien future, and "Rachel in Love" describes the difficulties of a chimpanzee scientifically imprinted with the human intelligence of a teenage girl. *The City, Not Long After* (1989), a fantasy inhabited by various human, machine, and nonhuman figures, is set in a world devastated by a plague that was caused by humans with misguided intentions. Most of the short stories collected in *Points of Departure* also feature a synthesis of universal human concerns with the elements of science fiction and fantasy.

The Falling Woman illustrates Murphy's recurrent themes. First, Murphy expands the alien encounter theme to develop dynamic characters and plot complexities. Liz is a stranger to her peers and her daughter. Zuhuy-kak, the *Doppelgänger* shadow from the past, the ghostly double who stresses her commonalities with Liz, is as alien to the present world as Liz would be to the past. Moreover, Diane is able to see ancient shadows, twisting the double displacement theme into a third level. A second thematic idea centers on the parent/child bonds. The mother/father/daughter unit, extended to include Tony Baker, offers a sharp thematic contrast: The father figure protects the daughter from a mother who may kill her. A third theme relates to the pursuit of personal power, which Zuhuy-kak repeatedly mentions as a reward if Liz agrees to sacrifice Diane. The answer to this question of what Liz is willing to sacrifice for success is crucial to her choice.

The power theme is also expressed at a symbolic level. One symbol relates to Zuhuy-kak, an archetypal figure representing the powerful, perhaps dangerous, influence of the dead past on present or future actions. Symbolic meanings of "falling," "treasure," "water," "caves" and other terms give additional depth to Murphy's fiction.

—*Betsy P. Harfst*

The Fantasy Worlds of Peter Beagle

A collection of Peter Beagle's works of fantasy, comprising two
short stories and two novels

Author: Peter S. Beagle (1939-   )
Genre: Fantasy—Magical Realism
Type of work: Collected works
Time of plot: Various, primarily the nineteenth and twentieth centuries
Location: New York City and England
First published: 1978 (includes *A Fine and Private Place*, 1960; "Come,
Lady Death," 1963; *The Last Unicorn*, 1968; and "Lila the Werewolf,"
1974)

The Story

The first story in *The Fantasy Worlds of Peter Beagle* is "Lila the Werewolf."
It might be called either a short novella or a lengthy short story. It follows the brief relationship between Joe Farrell and Lila Braun. Shortly
after Lila moves into Farrell's apartment, Farrell begins to notice that
Lila acts strangely during a certain part of the month. He soon discovers
the reason for this behavior: Lila Braun is a werewolf. Although their relationship continues for a short time, it finally disintegrates when Farrell
and Lila's mother follow Lila, who is in wolf form, as she makes her
rounds of New York City. Years later, Lila's mother calls Farrell to inform
him of Lila's wedding to a research psychologist, whose interest in Lila
is both romantic and professional.

The next story in the collection is *The Last Unicorn*. This novel focuses
on the adventures of a female unicorn who leaves the safety of her forest
in order to find others of her kind. Along the way, she gains the companionship of Schmendrick the wizard, whose success at wizardry is spo-
radic at best, and Molly Grue, a tender-hearted but tough-speaking
woman. Their search leads them to the heart of the kingdom of King
Haggard, a monarch whose desire to possess beauty and immortality
led him years before to imprison unicorns within the waves of the sea.
When confronted by King Haggard's mighty Red Bull, the unicorn almost meets the same fate as her kindred, but Schmendrick changes her
into the shape of a frail, beautiful woman, Lady Amalthea. Prince Lír,
King Haggard's adoptive son, soon falls in love with Lady Amalthea,

but because of her true nature, she cannot fully reciprocate his love. The novel ends with the fall of King Haggard, the ascent of Lír to the throne, and the freeing of the unicorns from the waves.

"Come, Lady Death" appears after *The Last Unicorn*. This short story centers on Lady Neville, an important aristocrat with a flair for the dramatic. So that she can host the most exciting party in London, Lady Neville invites Death to be the guest of honor at her next ball. Death shows up in the guise of a beautiful young woman. By the end of the story, Death trades places with Lady Neville.

The final story in the collection is the novel *A Fine and Private Place*. The story is about Michael Morgan, a young college professor who suddenly finds himself dead, even though he retains consciousness. He is in a state of limbo. In the graveyard, he meets Jonathan Rebeck, a misfit from society who has lived in the graveyard for two decades. Morgan also meets Laura Durand, a ghost like himself, and the two of them fall in love. The novel follows two main plots: the relationship between Morgan and Durand and the relationship between Rebeck and a widow, Gertrude Klapper. Morgan and Durand's relationship is threatened by the exhumation of Morgan's body because of Morgan's apparent suicide (he is buried in a Roman Catholic plot). Rebeck and Klapper's relationship is strained by Rebeck's inability to cope with the outside world. Finally, Morgan and Durand are reburied in another cemetery, and Rebeck, with Klapper's support, re-enters society.

Analysis

This collection displays the variety of topics with which Peter Beagle is able to work in his artistry. He possesses the ability to produce extremely realistic stories set in ordinary places during the twentieth century. Excepting the few strains of the fantastic arising within "Lila the Werewolf" and *A Fine and Private Place*, those stories are believable tales. Beagle's writing style is reminiscent of that of other twentieth century realists such as Sherwood Anderson, William Faulkner, and Ernest Hemingway, yet Beagle is also an accomplished writer of fantasy fiction, able to transport the reader into magical worlds brimming with extraordinary people and creatures.

The Last Unicorn falls into this category and is arguably Beagle's masterpiece of fantasy fiction. Because of his mastery of fantasy fiction, critics and scholars often compare Beagle to other twentieth century fantasists, including J. R. R. Tolkien and C. S. Lewis. *The Fantasy Worlds of Peter Beagle* allows the reader a chance to witness a writer exercising his skills in versatility.

For this collection of stories, Beagle wrote an introduction providing his personal insights into the creation and publication of each story found within the volume. This introduction, providing Beagle's explanation of why he writes works of fantasy, will be of interest to scholars, lovers of fantasy fiction, and avid Beagle fans. The introduction serves as a means for Beagle to give his views on the topic of fantasy fiction but also affords the reader a glimpse into the activity of writing fantasy fiction. Beagle discusses how and where he wrote the stories, the means of publication, and his retrospective opinions about them. In essence, he provides a short critique of each work.

—*Trevor J. Morgan*

The Female Man

An emissary from an all-female planet of the future travels to the present to observe male/female relations

Author: Joanna Russ (1937-   )
Genre: Science fiction—feminist
Type of work: Novel
Time of plot: An alternative 1970's and two possible futures
Location: Earth and Whileaway
First published: 1975

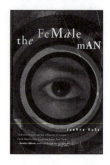

The Story

The novel is polyphonically composed, using six alternating female narrators (a group called the four J's, a teenager, and the author). Each brings her own perspective, shaped in some cases by life in an alternative reality.

The first of the J's, so named because their names begin with that letter, is Janet Evanson. She is an inhabitant of Whileaway, a possible future Earth whose entire population is women. She has been sent back to a possible present to study mores in a land where men still exist. Janet finds two women whom she wants to take back to her time: Joanna, her tour guide, and Jeannine Dadier, a librarian. A large part of the book describes the relatively uneventful daily lives of these two women.

Jeannine has a noncommittal sexual relationship with the unambitious Cal. He is a male chauvinist who matter-of-factly expects Jeannine to do his laundry and prepare his meals, even though both work and he contributes nothing to her support or nurture. Jeannine's passive behavior is contrasted sharply to Janet's no-holds-barred actions. Taken to a party by Joanna, Janet evades the attentions of the drunken host by punching him in the nose and breaking his arm.

Yet another unfulfilled character is introduced when Janet Evanson moves in with a suburban family. The family's seventeen-year-old daughter, Laura Rose Wilding, is a budding writer who has been frustrated by others, who label her aspirations unfeminine. The girl initiates a love affair with Janet, who is the first person she has met who respects her intellect and dreams.

The plot takes yet another unexpected turn when Alice-Jael Reasoner, called Jael, arrives to transport the women to another future. Jael lives on an Earth where women and men live in opposed, armed camps. Her nation has wanted to contact Whileaway but has been unable to because of peculiarities of the time-space continuum. Now that Whileaway can be approached by way of Jeannine and Joanna's world, Jael asks if the female planet can be used as a training camp and if Earth can serve as a transfer point.

The book ends with the answers to these questions. Janet, not particularly impressed with Jael's world, says no. Jeannine, sick of her planet's patriarchal arrangements, agrees to assist in a war to exterminate men.

Analysis

The Female Man appeared during the high tide of the women's liberation movement. At this time, authors such as Kate Millett published books denouncing the stereotyping of women as inferior and the carryover of these stereotypes into inequitable social practices, such as paying women and men differently for equivalent work. These books were products of a broader social current of women who protested against injustices.

This upheaval sparked a questioning of sexual roles by imaginative writers. During this period, the most acclaimed attempt by a science-fiction author to rethink biological bias was made in Ursula K. Le Guin's *The Left Hand of Darkness* (1969). In the universe Le Guin portrayed, there was no question of one sex dominating, because all the humanoids were hermaphrodites. Joanna Russ's vision is more combative than this. She is not interested in simply drawing the type of implicit contrast found in *The Left Hand of Darkness,* in which the viability of a different biological setup is explored. Russ savagely compares contemporary sexism to the milder, freer life on all-female Whileaway.

One of the author's strengths arises from her need to give an accurate rendering of modern life to serve as a basis of comparison. It is often overlooked that some of the greatest writers of science fiction, such as Philip K. Dick, achieve much of their authority because they bring to their speculative writing realistic portraits of their times. In Russ's case, some of the best parts of this book are her faithful portraits of contemporary women, as in her depiction of Laura's yearning for support and Jeannine's ambivalence toward marriage. Such writing as easily might have filled a place in a mainstream realist novel as in a work of futurology.

When such slices of life are interrupted by visits from extraterrestrials and the narrative is intercut with views of future Earths, the book firmly establishes its science-fiction credentials. Inclusion of two manners of intervention allows Russ to make her sharpest comments in relation to the sexism in American society. On one hand, Janet, who has been socialized outside of patriarchy, is a determined, independent woman, more capable and generally likable than the Earth women. On the other, life on Whileaway, without men, is treated as attractively natural, festive, and well suited to the all-around development of individual potential.

This is not to say that Russ presents a blinkered view of either Janet as a faultless heroine or of her world. Janet is cold and can be self-absorbed, and her planet, which still allows the brutality of duels, arbitrarily and undemocratically assigns people to jobs they may not want.

The introduction of Jael's planet hints that social structure determines a world's negative or positive nature. Jael's female civilization is warlike, murders men without compunction, and is not above keeping slavish gigolos for its elite women. This culture, at war with all men, makes the female/male dyad the central equation in the society's worldview, and this twists its existence, even though men do not live within the community. Russ implies that it is the use of this dyad to establish difference, rather than inherent biological traits, that poisons human relationships. This point does not reduce the causticity of Russ's critique of the injustices perpetuated by men in the United States.

—*James Feast*

Fire and Hemlock

A modern reworking of the ballad of Tam Lin, in which Polly must solve the mystery surrounding Thomas Lynn

Author: Diana Wynne Jones (1934-   )
Genre: Fantasy—magical world
Type of work: Novel
Time of plot: The 1980's
Location: Middleton and Bristol, England
First published: 1985

The Story

In the middle of packing to return to college, Polly suddenly becomes aware that she seems to have forgotten several years of her life, or rather that she seems to have two parallel sets of memories, one featuring a man called Thomas Lynn. In trying to figure out this puzzle, she is obliged to work back through her adolescence, recalling events.

Readers see Polly at the age of twelve. She has been sent to her grandmother's home because her parents are quarrelling. There, with her friend Nina, she undertakes a madcap set of adventures that lead her to the mysterious Hunsdon House, where she inadvertently steps into a funeral and attends the reading of the will. She is rescued by a young man called Thomas Lynn, with whom she strikes up a friendship. They quickly discover that they share a love of heroic tales and begin to invent one concerning Tan Coul, who is Lynn, with Polly as his assistant.

The friendship and the storytelling continue by letter. Thomas gives Polly many books suitable for assistant heroes. Polly becomes aware, however, of her grandmother's disapproval, and also of an unhealthy interest from the occupants of Hunsdon House, who seem to punish her and Thomas for any contact.

This friendship against the odds is counterpointed by Polly's miserable daily life. Her parents separate and eventually divorce, and Polly comes to realize that neither of them really wants her. Her mother moves from one partner to another, and her father begins living with a woman who clearly dislikes children. In one particularly appalling scene, Polly's mother sends her to live with her father permanently, but he has not told his new partner that Polly is coming. Only through the intervention of

Thomas Lynn and Polly's grandmother is disaster averted.

As Polly grows older, she finds that her life remains inextricably mixed up with that of Thomas Lynn and the Leroy family but is unable to work out what is happening. Sebastian Leroy, the child of the family, dogs her footsteps and eventually asks her to marry him, but she refuses. Only the combination of the book she is reading and the picture Thomas Lynn gave her many years earlier suddenly alert her to the curious nature of her memories. She then discovers that no one else can remember Thomas Lynn and begins to doubt her own sanity. Her flatmate, however, reveals that she remembers him, and Polly finds that Thomas Lynn's Dumas Quartet has become well known in the musical world.

Reading at last the book of fairy stories he once gave her, she realizes that the story of Tam Lin is being reenacted, with the Queen of the Fairies keeping a man for seven years and then consigning him to Hell. Her role, like that of Janet, is to hold onto Thomas Lynn and save him from this. A final confrontation with the mysterious Laurel rescues Thomas Lynn. The novel is resolved ambiguously, with a hint of a future relationship between Polly and Thomas.

Analysis

By the time *Fire and Hemlock* was published, Diana Wynne Jones was well established as the writer of a particularly joyous and imaginative style of fantasy that tended to be regarded as suitable for children and young adolescents. *Fire and Hemlock* was one of her first attempts to move into the area best characterized as "young adult fiction." The work is darker in tone than her readers were accustomed to, dealing with a young girl's platonic relationship with an older man who shares her love of reading. A counterpoint is provided by the failing relationships of the girl's own parents, both with each other and with new partners. Jones is very skillful in creating the ambiguities of the relationship between Polly and Thomas, from Polly's delight in meeting someone who shares her pleasure in reading and is able to recommend new books to her, to her jealousy when Tom introduces her to Mary Fields, who seems to be his girlfriend. Jones also lovingly creates the world of the teenage girl, neither adult nor child, torn by confusing signals from all around her: the disentangling of childhood friendships, the new interest in boys, and the realization that adults are not to be relied on and can indeed let one down badly. On top of all this is the magical component of the story, a dark magic entirely unlike that found in most of the story books with which Polly is familiar.

Jones updates one of the most enduring and most menacing of the old ballads without losing any of its power. Instead, she heightens its effect by showing the faeryfolk capable of functioning, apparently with impunity, in the mundane world, exercising power of life or death as they wish, entirely unquestioned. A hero, which is how Polly casts herself, may yet triumph and save the day. The fact that Polly is a hero in many other ways, surviving her parents' callous disregard, remains unstated but nevertheless is clear. Jones has never shirked from pursuing an amalgam of magic, fantasy, and the grim reality of everyday life. This novel shows creation of such an amalgam in her best style.

—*Maureen Speller*

A Fire upon the Deep

As a great evil power, the Perversion, devours the thinking galaxy, a small band of sentients struggles to activate a counteragent that was liberated when the Perversion was created

Author: Vernor Vinge (1944-   )
Genre: Science fiction—catastrophe
Type of work: Novel
Time of plot: Org years 52089-52091
Location: Relay, Tines World, Harmonious Repose, and on board the spaceship *Out of Band II*
First published: 1992

The Story

A Fire upon the Deep tells the story of the Perversion's attack on civilization and of the countermeasures taken against it. The Perversion is unwittingly unleashed by an advanced society, but the process also produces a countermeasure. As the Perversion advances, the unusual crew of the spaceship *Out of Band II* races to activate and guide the countermeasure. They succeed, and the galaxy is saved, although a substantial piece of high civilization has been set back for some period of time.

In the environment of *A Fire upon the Deep*, shells of potential, shaped roughly like a child's toy top, define activity in the Milky Way. Even thought cannot exist in the central Unthinking Depths. The closer that sentients approach this limit, the less intelligent they become. The next shell out defines the Slow Zone, where any information transfer is constrained by the speed of light. The outermost boundary separates the Beyond, where advanced civilizations dwell, from the Transcend, where the Powers dwell.

On a planet barely inside the Transcend, the Straumli Realm accidentally unleashes a great evil power, the Perversion. As researchers escape their laboratory, they take with them a countermeasure to the Perversion. This countermeasure lands on Tines World, very near the Slow Zone. As they emerge from their ship, the humans are massacred by large, somewhat doglike creatures. Only two children survive: Jefri Olsndot stays in the Flenser Republic and is carefully nurtured; Johanna Olsndot is skillfully spirited away to the Woodcarvers' domain.

On Relay, a prime location in the communications network of the Beyond civilizations, Ravna Bergsndot happily works as a student librarian. She is pulled from her accustomed duties to orient a revived primitive spacefaring human, Pham Nuwen, to work for a Power known as Old One. As Ravna and Pham get to know each other, they meet and become acquainted with two Skroderriders, plant intelligences named Blueshell and Greenstalk, who fly *Out of Band II* as interstellar traders.

Pham turns out to be a creation of Old One. As Straumli Realm falls, Jefri calls for help. The administration of Relay commissions *Out of Band II* to rescue Jefri and activate the countermeasure, instituting a multifunction refit of the ship. When the Perversion attacks Relay and kills Old One, Old One Godshatters, turning into Pham. Ravna, Pham, and the Skroderriders run for Tines World in *Out of Band II*.

As *Out of Band II* arrives at Tines world, the situation is desperate. War has broken out between the Flenser Republic and the Woodcarvers' domain, and the Perversion is advancing fast. The crew of *Out of Band II* rescues the children and activates the countermeasure, which causes a wave out of the Slow Zone that extends into the Transcend. This eliminates the Perversion and all Beyonder civilizations in its path.

Analysis

From prologue to epilogue, *A Fire upon the Deep* fills its reader with a sense of wonder. A unique structure for cognitive processes fills the galaxy, from the Unthinking Depths to the supercharged Transcend. Civilizations can evolve from limited organizations in the Slow Zone, through increasingly sophisticated societies in the Beyond, into Powers in the Transcend, and perhaps into something beyond the Powers. A vast communications network unites the few human and many alien civilizations of the Beyond. The conflict of the novel occurs when an advanced human civilization dabbling in the wonders of the Transcend inadvertently releases a Perversion that threatens to subvert the entire Beyond and a good portion of the Transcend.

The tradition of grand scope into which this novel falls extends at least from H. G. Wells's *The Time Machine* (1895), which describes the near and far futures of the Earth, through the science-fiction magazines of the 1930's and 1940's. John W. Campbell, Jr.'s novel *The Black Star Passes* (1953) deals with threats to Earth and the entire solar system, and his *The Mightiest Machine* (1947; serial form, 1934) envisions conflict between galaxies. E. E. Smith's Lensman series, from *Triplanetary* (1948; serial form, 1934) to *Children of the Lens* (1954; serial form, 1947-1948), extends through six books, envisioning a conflict between high forces of good and evil involving the entire Milky Way and multiple races. Isaac Asimov's Foundation trilogy (1951-1953) centers on institutions whose purpose is to save essential civilization as a galactic empire crumbles.

The tradition of grand scope extends into the 1980's and 1990's with work such as Michael Resnick's novels of the Inner Frontier: *Santiago: A Myth of the Far Future* (1986), *Ivory: A Legend of Past and Future* (1988), *Soothsayer* (1991), *Oracle* (1992), and *Prophet* (1993). The worlds in them are modeled on the American Wild West and populated by legendary aliens.

Vernor Vinge informs *A Fire upon the Deep*, his contribution to the tradition of grand scope, with his background as a professor of computer science. His background breathes life into both the communications network that links the civilizations of the Beyond and the information mining that awakens the Perversion.

This novel shows the continued growth of Vinge's writing. In *Marooned in Realtime* (1986), Vinge envisions a few pockets of humanity living in stasis while some force eliminates humankind. Their problem is uniting the pockets so that humankind can continue. Vinge's background in information theory shows up again in this book: The first hurdle to be overcome is communication between stasis bubbles. What Vinge adds in *A Fire upon the Deep* is a greater richness of detail. The context of the novel is a galaxywide society of diverse civilizations populated by a variety of mutually alien races. Two particularly delightful alien races are fully realized.

—*Joseph Minne*

The Fisher King Trilogy

In this action-packed trilogy, various characters interact with ghosts, mythological figures, and black-magic tarot cards in a drama of suffering, redemption, and apotheosis in the American West

Author: Tim Powers (1952-   )
Genre: Fantasy—Magical Realism
Type of work: Novel
Time of plot: 1990-1995
Location: Southern California and Las Vegas, Nevada
First published: *Last Call* (1992), *Expiration Date* (1996), and *Earthquake Weather* (1997)

The Story

The Fisher King trilogy chronicles the apotheosis of Scott Crane, the son of a corrupt gangster who rules a mystical realm of nebulous boundaries in the American West. Scott and his father, Georges Leon, possess magical powers that are explicitly associated with those of the Fisher King of Arthurian legend. Scott must challenge his father and assume the kingship of the West in order to save what has become a political, financial, architectural, and spiritual wasteland. Dramatizing the stages of the symbolic life of the Fisher King, each novel is set in a different season: *Last Call* in spring, *Expiration Date* in autumn, and *Earthquake Weather* in winter.

In *Last Call*, Scott attempts to reclaim the life his father stole from him. As a child, Scott was nearly turned into a soulless vessel by Leon, who uses black magic in the pursuit of longer life. Saved by his mother, Scott fled and was adopted in Los Angeles by Ozzie Crane. His legacy is the loss of one eye, a casualty of the Page of Swords card in an evil tarot deck hurled by his father. Scott becomes an avatar of the Page of Swords, also known as the One-Eyed Jack (the Jack of Hearts) and the crown prince of the King of Hearts (the Fisher King). Years later, Scott symbolically loses his life to his father again, this time in a card game called assumption, a variation of poker played with Leon's tarot deck.

Later, at the age of forty-seven, Scott loses his beloved wife and the life they shared. Joined by his friend Archimedes "Arky" Mavranos,

Ozzie Crane, and his foster sister Diana, Scott defeats his father, reclaims his life, and becomes the new Fisher King.

Expiration Date introduces Koot Hoomie Parganas, an eleven-year-old candidate for the position of Fisher King, who accidentally sets free the curmudgeonly ghost of Thomas A. Edison in Los Angeles. Pursued by a one-armed madman called Sherman Oaks (after the name of a Los Angeles suburb) and Loretta deLarava, a ghost-obsessed documentary producer, Koot navigates the dangerous streets of an unfriendly city with Edison's help.

Koot's story is interwoven with that of Pete Sullivan, busy fleeing ghosts of his own as he finally returns to Los Angeles. After witnessing the death of their father years before, Pete and his twin sister grew up in that city and began working for deLarava. The siblings eventually realized that deLarava planned to capture the ghost of their father, and they parted ways, always running from the past. However, Pete is drawn back to the city to seek absolution from his father's ghost and a resolution to the mystery surrounding his murder.

Earthquake Weather opens with the murder of Scott Crane. Janice Cordelia Plumtree, host to multiple personalities, surrenders herself to the authorities as the assassin after suffering possession by a ghost. Joined by Sid "Scant" Cochran, a vineyard worker marked with a scar on his hand from Dionysus, Janice seeks to restore Scott to life. Arky Mavranos and Diana follow magical guidance and take the king's body to Pete Sullivan and Koot. The two groups join in a quest to bring Scott back to life or to replace him with a new Fisher King, racing against time to save the failing Kingdom of the West.

Analysis

The Fisher King Trilogy succeeds in adapting the myth of the Fisher King into eminently readable novels set in the 1990's. Filled with rituals, legends, magic, gods and ghosts, each novel reflects extensive research and the deft writing needed to blend these elements into fast-paced, engaging stories.

The character Scott Crane is aptly named. In ancient Greece, cranes were sacred to Demeter, the goddess who renewed the earth each spring when her daughter was released from the Underworld. They are also symbolic of resurrection, and throughout the novels Scott Crane seeks the rebirth of the wasteland created by his father. The bird most closely related to the North American crane is the coot, and, as the series progresses, Koot becomes an "heir" to Scott Crane's throne.

The novels rely heavily upon Arthurian myth. Like the Fisher King of lore, both Scott and Koot develop a wound which will not heal. In order to succeed, Scott must challenge and defeat a Green Knight figure, Vaughan Trumbill. The discovery of the essential tarot deck occurs only after he has removed a pocketknife stuck in a brick, a symbolic Sword in the Stone. According to legend, the Fisher King can be healed only when an innocent fool asks the question, "Whom does it serve?" In *Earthquake Weather*, Koot's first question to Arky and Diana refers to the color of the truck carrying the dead king. By mistakenly asking the wrong question, Koot sets in motion the quest to restore Scott to life.

Powers interweaves subtexts from Charles Dickens, Shakespeare, T. S. Eliot, Alfred Lord Tennyson, Lewis Carroll, and others to provide greater depth through allusions to both tragedy and irrationality. The humor for which Powers is famous is present throughout. For instance, while seeking Koot Hoomie Parganas, Scant and Janice ask around for someone whose name sounds like "Boogie Woogie Bananas." Like Carroll, Powers has a gift for comic invention when dramatizing miscommunication.

Powers's Catholic beliefs fully inform his works. Redemption, forgiveness, salvation, and resurrection are essential to the madcap adventures he depicts. A work not explicitly alluded to by Powers, C. S. Lewis's famous Space Trilogy, nonetheless presents powerful parallels. These books also deal with Christian motifs and Arthurian myth, and the concluding volumes of both trilogies painfully dramatize the themes of sacrifice and redemption.

—*Michael-Anne Rubenstien*

Flowers for Algernon

Experimental surgery enables Charlie Gordon, a retarded man, to attain an extremely high level of intelligence

Author: Daniel Keyes (1927-   )
Genre: Science fiction—superbeing
Type of work: Novel
Time of plot: The 1960's
Location: New York City
First published: 1966 (expanded version of a short story in *The Magazine of Fantasy and Science Fiction*, 1959)

The Story

Flowers for Algernon unfolds in a series of diary entries. In the first, dated "march 3," Charlie describes himself as a thirty-two-year-old man who works at a bakery and attends "Miss Kinnians class at the beekmin colledge center for retarted adults." Ensuing entries chronicle Charlie's progress as the first human subjected to an intelligence-boosting surgical procedure.

Before the operation, Charlie undergoes a series of tests that measure his intelligence. In one, he tries in vain to pencil through a maze faster than Algernon can run it. Algernon is a laboratory mouse that already has undergone the surgical procedure. After the surgery, sleep learning accelerates Charlie's mental development. By the end of the month, he outraces Algernon. In early April, he comprehends a grammar book overnight and shows signs of increased self-awareness, staying home from Donner's Bakery after realizing that he has long been victimized by coworker "friends" Joe Carp and Frank Reilly.

Counseling Charlie is Dr. Jay Strauss, a neurosurgeon and psychiatrist who, with Professor Harold Nemur, is responsible for the experiment. Together with lab assistant Burt Selden and teacher Alice Kinnian, they guide Charlie as he begins a long-delayed maturation process.

Two months after the operation, Charlie is able to converse intelligently with college students but is stymied in acting on his amorous feelings for Alice. Although she is attracted to him, both fear that they may jeopardize his development.

As Charlie accumulates knowledge at a breathtaking rate, his illusions are shattered at a similar clip. He sees the fallibility of his mentors and realizes that their interest in him stems largely from selfishness. Charlie rebels at a scientific conference in Chicago, where he and Algernon are put on display. Freeing the mouse from its cage, Charlie takes his counterpart back to New York and moves into an apartment near Times Square.

Independent after years of institutionalization, Charlie initiates a new phase of his education, entering into an affair with free-spirited Fay Lillman and visiting his father, Matt, who fails to recognize him. Charlie also applies his brainpower to studying Algernon's regressive tendencies. Suspecting that he also may regress, Charlie visits the Warren State Home and Training School, where his doctors and family had arranged to send him if the experiment failed.

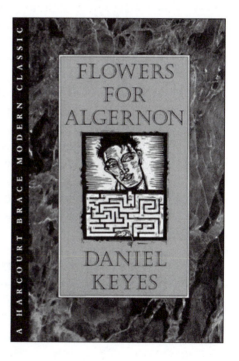

In late August, Charlie concludes that the experiment's results are indeed temporary and potentially fatal. After Algernon dies on September 17, Charlie spares the mouse from laboratory incineration by burying its remains in his backyard.

Mindful of his inevitable decline, Charlie visits his mother, Rose, and sister, Norma, both of whom he remembers as hostile. He finds that Rose has entered senility and Norma feels remorse over her past unkindness toward him.

Charlie consummates his relationship with Alice on October 11. Though heartened by their shared love, ten days later he tells her to leave in a fit of anger over his deterioration. Having already lost his multilingual abilities, he rapidly loses his typing prowess and command of English. Isolating himself from the Beekman staff, he returns to Donner's Bakery, where newly sympathetic coworkers welcome him.

In his last entry, dated "nov 21," Charlie writes of his decision to go to Warren. Bidding farewell to Alice and the others at Beekman, he asks that the reader "put some flowrs on Algernons grave in the bak yard."

Analysis

After the short story "Flowers for Algernon" received a Hugo Award in 1960, the tale of Charlie Gordon was embraced by a wide mainstream audience. In the early 1960's, a television adaptation titled "The Two Worlds of Charlie Gordon" appeared on *The U.S. Steel Hour*, with Cliff Robertson playing Charlie. After the Nebula Award-winning novel appeared in 1966, a feature film adaptation, *Charly* (1968), also starred Robertson, who received an Academy Award for his portrayal. Widely anthologized and taught in schools throughout the United States, the story also was the basis for a 1980 Broadway musical.

At the heart of its appeal is its unsensational use of a speculative premise, that surgery can radically boost intelligence, as the basis of a moving allegory. Charlie is like many people who reach a peak only to foresee and then experience their inevitable decline. Although the novel is considerably longer than the short story (its extended time frame approximates the human gestation period), both use compression to intensify the drama of this experience.

Notwithstanding the fact that the novel has been criticized as inferior to the short story, its extended narrative enabled Daniel Keyes not only to exploit his story's commercial potential but also to explore a variety of story elements in greater depth. The cultural tendency to look on the retarded Charlie as a nonperson is one such element. Charlie's psyche also is delineated in greater detail.

Although *Flowers for Algernon* bears some resemblance to Mary Wollstonecraft Shelley's *Frankenstein* (1818)—the animus of Charlie and his doctors softly echoes that of the monster and Victor Frankenstein—significant links also can be made between the novel and other, nonspeculative works, including Anne Frank's *The Diary of a Young Girl* (1947; English translation, 1952), the entries of which record key years of growth in the life of a girl doomed by a Nazi culture that deems her subhuman. Charlie's experience also parallels that of actual human test subjects, such as those in the infamous Tuskegee syphilis study of the 1930's and the catatonic patients given L-dopa by Dr. Oliver Sacks in 1969. Although the influence of *Flowers for Algernon* can be seen in science-fiction works, including Thomas M. Disch's *Camp Concentration* (1968), its legacy may be most evident in Sacks's book *Awakenings* (1973) and its 1990 screen adaptation. Keyes himself continued to delve into unusual psychological states in science fiction and nonfiction genres.

—David Marc Fischer

The Forever War

William Mandella is drafted, trained as a spaceborne infantryman, and sent into combat against the alien Taurans

Author: Joe Haldeman (1943-   )
Genre: Science fiction—future war
Type of work: Novel
Time of plot: 1997-3143
Location: Earth and various planets
First published: 1974

The Story

The story concerns the experiences of William Mandella during a protracted interstellar war between humanity and an alien race known as the Taurans. The novel begins in 1997 (a future date at the time the novel was written), when the war already has been escalating for some years. Mandella has been drafted into the United Nations Exploratory Force (UNEF) under the terms of a conscription act intended to select the physical and intellectual elite of Earth to defend humanity against the Tauran menace. Among the UNEF's more unusual policies are toleration of drug use and compulsory sexual promiscuity, enforced through rotating rosters of bunkmates.

Mandella's first combat mission is an attack on a Tauran base located on a planet in a system near a collapsing superdense star. This mission includes capturing a prisoner. On its march to the target, the strike force encounters a group of alien creatures. When Sergeant Cortez gives the order to fire, the soldiers slaughter what turn out to be members of the sentient indigenous population, creating tremendous guilt in Mandella, Marygay Potter, and other soldiers. Cortez triggers a posthypnotic suggestion to the soldiers to kill indiscriminately when the time for the actual attack arrives. The result of the first campaign is at best ambiguous, because the soldiers fail to capture a Tauran and a number of soldiers go insane after realizing what they have done to an almost helpless enemy.

Because of the time-dilating effects of travel at near the speed of light, when Mandella and Potter return to Earth after their first combat tour, they discover that twenty-six years have passed on Earth while they have experienced only two years in their own frame of reference. The two have fallen in love despite the UNEF's attempts to regulate personal lives, and they want to leave the UNEF at the end of their enlistments and resume their lives on Earth. They are shocked by the social and economic changes on Earth. The United Nations has become a planetary government dedicated to reorganizing society to support the war effort. Unable to adjust to the radical changes at home, Mandella and Potter decide that their best choice is to re-enlist in the UNEF.

More than three hundred years elapse while Mandella and Potter are on their next combat tour. When both are wounded, they are sent to convalesce on the planet Heaven. The pattern of social changes that Mandella and Potter found so disturbing on Earth has continued. Humanity is now almost completely homosexual, and people are conditioned from birth to support the policies and goals of the UNEF. Recovered from their wounds, Mandella and Potter are assigned to different strike forces. They realize that because of the effects of relativity, centuries of subjective time will separate them after their next combat tours, should they survive.

Assigned to command his own strike force, Mandella finds himself leading soldiers who are almost as alien to him as the Taurans. The men and women under his command are a group of eugenically controlled and scientifically reared homosexuals, bred in vitro, who fatalistically accept that they live and die to serve the UNEF. Mandella's assignment is to secure a portal planet orbiting a collapsar (a kind of neutron star) that could be pivotal in the Tauran war strategy. The strike force defeats the Taurans in a Pyrrhic victory in which only twelve percent of Mandella's command survives.

Mandella and the other survivors return to Stargate and find that the war ended more than two centuries earlier. Under the UNEF's policies, humanity has evolved into a race of telepathic male and female clones of a single individual, Corporal Kahn, who is presumed to be the perfect prototype for humanity. Mandella is offered a choice of ways to integrate himself into the Kahn-clone world of the UNEF, but he rejects the idea. Only when he studies a printout of his military record does he find a solution. Potter and other survivors of the war have settled the planet Middle Finger, where some individuals cheat time on a "relativistic shuttle" waiting for other returnees to join them. The UNEF tolerates the aberrant society, in which people breed in the conventional manner, as a eugenic control baseline for human diversity. The novel concludes with the press announcement of the natural birth of a son of the two oldest survivors of the Forever War.

Analysis

The Forever War, Joe Haldeman's first science-fiction novel, is a significant example of the future-war novel and military *Bildungsroman*. The novel should be read in the context of the Vietnam War, the author's own participation in that conflict, and its analogs in Robert A. Heinlein's Cold War-era novel *Starship Troopers* (1959) and Orson Scott Card's postdétente *Ender's Game* (1985). *The Forever War* won both the Hugo and Nebula Awards as best science-fiction novel.

The first section of Haldeman's novel is a science-fictional rendering of American involvement in Vietnam. The subsequent sections of the novel continue the parallels with Vietnam but also expand on the major theme of the novel, the importance of individuality and free will in the face of authoritarian government and social pressures toward conformity. The UNEF's drive toward conformity starts with screening the population for sociopathic traits. The trend continues with the eugenically controlled population that provides the soldiers for Mandella's strike force and the Kahn-clone "humanity" that appears at the conclusion of the novel. Government policies are geared toward producing a uniform and predictable population of workers and soldiers for the war effort. This theme is accompanied by a series of images of the increasing mechanization of human society, starting with Mandella's vision of his relationship with Marygay Potter reduced to copulating fighting suits and his dream of being an animated fighting suit with the UNEF at the controls. These images culminate with Mandella's realization that wounded soldiers have become "soft machines" to be repaired or replaced in the service of the UNEF.

The ending of the novel is problematic in that, from the UNEF's perspective, Mandella, Potter, and the other returnees on Middle Finger are maladjusted veterans unable to incorporate themselves into postwar society. From the perspective of Mandella and Potter, however, Haldeman has provided the happy ending impossible for many Vietnam War veterans.

—*Peter C. Hall*

The Forgotten Beasts of Eld

The wizard Sybel, living alone on a mountain among a collection of fabulous animals, takes in a baby boy to rear, an action that ultimately involves her in a dynastic war

Author: Patricia A. McKillip (1948-   )
Genre: Fantasy—high fantasy
Type of work: Novel
Time of plot: The present
Location: The land of Eldwold
First published: 1974

The Story

In *The Forgotten Beasts of Eld*, the beautiful wizard Sybel has the power to call and tame a collection of wondrous animals. Her calm life is shattered when she takes in Tamlorn, a supposedly orphaned boy who is at the center of a long-standing war. As Tamlorn grows up and becomes aware of his heritage, Sybel is forced to become involved in the outside world. When confronted with conflicting needs of love and revenge, Sybel must struggle to overcome her betrayal of both herself and those she loves most.

Sybel, the daughter of wizards, lives contentedly alone atop her mountain until Coren, a warrior of the House of Sirle, brings to her a baby boy. Coren tells Sybel that the baby's dead mother was Sybel's aunt and the queen of Eldwold, and that his father, Coren's brother, was slain in the recent battle in which Sirle was soundly defeated. Now little Tamlorn is endangered by the war between Sirle and Eldwold. Coren begs Sybel to care for Tamlorn, and she reluctantly agrees. She is assisted by Maelga, an old witch living nearby.

As Tam grows up among Sybel's fantastic menagerie, Sybel comes to love him dearly. She knows that Tam actually is the son of Drede, the king of Eldwold and sworn enemy of the House of Sirle. Rok, the lord of Sirle and Coren's eldest brother, desperately wishes to overthrow Drede. He sends Coren back to Sybel to try to persuade her to use both Tamlorn and her considerable wizardly powers to defeat Drede. Coren, who has fallen in love with Sybel, is unable to coax her into fighting for Sirle. Tam has also discovered his parentage and wishes to live with his real father. Drede, pleased to have his son back but fearing that Sybel will use her powers against him, hires a wizard to control Sybel. She is able to defeat the wizard with the help of one of her magical beasts, and Coren takes her to Sirle as his wife.

Sybel harbors hatred for Drede and desires revenge as much as the Sirle brothers. She conspires with Rok to use her powers and her animals—including a dragon, a lion, and a riddle-spouting boar—to destroy Drede. Sybel thus betrays the trust of both Coren and Tam, who believed she had given up her need for revenge.

Maelga and Cyrin the boar reawaken twinges of guilt in Sybel over what she has done. Then, on the eve of battle, Sybel herself is almost destroyed by one of her more fearsome and not easily controlled beasts. Realizing that the price of revenge is too high, Sybel releases all her animals from her control and returns to her isolated mountain to let fate decide the battle's outcome. Even without Sybel to command them, her animals destroy Drede, rescue Tamlorn, and lure the soldiers away from the battlefield to stop the war before it starts. By facing and overcoming the ugliness within her own heart, Sybel is able to save her relationships with Coren and Tam and achieve her heart's desire.

Analysis

The Forgotten Beasts of Eld was published before Patricia McKillip's *The Riddle-Master of Hed* (1976), the first book of her *Riddle of Stars* trilogy (1979 as trilogy; also known as the Riddle-Master trilogy), for which she is probably best known. Like the trilogy, *The Forgotten Beasts of Eld* overflows with elements typical in fantasy: fabulous, mythical animals; powerfully magical wizards; and kings, princes, and wars. To this familiar fantasy background, McKillip adds a host of distinctive and all-too-human characters. The rich, poetic language does not overwhelm this story of love, betrayed trust, revenge, and, above all, taking responsibility for one's actions. All the characters, including the beasts, display conflicting loyalties and motives as they struggle to attain their innermost desires while trying not to hurt those they love.

McKillip's fantasy novels are noted for their excellent characterizations. *The Forgotten Beasts of Eld* allows for exploration of the souls of all the characters. Even the emotional motivations of the villains are somewhat understandable. Drede is driven by fear to try to entrap Sybel, but his devotion to his son is evident. Coren remains hopelessly in love with Sybel even when she tampers with his thoughts and manipulates him as if he were another of her captured animals. Sybel herself seems remote and aloof, far removed from the turmoils of the feuds outside her mountain oasis, but she is also drawn into a fray of tangled emotions when she allows herself to feel love, first for Tam, then Maelga, then Coren. She must learn to deal with both the benefits and strengths, as well as the vulnerabilities and risks, of forming relationships. Readers can identify easily with these believably inconsistent and often confused characters, who love and hate and love again.

Reviewers have also commended McKillip's compelling style of storytelling in this novel. McKillip herself has stated that she was a storyteller for her younger siblings before she ever began writing. *The Forgotten Beasts of Eld* draws the reader into an increasingly complicated web of political and emotional intrigue. Tantalizing hints are dropped that each of Sybel's animals could tell a story of its own, giving the novel a rich backdrop and a mystical ambience that is maintained throughout.

Although McKillip did not write *The Forgotten Beasts of Eld* specifically for children, it is usually classified by booksellers and librarians as a young adult novel. Reviews were favorable, although some reviewers objected to the somewhat flowery language and imagery. The novel received the World Fantasy Award in 1975.

—*Quinn Weller*

The Foundation Series

Mathematician Hari Seldon, creator of the science of psychohistory, creates a grand scheme for arresting the decline of the Galactic Empire and controlling its future

Author: Isaac Asimov (1920-1992)
Genre: Science fiction—future history
Type of work: Novels
Time of plot: 12,020-14,000
Location: The Galactic Empire
First published: *The Foundation Trilogy* (1963; as trilogy); previously published as *Foundation* (1951; serial form, *Astounding Science-Fiction*, 1942-1944), *Foundation and Empire* (1952; serial form, *Astounding Science-Fiction*, 1945), and *Second Foundation* (1953; serial form, *Astounding Science-Fiction*, 1948-1950); additions to the series include *Foundation's Edge* (1982), *Foundation and Earth* (1986), *Prelude to Foundation* (1988), and *Forward the Foundation* (1993)

The Story

The vast Galactic Empire, composed of 25 million worlds and quadrillions of human beings, is in decline. Mathematician Hari Seldon, a provincial scholar from the distant planet Helicon, presents his learned hypothesis about the mathematical possibilities of what he calls "psychohistory" to a conference held on Trantor, the imperial capital. Seldon understands that his hypothesis is incomplete and untested. Nevertheless, it offers the prospect of mathematically predicting the empire's future and, with this knowledge, influencing events so as to lay the groundwork for a Second Galactic Empire.

Seldon's psychohistorical predictions do not apply to specific events or personalities; rather, they deal with the aggregate of the empire's myriad worlds and peoples in sweeping ways. Psychohistory is a science of masses, of mobs in their billions. Intelligent people suspect that the empire is declining, and Seldon himself believes that the empire will soon confront thirty thousand millennia of wars and barbarism.

The potential of psychohistory to shorten this period draws the attention of Emperor Cleon I; his most influential aide, Demerzel; and female historian Dors Venabili. *Prelude to Foundation* chronicles Seldon's trials and adventures, as the emperor, Demerzel (a robot in various human guises), and Dors (another humanized robot) alternately menace Seldon and encourage him to refine his thesis and to make it practical enough to allow prediction, manipulation, and control of social and economic change that will lead to a new empire.

The fall of the empire is inevitable, but to abbreviate the ensuing period of chaos to less than a millennium, Seldon establishes two Foundations at opposite ends of the Galaxy. The First Foundation, on Terminus, far from Trantor, is begun as a settlement of physical scientists who labor to compile the *Encyclopedia Galactica*, a compendium of universal knowledge. During the empire's long decline, the First Foundation becomes a center of advanced science. The Second Foundation, a mysterious body devoted to the expansion of the powers of the intellect, is established simultaneously at a secret location.

Forward the Foundation recounts the events of Seldon's later life, a time focused on elaboration of his predictive plan, on his preparations to reappear in a special vault as a holograph during future crises in order to dispense additional counsel, and on his symbolically significant death. Soon afterward, as recorded in *Foundation*, the Empire shatters into independent kingdoms that quickly threaten the First Foundation's existence.

Because of the political skill of Salvor Hardin, the First Foundation's mayor, the Foundation maintains its independence. Because the First Foundation is the sole remaining possessor of atomic power and a repository of superior science, it also gains ascendancy over much of the galaxy. As centuries pass, the First Foundation evolves a trading economy based on the sale of compact atomic devices. Its traders penetrate the periphery of the galaxy, defeat the Foundation's rivals, and prepare for clashes with the dying empire's remaining forces—a story told in *Foundation and Empire*.

Because Seldon's psychohistory cannot account for the actions of individuals, the First Foundation is ruined eventually by the mind-shaping powers of the Mule, a mutant. Thus begins the search by the Mule, as well as by the survivors of the First Foundation, for the secret location of the Second Foundation, whose leaders are recognized as "mentalists," masters of mind control. A remarkable woman, Batya Darell, defeats the Mule, leaving the First Foundation technologically ascendant but eager to discover the location of the Second Foundation.

In *Foundation's Edge*, which is set 498 years after the founding of the

First Foundation, this search is pressed by a young Terminus councilman, Golan Trevize, who is joined by historian Janov Pelorat. Traversing the galaxy searching for the Second Foundation as well as for Earth and the origins of life, Trevize and Pelorat arrive at Gaia, a peaceful, ecologically harmonious world that has evolved as a collective mind. Because of the "objective rightness" of Trevize's intuitions, during a critical confrontation between representatives of the First and Second Foundations, the Gaians allow Trevize to decide the future of the galaxy; that is, to determine whether creation of the Second Galactic Empire should be directed by either of the Foundations. Trevize chooses a third way, the Gaian way: creation of a harmonious, collectivist Gaian-style "Galaxia" instead of an Empire. Believing that he has made the right choice, Trevize nevertheless harbors doubts. Gaia is a collective mind, and Trevize is an individualist; he wants hard facts to undergird his intuitive decision.

Trevize, Pelorat, and Pelorat's Gaian love, Bliss, continue the search for Earth and the origins of life in *Foundation and Earth*. The trio's quest ensnarls them in adventures on three variously hostile planets. They backtrack their way through evidence of galactic colonization only to discover that Earth is radioactive and lifeless. They find the Moon, however, inhabited underground by the twenty-thousand-year-old robot Daneel, who gives them information about the origins and galactic spread of humans and their robots. Meanwhile, the searchers acquire a precocious hermaphrodite child, Fallom, whose evolved transducer lobes give it awesome and sinister powers.

Analysis

At his death in 1992, Isaac Asimov had published at least 475 books, ranking him as one of the world's most prolific authors. *The Foundation Trilogy* rapidly earned status as a science-fiction classic, while two other novels in the series became long-term best-sellers. A learned student of science—he held a Ph.D. in chemistry and was a professor of biochemistry—and a devotee of history, Asimov virtually founded the science-fiction subgenre of future history. He earned many major awards, including numerous Hugos and Nebulas, and was named a Nebula Grand Master in 1987. Throughout the Foundation series novels, Asimov's scientifically or technically trained leading characters are aided or guided by historians. In the Foundation series as elsewhere in his writings, Asimov acknowledges drawing heavily on themes embodied in widely influential historical and metahistorical studies, notably Edward Gibbon's *The History of the Decline and Fall of the Roman Empire* (1776-1788), Arnold J. Toynbee's *A Study of History* (1934-1954), and Oswald Spengler's *The Decline of the West* (1926-1928). Although differing in their subject matter and their perspectives, each of these works is concerned, as was Asimov, both with identifying recurrent patterns in history and with tackling the venerable historical question of whether such patterns are determined primarily by profound social forces or instead by individual actions or chance. The mutant genius the Mule, for example, temporarily upsets the Seldon Plan.

The unfolding of Seldon's psychohistorical plan, around which the plotting of the entire Foundation series occurs, suggests that Asimov at one time believed in the existence of mathematically quantifiable, predetermined collective forces that drive historical processes. By 1955, however, he held an opposing view, which he expounded in *The End of Eternity*. In fact, over time, Asimov led his readers to wonder if he had resolved these great questions himself. In the Foundation series, after all, it is Seldon, an individualist, rather than a collective mind who develops the "law" of psychohistory.

A few writers of future histories, such as Mark Twain and H. G. Wells, anticipated Asimov's grappling with the causes of historical development. Others such as Frederik Pohl, Cyril Kornbluth, and Frank Herbert began publishing their writings as Asimov's Foundation series evolved, and others have followed. For intellectual breadth, imaginative interplay of science and history, and sheer engaging volume of work, however, the Foundation series remains unsurpassed.

—*Mary E. Virginia*

Frankenstein

Victor Frankenstein discovers the secret of life and creates a monster whose despair and anger ruin the lives of Frankenstein and his family

Author: Mary Wollstonecraft Shelley (1797-1851)
Genre: Science fiction—cautionary
Type of work: Novel
Time of plot: The late eighteenth century
Location: Europe and the great northern polar seas
First published: 1818

The Story

Frankenstein: Or, The Modern Prometheus is framed as a series of letters written by polar explorer Robert Walton to his sister, Margaret Saville, who is home in England. He relates to her his adventures, including a story told to him by a young man, Victor Frankenstein, whom his ship has rescued from the polar ice.

As a young university student at Ingolstadt, in Bavaria, Frankenstein is determined to find the secret of life. He studies constantly, ignoring his family back in Geneva, Switzerland. He steals body parts from charnel houses and medical laboratories, then uses the power of electricity to create a living being. He immediately knows he has erred: His creature is ghastly. It leaves Frankenstein's quarters but remains in his life.

Frankenstein next sees the creature back in Geneva, where he has returned following the death of his young brother William. Although a servant girl, Justine, is accused of causing William's death, Frankenstein sees the creature lurking near the place of the murder and knows he is the killer. Frankenstein's anguish is intensified when innocent Justine is executed for the murder. In his agony, Frankenstein leaves home to wander in the mountains. The creature confronts him and tells him his own story.

After leaving Ingolstadt, the creature wanders throughout the countryside. He discovers quickly that he is frightening and repugnant to humans and takes to traveling at night and hiding during the day. The creature learns to speak and to read during a long stay in a hovel attached to a poor farm family's hut. During his stay, he performs many kindnesses for the family and feels sympathy for their poverty. He be-

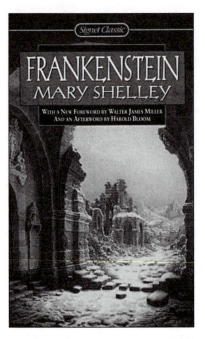

friends the old father, who is blind. As soon as other family members return and see him, they flee. In anger, the creature sets their farm on fire.

He makes his way to Geneva, saving a small child from drowning along the way. Every time he tries to perform an act of kindness, however, he causes a reaction of horror. On the mountaintop, the creature begs Frankenstein to make him a mate so he need not be lonely. Then, he says, he will leave humankind alone and live with his mate in seclusion. If not, he says, he will be with Frankenstein on his wedding night.

Frankenstein promises to make him a mate but questions his wisdom. He travels to England with his friend William Clerval, then goes alone to an isolated spot in Scotland to carry out his promise.

He cannot finish the job. He abandons it and prepares to return home. The creature, infuriated by Frankenstein's unwillingness to keep a promise, kills Clerval, then returns to Geneva to kill Frankenstein's bride, his adopted sister Elizabeth, on their wedding night.

The tragedy and the guilt are too much to bear. Frankenstein resolves to pursue the monster until one of them is dead. He travels by dogsled across the snowy expanses of Russia toward the North Pole. He is picked up by Robert Walton's ship during his pursuit and dies on the ship after telling Walton his story. The creature appears and tells Walton of his remorse for his deeds, then sets off into the cold to build his own funeral pyre.

Analysis

Mary Shelley wrote *Frankenstein* as part of a friendly ghost-story writing competition with her husband, Percy Bysshe Shelley, and friend Lord Byron when she was eighteen years old. The novel has prompted many melodramatic takeoffs in film and much critical interest. It is one of the earliest works of science fiction, and the scientific techniques described in it are shadowy at best, yet they represent adequately the scientific knowledge of the time.

The book's subtitle links it to the Prometheus myth, popular in the Romantic era. Both Percy Shelley and Lord Byron wrote Promethean poems. Prometheus, a Titan, stole fire from the gods and gave it to humans, allowing them to thrive and create. Frankenstein's creature was brought to life through the "fire" of lightning. In both cases, the reader must wonder whether the powers given to humankind are blessings or curses. The novel questions what responsibility humankind has in the face of achievements that can have both good and bad results. Frankenstein's suffering clearly shows that he realizes too late that he miscalculated the destructive potential of his discovery.

The novel is filled with imagery of light and dark. The creature, brought to life through the power of lightning, is always in the shadows of darkness, and he commits dark deeds.

The Romantic writers with whom Shelley can be connected wrote in part as a revolt against the Enlightenment assumption that scientific advances and education represent the highest possibilities of humankind. If scientific achievement is paramount to Frankenstein, it comes at the expense of humanity, including the lives of everyone whom Frankenstein loves. *Frankenstein* offers interesting views of the psyche of man in both Frankenstein and his creature, and of the social damage that can result when love is denied, as it was to the creature, or relegated to low status, as it was by Frankenstein. A psychological inquiry also suggests the idea of the creature being the double, or dark side, of Frankenstein.

One interesting stylistic device in the novel is the lack of a constant or reliable narrator: Robert Walton, Frankenstein, and the creature all tell their own stories. The reader thus is given different points of view from which to judge the story. Another point of interest is the consideration of gender: The novel has a female author, employs stereotyped female characters, and shows contrasts between the typically male and female motives of ambition and love.

—Janine Rider

The Gate to Women's Country

Although in a postconvulsion world women live with a few nonviolent males in communities separate from garrisons of warlike men, they secretly devise ways to dominate and to breed nonviolent children

Author: Sheri S. Tepper (1929-   )
Genre: Science fiction—feminist
Type of work: Novel
Time of plot: The twenty-fourth century C.E.
Location: The fictional community of Marthatown
First published: 1988

The Story

Three centuries after most of Earth is devastated and left radioactive by wars, human survivors have evolved a dual civilization. Most men, as well as boys from an early age, live in military garrisons learning martial arts and military values. All women, aided by a handful of pacific male servitors and small children, live in women's country, small communities dominated by females and by the feminine values of nurturance, nonviolence, and love. Sexual intercourse between members of the women's towns and garrison males is permitted only during periodic Carnival Times.

In Sheri S. Tepper's feminist, post-holocaust novel, *The Gate to Women's Country*, the principal women's community is Marthatown (there are a dozen others). Its main figures are Morgot, the chief medical officer and a Council member; her children, Stavia, Myra, and Jerby; and her old male servitors, Jik and Joshua. The male garrison, which has dwindled gradually in numbers, is led by Stephon, Michael, and Besset, officers who suspect that Marthatown's women possess a secret that might strengthen garrison forces as they prepare for the day when they may conquer women's country.

To ferret out the women's secret, the garrison command enlists Chernon, a young warrior eager to win their approval. He is the son of Morgot's friend Sylvia. Cold-bloodedly, Chernon cultivates the affections of Morgot's daughter, Stavia, in the hope that Stavia can learn and pass on to him the secret of whatever weapon the women possess. Stavia is an unwitting victim of Chernon's guile until, on an expedition to find the limits of habitable territory, a magician, Septimius the Bird, and his two paranormal daughters alert Stavia to Chernon's untrustworthiness.

Before learning the women's secret, however, the garrisons, Chernon among them, decimate one another in one of the periodic wars women arrange to keep down the number of violent men. The men never discover that the "weaker" sex, under Morgot's auspices as medical officer, have been inoculating Marthatown's girls with contraceptives and that the fathers of Marthatown's children are not the garrison's warriors, as the warriors believe, but are Marthatown's seemingly innocuous, usually nonviolent male servitors. The garrison warriors had boasted, amid their carouses and macho displays, of how well Marthatown's women fed, clothed, and furnished them with sex and sons as recruits. They failed to comprehend why their numbers have been dwindling and that the women have always controlled their own as well as the warriors' destinies. Garrison males never understand how subtly and effectively they have been deceived in the name of women's reverence for life and love.

Analysis

A native Coloradan who began writing following her retirement from another career in 1986, Sheri S. Tepper has produced an impressive body of high-quality science-fiction and fantasy novels. Like *The Gate to Women's Country*, *After Long Silence* (1987), *Grass* (1989)—a Hugo nominee and a Notable Book named by *The New York Times*—and *Raising the Stones* (1990), the novels have won critical praise for their taut plotting and imaginative creations both of otherworldly locales and of plausible characters. Equally important, her novels have been commended for their deft, judicious explorations of relationships between the sexes, for observations on miscommunication between the sexes, and for drawing recognizable distinctions between widely prevalent male and female values.

In *The Gate to Women's Country*, for example, the male warrior values of Stephon, Michael, and Chernon contrast sharply with the feminine values of Morgot and Stavia—indeed, with the values of nearly all of Marthatown's women. By her careful characterizations, Tepper makes sensible allowance for the vitally important exceptions. For example, Morgot's male servitors, Jik and Joshua, like most of Marthatown's handful of males, are comforting figures, warmly paternal, nonviolent, secure, and wise, though when necessary they are lethal defenders and, like the women, better fighters than men of the garrison. Similarly,

Septimius the Bird, the itinerant magician who eventually settles in Marthatown, is drawn as bright, articulate, shrewd, discerning, caring, and trustworthy.

Conversely, not all of Tepper's women are models of abstract bourgeois virtue. Marthatown's girls and their mothers show lusty interest in sex aside from the permissible revels of Carnival Time, and whores and wayward youngsters are always busy in the warriors' Houses of Assignation. Tepper's strong and admirable concentration on Marthatown's women never degenerates into facile male-bashing. Nevertheless, by means of both her dialogue and her descriptions, Tepper consistently deplores the sacrifices required of women to maintain their masked dominance. She dramatically emphasizes this theme by having Morgot, Stavia, and other female characters reenact each year Marthatown's theatrical version of the ancient Greek legend of Iphigenia. Over the years, nearly all of Marthatown's abler girls and mothers are expected to speak their prescribed roles in the play, an instructive rite of passage for girls approaching maturity and a grimly reflective exercise for Marthatown's matrons. Iphigenia was the daughter of the Greek warrior hero, Agamemnon. When Agamemnon and his fleet were delayed by contrary winds on their way to join the Trojan War, Agamemnon's lord informed him that the goddess Artemis demanded the sacrifice of Iphigenia. Reluctantly and despite his wife's protestations, Agamemnon agreed to the sacrifice, and beautiful young Iphigenia consented to die for the glory of Greece. In women's country, ostensibly at the mercy of its male garrisons, only brains and resilient character, as Tepper makes manifest in her novel, could forestall or circumvent such realities.

—*Mary E. Virginia*

The Godhead Trilogy

God's two-mile-long body falls into the Atlantic Ocean, raising a multitude of questions, from whether he is is really dead to what happens next

Author: James Morrow (1947-   )
Genre: Fantasy—Magical Realism
Type of work: Novel
Time of plot: 1992-2025
Location: Earth
First published: *Towing Jehovah* (1994), *Blameless in Abaddon* (1996), and *The Eternal Footman* (1999)

The Story

In *Towing Jehovah*, winner of the prestigious World Fantasy Award, the body of God falls from Heaven and lands in the Atlantic Ocean. Afterward, the Vatican calls on disgraced oil tanker captain Anthony Van Horne to tow his body to a final resting place in the Arctic. Thomas Ockham, a Jesuit priest interested in cosmology, accompanies Van Horne on the voyage in order to protect the Vatican's interests. Both are searching for something: Keith seeks redemption for his role in the colossal oil spill that decimated Matagorda Bay, and Thomas wishes to discover the answer to the question, "Why did God die?" While they fail to transport God's body in time to preserve his brain activity, they overcome obstacles including Cassie Fowler, a militant atheist who believes the feminist cause is threatened by the body's very existence; a deranged World War II re-enactment society bent on destroying his corpse; and a side trip to a pagan island in order to put God's body—the Corpus Dei—to rest in an iceberg.

Blameless in Abaddon begins as an arctic earthquake reveals God's dead body to the world and the Vatican arranges to hook it up to machines in order to preserve the newly discovered signs of activity in his brain. The Corpus Dei, sold to the Baptists, becomes the main attraction in a religious theme park in Orlando. Martin Candle's visit to the park fails to cure his cancer, his wife dies, and suddenly this contemporary Job decides to put God on trial for crimes against humanity. Presenting testimony ranging from natural disasters to existential evil, Martin hopes to hold God accountable for the pervasive and unending torment visited upon humanity. In the end, the World Court finds God not guilty, and Martin destroys the life-support machines sustaining God's body.

No longer maintained by machines or preserved by ice, the Corpus Dei explodes piece by piece, until only its head remains. God's skull goes into orbit above the Western Hemisphere, and in its shadow a new plague is visited upon humanity. *The Eternal Footman* chronicles the existential sickness, referred to as "death awareness," and explains that victims are visited by a personification of death called a fetch. Confronted by their mortality, most victims succumb to this "abulic plague" by losing their will to live. Nora Burkhart sets out to save her son Kevin from this deadly disease.

Analysis

James Morrow's satirical trilogy presents the premise of the physical death of God with compassion, intellect, and scathing wit. Thomas Ockham, named by Morrow for the scientist who theorized that simple explanations are to be preferred over complex ones, believes that the Heavenly Father killed himself in order to allow humanity to grow up. According to Thomas, "A father's ultimate obligation is to stop being a father." Stifled by mysticism, constrained by a complex yet irrational belief system, people cannot grow and learn as individuals until they are free. "In the post-theistic age, let Christianity become merely kindness, salvation transmute into art, truth defer to knowledge, and faith embrace a vibrant doubt." Morrow dramatizes strong relationships among his characters, particularly among parents and children, and in his trilogy God's death is the ultimate gift of love to his children.

Existential pain takes center stage in *Blameless in Abaddon*, as Martin presents evidence of plane crashes, incurable diseases, murders, and natural disasters in his case against God. Theodicy, reconciling God's goodness with the world's evils, provides an excellent backdrop for the question of God's culpability in the matter of human suffering. Morrow said in an interview that "the harder you try to acquit God of complicity in human suffering, the closer you come to trivializing that suffering."

In *The Eternal Footman*, Morrow observes that fear of death prevents people from living life to the fullest. In a world without God influencing people's behavior, the next step in realizing humanity's potential is addressing the paralyzing obsession with mortality. Kevin's fetch explains: "The invention of death made possible the individual, in all its astonishing variety. Death broke life free of immortality's chains."

—*Michael-Anne Rubenstien*

Good News from Outer Space

> When two tabloid journalists investigate an alien invasion and a televangelist who preaches the advent of a New Age, they find themselves involved in a bizarre series of interconnected events

Author: John Kessel (1950-   )
Genre: Science fiction—invasion story
Type of work: Novel
Time of plot: 1999, with a scene in April, 2000
Location: The United States
First published: 1989

The Story

Three chapters of *Good News from Outer Space* were published independently as short stories in 1987 and 1988, but they were rewritten extensively and now contribute to the novel's intricate plot, a satire about religion, politics, and the mass media in 1990's America. The main characters are Lucy, a lawyer; her husband George, a reporter at a tabloid news television program; and Richard, George's editor. Lucy is the most sympathetic character, though George learns kindness and consideration, and Richard's manic personality has its own appeal.

George becomes interested in two sinister developments: the increasing popularity of televangelist Jimmy-Don Gilray and a growing mass hysteria that malicious aliens have invaded the country. He grows obsessed with the latter reports and even abandons Lucy to track down the aliens.

Lucy naturally is upset, and when Richard visits her, showing no concern for George but demanding to know what story he is pursuing, she recklessly attacks him. She then hides from the law by taking refuge with some feminist bioterrorists who plan to spread a plague that will make men mentally and emotionally more like women.

Richard, always reckless himself, decides to scoop George's televangelism article by becoming a publicist for the Reverend Gilray. Gilray rightfully suspects Richard of being a spy but is intrigued enough to hire him. Ironically and amusingly, Richard himself becomes such a superstar in his new role that the televangelist proclaims Richard to be a prophet.

George's travels across the country reveal that humanlike aliens are spreading fear and dismay with their bizarre behavior, yet they always elude him. He decides that Gilray is allied with the aliens and decides to assassinate him. Returning to Raleigh, North Carolina, the site of Gilray's headquarters, he finds millions of pilgrims there. Starving and desperate, these believers wait for Gilray's promised event—the appearance of Jesus Christ in a spaceship on the eve of the millennium. During these activities, Lucy is arrested and imprisoned. She escapes, only to be captured by Gilray, who declares her as his destined bride for the New Age. In a brief and bitter meeting with George, she orders him to undertake a mysterious mission. The item he secretly brings to her contains the bioterrorists' potion to feminize men.

When December 31, 1999, arrives, aliens infiltrate Gilray's headquarters, bewildering everyone by appearing as the different main characters. Gilray meets one disguised as Lucy, is frightened when it tries to seduce him, and flees. Lucy meets an alien appearing as Gilray and tries to persuade it to drink the potion, mixed into a glass of wine, but it knows better. When George leaps out of a closet to surprise them, he accidentally shoots her. At this point the alien offers to tell George all the answers he has dreamed of finding and has pursued for so long, but George chooses to ignore the alien so that he can save Lucy's life. In his relief, afterward, he drinks the doctored wine. Meanwhile, Richard and Gilray abandon their desperate followers, who realize that there will be no Second Coming.

After the unfolding of this madcap climax, the final chapter, set the following spring, reveals that although America has been shaken by Gilray's reign and revolt, some normality is restored. George acts more tenderly toward Lucy. They renew their love and turn to raising their own food. Perhaps the aliens are still on the loose, but friendship and honesty matter more, in the end, than the mystery of alien deceptions.

Analysis

John Kessel has a gift for comic invention. The humor, mysteries, and chills of the story begin on the first page. When George is introduced, readers realize that the novel will be darkly whimsical because the reporter, like the subject of a typical tabloid tale, recently has been revived from the dead. Through his minor characters and scenes of an unraveling culture, Kessel targets the ignorance and sloth underlying the popularity of tabloid journalism in modern America. The success of Gilray's preachings and the demoniac magnetism of Richard's charisma reveal Kessel's distaste for the fear mongering and greed of televangelism.

Kessel's satirical tone is effectively funny and grim, and his novel takes potshots at everything from the social conditions of modern America to earlier science fiction. The alien invasion suggests a number of familiar plots, beginning with H. G. Wells's *The War of the Worlds* (1898) and including Arthur C. Clarke's *Childhood's End* (1953) and Jack Finney's *The Body Snatchers* (1955), but Kessel coyly declines to explain the motive behind the invasion, unlike these classic texts. The invasion story by its nature conveys and expresses paranoia, which Kessel increases by portraying aliens who deceive, frighten, and abuse ordinary Americans for no apparent reasons other than curiosity and *Schadenfreude*, the joy in others' misfortunes. This disinclination to explain everything operates throughout the novel; for example, has George actually been "feminized," or has he learned to value his wife's love?

Science fiction traditionally presents a problem that humans solve, in the process becoming more enlightened and heroic. Kessel alludes to recent paradigms such as quantum theory, which reveal the search for complete knowledge to be in vain, even as he casts doubt on many recent human endeavors. The traditional figure of the noble private investigator who discovers inner truths is likewise parodied when Richard, wondering where George has gone, puts a detective on his tail. The comedy of errors becomes horrific when readers realize that the detective is a crazy paranoiac who thinks she has been commissioned to assassinate George. Her mission contributes to the humor and suspense.

Good News from Outer Space was nominated for the Nebula Award and the John W. Campbell Memorial Award. It has been translated into several languages.

—*Fiona Kelleghan*

Gravity's Rainbow

Paranoia increases and apocalypse nears as characters seek the source of a rocket during World War II

Author: Thomas Pynchon (1937-   )
Genre: Science fiction—alternative history
Type of work: Novel
Time of plot: 1944-1945
Location: Europe
First published: 1973

The Story

Although *Gravity's Rainbow* is often considered a culmination of his earlier novel, *The Crying of Lot 49* (1966), Thomas Pynchon created his magnum opus with this book. It is particularly difficult to categorize a work of this scope in any specific genre because it has been called revisionist history, apocalyptic, picaresque, a Grail quest, satire, social criticism, Magical Realism, and encyclopedic narrative, among others. It does, however, fall under the broad parameters of science fiction given its preoccupation with machinery—the fact that the rocket becomes the protagonist of the work and that the multiple technological crises presented overshadow or eliminate human emotions and human worth. Although it was nominated for a Pulitzer Prize, and many critics believed it was the best novel of that or any year, the committee rejected the book as being "obscure and obscene."

With a circuitous romp through subplots, minor characters who appear and disappear without warning, technological and mathematical jargon, and world-class wordplay, Pynchon introduces the reader to a revised history of the latter days of World War II in Europe. In fact, not until at least one-third of the way into this massive tome does it become evident that the protagonist is Tyrone Slothrop, an American who has been assigned to the experimental whims of Pavlovian scientists who are attempting to prove a correlation between Slothrop's sexual encounters and the striking zone of the German A-4 rocket.

Paranoia is an integral part of Slothrop's personality, and he grows increasingly more paranoid as the experiments intensify and threaten imminent bodily harm. He is permitted a holiday, although it is under supervision. While staying at a resort in the south of France, where he has a strange encounter with his "supervisor," Katje Borgesius, and a trained octopus, Slothrop realizes that he can never outwit surveillance by The Firm until he physically escapes. He runs for his life and vanishes into the Zone, the interior of war-torn, mainland Europe. It is his näive assumption that if he can locate the source of the rocket and the mysterious propellant, S-Gerat, he can purchase his freedom with the information.

In picaresque fashion, Slothrop slides into and out of life-threatening situations while encountering scores of rogues, renegades, and reprobates. Because of his proclivity for each, the encounters involve sexual antics, drug deals, hallucinations, disguises, extraordinary heroics, and increasing paranoia.

While in the Zone and using changes in identity and costume, Slothrop is forced to live by his wits, surviving off the land and the kindness of strangers—usually female. With a false identification card, he slips across border checkpoints as the actor Max Schlepzig; he cohabits in a bombed-out building with an apprentice witch, Geli Tripping; he escapes his pursuers in a cream-pie-laden hot-air balloon; he stows away on an orgiastic ship of fools going nowhere; he dons a cape and a Viking helmet to become Rocketman and smuggles hashish out of the occupied Zone; and he accepts the role of Liberator Pig God in an ancient village ritual and escapes in the pig's costume. Appropriately, he spends the majority of his time as Rocketman, the merger of the rocket and the man, and as the pig, having started his peripatetic quest as a guinea pig.

Eventually, through the multiple changes in identity, Slothrop loses his own, as well as any interest in pursuit of the rocket. As with many of the minor characters, he simply vanishes from the novel's pages, and the reader is left to fill in the blanks. The story does not end there, however, for others also seek the rocket and the propellant. Only one man has the answers as well as the rocket: Captain Blicero knows that the mysterious propellant, S-Gerat, is really a human being. He methodically places his lover on board the rocket, begins the countdown, and incinerates himself in the afterburn.

Analysis

It is virtually impossible to treat the scope of this novel in a short summary. The book should be read slowly, considered, digested, and then read again. As with any work of this magnitude, critical reception has been polarized: One either loves the book or hates it, but few claim to understand it completely. The parameters of Pynchon's knowledge are seemingly boundless and often beyond the grasp of the average reader, but that should not deter the effort. Whether one understands the book completely or not, it is a labyrinth of literary surprises, offering something for everyone who reads it.

Gravity's Rainbow juxtaposes the apocalyptic and the comic. Because the reader knows the time frame and the historical outcome of World War II, he or she should also be aware that the work is fiction. Because of Pynchon's attention to historical detail and his use of real names throughout the work, the reader cannot help but question the truth of the extant version of history. Although it is apocalyptic in tone, the work predicts not the destruction of the world but the destruction and subsequent rebuilding of culture by revealing how human and machine essentially have become one and how the machine has gained preeminence. Although it addresses such issues as war, genocide, mental illness, and sexual depravity, *Gravity's Rainbow* is not entirely pessimistic, for Pynchon admits glimmers of a brighter tomorrow.

An underlying theme present in this work and others by Pynchon is entropy, the theory that the world is winding down and depleting its own energy. Entropy, based on Isaac Newton's second law of thermodynamics, is best represented by Slothrop, who is too lazy to maintain his self-appointed quest and too prone to distraction to notice the obvious clues that are strewn in his path. For Slothrop, seeking information is entirely too much trouble.

Whether one accepts Pynchon's premise or understands his encyclopedic scope is irrelevant. *Gravity's Rainbow* should be devoured like the literary smorgasbord it is.

—*Joyce Duncan*

Gulliver's Travels

Lemuel Gulliver goes on a series of sea voyages and has a variety of encounters in which his psychic deterioration as a human being is revealed

Author: Jonathan Swift (1667-1745)
Genre: Fantasy—cultural exploration
Type of work: Novel
Time of plot: 1699-1715
Location: Various island communities
First published: 1726

The Story

Gulliver's Travels, as the book is now known, first appeared anonymously. Capitalizing on the lively interest in voyages at the time, Jonathan Swift called it *Travels into Several Remote Nations of the World* and ascribed it to "Lemuel Gulliver, First a Surgeon, and then a Captain of Several Ships." Swift published the book anonymously partly because of the occasional scatological references but more pressingly because of the thinly veiled political satire of England's powerful first prime minister, Whig party leader Sir Robert Walpole, whom Swift detested and whom contemporaries would have immediately recognized in the ridiculous figure of the tightrope dancer, Flimnap, the treasurer of Lilliput, in part 1.

The first two parts of *Gulliver's Travels* form a nicely balanced pair. In Lilliput, where Gulliver first is shipwrecked, he is twelve times as tall as the diminutive local inhabitants. Everything is kept to this scale except for their senseless warring and hypocrisy, which are out of all proportion to their size and therefore seem the more alarming; one, illogically perhaps, expects decent conduct from tiny people. Flimnap, however, so inflated is his ego, accuses Gulliver of having an affair with his six-inch-tall wife.

On the second island on which Gulliver is marooned, the natives are twelve times as tall as he is. He displays all the moral blindness of the Lilliputians in his dealings with the reasonable and generous Brobdingnagians. Gulliver, from his own over-inflated notion of his six-foot self, is offended that the local women do not cover themselves when undressing in front of him. Evidently, like Flimnap in part 1, Gulliver believes that he is at least their equal. After two years, Gulliver escapes to sea and returns to England.

Gulliver's third voyage, actually written by Swift after the fourth, is the most scattered in its focus. It is largely political and for this reason is usually not as well received by critics. Gulliver travels to Laputa and encounters scientists and intellectuals whose work is, for the pragmatic parish priest in Swift, altogether too far removed from real life. Attempting to distill sunlight from cucumbers is one of their projects. The Laputan Projectors, in their flying island, tyrannize the inhabitants of Balnibarbi and waste this fertile land. Visiting nearby Luggnagg, Gulliver for a moment envies the Struldbrugs, who live forever, though he quickly changes his mind when he discovers that the immortals do age in the normal way.

His fourth voyage, to the land of the Houyhnhnms (named after the whinnying sound horses make), is the climax of Gulliver's personal regression. That he cannot approach the level of rationality of the equine race who are in control drives him insane. His much closer resemblance to the bestial, greedy, bellicose, and irrational Yahoos, who are the other native inhabitants, depresses him severely. Viewing him as a possible subversive, the Houyhnhnms invite him to leave their rational world. Finally home again in England, he prefers the stable to his home and can no longer tolerate the company of other humans. Feeling oneself superior to the entire human race, as Gulliver does, is by most definitions a position of insane pride.

Analysis

As a product of an age that celebrated reason and was then apt to think of life as a comedy, *Gulliver's Travels*, it should not go unsaid, is frequently funny. As an Irishman born in Dublin, Dean Swift of St. Patrick's Episcopal Cathedral was inclined to blame the Whig administration in London for Ireland's social ills. Satire is the outsider's mode, and Swift here uses and makes fun of the popular, first-person, sea voyage account. William Dampier's books of the late seventeenth century had been extremely successful in establishing the genre. Daniel Defoe had published the successful *Robinson Crusoe* in 1719, seven years before Swift's book appeared. Swift supported Irish aspirations for freedom from English domination and published his equally incendiary *The Drapier's Letters* anonymously in 1724. The Anglican clergyman in him also appreciated that some moral rearmament must accompany any political solution. It is this moral dimension, this focus on humankind's universal propensity to delude itself, that is the main appeal of the work for subsequent generations of readers, for whom the machinations of eighteenth century Westminster politicians mean very little.

Swift deliberately sets up Gulliver's voyages in a realistic voyage framework. He provides maps of the voyages, complete with decorative, tiny, spouting whale drawings just like real maps. He also mixes actual places (Japan and Sumatra) with the imaginary.

Gulliver's level of pride is fairly stable in part 1, where he has the physical and moral advantage over the tiny Lilliputians. In part 2, however, he reveals himself to be suffering from their destructive, hubristic attitude. Having boasted of the political and social situation in England, and then having offered the king of Brobdingnag gunpowder, Gulliver is roundly deflated by that monarch, who informs him that he must represent "the most pernicious race of little odious vermin nature ever suffered to crawl upon the surface of the earth." In part 3, Gulliver's pride expands even further when for an instant he envies the Struldbrugs' immortality. His normal high level of this vice, the most damning in the Christian scheme of things, returns in part 4, where he resents being treated like a Yahoo and envies the superrational Houyhnhnms.

Humankind exists, Swift suggests, between the animal world of the Yahoos and the rational world of the Houyhnhnms. Gulliver's recourse to living in the stable with his horses on his return to England is hardly a solution. To be out of step with the entire human race is to be insane; some kind of balance, however precarious, is Swift's proposal in this, his only trip into the world of fantasy voyages.

—Archibald E. Irwin

The Handmaid's Tale

Offred, a legal concubine in a totalitarian state, tells the story of her experiences and the adjustments she makes to survive

Author: Margaret Atwood (1939-   )
Genre: Science fiction—feminist
Type of work: Novel
Time of plot: The early twenty-first century
Location: Gilead, in what was once the United States
First published: 1985

The Story

In the late 1980's, an ultraconservative religious group toppled the U.S. government and established a totalitarian regime called Gilead. The leadership is strictly Christian in nature and ruthlessly fascist in practice. Using the former society's plummeting birth rates as an excuse, the Gilead leaders force women into restricted roles in society, with little freedom or power. Couples in the upper classes who are without children are assigned Handmaids, who essentially are legal concubines intended to bear their hosts' children. These Handmaids are fertile women who were politically unsafe, divorced, or in second marriages.

The narrator is a Handmaid assigned to the family of a high-ranking commander. She loses her identity and original family, and she is renamed "of Fred" (the commander's first name), or Offred. Offred is cared for by the family in exchange for having sex with the commander. In an elaborate ceremony required by the society, Offred lies between the legs of Fred's wife during the act, making her resemble a substitute womb for the wife. This ritual enacts a literal translation of the Old Testament, in which Rachel says to Jacob, "Behold my maid Bilhah, go in unto her; and she shall bear upon my knees, that I may also have children by her" (Genesis 30:1-3).

Even this tightly controlled society has hidden rebellions. The commander arranges clandestine meetings with Offred. They talk and play Scrabble. Such relationships of Handmaids and their hosts are forbidden, as Handmaids are meant solely for procreation. Offred's walking partner, Ofglen, reveals another rebellion, a resistance group called Mayday, of which she is a member.

The commander's wife arranges for Offred to have an affair with Nick, the chauffeur, so that she might become pregnant even if the commander is sterile. Offred begins to fall in love with Nick and loses all desire for the rebellion encouraged by her friends in Mayday.

Offred's tenuous situation becomes more precarious when the commander's wife learns of Offred's secret meetings with the commander. Ofglen is discovered to be part of Mayday and is killed. Offred's story ends in a dramatic climax. The black death van of Gilead arrives at the house to take Offred. At that moment, it is unclear why the van came for her. To her surprise and dismay, Nick appears at her door with the military men and hands her over. As she passes him, he whispers in her ear to go with them because they are from Mayday and will take her outside Gilead. Offred goes into the van. Her ultimate fate, whether betrayal or salvation, is not revealed.

The final chapter of the novel is an epilogue set two hundred years after the story of Offred. The keynote speaker at a symposium on Gileadean studies is a professor who has been studying a document called "The Handmaid's Tale." He makes a few comments on the possible au-

Margaret Atwood. (© Washington Post; reprinted by permission of the D.C. Public Library)

thenticity of this document, which was discovered shortly after the regime of Gilead fell. It remains unclear whether Offred escaped safely or, instead, that only her story survived.

Analysis

The epilogue creates an interesting effect on building a possible future on top of a possible future. Margaret Atwood satirizes at two levels— modern society as a whole in the main story and the world of academia in the epilogue. Reminiscent of George Orwell, Atwood criticizes modern society by showing the horrible extent to which many current problems could advance. Like Orwell, Atwood presents criticism at the most obvious, political, level. She especially satirizes the workings of nations that impose strict control over their citizens.

Atwood has said that she borrowed every aspect of Gileadean oppression from something similar in known history. Some familiar tactics employed by Gilead include using religion to control people for the government's purposes; being constantly at war, as in Orwell's *Nineteen Eighty-Four* (1949), to keep people quiet in the name of national security (there are numerous hints that the war may be staged); and emphasizing the need for children and women's role as childbearers to keep women in limited roles. The novel focuses on the oppression of women, and it is commonly cited in the context of feminist criticism. Although men of lower classes also are shown to be limited in their choices, clearly the worst victims of the Gileadean regime are women. Even women higher up in the hierarchy, such as Aunts (who train the Handmaids) and Wives, are often as miserable as the others.

One of the most insidious tactics used to control Gilead's citizens, especially women, involves control over language. Atwood often addresses the role of language in human lives. In *The Handmaid's Tale*, language symbolizes power. All use of language is regulated by the regime. Handmaids are not allowed to write, read, or even carry on a free conversation. Only certain prescripted greetings are allowed, and even the signs on stores are pictorial symbols.

Against these kinds of limits, Offred's rebellion comes in strange forms, such as playing illicit games of Scrabble, speaking freely with her walking partner, and ultimately leaving behind a subversive record of her experiences for future scholars to discover. These rebellions are powerful because they involve the uninhibited use of language. Her name is symbolic of Offred's semantic rebellion. It could be read as "of Fred," or it could be "off-red," suggesting that she is not fully integrated into the role of the red-clad Handmaids.

The true effect of Offred's final document is uncertain, pointing to the ambiguous nature of language. Subversive words are powerful in this context but also problematic, because they are always subject to interpretation. In the epilogue to the novel, the professor working on Offred's story finds little evidence to support her statements and questions their authenticity. In a chatty, joking tone, he talks in general about Gilead and points to some discrepancies between the story and his own historical findings. The contrast between Offred's heartrending, urgent story and this skeptical, analytical conversation among scholars may present pain and frustration to the reader. Atwood frustrates her readers purposefully to make some pointed remarks about the world of academia.

—Susan Hwang

The Helliconia Trilogy

On Helliconia, the chief planet of a binary system, seasons are centuries long and winters are so severe that survivors must rediscover civilization as the planet emerges from its glacial ages

Author: Brian W. Aldiss (1925-   )
Genre: Science fiction—alien civilization
Type of work: Novels
Time of plot: Indeterminate future relative to Earth
First published: *Helliconia Spring* (1982), *Helliconia Summer* (1983), and *Helliconia Winter* (1985)

The Story

The first section of *Helliconia Spring* tells the story of Yuli, who finds an underworld where a perverted religion—the virtual worship of darkness—holds sway. He works his way back to the world of day and founds a city called Oldorando. There, as the planet emerges slowly from its centuries-long winter, the tribes of the equatorial continent emerge from their hiding places. They begin to do battle, not only for survival but also to dispute possession of the planet with the ferocious phagors. In the central city, all the appurtenances of civilization—love, trade, coinage, history, and science—are being rediscovered. Yuli's descendants hail him because he rejected his faith in favor of his people.

Other characters emerge in this episodic novel, which spans centuries. Helliconia eventually undergoes still another violent change as winter yields to a triumphant spring. Above the planet, five thousand astronauts from Earth orbit the planet in space station *Avernus*. They are prohibited from intervening in the affairs of Helliconia because some aspect of its atmosphere is poisonous to humans. They relay the day-to-day activities of Helliconia back to Earth, where Helliconian events have become a space opera on the "Eductainment Channel."

Helliconia Summer covers a time span of only a few months. Its plot events center on the king, Borlien, and his queen, MyrdemInggala. Borlien, for political reasons, decides to divorce his queen and marry the princess of ancient Oldorando. The scene shifts rapidly from continent to continent until an Avernian Earthman, Billy Xiao Pin, attempts to intervene in the affairs of Helliconia, with predictably tragic and fatal results.

In *Helliconia Winter,* as Helliconia moves away from its larger sun, auguries of winter begin to haunt the planet. Snow falls, crops fail, and tyranny tightens under the sway of the Oligarch. On Helliconia, Luterin Shokerandt begins a pilgrimage of terror to the arctic regions of the planet. He enters the Great Wheel of Kharnabhar, where prisoners are supposed to row their planet back to light. This action has become almost a religious ritual, and all the trappings of the Darkness religion, first glimpsed in *Helliconia Spring,* are given new meaning. Coupled with the main story is the continuing saga of the observer space station, *Avernus,* and events on post-apocalyptic Earth that parallel those on Helliconia, separated by 1,500 light-years of time.

Analysis

Little question exists that the Helliconia Trilogy is Brian Aldiss's epic masterpiece and one of the masterpieces of science fiction. The planet and binary sun system Aldiss created is one of the most complex ever to spring from the pages of science fiction. It is also one of the most human—and most humane—as well as the most germane. Readers seem to share the fascination with the planet that spurs the activities of the observers on *Avernus.* They can readily understand how Earth dwellers are virtually hypnotized by the long-running epic saga of Helliconia.

The Helliconia Trilogy is far more than a science-fiction epic. It is a fully fleshed artistic creation in which Aldiss wishes not only to tell a series of loosely connected stores, both epic and miniature, but also to relate a parable about humanity's ability to ignore "reality" and revel in "eductainment." The three Helliconia novels are as much about Earth and its ways of approaching reality, its methods of ignoring the "shadow" side of itself, its headlong flight from unpleasantness, and its ability to revel in distancing itself from problems as it is about the multifaceted panorama of the Great Year and its effects on Helliconia.

Aldiss appears to ask if people could become so fascinated by distant drama, made unreal by distance and time, that they could fail to see the approaching apocalypse. Seeming to echo German physicist Werner Heisenberg, he asks if the very act of observing changes both the observer and the observed. Are the people of Earth changed by their ages-long observation of Helliconia? Can the five thousand exiled residents of *Avernus* remain unchanged because they can only observe but never interfere? What about the Helliconians themselves, unaware that they have provided "eductainment" to millions on a faraway planet? Is their climate so inexorable that change is forced upon them, albeit with glacial slowness?

Aldiss has returned in this trilogy to one of his most elemental themes, the question of change. The theme of awareness of change (or lack of awareness) pervades many of his novels and short stories, and he frequently explores the effects of change or the results of stasis. Rarely are these questions asked without some relevance to art. In these novels, the "art" is Helliconia itself as well as the interstellar space opera it has engendered.

Perhaps the most telling section of this remarkable series of novels occurs toward the end of *Helliconia Winter*, in one of the italicized passages that concern Earth or *Avernus* rather than Helliconia. More than seven thousand Earth years have passed since the common era began, yet the memory of Helliconia still haunts the survivors of the apocalypse, and a new glacial age brought about by the overuse of fossil fuels stalks them. One character then advances the Gaia hypothesis: Earth itself may possess life, and humankind has to learn not to try to possess Earth or to ignore its needs.

Another major question raised by Aldiss is the nature of the ferocious phagors. Reminiscent of demoniac creatures, nightmarish minotaurs, and other hateful and hated monsters, they may provide some hideous balance with the humans they ceaselessly wage war against. Aldiss seems to ask if they are in some way the same as humans, merely in another guise or form.

Multiple meanings, all of them intended and many of them ironic, are found in the name of the planet Helliconia. The name draws upon the words halcyon, helix, and helios, as well as the flower helliconia itself. All give some hints of how Aldiss works: He provides questions rather than answers, and he suggests, hints, or alludes rather than being simplistic. Aldiss would be the first to insist that he is not in the business of writing to provide answers. He might maintain that there are no definitive answers to the questions he raises, that in fact the position of the artist is simply to question, to require the reader to think and to probe, not merely to be entertained. His requirement of careful thought is perhaps the best single reason to ponder—and be entertained by—the Helliconia Trilogy.

—*Willis E. McNelly*

Her Smoke Rose Up Forever

Stories of disease, love, sexuality, death, and alien contact illustrating human and alien biology and alienation both across and within species

Author: James Tiptree, Jr. (Alice Hastings Bradley Sheldon, 1915-1987)
Genre: Science fiction—alien civilization
Type of work: Stories
Time of plot: Various times in the future
Location: Various locations on Earth and planets throughout the galaxy
First published: 1990

The Story

This collection of eighteen stories, published three years after her death, represents the best of James Tiptree, Jr.'s short fiction. The collection, subtitled *The Great Years of James Tiptree, Jr.*, was edited by James Turner and contains stories originally published between 1969 and 1981. Under the pen name of James Tiptree, Jr.—taken from the label of a marmalade jar—Alice Sheldon began publishing science fiction in 1968. She earned critical acclaim, and interest rose in the mystery of her identity, which was not revealed until 1977.

All the stories in this collection are about death as an inextricable part of the striving and dreams of living beings. In the title story, "Her Smoke Rose Up Forever" (1974), enigmatic alien visitors somehow cause moments of love, violence, and loss in the life of one man to be relived on the cinders of a dead Earth. In "Slow Music" (1980), two of the last people on Earth are betrayed by their love to follow the rest of humanity into a mysterious "River" of alien, bodiless sentience. In "The Man Who Walked Home" (1972), an experimental subject thrown into the far future "walks" back to the moment of the experiment by sheer willpower, appearing and reappearing on the post-apocalyptic Earth at the point of the civilization-destroying explosion caused by his return. In "The Last Flight of Dr. Ain" (1969), a biologist, in despair at the destruction of a "beautiful woman"—Earth—creates a humanity-destroying plague.

In many of the stories, the sex drive itself is a form of death. In "The Last Afternoon" (1972), a human colony is unable to stop waves of giant sea creatures who thrash ashore to mate in an orgy of sexual destruction. In "Love Is the Plan, the Plan Is Death" (1973), an alien being struggling toward sentience is trapped in a biological life cycle in which the females eat the males. The author also represents the human fascination with alien beings as itself a form of self-destruction. In "A Momentary Taste of Being" (1975), the first interstellar expedition, desperate to find new planets to relieve pressures on an overcrowded Earth, finds that humans are merely sperm for fertilizing the ovum of an unknown life-form.

Tiptree's most famous stories deal with relations between the sexes in which the sexual aggression of men makes them deadly and alien to women. In "Houston, Houston, Do You Read?" (1976), a ship of NASA astronauts is thrown forward in time to an Earth sparsely populated by female survivors, all clones, of a plague that has destroyed humanity's ability to reproduce. The author represents the men as painfully driven by "alpha male" aggression and misogyny. In "The Girl Who Was Plugged In" (1973), a young man falls in love with a literally brainless, beautiful body that is animated by remote control by a woman whose own ugly body makes her a social outcast. In "The Women Men Don't See" (1973), a mother and a daughter leave Earth willingly on a thoroughly alien ship. The mother says to the shocked male narrator, "We survive by ones and twos in the chinks of your world-machine. . . . I'm used to aliens."

Analysis

Tiptree's stories are a distinctive contribution to science fiction. In their settings and the way the plots are established, many of the stories evoke the "Golden Age" of science fiction in the early twentieth century. The author conjures up corrupt galactic empires, distant futures, amazing occurrences, bug-eyed and exotic aliens, and alien worlds with the stroke of a pen. Whereas older science fiction aimed at "amazing stories," Tiptree's work aims at unsettling and idiosyncratic explorations of the psychology and biology of love and death. Like the New Wave writers of the 1960's and 1970's, she uses her settings and plots metaphorically, occasionally experimenting with unusual narrative voices, as in "The Girl Who Was Plugged In," a Hugo Award winner. Unlike many of the New Wave writers, she pursues her themes with an expository directness.

A strand of her work, composed of her most famous stories, can be identified clearly as feminist and therefore related to the feminist science fiction of the 1970's and 1980's. It is easy to read some of her fiction as representing a radical feminism. She consistently portrays the male sex drive as violent, most shockingly perhaps in "The Screwfly Solution" (1977, as Raccoona Sheldon), a Nebula Award winner. In that story, human males sprayed with an alien hormonal "pesticide" kill all women. She evokes visions of women's societies as happily separate from men and of women as severely damaged by men, as in "Houston, Houston, Do You Read" (1977 Hugo Award and 1976 Nebula Award winner) and "Your Faces, O My Sisters! Your Faces Filled with Light!" (1976). She shows male culture as destructive of and contemptuous of women who do not fit male stereotypes of women, as in "With Delicate Mad Hands" (1981). Given all this, it is remarkable that the science-fiction community initially took Tiptree to be a male writer.

As angry and satirical as her representation of male and female differences is, it lacks the drive of most feminist writing to reform and enlighten ideologically. Most of her narrators are male, and woven in with the anger, sharp social satire, and even contempt of their portrayal is a strand of sympathy or understanding. Tiptree tends to present men and women, and all living beings, as trapped in their biology and mortality. "Love Is the Plan, the Plan Is Death" (Nebula Award winner) is perhaps the archetypal Tiptree story in this respect. Dark as her vision is, her fatalism allows space for appreciation of the doomed strivings of the spirit for love and transcendence.

—*D. Barrowman Park*

The Hitchhiker's Guide to the Galaxy Series

Arthur Dent, an ordinary Englishman, is drawn into an extraordinary galactic adventure involving personal danger and revelations about the meaning of life, the universe, and everything

Author: Douglas Adams (1952-2001)
Genre: Science fiction—cultural exploration
Type of work: Novels
Time of plot: Before Earth existed to the end of time
Location: Throughout the universe
First published: *The Hitchhiker's Guide to the Galaxy* (1979), *The Restaurant at the End of the Universe* (1980), *Life, the Universe, and Everything* (1982; with the first two novels as *The Hitchhiker's Trilogy*, 1983), *So Long, and Thanks for All the Fish* (1984; with the first three novels as *The Hitchhiker's Guide to the Galaxy: A Trilogy in Four Parts*, 1986, in Great Britain and as *The Hitchhiker's Quartet*, 1986, in the United States), *The More than Complete Hitchhiker's Guide: Five Stories* (1987; contains the first four novels and a related short story, "Young Zaphod Plays It Safe"), *The Original Hitchhiker Radio Scripts* (1985), and *Mostly Harmless* (1992)

The Story

The Hitchhiker's Guide to the Galaxy series is a unique "trilogy," as it originally was called, in that by 1992 it consisted of five novels and a short story and still had yet to be concluded definitively. It began as a radio series broadcast by the British Broadcasting Company (BBC) beginning in 1978 and ending in 1980. Many fans of the story became acquainted with it through recordings of the old radio shows, the scripts of which were published as *The Original Hitchhiker Radio Scripts*. A television version of the series was broadcast by the BBC in 1981. There are, therefore, three versions of the Guide: radio, television, and print. Although all were written by Douglas Adams, these versions are not altogether consistent with one another. What follows is a summary of the five novels and the short story.

The Hitchhiker's Guide to the Galaxy begins with Arthur Dent, an ordi-

nary young Englishman, waking to find that his home has been scheduled for demolition to allow construction of a new motorway bypass. In
protest, Arthur lies prostrate between the bulldozer and his house. Arthur's friend, Ford Prefect, talks Arthur into giving up his protest (at
least temporarily) and going to the local pub. There, Ford completely
perplexes Arthur by claiming to be an alien and telling him that they
must leave Earth immediately because it is about to be demolished to
make way for an intergalactic bypass.

Thus begins Arthur's adventure. He and Ford, a researcher for and
proud owner of the encyclopedic *Hitchhiker's Guide to the Galaxy*, man-
age to get on board a ship of the Volgon fleet, which has just demolished Earth. They are captured by the Volgons and expelled into the
void of space. Fortunately, they are picked up by Ford's two-headed
cousin, Zaphod Beeblebrox, and his companions, Trillian, an Earth
woman Zaphod recently picked up, and Marvin, a chronically depressed robot. Zaphod's stolen ship, the *Heart of Gold*, is equipped with
the prototype of an "improbability drive," which is what enabled them
to rescue Arthur and Ford.

Zaphod is en route to Magrathea, a legendary planet that once was in
the business of producing custom-made planets to order. After a brush
with two deadly missiles, the travelers land on Magrathea. The planet
seems to be shut down but is not. A new project is under way: the reconstruction of Earth.

As it turns out, Earth actually was a massive computer designed by
advanced aliens from another dimension who took the form of laboratory mice on Earth. Its purpose was to determine the ultimate question
of "life, the universe, and everything." The ultimate answer, the number
forty-two, already had been derived by "Deep Thought," Earth's cybernetic predecessor, but the Volgons destroyed Earth five minutes before
Deep Thought's main program was to be completed and the question
delivered.

Upon discovering that Arthur is human, the mice cancel the order for
another Earth, believing that they can get the answer they seek from an
examination of Arthur's brain. Zaphod's pursuers arrive and are about
to blast him and his companions when Marvin, the depressed robot, accidentally saves them all. The novel comes to a conclusion with the
group back on the *Heart of Gold*, heading for the Restaurant at the End of
the Universe.

The subsequent novels do not take this narrative forward systemati-
cally, although they occasionally present new variations on the theme.
The Restaurant at the End of the Universe begins with the travelers being

pursued by a Volgon fleet. The Volgons have been hired by Zaphod's psychoanalyst, who, it is revealed, arranged to have Earth destroyed. The answer to the riddle of life, the universe, and everything, he feared, would put psychoanalysts out of business, or at least drastically reduce their income.

With the help of one of Zaphod's long-dead ancestors, the travelers escape, but Zaphod disappears from the *Heart of Gold*. He finds himself drawn to a character named Zarniwoop, first experiencing the mind-zapping "total perspective vortex." Zarniwoop wants the *Heart of Gold*. Zaphod manages to escape, and the travelers resume their journey to the restaurant.

After a hearty meal, during which they watch the destruction of the universe, the travelers leave on another stolen ship, one that is pro-grammed to crash into the heart of a nearby sun. Fortunately, the ship has a transporter. Marvin stays behind to work the contraption (never-theless appearing in future novels), and the others are transported off the ship.

Zaphod and Trillian are transported to a further adventure with Zarniwoop. More in line with the plot of the series, Arthur and Ford wind up on a spaceship containing human rejects—cosmeticians, hair-dressers, telephone cleaners, and the like—from a planet called Golga-frincham. Their destination is prehistoric Earth. Once on Earth, Arthur and Ford find mates and settle down.

Life, the Universe, and Everything touches only peripherally on the main themes and plot line of the series. As the novel opens, Arthur and Ford are still on prehistoric Earth, but a time and space anomaly enables them to escape to a modern cricket match being played at Lord's. The universe is saved from disaster, and the fictional origin of cricket is revealed.

So Long, and Thanks for All the Fish is more closely connected to the pri-mary plot of the series. In it, Arthur hitches a ride back to Earth, which somehow has been restored to its former condition, minus dolphins. In typically complicated fashion, Arthur finds Fenchurch, a young woman who also has been profoundly affected by the Earth's (alleged) demoli-tion. The two fall in love, enjoying both mutual attraction and a shared cosmic consciousness. At the conclusion, it is revealed that dolphins saved Earth before departing, leaving the message contained in the book's title. Arthur and Fenchurch remain in a blissful state of uncer-tainty, tempered by love and companionship, as the novel closes.

For readers who like a happy ending, that would have been a good place to end the "trilogy." *Mostly Harmless* begins with Fenchurch already killed in an accident and Arthur adrift in the universe, searching for an Earth-like planet on which to settle. He finds one that is suitable and makes a home for himself. In short order, however, a mysterious daughter appears (and bolts), and Ford appears. Together, he and Arthur must rescue the universe from the new publishers of the *Hitchhiker's Guide to the Galaxy*, who are allowing different dimensions and universes to leak into one another, threatening the little meaning and stability left to the galaxies' inhabitants. The novel ends anticlimactically, allowing the possibility of further adventures.

Analysis

The Hitchhiker's Guide to the Galaxy series is a unique experiment combining humor and science fiction. As humor, it lampoons everything from philosophers, psychoanalysts, and economists to the BBC, American television, and the publishing business. The trilogy also deals in high irony. For example, while the authorities are planning to demolish Arthur's house and coming up with all kinds of morally bankrupt reasons for doing so, they are about to have their habitat demolished, for equally vacuous reasons. Likewise, the rejects from Golgafrincham are portrayed as inept, useless idiots, but they survive while their fellow Golgafrinchams are wiped out by a plague contracted as a result of a dirty telephone.

As science fiction, the series creates a universe that becomes real to readers, although, again ironically, it is one in which reality is elusive, conditions constantly shift, and the meaning of life may be completely unknowable. Douglas Adams's universe is an existential one in which there is no knowable godhead to supply authoritative guidance and morals are relative. In the fourth novel, Adams offers love as an answer, but it is not a dominant theme in the work. As in Voltaire's *Candide* (1759), readers might draw the lesson that one should simply mind his or her own business, but Arthur is not allowed to do that. Trouble finds him, whether he is looking for it or not. Thus, Adams gives urgency to the questions he raises, though he gives no answers.

There is, in addition, an occasional environmental theme, as in the story "Young Zaphod Plays It Safe." As might be expected, no such crusade could long be sustained in this work, because environmentalists, like everyone else, must be lampooned. Their cause rests on the same flimsy philosophical foundations as all human ideals and principles.

—*Ira Smolensky*

The Hobbit

Bilbo Baggins, a hobbit, unwillingly accompanies the wizard Gandalf and thirteen dwarves on a quest for the treasure of the dragon Smaug

Author: J(ohn) R(onald) R(euel) Tolkien (1892-1973)
Genre: Fantasy—heroic fantasy
Type of work: Novel
Time of plot: The Third Age
Location: Middle-earth, an imaginary land
First published: 1937 (2d ed., 1951; 3d ed., 1966)

The Story

Although J. R. R. Tolkien drew extensively from northern European myths in developing various inhabitants of his imaginary world, Middle-earth, *The Hobbit* (subtitled *Or, There and Back Again*) focuses on a new race of beings he created. His hobbit hero Bilbo Baggins likes the snug comforts of home with no adventures to interrupt his ordinary life. The wizard Gandalf draws Bilbo out of this sheltered and complacent life by sending him on an adventure—a quest with the dwarf Thorin and his twelve companions to recover the treasure that the dragon Smaug stole. Gandalf employs Bilbo as the dwarves' "burglar," engaging him against his will to steal back Smaug's hoard.

As the dwarves journey toward Smaug's lair in the Lonely Mountain, Bilbo learns to live up to Gandalf's expectations. He fails at first when he unsuccessfully tries to pick a troll's pocket, and Gandalf has to rescue the group. When they are captured again, this time by goblins, Bilbo is separated from his companions and must rescue himself. He finds a magic ring that makes the wearer invisible and uses it to escape first from Gollum, a threatening creature he encounters, and then from the goblins. He rejoins the dwarves and Gandalf, who have also escaped. Wolves (called "wargs") and goblins attack again, but the group is finally rescued by eagles and aided by Beorn, a man who can transform himself into a bear.

After Gandalf leaves the dwarves at the entrance to the forest of Mirkwood to pursue his own errand, Bilbo begins to lead the group, using his ring to save them from giant spiders and then from the dungeons

J. R. R. Tolkien. (Houghton Mifflin Co.)

of the Elvenking. When the dwarves arrive at the Lonely Mountain, Bilbo finds the secret door to Smaug's lair, then arouses the dragon's anger by stealing a cup. Seeking revenge, Smaug destroys nearby Lake-town, but he is killed by Bard the bowman, leader of the townsmen. Thorin refuses to share the treasure with the Lake-men and elves, despite their legitimate claim on part of it. Bilbo tries to prevent a war by offering Bard the Arkenstone, the fabulous gem Thorin values above all the rest of the hoard. Despite Bilbo's efforts, the competing races are about to fight when they are attacked by goblins and wargs. Working together, the dwarves, elves, and men defeat the enemy, although Thorin is killed in the battle. Bilbo refuses a large reward, desiring instead simply to go home. The book ends on a comic note as Bilbo returns to find that he has lost his reputation as an unadventurous and thus respectable hobbit.

Analysis

Although many people read *The Hobbit* only as a precursor to Tolkien's masterpiece, *The Lord of the Rings* (1968 as omnibus; original volumes *The Fellowship of the Ring*, 1954; *The Two Towers*, 1955; and *The Return of the*

King, 1955), the earlier book deserves discussion for its own considerable merits. The third edition, revised from the original, is considered the standard.

Tolkien is one of the preeminent fantasy writers of the twentieth century. For many readers, his books provide the standards by which to judge all other fantasy. Tolkien's success lies in his ability to "subcreate," a process he defines in his essay "On Fairy Stories" as the artist's ability to create a "Secondary World" that follows consistent internal rules. By describing in depth the peoples, geography, and history of his invented world, Tolkien offers an imaginary world so vividly portrayed in its complexity that readers do not so much "suspend disbelief" while reading as much as simply believe in Middle-earth.

One component of Tolkien's success as a "sub-creator" is his profound knowledge of Anglo-Saxon and Old Norse literature. He freely borrows its trolls, goblins, dwarves, elves, and dragons, as well as the quest motif. The quest is an archetypal pattern of fantasy literature present in fairy tales, romances, and epics; it provides structure for both the plot and character development in *The Hobbit*. Quest stories depict people, most often young, who leave home in search of some object. On the journey the protagonists pass a series of tests, often encountering evil and attempting to destroy it. At the end, the heroes return home fundamentally altered, with their identities reshaped.

Bilbo is a model quest hero. Readers easily identify with him. At the beginning of his travels he is not particularly imaginative, brave, or competent, but he develops these qualities as events demand them of him. Leaving his quiet, unchallenging home for the quest forces Bilbo to grow psychologically during his travels. One fundamental characteristic never changes: He remains good-hearted throughout the story, and much of his success comes from his best qualities of loyalty, perseverance, kindness, and unselfishness. In contrast with Bilbo, the dwarves, elves, and men lack these qualities; their greed over the dragon's treasure causes the clash among them that precedes the Battle of Five Armies.

The Hobbit has a reputation as a children's book, but it appeals to a broader audience because it is simultaneously amusing and serious. It deals with important themes in a humorous narrative style. The narrator is intrusive, addressing his audience directly to comment on the action or give information, a trait that younger readers enjoy but that some older readers may occasionally find tiresome. The novel reads aloud well to children, partly because of Tolkien's use of comic verse and onomatopoeic words.

The Lord of the Rings, the trilogy sequel to *The Hobbit*, differs vastly in its epic scope and thus is appropriate for adult readers rather than children. It tells the story of Bilbo's nephew Frodo, who must destroy the Ring of Power of Sauron, the Dark Lord. It explores the same themes of heroism and conflict between good and evil that are present in *The Hobbit*, but in far greater complexity and intricacy of detail. Although critics frequently favor the epic over its precursor, the two differ so much in aim that comparisons are unfair. *The Hobbit* furnishes an incomparable introduction to *The Lord of the Rings*, and its readers often wish to go on to the trilogy, but *The Hobbit* can stand alone as a rich fantasy experience.

—*Kara K. Keeling*

Hyperborea

A series of exotic fantasies set on a mythical polar continent

Author: Clark Ashton Smith (1893-1961)
Genre: Fantasy—magical world
Type of work: Stories
Time of plot: About 15 million years ago
Location: Hyperborea
First published: 1971

The Story

In "The Tale of Satampra Zeiros" (1931), two thieves, unwisely un-
daunted by the evil reputation of a certain ruined city, attempt to plunder
a shrine erected to the dark god Tsathoggua. The protagonist escapes,
though badly maimed, after seeing his companion horribly killed.

In "The Door to Saturn" (1932), the priest Morghi pursues the sorcerer Eibon through a doorway to another world. The two adversaries
are forced to combine forces in order to survive in a wilderness of wonders until they find a place to settle.

"The Testament of Athammaus" (1932) is the tale of a hapless heads-
man appointed to execute a demoniac bandit. Every time his head is
struck off, the bandit miraculously rises from the dead, becoming gradually more monstrous. In the end, the bandit degenerates to the point that
further beheadings become impractical. In "Ubbo-Sathla" (1933), a
modern occultist finds a magic lens that unites him with the personality
of its wizard owner and allows him to share that owner's visionary
quest to find the hideously repulsive mass of protoplasm that is parent
to all Earthly life.

In "The Seven Geases" (1934), the vainglorious magistrate Ralibar
Vooz falls prey, while out hunting, to the wrath of the sorcerer Ezdagor.
Ezdagor places Vooz under a geas, which requires him to descend further into the Tartarean realm to present himself as a blood offering to
Tsathoggua. Tsathoggua has no need of him and sends him deeper into
the bowels of the earth. The pattern repeats as Vooz delivers himself in
turn to the web of the spider-god Atlach-Natha, the palace of the "ante-
human sorcerer" Haon-Dor, and the Cavern of the Archetypes. Finally,
he arrives in the slimy gulf of Abhoth, "father and mother of all cosmic

uncleanliness." By this time, he is in a realm so remote that his own ordered world is known only by ominous rumor, so Abhoth can think of no more awful place to send him than home. The journey back is fraught with far too many dangers for it to be made safely.

"The Weird of Avoosl Wuthoqquan" (1932), "The Ice-Demon" (1933), and "The Coming of the White Worm" (1941) are all tales whose leading characters are drawn by avarice to some ironically bizarre end. The Hyperborean series also includes the sentimental extended prose-poem "The White Sybil" (1935) and the lackluster "The Theft of the Thirty-Nine Girdles" (1958). The collection also includes a group of prose-poems grouped under the heading "The World's Rim," including one extended account of "The Abominations of Yondo" (1926).

Analysis

The balmy polar continent of Hyperborea, mentioned frequently in Greek mythology, was the third setting that Clark Ashton Smith set out to explore in some detail, following the imaginary French province of Averoigne and the legendary continent of Atlantis. Being even more remote in time than Atlantis (its obliterated civilizations flourished in the Miocene era, according to the occultist in "Ubbo-Sathla"), Hyperborea could more easily accommodate the kind of exotic landscapes, flora, and fauna that Smith earlier had attributed to the desert of Yondo near the world's rim.

Hyperborea retained one crucial limitation, by virtue of belonging to the past rather than the future: It was subject to the destiny of giving way to the mundane world of the present. For this reason, it was to be superseded by the far-future scenarios of Zothique when Smith wanted to push his vivid imagination to its most earnest limit, but it remained the location of choice for his lightest and most playful tales.

The characterization of the monsters and evil deities in these stories owes something to H. P. Lovecraft, to whose Cthulhu Mythos the god Tsathoggua sometimes is attached and to whose eccentric library of forbidden books Hyperborea contributed *The Book of Eibon*. Smith's handling of such material herein is, however, far more ironic than Lovecraft's ever was. Smith called these tales "Hyperborean grotesques," and they are indeed exercises in calculated grotesquerie, with a strong element of black comedy. The author's perennial fondness for tongue-twisting nomenclature is given its freest and most exuberant rein in "The Door to Saturn" and "The Weird of Avoosl Wuthoqquan." The best of the Hyperborean tales, "The Testament of Athammaus" and the magnificently bizarre "The Seven Geases," are redolent with a macabre sarcasm no other writer ever matched.

A theme that recurs in several of the stories is that of regression from order to chaos. In "The Testament of Athammaus," the sequence of the bandit's resurrections is from human being to a near-formless mass of primordial slime, a state of being highly reminiscent of that credited to the ultimate ancestor of all Earthly life in "Ubbo-Sathla." A similar degenerative sequence is provided, with more elaborate stages, in "The Seven Geases," but the endpoint is the same: Underlying all other notions of identity is an utterly loathsome, slimy mess.

The revelation that the ultimate reality is both degrading and disgusting is another echo of Lovecraft, but Smith's disgust at the concept of degradation is much less heartfelt than Lovecraft's. Smith's imagination agrees with Lovecraft's in reducing humankind to virtual insignificance in a vast and hostile universe, but Smith's vision is not straightforwardly horrific; it is extraordinarily lush and marvelously fecund. Smith's imagined universe is by no means dismal; it is very colorful and full of bizarre life. Smith's is a universe in which there are not merely more things than are dreamed of in the dour Lovecraftian philosophy, but more things than are dreamed of in any philosophy. That is what makes Smith a uniquely precious writer.

—Brian Stableford

The Hyperion Cantos

Future humanity is caught in a conflict between rival groups of artificial intelligences seeking to control the universe

Author: Dan Simmons (1948-   )
Genre: Science fiction—artificial intelligence
Type of work: Novels
Time of plot: The distant future
Location: The planet Hyperion, cyberspace, and various unidentified planetary locations
First published: 1990 (previously published separately as *Hyperion*, 1989, and *The Fall of Hyperion*, 1990)

The Story

The two books of *The Hyperion Cantos* take their titles and themes from two unfinished poems by the Romantic poet John Keats (1795-1821) that deal with the displacement in Greek mythology of the old gods, the Titans, by the new gods, the Olympians. In Dan Simmons's work, Old Earth has been destroyed by a black hole, and humans are spread across two hundred worlds and moons scattered throughout a thousand light-years in space. Communication and travel are achieved through fatlines and farcasters, operated by Technocore Artificial Intelligences, who inhabit singularity environments and cyberspace. The artificial intelligences evolved in a symbiotic relationship with humankind but have decided that humans are no longer necessary.

There are three factions of artificial intelligences: the Volatiles, who want to remove humans altogether; the Ultimates, who are prepared to make way for a negotiated new order; and the Stables, who believe in continued coexistence. The fate of the universe depends on which of these groups is able to take control of the unforeseen variables occurring on the planet Hyperion. As the story opens, a number of futures theoretically are possible.

A cosmic conflict looms between the logically predestined Artificial Ultimate Intelligence and a newly evolved human Ultimate Intelligence, which is a triune god composed of Intellect, Empathy, and The Void Which Binds (or Quantum Reality). The Empathy part of this trinity has fled backward in time to avoid the conflict. To lure it back into the struggle, the artificial intelligences have accessed the worst nightmares of billions of humans to create an Avatar of Pain, called the Shrike. The idea is that the Shrike, which has impaled thousands of suffering humans on the branches of its Tree of Pain, will broadcast enough agony to drive Empathy out of hiding.

The Stable Artificial Intelligences also have constructed the perfect bodily trap for Empathy, a combination of a nearly divine human consciousness and an artificial imagination capable of spanning space and time. This body takes the form of cybrid (cyborg hybrid) personality retrieval projects based on John Keats. The Keats cybrids prove to be disinclined to accept godhood and prefer identification with humanity.

Also involved in the conflict is a third group, the Ousters, a highly evolved branch of humanity that is interfering retroactively to favor humankind. They have modified the actions of the Shrike by creating Time Tombs on the planet Hyperion. They also have trained Rachel/Moneta to be the Shrike's companion, nemesis, and keeper, traveling backward in time with the Tombs and the Shrike toward the present of the text.

Ordinary humans are caught in the crossfire of this conflict between gods and quasi gods. The human action begins when the Church of the Final Atonement decides to send a final group of seven pilgrims to the Time Tombs. These pilgrims represent the major human religious factions in the galaxy. Lenar Hoyt is a Catholic priest; Sol Weintraub is a Jewish philosopher; Fedmahn Kassad is a soldier of Islamic origin; Martin Silenus is a pagan poet; Het Masteen, the True Voice of the Tree, is a Templar conservationist; the nameless Consul is an atheist; and Brawne Lamia is a romantic agnostic.

The first book follows the model of Geoffrey Chaucer's *The Canterbury Tales* (1380-1390), with each of the pilgrims recounting a tale of relevant personal experiences. One of these, the Consul's tale, was published separately as "Remembering Siri" (1983). The pilgrims interact, but each has a separate role to play in the resolution of the conflict. Each of them is connected to the fate of humankind through the overriding motif of death and resurrection; each is approaching a form of apotheosis; and each apotheosis is controlled in some way by the Shrike, which functions as an agent of predestination.

The second book narrows the narrative focus to concentrate on the Keats cybrid. This part of the story is recounted by the Joseph Severn persona of Keats, who dreams much of the complicated action from his deathbed in a reconstructed cyberspace version of old Rome. The multiple story lines are drawn together through the agency of the Shrike. The political and philosophical actions eventually are united through an authorial suggestion that love is the reason for predeterminism in the universe. It is this love that links the imminent birth of Keats and Lamia's divine girlchild with the sacrifice of Weintraub's time-trapped daughter Rachel, which will enable her to be born into the future. The universal conflict is resolved by the humans with much help from the Ousters and the Keats cybrid. The TechnoCore is destroyed, and with it the farcaster system that had both aided and enslaved humanity.

Analysis

Simmons's early fiction was largely horror, with some fantasy, but *Hyperion*, which won the 1990 Hugo Award, is science fiction. *The Hyperion Cantos* might be described as metaphysical science fiction in that it deals with concepts relating to the universe as a whole. The two books are theological in that they offer a discourse on eschatology and predestination, as well as philosophical in their adaptation of the early Romantic concept of perfectibility as pure abstract process.

This work also falls within the category of recursive science fiction, which treats real people and the fictional worlds that they create as having equivalent reality. In placing a reconstructed John Keats persona at the center of the text, Simmons aligns this work with a number of other recursive texts, such as Tim Powers's *The Stress of Her Regard* (1989), that make extensive use of the already self-reflexive lives and works of the major late Romantic figures, particularly George Gordon, Lord Byron (1788-1824), Percy Bysshe Shelley (1792-1822), Mary Wollstonecraft Shelley (1797-1851), and John Keats. To these Romantic writers, the proper function of memory is to provide a path to the divine, using the mythopoeic powers of the imagination to transform base nature into transcendent reality. In postmodern fiction, especially in works dealing with cyberspace, the inspired order of memory has been reduced to the accumulation of data. This means that the inspired human memory is devalued as being less accurate than electronically recorded information that can be used to reconstruct "reality." The more humans rely on artificially recorded data, the less able they are to perform the romantic apotheosis. This problem is explored in *The Hyperion Cantos*, in which the role of the dreaming poet as creator has been usurped by the artificial intelligences.

The overall structure is a space opera on a grand scale, containing complexly interwoven strands of action. Simmons's technique is a self-consciously allusive postmodern collage of literary styles. His characters are drawn from a wide range of literary sources. Within the overtly Chaucerian framework of the first book, each of the pilgrim's tales is narrated in a completely different style, ranging from the romance of the Consul's tale, through the *Bildungsroman* of Silenus the poet's tale, to the tough, short-sentence detective form of Brawne Lamia's detective's tale.

This technique is not sustained in the second book, which is more uniform in authorial tone, concentrating on the complexities of plot resolution. There, Keats's notion of spiritual growth through creative suffering is given literal form in the multiple deaths, quasi deaths, and resurrections inflicted on the characters in their search for reconciliation between human and machine, creator and created. The emphasis rests, finally, on a metaphoric structure of birth and rebirth.

The Hyperion Cantos has given Simmons a prominent place in the science-fiction field. Simmons later resumed the Hyperion series with *Endymion* (1996), which follows the adventures of the hybrid girl Aenea and her lover and protector, Raul Endymion. Simmons concluded the series with *The Rise of Endymion* (1997), in which Raul and Aenea continue their journey in their search for the meaning of the universe. His other works include *The Hollow Man* (1992; a much expanded version of "Eyes I Dare Not Meet in Dreams," 1982) and the horror novel *Children of the Night* (1992). Neither of these works has received the acclaim accorded to *The Hyperion Cantos*.

—Janeen Webb

I Am Legend

After a worldwide plague, the only surviving human must face grief, loneliness, and the marauding victims of the disease: a new race of vampires

Author: Richard Matheson (1926-   )
Genre: Science fiction—apocalypse
Type of work: Novel
Time of plot: January, 1976-January, 1979
Location: Los Angeles, California
First published: 1954

The Story

As *I Am Legend* begins, in January, 1976, Earth has been ravaged, first by nuclear war, then by a mysterious plague that transforms its victims into vampires. One normal human being, Robert Neville, remains. Through him, Richard Matheson dramatizes humanity's desperate struggle to overcome a catastrophe that it perhaps brought upon itself.

In the first of the novel's four parts, Neville has barricaded himself in his home against the nightly onslaughts of the vampires, among them his former friend and neighbor, Ben Corman. While Corman shouts for him to come out, Neville attempts to block the horror with classical music and alcohol. By day, while the vampires sleep, he repairs the damage to his house and hunts his tormentors. This has been his life for five months. He avoids the past, particularly memories of his wife, Virginia, and daughter, Kathy, both victims of the plague. Instead, he exists alone in the terrifying present, eating, drinking, listening to Beethoven, and killing scores of vampires.

When part 2 opens in March, 1976, Neville has refortified and sound-proofed his house. More secure, he begins to diverge from his obsession with destroying vampires and seeks to understand them and the disease that engendered them. Thus begins a clever scientific inquiry that trans-forms into science fiction what has been so far a rather ordinary horror story. With microscope and science book in hand more frequently than mallet and stake, Neville discovers a bacterial cause for the vampirism. He also carefully observes vampire behavior and conducts "experi-ments" to solve mysteries surrounding the vampires. This scientific inquiry transforms Neville as well as the novel. Compelled to search his memories of the past for clues about the plague, he cannot help but recall his own losses. His resulting pain and grief display a compassion and vulnerability previously missing, as does his touching attempt to befriend a terrified stray dog.

By June, 1978, when part 3 opens, Neville seems to have adjusted to his solitary life and resigned himself to living only in the present. On a leisurely daytime hunt for Ben Corman, he sees, pursues, and captures a woman who may be normal. During their day and night together, Neville makes several startling discoveries that challenge his existence. Not only do his few hours with Ruth reveal the emptiness of his solitary life, but her true identity and purpose also radically transform his understanding of the vampires and of himself. A member of a new society of living vampires who have developed a treatment for the plague, Ruth was sent to spy on Neville, the monster who has been indiscriminately slaughtering and experimenting on both the reanimated dead and her kind. Although puzzled by the two different types of vampires, Neville had decided that both were monsters he must kill for the sake of his own survival. Now he must confront the awful truth.

Part 4 finds Neville resignedly awaiting his fate. When the new humans come for him, they display the same hatred and brutality that led to nuclear war. They ruthlessly slaughter the reanimated dead, including a pitiful Ben Corman, and then capture an appalled Neville. Humankind has mutated, but it has not changed. It remains painfully "normal." Whether Neville chooses suicide with Ruth's assistance or public execution, he will be a new terror, a new superstition, a new legend for humankind.

Analysis

Published less than ten years after the end of World War II and the detonation of two atomic bombs, *I Am Legend* was part of a revival of disaster theme literature. Earlier in the century, literature of this sort was less common and usually centered on natural catastrophe. Notable examples of this earlier type include Jack London's *The Scarlet Plague* (1915) and S. Fowler Wright's *Deluge* (1928). In England, post-World War II disaster literature continued this emphasis on natural catastrophe, for example in John Wyndham's *The Day of the Triffids* (1951) and John Christopher's *The Death of Grass* (1956). U.S. science-fiction writers, on the other hand, concentrated on disease, with George R. Stewart's *Earth Abides* (1949) preceding *I Am Legend* by several years. Other noteworthy examples include Algis Budrys's *Some Will Not Die* (1961), Michael

Crichton's *The Andromeda Strain* (1969), and Stephen King's *The Stand* (1978; text restored, 1990).

I Am Legend was Matheson's first science-fiction novel, and it established his reputation in the field. He followed it with two others, *The Shrinking Man* (1956) and *Bid Time Return* (1975), which won the World Fantasy Award for best novel of 1975. For the most part, Matheson's writing blends fantasy and science fiction in a combination that is more mysterious than explicable, more fanciful than possible. Critics and scholars have noted that the major theme in nearly all of Matheson's work has been paranoia. Thus, in *I Am Legend*, to preserve his own life Robert Neville is driven to annihilate the vampires who threaten him. Likewise, the living vampires become obsessed with destroying their enemies: the reanimated dead and the monster, Neville. In dramatizing this theme, Matheson recasts the legend of Count Dracula and his legion of the undead, substituting the objective, rational, systematic inquiry of science for the subjective, illogical, impressionistic observation of superstition. When *I Am Legend* concludes, however, humankind clings to the old ways.

In his writing, Matheson elevates fantasy and horror above science fiction. It is not surprising, then, that although he initially was considered to be a science-fiction writer, by the late 1950's he was mainly creating, with enormous success, terror and fantasy for television series such as *The Twilight Zone, Star Trek*, and *Rod Serling's Night Gallery*; for television films such as *Duel* (1971), directed by Steven Spielberg; and for theatrical films, particularly Roger Corman's adaptations of Edgar Allan Poe's horror stories. Matheson adapted *I Am Legend* into a screenplay for the 1964 film *The Last Man on Earth* but demanded that his name be removed when the screenplay was rewritten. Matheson was not involved in the better-known film adaptation, *The Omega Man* (1971).

—*Joseph M. Nassar*

I Have No Mouth and I Must Scream

A collection of stories using fantasy and science fiction to explore extreme emotional states

Author: Harlan Ellison (1934-   )
Genre: Fantasy—inner space
Type of work: Stories
Time of plot: Various times between the 1960's and centuries into the future
Location: Various locations in the United States and outer space
First published: 1967

The Story

The seven stories in *I Have No Mouth and I Must Scream*, originally published in science-fiction and men's magazines between 1958 and 1967, include both science fiction and fantasy. They are united by Harlan Ellison's introductions for each of the stories, in which he discusses their personal significance to him, as well as by their focus on powerful emotions. In each story, people are confronted with their deepest fears or desires.

"I Have No Mouth, and I Must Scream" is narrated by Ted, one of five people trapped below the surface of the earth in a sentient computer called AM. The computer has taken over the world and killed everyone except these five people. Programmed to wage war, the nearly omnipotent AM has kept these five alive and tortured them for 109 years. Ted relates their brutal sufferings, revealing in the process his extreme paranoia. He is capable of love for Ellen, the only woman in the group, and of self-sacrifice. When the group arrives at an ice cavern in search of food, he seizes a moment of confusion to initiate a mercy killing of the others. In rage, the computer reduces Ted to a hideous blob, able to be tortured for eternity and to think but not to act. In his reflections, Ted hopes he did the right thing.

The narrator of "Big Sam Was My Friend" is also tested but falls short. A member of an intergalactic circus, Johnny Lee befriends a teleporter named Sam, who believes that heaven is in space and is looking for a dead girl he loved on Earth. When the circus performs on Giuliu II, its employees are invited to a royal ceremony, which to their surprise involves a virgin sacrifice. Sam mistakenly thinks the girl to be sacrificed is his lost love and rescues her, offending their host. He agrees to take the girl's place. The narrator bitterly notes how neither he nor anyone else tried to prevent Johnny Lee's sacrifice.

In "World of the Myth," three explorers crash on an alien world and encounter antlike beings that project the characters' inner thoughts. Although the protagonist feels weak throughout the story, his rival cannot face his true self and commits suicide.

The fantasy stories also deal with characters facing their true selves. In "Lonelyache," a philanderer recently separated from his wife watches a threatening black beast take shape and grow in his living room as he engages in meaningless one-night stands. He finally commits suicide in a combination of courage and despair. In "Delusion for a Dragon Slayer," the protagonist, shortly before being crushed by a wrecking ball, gets the opportunity to earn the heaven of his dreams. Transformed from a mild-mannered man into a Teutonic demigod, he sails through a phantasmagoric landscape and learns from a wizard that he must defeat a demon and win the love of a fair maiden. In his overconfidence, he wrecks his ship, killing his crew; and in his cowardice he allows the demon to take the maiden and then slays it from behind. Having fallen short, he loses his chance at heaven.

Other stories in the volume are allegorical. "Eyes of Dust" is set on a planet where everything is beautiful except a couple who defy the law to produce a hideous son with the soul of a prophet. The authorities kill the couple and destroy the son, but in doing so they mar the beauty of their world. Set in Las Vegas, "Pretty Maggie Moneyeyes" involves a man, down on his luck, who plays a slot machine possessed by a woman. Manipulating his need for love, she manages to free her own soul while trapping his in the machine.

Analysis

Although he gained recognition as a writer of science fiction, Ellison's work has never been described adequately by the label. The weakest stories in the book—"Big Sam Was My Friend," "Eyes of Dust," and "World of the Myth"—are from the first decade of his professional career. Although they contain themes that are important in his work, they are more conventional in subject, drawing on standard science-fiction tropes of the late 1950's and early 1960's. They combine Ellison's typically expressive style with passages of self-conscious writing. In the mid-1960's, Ellison perfected his voice, and from that point his work, though often drawing on science fiction and fantasy, is a unique juxtaposition of emotional expression, wild imagination, and stylistic experimentation. Many critics saw such experimentation as part of science fiction's New Wave in the late 1960's and early 1970's, but no one associated with the label—many of them contributors to the anthology *Dangerous Visions* (1967), which Ellison edited—wrote like Ellison wrote, and even he rarely repeated himself.

Although "I Have No Mouth, and I Must Scream" employs a science-fiction concept, the story uses narrative and typographical techniques seldom seen in earlier science fiction. The story also makes free use of mythical elements and literary allusion. "Delusion for a Dragon Slayer" combines "sword-and-sorcery" elements with psychedelic imagery, all framed by a mundane experience in a modern city. The protagonist of "Lonelyache" is haunted by a beast in his living room, and "Pretty Maggie Moneyeyes" mixes the life stories of a prostitute and a drifter with highly experimental passages describing her death and the story's fantastic premise.

Critical response to Ellison's work has always been mixed, with some readers finding fault with his personal tone and hyperbolic style as others praise him for his imagination and the emotional power of his writing. Frequently anthologized and the winner of the 1967 Hugo Award for best story, "I Have No Mouth, and I Must Scream" is one of Ellison's best-known works. A corrected version of the story collection was published in 1983.

—*Darren Harris-Fain*

The Illustrated Man

A collection of classic science-fiction short stories centered on the prophetic tattoos drawn by a witch on a circus worker

Author: Ray Bradbury (1920-   )
Genre: Science fiction—cautionary
Type of work: Stories
Time of plot: The 1950's, with flashforwards and flashbacks
Location: Various
First published: 1951

The Story

This book was published following serial publication of its component stories in a variety of sources. The thread connecting the stories is the narrator's tale of meeting a tattooed man while on a walking tour of Wisconsin in the 1950's. The tattoos move and change at night, each telling a different story predicting the future. The narrator befriends the illustrated man and watches the tattoos become the eighteen tales collected in this volume.

Ray Bradbury questions the need for technology in many of the stories. George Hadley buys a Happylife Home (the ultimate virtual reality house) for his family in "The Veldt." His children, named after Peter Pan characters, seek their own never-never land in a nursery where thoughts materialize. When George threatens to turn off the house, the children revolt by turning the nursery into an African veldt where lions attack and eat their trapped parents.

Another story of technology gone awry is "Marionette, Inc." A man buys a robot to replace himself in daily life so he can take a vacation, but the robot replaces the man by killing him and running off with his wife. In "The Rocket," another story of the wish-fulfillment powers of technology, a man spends his life savings to simulate a rocket trip for his family because he cannot afford a real rocket trip.

Space travel is a common theme in science fiction. "The Rocket Man" depicts a husband and father unable to trade the lure of space for a home life. He stays with his family for only three days at a time before he feels compelled to voyage to the stars. In "Kaleidoscope," men hurtle into space when their rocket blows up. Hollis realizes that his life has been full of dreams rather than memories. As he hits Earth's atmosphere, he burns like a meteor, and a young boy in Illinois wishes upon him as if he were a falling star.

In "No Particular Night or Morning," a space traveler realizes that he cannot connect to his own identity and commits suicide. In "The Long Rain," a spaceship crash leaves men stranded on Venus, where they walk through incessant rain in search of a sun dome for shelter, only to find that one after another is inoperable. The showers turn into a Chinese water torture, driving them mad. Only one man succeeds in making his way to safety.

Bradbury explores the potential for good in human life on other planets in "The Other Foot." Hattie Johnson, a black woman, lives on Mars. Hattie's husband organizes the colony to greet the first white man on Mars. When the white man arrives, he announces that Earth has been destroyed, and with it, racism. The colony has the opportunity for a new start with everyone on the same level. The "Fire Balloons" is the story of missionaries who find that they have landed where there is no sin.

Bradbury also explores the evil side of humanity. In "The Exiles," all the great authors are kept alive by the spirit of their books, but intolerant book burners extinguish the writers from existence. Invading Martians in "The Concrete Mixer" are overwhelmed by commercialized and materialistic Earthmen. "The Visitor" is a man who offers hope to a planet of people dying of a debilitating disease. Instead of treating the visitor kindly, the people kill the only person who can help them. A couple escape from a future of repression only to be recaptured and sent back by people they thought were friends in "The Fox and the Forest." The children in "Zero Hour" are the only people who can see the invaders who brainwash them into killing parents who do not pay attention to them. In "The Man," a crew of spacemen land on a planet that has been visited recently by God. The captain initially believes the visitor to be his rival, and his pride gets in the way of him meeting with God.

The end of the world is another theme. In "The Highway," Hernando stands in his field and watches cars pass on the highway, their passengers fleeing atomic war. One driver informs him that the world is going to end, and he wonders what "the world" could mean, so separate is his life from the rest of civilization. "The Last Night of the World" is the tale of a dream shared by everyone the night before the end of the world and the calmness with which they all meet their last moments. The framing story ends when the narrator sees a clear picture of the illustrated man waking and strangling him. He runs off to the next town before this prophecy can come true.

Analysis

Although *The Illustrated Man* is classic science fiction, written early in Bradbury's career, it is more concerned with ideas than with science, although Bradbury often questions the consequences of science. The book contains characters from middle America. The heroes are not mythical figures but everyday people. Technology is depicted as failing to make human life better, and Bradbury shows in several stories that a return to

Ray Bradbury. (Thomas Victor)

a simpler life is desirable. He looks at space travel as a romantic journey into the unknown ending in death rather than as an epic journey into adventure.

Bradbury's body of work is voluminous, from short-story collections, including *The Martian Chronicles* (1950) and *Dandelion Wine* (1957), to his novel *Fahrenheit 451* (1953), which was made into a film in 1966. *The Illustrated Man* also was filmed, in 1969. Bradbury has written plays, poems, children's stories, and nonfiction. He received the O. Henry Award in 1947 and the Nebula Grand Master Award in 1989. He has written under a number of pseudonyms, including Guy Armory, Edward Banks, and Anthony Corvais.

—*Dianna Laurent*

The Incomplete Enchanter

Psychologist Harold Shea travels to mythical lands, where he embarks on quests, discovers romance, and dabbles in magic

Authors: L(yon) Sprague de Camp (1907-2000) and Fletcher Pratt (1897-1956)
Genre: Fantasy—heroic fantasy
Type of work: Novels
Time of plot: The 1940's and medieval times
Location: Garaden, Ohio, and various mythological places
First published: *The Incomplete Enchanter* (1941; includes "The Roaring Trumpet," serial form, *Unknown*, 1940, and "The Mathematics of Magic," serial form, *Unknown*, 1940), *The Castle of Iron* (1950; serial form, *Unknown*, 1941; first two books published as *The Complete Enchanter: The Magical Misadventures of Harold Shea*, 1975), *The Wall of Serpents* (1960; includes "The Wall of Serpents," serial form, 1953, and *The Green Magician*; published with the previous material as *The Intrepid Enchanter*, 1988, and as *The Complete Compleat Enchanter*, 1989), and *The Green Magician* (1954)

The Story

Harold Shea, a psychologist for the Garaden Institute in Ohio, hungers for travel and adventure. His coworkers tease him about the activities he takes up and subsequently drops, such as fencing and horseback riding. None of them satisfies his longing.

Shea's superior, Dr. Reed Chalmers, has hypothesized the existence of parallel worlds that can be reached by people who can attune themselves to receive a different series of impressions of reality. These parallel worlds have been made known to humankind through such classic works of literature as Edmund Spenser's *The Faerie Queene* (1590 and 1596). The possibility of travel to these other worlds captures Shea's imagination, and in a rash moment, he puts Chalmers's hypothesis to the test.

Aiming for the lush green fields of the Ireland of Cuchulainn and Queen Maev, Shea ends up instead in the snowy, frozen wasteland of Scandinavian myth in the first story of the series, "The Roaring Trumpet." There, Shea embarks on a quest with the Norse gods Thor and Loki to recover Thor's great hammer from the giants. The hammer is needed in the coming legendary battle, the Ragnarök. Although Shea, a mere mortal, proves useful in recovering it, he and another god, Heimdall, are taken prisoner. Shea again proves his worth by escaping with Heimdall from the giants' dungeon by the use of psychology—a foreign concept to the gods—and magic. At the Gates of Hell, however, as Heimdall blows his trumpet, signaling the beginning of the battle, Shea is thrust back into his own world.

In this first adventure, Shea discovers the secrets of travel to parallel universes. He discovers, much to his dismay, that his modern tools, such as a Colt .38 revolver, a flashlight, and a box of matches, do not function there. Instead, he finds that his fencing lessons stand him in good stead. Magic works because the parallel worlds are governed by a set of natural laws different from those of Shea's world. As Shea masters the fixed principles of magic for the time and place in which he finds himself, he gains the ability to cast spells, many of them with comic results.

In "The Mathematics of Magic," Dr. Chalmers accompanies Shea to the land of *The Faerie Queene*, where both men meet and fall in love with beautiful but quite different women. The object of Shea's desire is an independent woodswoman named Belphebe. The more mature Chalmers, however, becomes smitten with a fragile young thing, Florimel, who is merely a magical creation made from snow. After many sword fights and magical incantations, Shea once again is blasted back to his own universe, but this time with Belphebe in tow. Chalmers remains behind.

As *The Castle of Iron* begins, Shea and Belphebe are husband and wife and living in Ohio. Belphebe mysteriously disappears during a picnic. Shea, his colleagues Walter Bayard and Vaclav Polacek, and a police officer named Pete Brodsky are snatched during an interrogation into the disappearance. They land in Samuel Taylor Coleridge's Xanadu, where they are force-fed milk and honey by beautiful women. Before they know what is happening, Shea and Vaclav then appear in the world of Ludovico Ariosto's *Orlando Furioso*

Chalmers seeks Shea's help in freeing Florimel from her enchantment and admits that he accidentally brought Belphebe to this world, where she lost her memory and believes that she is now a woman called Belphegor. Apparently, Spenser based *The Faerie Queene* on Ariosto's *Orlando Furioso*, so there are many similarities between the worlds of these two works. Shea agrees to help Chalmers render Florimel a human, all the while keeping her out of the lecherous hands of the magician Atlantès. He also must find and woo back his beloved Belphebe. At the novel's end, Shea and Belphebe return to Ohio, Chalmers and Vaclav remain in the world of *Orlando Furioso,* and Bayard and Brodsky are stuck in Xanadu.

In "The Wall of Serpents," Shea and Belphebe travel to the world of the Finnish epic *The Kalevala* in search of a magician powerful enough to retrieve Bayard and Brodsky from Xanadu. This accomplished, the foursome become involved in master magician Lemminkainen's revenge plot against a neighboring family and barely escape death by transporting, accidentally, to the land of Irish myth, the land Shea had tried to find on his first venture. Thus the last story, *The Green Magician,* finds Shea, Belphebe, and Brodsky working for Cuchulainn in his fight against Queen Maev and the Connachta in exchange for passage via a magician back to Garaden, Ohio. The threesome finally returns to Ohio.

Analysis

In an afterword to *The Compleat Enchanter* titled "Fletcher and I," L. Sprague de Camp reveals that it was Fletcher Pratt who first proposed this collaboration between the two. "The Roaring Trumpet" first appeared in John W. Campbell, Jr.'s fantasy magazine *Unknown* in May, 1940. "The Mathematics of Magic" followed in August, 1940, and "The Castle of Iron" in April, 1941.

The project stayed on hold until after World War II, when the two authors rewrote and expanded "The Castle of Iron," eventually republishing it in book form in 1950. The last two novellas in the series, "The Wall of Serpents" and *The Green Magician,* also saw magazine publication before being combined in a single volume. Besides the Harold Shea stories, the two also collaborated on other works of fantasy. Although other adventures were planned for Shea, such as having him travel to the world of Persian myth, they were never written because Pratt died suddenly in 1956 of cancer.

According to de Camp, Pratt furnished the imaginative element and de Camp the controlling logic. Their relationship calls to mind that between their two main characters, Shea and his older mentor, Chalmers. De Camp notes that Pratt despised Robert E. Howard's Conan stories and, surprisingly, J. R. R. Tolkien's *The Lord of the Rings* trilogy (1954-1955), considered by many to be the classic fantasy adventure, for their occasional crudities and lapses of logic.

David Drake, in his preface to *The Complete Compleat Enchanter,* classifies the Harold Shea stories as rigorous fantasy with humor. He states that the rigor appears through the authors' display of their expert knowledge both of the myths that form the framework for the novellas and of the real conditions of the worlds on which the myths are based.

A key element in all the stories is their humor. Pratt and de Camp's apprentice magician, whose spells misfire as often as not, is an appealing hero. When Shea turns ordinary broomsticks into flying ones in "The Roaring Trumpet" or an ordinary carpet into a magic one in *The Castle of Iron*, the maiden voyages of these vehicles are fraught with hair-raising adventure. Their riders' lives are in as much danger in the air as they were on the ground. Chalmers, too, has difficulty making his spells come out right. In "The Mathematics of Magic," his attempt to turn water into wine at a castle dinner party results instead in a very potent Scotch whiskey, causing many a medieval hangover the next morning.

Integral to the stories' humor is their use of colloquial English, as opposed to the pseudo-Elizabethan English often employed in heroic fantasy. For example, the Frost Giants of "The Roaring Trumpet" talk and act like Brooklyn gangsters. According to Drake, de Camp was one of the first to defend publicly the use of colloquial English in heroic settings.

A product of a time that has been categorized as the Golden Age of science fiction, the series experienced a rebirth in the 1990's with the publication of L. Sprague de Camp's *The Enchanter Reborn* (1992) and *The Exotic Enchanter* (1995). These two titles encompass several shorter novellas by different authors, written in the spirit of the originals by Pratt and de Camp.

As noted by Christopher Stasheff in his introduction to *The Enchanter Reborn*, the purpose of the original stories was to teach as well as to amuse. Through the adventures of Harold Shea, the reader is introduced to such works of classical literature as *The Faerie Queene, Orlando Furioso*, and *The Kalevala*, as well as the worlds of Norse and Irish mythology. The Incomplete Enchanter stories continue to entertain because they embody certain fundamental truths, foremost of which is the desire of modern people to escape the technological, impersonal life of the big city for a simpler one where people live by their wits in an edenic countryside.

—C. K. Breckenridge

The Infernal Desire Machines of Doctor Hoffman

> The minister of determination commissions Desiderio to assassinate Dr. Hoffman, who is attempting to destroy a world of reason and create a world of dreams

Author: Angela Carter (1940-1992)
Genre: Fantasy—Magical Realism
Type of work: Novel
Time of plot: Undefined
Location: Various locations on Earth
First published: 1972 (also published as *The War of Dreams*, 1974)

The Story

Desiderio, an old man, tells the story of the Great War between reason and unreason in which, fifty years earlier, he played a heroic role. The war begins when Dr. Hoffman's infernal desire machine destroys the forces of reason in the Capital and installs a world of desire. The Capital's ruler, the minister of determination, sends his twenty-four-year-old aide, Desiderio, to destroy Hoffman and his machine. Desiderio, already unconsciously desirous of Hoffman's daughter, Albertina, sets off on a quest that is both heroic and romantic.

At his first destination, a seaside village, he meets Hoffman's old teacher, now the blind proprietor of a peep show. Desiderio, accused of murdering a woman and sought by the police, takes refuge among the River People, who are Indians. Part Indian himself, he becomes one of them. On the eve of his wedding, however, Desiderio realizes that the River People are about to cannibalize him. After escaping, he again meets the peep show proprietor, now traveling with a carnival. Desiderio joins the carnival, masquerading as the proprietor's nephew.

The proprietor, he learns, is allied to Hoffman; indeed, Albertina has commanded him to bring Desiderio safely to Hoffman's castle. Desiderio's love and desire for this woman he has never met increases, and his desire fuels his vision.

Desiderio is attracted to the carnival's grotesque but friendly performers. Most intriguing to him are the little Acrobats of Desire, religious ascetics who practice an erotic and sadomasochistic dismemberment act from which they take no pleasure. They perform a ritual gang rape on Desiderio. When he finally escapes to a place overlooking the town, he watches a landslide bury it.

A black-robed count and his servant, Lafleur, who is Albertina in disguise, ask Desiderio to accompany them. At a whorehouse run by a madam (Albertina), they participate in grotesque sexual acts until flames destroy the place. Desiderio and his companions escape and board a ship, from which they move to a pirate vessel. By now aware that Lafleur is Albertina and that she has protected him, Desiderio waits eagerly to consummate his love for her.

A storm destroys the ship and lands them in Africa. There the count is killed, but Desiderio and Albertina escape to "Nebulous" time and space and a world in which centaurs worship a god called the Sacred Stallion. The male centaurs are privileged; the female centaurs are oppressed. The centaurs religiously gang rape Albertina before her father's helicopters arrive to free them both. Albertina leads Desiderio to Dr. Hoffman. He destroys Hoffman, Albertina, and the machine. Reason is restored, and Desiderio is a hero.

Analysis

Angela Carter's *The Infernal Desire Machines of Doctor Hoffman* brings to prominence elements that were undertones in her earlier, more realistic works, such as *Heroes and Villains* (1969). She has been compared with such contemporaries as Thomas Pynchon and Gabriel García Márquez; she uses the philosophical, surrealistic, and erotic to create predominantly imaginative yet familiar landscapes.

The fantasy war between the minister of determination and Dr. Hoffman dramatizes the philosophical question of the relationship between reason and imagination, the real and the illusory, the objective and the subjective. The drama has faint traditional structures: Desiderio's linear journey is a quest and a love story. A strong additional textual element is gender: Women are totally and complicitly victims of violent sex.

Carter's dramatization of a philosophical debate succeeds as narrative first because of its familiar elements of linear time, quest story, and romance, and second because of Desiderio's first-person narrative voice. Through these, the writer succeeds in keeping the reader in the story itself rather than in the philosophical debate it dramatizes. At the same time, the story makes the complexity of the issue come to the fore in two ways. First, Desiderio is, paradoxically, unaware until late in his journey that what he experiences—and thus what the reader experiences—are manifestations of his own unconscious, his own desires, his own internal dream machine. What he seeks to destroy also seduces him. Second, a conversation between Hoffman's ambassador and the minister of determination reveals that what both want is control, the minister through logical coercion and Hoffman through imaginative seduction.

For a long time, Desiderio journeys through chronological time observing landscapes and populations that, though grotesque, are at least minimally based on the real. He eventually enters "Nebulous" time, a creation of Hoffman. What is wrong is not that time and space disappear as structures but that humanity disappears when fantasy rules. The nameless centaurs, in which the horse portion dominates, are not merely ludicrous in their religion (as perhaps Carter perceives religious humans); they are also nonhuman. When Desiderio and Albertina proceed to Hoffman's castle and the site of his infernal desire machine—a technological thing that creates a fantasy world—Desiderio realizes that his power has made Hoffman absolutely bland. After Desiderio destroys Hoffman's castle and returns home a hero, he, too, loses all passion for life.

What is most effective in this novel is language. Carter's lucid descriptive power pulls the reader from the realm of ideas into the dramatic energy of a captivating story. Vividly, humorously, and poetically, Carter presents the philosophical dilemma of the interactions and subversions of the ordered world that the human mind demands and the chaotic world that human imagination desires. Although sadism and destruction are everywhere, the voice of the narrator never drags, and the rich prose details speed the reader through this disturbing landscape.

—*Francine Dempsey*

The Instrumentality of Mankind

Stories that relate events in humankind's development, from the forgotten First Age of Space to the discovery of space[3]

Author: Cordwainer Smith (Paul Myron Anthony Linebarger, 1913-1966)
Genre: Science fiction—future history
Type of work: Stories
Time of plot: Various times between the close of World War II and 15,000 C.E.
Locations: Earth, Venus, various other planets, and aboard spacecraft
First published: 1979

The Story

Nine stories in this collection are part of Cordwainer Smith's future history, several involving the Instrumentality. The last five stories are not part of the common future history, although Smith pursues his usual themes in them.

"No, No, Not Rogov!" is set shortly after World War II. Rogov and his wife, both scientists and members of the Soviet elite, work on an espionage machine (often killing human test subjects) by which they will be able to tune in and confuse the thoughts of others. When Rogov tries the completed machine, a slight miscalculation causes him to see the beautiful celebration of The Glory and Affirmation of Man being held in 13,582 C.E. As a result of seeing this celebration, he falls into a permanent trance. Rogov's wife, who caught a glimpse of the fabulous vision, refuses to continue the experiments.

In "War No. 81-Q," set in 2127 C.E., the Mongolian Alliance and the Americans receive permission to wage war with radio-controlled aeroships. When Jack Bearden takes control of the remaining American ships, he falters, realizing that he is an overrated hero. He goes on to eke out a victory and gain fame as the Charles Lindbergh of the twenty-second century.

"Mark Elf" is set in the era following the Ancient Wars. Laird, a telepath, locates an ancient satellite carrying Carlotta vom Acht in suspended animation. In the forest where she lands, Carlotta confronts the strange creatures roaming Earth, including Mark Elf, a machine that kills anybody not having German thoughts. She is protected by a talking bear, who tells her that Laird, who sees in her the regeneration of the True Men, will be her husband.

In "The Queen of the Afternoon," the sequel to "Mark Elf," Carlotta, unable to rejuvenate, has grown old and decrepit, unlike Laird, who remains youthful. He calls down a second satellite, one containing Juli, Carlotta's sister. Upon Carlotta's death, Juli marries Laird and helps him overthrow the Jwindz overlords who held mind control over humanity. Juli grows old in her turn, but Laird refuses rejuvenation, choosing to die with her. The last sister called down, Karla, will work out her own fate.

In "When the People Fell," Dobyns Bennett is working at the Experimental Area on Venus when the Chinesians parachute down 83 million people in a single day. Despite countless casualties, they set up home and eliminate the competitive Martian life-form. Bennett meets, comes to love, and marries Terza, daughter of Scanner of Vomact (one of the descendants, presumably, of the vom Acht sisters who show up in minor roles throughout Smith's fiction).

"Think Blue, Count Two" is about Veesey, a young girl who is a crew backup on a long-term interstellar flight. Awakened en route, she tries to prevent violence between the male crew members, Trece and Talatashar. Out of jealousy, Talatashar overpowers Trece and Veesey, threatening to carry out unspeakable atrocities against them and all the passengers in cold storage. They are saved by a device that Veesey activates by remembering a poem. At their destination, the vast loneliness of space behind them, Veesey and Talatashar find that they are attracted to each other.

"The Colonel Came Back from Nothing-at-All" concerns Colonel Harkening, who appears from nowhere and is unable to respond to stimuli. A young girl makes telepathic contact with the colonel, who has been in space^2 where faster-than-light travel is possible. His adventures bring humankind into the age of planoforming.

In "From Gustible's Planet," the aliens from Gustible, the obnoxious Apicians, so love human food and liquor that they flock to Earth to gorge on its treats. Humans discover that the ducklike creatures are extraordinarily tasty, so the Apicians, to avoid being eaten, retreat to their home planet.

In "Drunkboat" (with obvious allusions to Arthur Rimbaud's "The Drunken Boat"), Lord Crudelta of the Instrumentality, to show the existence of space^3, places Artyr Rambo a galaxy away from his beloved Elizabeth. To return to her, he must travel in space^3, where movement is instantaneous from any spot to any other, no matter the distance. Rambo describes space^3 as a realm of fantastic visions, though it is not a place he wants to revisit. The discovery of space[3] brings humankind to the brink of a new age.

Analysis

The stories in this collection fill in some of the blanks in Cordwainer Smith's future history, particularly events occurring in the forgotten First Age of Space and in the aftermath of the Ancient Wars. Smith gives details on that era, during which animals acquired human capabilities, speech in particular. These animals are similar to the beings that, in *The Best of Cordwainer Smith* (1975) and the novel *Norstrilia* (1975), are presented as the underpeople.

The Instrumentality of the title is perhaps a theological term, indicating the power vested in the priest who carries out the will of God. In Smith's work the Instrumentality is a priestly bureaucracy leading humankind through its travails. Although the stories of *The Best of Cordwainer Smith* are more important in characterizing the Instrumentality, *The Instrumentality of Mankind* fills in important details on its early history and its inner working.

"War No. 81-Q" suggests a sterile, bureaucratized future, but the stories otherwise show the tremendous drama inherent in the future. Rogov's wife stops unethical experiments when she sees the beautiful thing that the future will become.

These stories show the power of love, a common theme in Smith's work. For love, Laird forgos the rejuvenation that will extend his life. Dobyns Bennett finds love in the midst of 83 million parachuting Chinesians, love is behind Veesey's dangerous situation in the depths of interstellar space, and Rambo jumps a galaxy to reach his beloved Elizabeth.

The stories also celebrate simplicity and innocence. Rambo is a simple soul, and it is a child who is able to recover Colonel Harkening. The animal people in "Mark Elf" (1957) and "The Queen of the Afternoon" (1978) exude innocence. These two stories mark an evolution in Smith's style. Written with the simplicity of a child's tale, they elicit a rich imaginary world in which the improbable and the possible mix and become real. This is the essence of Smith's work.

—Steve Anderson

Inter Ice Age 4

Professor Katsumi's development of a computer that can predict the future provides a basis for exploring the dilemma of how to use that information

Author: Kōbō Abe (1924-1993)
Genre: Science fiction—future history
Type of work: Novel
Time of plot: The mid-twentieth century
Location: Tokyo, Japan
First published: *Daiyon kampyōki* (1959; serial form, 1958-1959; English translation, 1970)

The Story

Inter Ice Age 4 is a thought-provoking, futuristic novel exploring the complications brought about by the development of a computer that can predict the future. As the novel begins, a computer that can make political predictions, named Moscow I, already has been developed. Professor Katsumi, at the Institute for Computer Technique (ICT), wants to build a similar machine of his own. He succeeds, and to parallel the Moscow machine, he names his machine ICT I. Frightened of the possible repercussions, the Japanese government bans application of the machine to any questions with political overtones. When Katsumi asks ICT I what to do, it suggests that it be tested on an individual because the government should not object to such a small-scale test.

When Katsumi's computer and its program are ready to be tested, the computer gives instructions that the person chosen to test the program must not know that he or she is being sought and that selection is to be random. It is determined ahead of time, by random choice, that the person will be male. Other "standards" dictate someone of "ordinary" appearance, but otherwise the choice, to be made by Katsumi and his colleague Tanomogi, is to be random.

Katsumi and Tanomogi decide on a man they see in a small cafe. When the man leaves, they follow him to an apartment building, where they observe some unexplained shadows of two men and a woman through the window. As the hour grows late, they return home without discovering explanations. The next morning's headlines reveal that the test subject, Tsuchida Susuma, has been murdered. ICT I still can read his mind, however, and the information that it reveals implicates Professor Katsumi himself in the murder.

Meanwhile, other complications develop. Katsumi's wife is forced to have an abortion, and a laboratory is found where fetuses are being turned into aquatic beings. The computer predicts a climactic shift, Inter Ice Age 4, that will put Earth's surface under water; hence the need for aquatic adaptation of humans. It becomes evident that during this inter ice age to come, humans will be faced with two choices: to resort to something of a reverse evolution—back to fins and gills—or to drown and be obliterated in the process. Neither horn of the dilemma is palatable.

As layers of unanswered questions continue to pile up, Katsumi intuitively senses some connection among the unexplained events but is unable to draw any conclusions. Meanwhile, the behavior of personnel in the ICT toward him seems strange, but this too is inexplicable. Katsumi becomes suspicious of everyone, no longer knowing whom he can trust. When ICT I finally reveals the blueprint of the future, Katsumi is not among those present. Upon inquiry, Katsumi is told, "No, Professor. You are long since. . . ." The developer of the computer has become its victim. It had predicted his opposition to development of an aquan form of human life and, through a Katsumi simulation developed within the computer, even hired an assassin to kill the real Katsumi. Katsumi thus is trapped within a conspiracy headed by himself, in simulated form.

Analysis

Inter Ice Age 4 belongs to the genre of science fiction because of its use of computer technology. Robots and other machines were popular vehicles for telling fantasy tales before the computer superseded some of them. In Fredric Brown's "Etaoin Shrdlu" (1942), for example, a linotype machine comes to life after being animated by a technician from an alien civilization.

Science fiction quickly made use of the computer when it appeared. Kōbō Abe uses the computer to address the moral and philosophical complexity that arises when a machine makes available information that forces humans to face a dilemma: whether to cease to exist or instead to adapt as a nonhuman form of life. *Inter Ice Age 4* addresses the question of human reaction to learning that catastrophe and total disruption of ordinary life are to occur. Death by drowning is an unattractive choice, but the alternative, regression to an earlier stage of evolution, is not viable to Katsumi. He cannot accept the notion that his unborn child, when aborted and sold to the fetus laboratory, will be turned into a fishlike creature. The plot employs a device common to Abe's fiction: inversion of roles. Katsumi's genius ironically becomes the vehicle of his defeat.

The original Japanese version of the book, *Daiyon kampyōki*, was among Abe's earliest works. E. Dale Saunder's English translation did not appear until 1970. Abe, a novelist and dramatist, was at his peak during the 1960's, though a number of his major works were not available in English translation until the 1970's. Although others of his works contain bizarre situations and behavior, they are not science fiction as such. *Inter Ice Age 4* shares themes with Abe's other writing, in terms of dealing with life's frightening and unnerving dilemmas and with feelings of isolation or alienation.

Abe is considered to be one of Japan's greatest modern writers. More than half of his longer works, including some plays, have been translated into English. Critics of the translated works have tended to verify the reputation that Japanese critics already had established for Abe. Because a translated work necessarily is judged in part by the quality of the translation, it is not always easy to separate the two. Abe's translator also enjoys a reputation for excellence.

—*Victoria Price*

Inverted World

An inhabitant of a city traveling perpetually through a strange
hyperboloid world discovers the truth about his reality

Author: Christopher Priest (1943-   )
Genre: Science fiction—closed universe
Type of work: Novel
Time of plot: The twenty-second century
Location: Portugal
First published: 1974

The Story

The setting and notion behind this novel first appeared in a short story
of the same title published in *New Writings in SF 22* (1973), though the
idea was more fully developed in the novel. The setting is Earth City, a
curious structure that is winched along a set of rails that are perennially
being removed from behind the city and replaced in front. The city must
keep moving or it will suffer a terrible fate. What this fate is, and why, is
revealed only gradually during the course of the novel.

Helward Mann, having reached adulthood, is apprenticed to the
Future guild, though he must first spend time working with each of the
other guilds that are vital to the city's survival. He begins with the track
layers and learns that the city must keep moving in pursuit of "the Optimum," though he does not yet know what the Optimum might be. He
also discovers that the sun is a flattened disc from which infinitely long
spikes protrude top and bottom.

Later, Helward learns more about the threatening nature of the world
when he escorts a group of native women back to their village. The further south from the city he goes, the more the landscape is distorted. A
deep chasm that delayed the city while a bridge was built has turned
into a narrow creek. The women start to grow shorter and fatter. He himself feels an almost irresistible pull, like centrifugal force, that nearly
sweeps him away. There are time distortions as well, so that a journey of
only a few subjective days in fact takes many months.

Helward pieces together the information he has about the city and
concludes that its inhabitants are survivors of an expedition from Earth
on a hyperboloid planet where the ever-moving optimum is the only

place where Earth-like conditions obtain. Elizabeth, whom Helward meets on one of his expeditions north of the city, reveals a different, more devastating truth: They are actually on Earth and are survivors of an experiment with a different sort of power made at the time of "the Crash." The experiment has inverted their perceptions of their world.

Analysis

The opening sentence of this novel is "I had reached the age of six hundred and fifty miles"; it has justly become one of the most famous in science fiction. In its skewed perception, it neatly encapsulates the radical and original idea that lies behind this book. The inverted world is one of the few truly original ideas to have been developed in contemporary science fiction.

The slow revelation of the nature of the world is beautifully handled, and Helward's journey to the South, full of vivid images, dramatically demonstrates both the nature and the threat of the world. Christopher Priest contrasts this closed universe with the closed society of the city, which, because of its isolation in a threatening environment, has become rigid and hierarchical. Helward starts by being opposed to the hierarchy and to the institutionalized secrecy, but as he learns more about the nature of his world he comes to accept the need for these restrictions, even though they come to separate him from his wife, Victoria.

In a devastatingly effective coup de théâtre, Priest produces a final revelation that twists everything that has gone before. The more Helward has accepted the hierarchy, the less he is able to accept the truth about the real nature of his world.

Elizabeth, the intruder from the normal world who appears at the end to reveal the truth about Earth City, is rather like a *deus ex machina*, nowhere near as fully realized as Helward or any of the other characters. Her explanation of the way the inhabitants of the city have been infected by their own source of power only ties off the loose ends. The real force of the ending lies in the fact that after their unknowing journey across Asia and Europe the inhabitants of the city have reached the shores of the Atlantic and can go no further: The optimum can never be achieved.

Dating from early in his career, *Inverted World* is untypical of Priest's work. His early novels, such as *Fugue for a Darkening Island* (1972), were austere New Wave takes on traditional British tropes such as the catastrophe novel. His later books, such as *A Dream of Wessex* (1977), are challenging and disturbing examinations of the nature of identity in which the science-fictional ideas are often only tangential to the psychological depth. There are elements of both of these approaches in *Inverted World*.

There is something coolly detached about the characterization that is typical of the British New Wave, for example, while the focus of the book is as much on the inverted world within Helward's mind as it is on the world around him.

There is an exuberance in the sheer science-fictional invention of the book that Priest has not approached, or even attempted, before or since. It is not his best book, for his writing has steadily gained greater depth and power as his career has progressed, but it remains one of his most popular. It won the British Science Fiction Association Award and is one of the key works of postwar British science fiction.

—*Paul Kincaid*

The Invisible Man

A demented research chemist invents a way to become invisible hoping that it will give him unlimited power, but he discovers that his invisibility limits his freedom and eventually unhinges his mind

Author: H(erbert) G(eorge) Wells (1866-1946)
Genre: Science fiction—superbeing
Type of work: Novel
Time of plot: The late nineteenth century
Location: Rural Sussex, England
First published: 1897

The Story

The Invisible Man: A Grotesque Romance begins on a wintry day in February. A mysterious, oddly dressed stranger arrives at the Coach and Horses pub in the town of Iping in rural Sussex. His entire body is covered: Even his face is swathed in a muffler, and his eyes are hidden behind dark glasses. Although the landlady and her husband, the Halls, are curious about his bizarre appearance, they readily agree to rent him a room because it is the off-season. The next day, the stranger's luggage arrives, consisting of several crates of chemicals and books. Because of his furtive and solitary nature, the stranger quickly becomes the object of local gossip.

Mrs. Hall, who believes he has been in a horrible disfiguring accident, soon perceives unbelievable things in her guest's eccentricities. It appears that he has no lower half to his jaw, for example, and as his brusqueness becomes more violent, she suspects that there is more to his behavior than can be explained by mere physical deformity. After he runs out of money, a rash of petty thefts in the village point to the strange lodger as the culprit. His invisibility finally is discovered when Mrs. Hall calls in Jaffers, the local constable, to evict him for not paying his bill. The village inhabitants panic.

Naked and on the run, the invisible man coerces a tramp, Thomas Marvel, to aid him in his escape. Marvel retrieves three scientific notebooks from the Coach and Horses and steals money for the fugitive. As news of the invisible man spreads around the countryside, he makes his way to Port Stowe, where he finds refuge with an old university mate of his, Dr. Kemp. Kemp harbors his friend, who is revealed to be named Griffin, and is fascinated by the achievement of his former classmate. Kemp becomes alarmed, however, as Griffin describes in gruesome detail the scientific experiments he carried out to perfect his invisibility and how, in his single-minded pursuit of his discoveries, he stole money from his father, causing his bankruptcy and eventually his death, events for which he seems to feel little remorse. It is apparent that the process has unhinged Griffin's mind as well as transforming his body.

An advertising poster for James Whale's film production of The Invisible Man, *starring Claude Rains and Gloria Stuart.*

As Griffin begins to rail about his newly found power over others and proposes a reign of terror to be visited by him on the general population in retaliation for the general neglect of his achievements, Kemp decides to turn him over to the authorities. Griffin, however, escapes once again and in a gratuitous act murders a man in broad daylight. Because of his betrayal, Kemp now becomes the object of Griffin's wrath. In cooperation with the police, he sets himself up as a decoy. The invisible man finally is cornered and killed by a smashing blow from a worker's spade. In death, he loses his invisibility and reappears.

The novel ends with a strange epilogue. The tramp, Marvel, with the money he stole for Griffin, buys a pub, which he names The Invisible Man. He regales his customers with tales of his exploits. After hours, Marvel peruses Griffin's notebooks, which contain his scientific notes. Marvel has hidden these notebooks from the police and Dr. Kemp. In the solitude of his pub, he dreams of rediscovering the formula for invisibility and achieving the power and wealth he assumes that such a state would afford.

Analysis

H. G. Wells wrote five "scientific romances" in the 1890's. It is on these novels that his reputation largely rests. *The Invisible Man* is the third, nestled between *The Island of Dr. Moreau* (1896) and *The War of the Worlds* (1898). Like Mary Shelley's *Frankenstein* (1818), it is a cautionary tale of how science can get out of control and do more harm than good.

Although Wells often is called the inventor of science fiction, *The Invisible Man* is not really a story of what is scientifically possible but rather is a moral romance about the corruption of power. As a contemporary critic remarked, the imagination is everything, the science nothing. Unlike Jules Verne, with whom he is often compared, Wells was less concerned with the accuracy of his science than with the consequences of it.

Wells was firmly anchored in the values and the preoccupations of his time, a period of intense speculation characterized by a feeling of weariness with the past and a foreboding about the future. There was a sense that the whole elaborate Victorian order was teetering on the brink of collapse, both intellectually and socially. *Fin de siècle* attitudes appeared in the literary work of Henrik Ibsen, George Bernard Shaw, Oscar Wilde, and, most obviously, Friedrich Nietzsche, whose ideas of the *Übermensch* figure prominently in *The Invisible Man*. The theories of Charles Darwin, Sigmund Freud, and Karl Marx that helped to overturn the intellectual and moral certainties of the nineteenth century and shaped the new world of the twentieth also can be found in Wells's early romances.

The Invisible Man contains a blend of fantasy and the everyday. It is a comic novel that plays with rural stereotypes of narrow-mindedness and credulity and yet does so with the serious intent of exposing the fragile security of modern life. As Griffin's invisibility allows animal instincts to surface in him, the threat to public safety stampedes the crowd. Griffin violates the ethics of modern science by pursuing knowledge as a means to power and not for its own sake. Like Dr. Jekyll in Robert Louis Stevenson's *The Strange Case of Dr. Jekyll and Mr. Hyde* (1886), Griffin releases in himself a dark side normally held in check by civilized codes of conduct.

The Invisible Man contains a fable in which Wells examines the myths of nineteenth century culture, particularly the hubris of science, with its pretensions of infallibility and progress. It is a nervous book, full of fear concerning collapse of the sureties of the past and yet apprehensive about the possibilities for the future.

—*Charles L. P. Silet*

The Iron Dragon's Daughter

A human girl grows up in a harsh, industrialized fairyland

Author: Michael Swanwick (1950-   )
Genre: Fantasy—magical world
Type of work: Novel
Time of plot: The 1990's
Location: Faerie
First published: 1994

The Story

Jane, a human changeling, is a child laborer in a grim factory in Faerie, where dragons, which are huge, sentient war machines, are manufactured. Her companions there are supernatural beings lead by Rooster, a Puck-like figure who plots to use witchcraft to kill their cruel overseer, Blugg. While attempting to steal Blugg's nail parings from his office in order to carry out the murder, Jane finds and takes a grimoire containing the specifications for a dragon. Jane begins memorizing the grimoire in order to take power over a dragon who is mentally contacting her.

During a test of new equipment, both Blugg and Rooster are killed. Jane forces the dragon's true name, Melanchthon, from him, and together they escape from the factory. Finally free, Jane lives secretly with the dragon, attends school, and learns shoplifting from Rat-snickle. Melanchthon desires that she become educated so she can become an engineer and complete his repairs. She must remain a virgin in order to work on him.

Jane meets Peter of the Hillside and Gwenhidwy the Green, the Wicker Queen. At year's end, Gwen is to be a human sacrifice and Peter will be castrated, but in the intervening year she can do or have anything she wants. Peter, although he loves Gwen, cannot have sex with her; he must remain a virgin in order to be her "sin eater," vicariously suffering Gwen's pain and guilt during her final year of life. Because Jane loves Peter, she seduces him and keeps him from the sacrifice. She also discovers that, like Rooster, his true name is Tetigistus.

Gwen is burned to death on schedule, with a substitute partner. Peter later hangs himself in guilt over not going through with the sacrifice. Melanchthon abandons Jane, because she is no longer a virgin.

Next, Jane attends a university, where she majors in alchemy. Her studies do not go well, and the "Teind" is coming, an anarchistic holiday in which one tenth of everything—including human life—is sacrificed. If Jane does not shape up, she will be on the Teind list. Fortunately, Jane's classmate Sirin tells her how to perform alchemical experiments successfully through sex magic.

Jane meets Puck Aleshire, a young man similar to Peter and Rooster. She is drawn to him but frightened of the consequences. She also begins visiting her human mother in dreams and tells her that she is studying to return to the human world. Because Jane needs money, she attempts to burglarize the elf-lord Galiagante. He captures her but spares her, promising employment if she survives the Teind.

Later, Jane unexpectedly discovers Melanchthon. He invites her to join him as pilot in an assault on the Goddess herself, the seemingly malevolent creator of Jane's universe and her perverse fate. She refuses, and at that moment the Teind begins, Jane is swept along by a mob and becomes part of it. She is rescued from a battle by Puck, who is later killed in a duel. Sirin also is killed. Both were avatars, or incarnations, of Rooster/Peter and Gwen.

Again Jane meets Melanchthon, who insists that the Goddess is only a cover for the meaninglessness of the universe and that it is the universe itself that he wishes to destroy. Jane finally agrees to help.

In her post-Teind role as a sycophant to Galiagante, Jane meets the dragon-pilot Rocket, the final avatar of Rooster/Peter/Puck. They fall in love and begin an affair. Jane returns from their tryst to find Melanchthon under attack and ready to begin the flight to Spiral Castle, the Goddess's stronghold. Rocket and his dragon squadron follow, and Jane kills him in the pursuit. Melanchthon is destroyed before reaching the castle. Jane is received in the castle by the Goddess in the form of Jane's mother, Sylvia, and is returned to her mortal body on Earth.

Analysis

The opening of *The Iron Dragon's Daughter* conveys an atmosphere reminiscent of Charles Dickens's work, with its exploited children and "dark, Satanic mills." The book is replete with references to other works of the fantastic, drawn from all eras. For example, Dr. Nemesis, Jane's alchemy professor, was a student of the unfortunate Friar Bungay, the hero of the Renaissance play *Friar Bacon and Friar Bungay*, in which an oracular brass head is brought to life. On another occasion, Jane receives a memo from the Office of Penitence and Truth, a title of the torturer's guild in Gene Wolfe's Book of the New Sun sequence (1980-1983). There are also

passing references to Ys (setting for a fantasy by Poul Anderson), Lyon-
esse (Jack Vance), and a host of other places drawn from modern fantasy
and traditional folklore.

Edward James defines the science-fiction genre of cyberpunk as a combination of "cyber," from cybernetics, the study of systems in machines and
animals, and "punk," from 1970's rock terminology referring to aggressive,
alienated, antiestablishment youth. *The Iron Dragon's Daughter* has been
called "fairypunk": It takes many elements of traditional fantasy and
fuses them with cyberpunk sensibilities and some of the motifs and concerns of urban fantasy. It shares with cyberpunk the gritty, industrial, urban settings; an aggressive pop-fiction sexuality; and a concern with the
brand-name details of imaginary technological systems. In this case, the
latter is a system of magic, consistent within its own frame of reference,
that makes playful use of alchemical, hermetic, tantric, kabbalistic, and
other esoteric systems, as well as every type of fairy lore imaginable. The
whole is spiced with references to drugs and technology, imaginatively
integrated with the fierce, cold elves of medieval legend.

—*George E. Nicholas*

Islands in the Net

Laura Webster travels in many lands attempting to avert bloody wars and a nuclear attack in a postmillennial age supposedly devoid of bullets and bombs

Author: Bruce Sterling (1954-   )
Genre: Science fiction—extrapolatory
Type of work: Novel
Time of plot: 2022-c. 2025
Location: Various locations on Earth
First published: 1988

The Story

Laura and David Webster, along with a small staff, run a guest house in Galveston, Texas, for the Rizome firm, a quasi-communal corporation structured loosely around a Japanese feudal system. David and Laura are associates of this multinational firm and have become coordinators to rear a family (they have an infant daughter, Loretta) and to make themselves visible to the Rizome dignitaries who vacation at the guest house.

Both Laura and David are on the fast track to success in their occupations when the company informs them that they will be hosting special guests for a conference. Through Emily, a close friend in Rizome, Laura learns these guests are data pirates, people who live on "islands" outside the established Net structure, stealing and selling data to whoever is willing to buy it. Laura soon finds herself entwined in the debates among three data pirate factions and Rizome.

The stakes are raised when, during the night, a Grenadian representative at the conference, a Rastafarian named Malcolm, is shot to death by a flying assassin drone as Laura watches. A terrorist group claims responsibility, but Grenada blames its rival data pirate, Singapore. Laura perceives an obligation, as a Rizome associate, to go to Grenada and help defuse the situation. This quickly involves Laura in an adventure that takes her from Grenada to Singapore to Africa and finally back to Galveston and the Rizome headquarters in Atlanta, Georgia.

The journey takes a little more than two years. During this time, Laura develops as an individual and as a member of humanity. She is exposed to myriad cultures and ideologies throughout her travels. By the end of the novel, Laura has matured. When she returns to her husband and child, she finds that her life will never be the same. *Islands in the Net* is thus a twenty-first century, feminist *Bildungsroman*.

Analysis

In an interview with Larry McCaffery in *Across the Wounded Galaxies* (1990), Bruce Sterling notes that *Islands in the Net* is "not really cyberpunk." Furthermore, Sterling admits that he either refutes or manipulates many of the tenets of cyberpunk and knows that he will be accused of trying to change or expand the nature of cyberpunk fiction rather than having critics recognize his novels simply as stories about the future. In most cases, Sterling has been correct in this assertion—most critics link this novel to the cyberpunk genre.

It is, however, more about the future than it is a traditional cyberpunk novel. There is "cyber," to some extent, in *Islands in the Net*, but there is no "punk," except for a few minor characters: Sticky, a Grenadian soldier/spy who can become an indestructible weapon by eating yogurt and activating bacteria in his stomach, and Carlotta, a New Age whore/nun of the Church of Ishtar who stays strung out on a romance-inducing drug.

Instead of typical cyberpunk characters, the novel uses a developing woman in the tradition of many *Bildungsroman* novels. Laura uses the Net as a means of communication, but she employs devices such as a portable wristwatch/monitor and a computer console to interact with it. These devices are more primitive than those typical in cyberpunk fiction.

Laura uses technology no more or less than other corporate individuals in the novel. Readers get a sense of cutting-edge technology, such as the video glasses that Laura and David wear in Grenada when they are "on-line" for Rizome, but this technology is new and expensive. It is not available to the everyday street hustler or consumer, as it is in most cyberpunk worlds. *Islands in the Net* has no brain implants, prosthetic devices, or genetic planning in its mainstream world. Technological breakthroughs do occur in the data havens, such as Grenada's darkening suntan lotion (which Rizome steals and, later, markets) and the black-market hormonal treatments in Singapore, but, for the most part, the world is not much different from that of today.

Sterling, in the McCaffery interview, correctly asserts that *Islands in the Net* will date quickly. The novel refers to the Soviet Union, which dissolved less than a decade after the novel was published, and the Internet of the real world has made some of the concepts of the fictional Net familiar to readers rather than being primarily speculative, as they were when the novel was published.

The human interactions that Sterling develops throughout the work, however, are what make this novel endure. Readers take part in Laura's inner struggles with the many ideologies that she must confront, then accept or deny. Most important, on her journey Laura experiences people, even ones not connected to information as she knows it, such as the inhabitants of Africa, which is a true "island" surrounded by a sea of inaccessible Net. She learns, accepts, and is even willing to die for some ideologies. Laura confronts the unknown terror of nuclear war and learns what it is to be human and vulnerable.

Sterling leaves readers with the feeling that Laura is a changed and enlightened individual. By doing this, he suggests that others who simply embrace technology and view it as progress can change. Finally, Sterling implies that the world is a somewhat better place for what Laura has done. Through the media, the Net's "army," she is able to expose the inner workings of the corrupted powers in the world. The novel does not espouse that utopia can be reached; rather, it suggests that technology is, in its own way, a powerful ideology to be studied before, and if, it is embraced.

—*Alan I. Rea, Jr.*

Journey to the Center of the Earth

A German scientist, his nephew, and their guide enter a volcano in Iceland, travel toward the center of the earth, and exit through a volcano in Italy

Author: Jules Verne (1828-1905)
Genre: Science fiction—planetary romance
Type of work: Novel
Time of plot: 1863
Location: Germany, Iceland, the volcanic island of Stromboli, and inside Earth
First published: *Voyage au centre de la terre* (1864; English translation as *Journey to the Centre of the Earth*, 1872)

The Story

The three major characters in Jules Verne's *Journey to the Center of the Earth* are a German mineralogist and geologist named Otto Lidenbrock, his nephew Axel, and their Icelandic guide, Hans. This novel is a first-person narrative told from Axel's point of view.

Otto Lidenbrock is a stereotypical scientist, obsessed with his research projects. He has little understanding of or patience with those who do not share his enthusiasm for scientific discoveries. His nephew Axel has a solid classical education, but his main interest in life is his love for Graüben, Lidenbrock's goddaughter.

Lidenbrock's hobby is collecting old books and manuscripts. One day, he discovers a mysterious message written in Old Icelandic by a sixteenth century scientist named Arne Saknussemm. Axel decodes this message for his uncle. They learn that Saknussemm claimed to have traveled from an Icelandic volcano toward the hollow center of the earth. Lidenbrock and Axel soon realize that no one before them had decoded Saknussemm's message. They decide to travel to Iceland and attempt to replicate Saknussemm's journey to the center of the earth.

After an arduous boat ride to Iceland, they hire a temperamental guide named Hans. The three of them go into the Mount Sneffels volcano in Iceland and discover an extraordinary world hidden beneath the crust of the earth. To their amazement, they observe massive mushrooms, plants, and fossils, along with an extensive series of lakes and

Jules Verne. (Library of Congress)

rivers. Several times, as they explore passages that lead nowhere, they almost run out of water, but each time they eventually find a path that appears to take them closer to the center of the earth.

Near the end of the novel, Lidenbrock, Axel, and Hans realize that they have begun to travel back toward the surface. When they exit from a volcano, they find themselves not in Iceland but rather on the volcanic island of Stromboli, near Sicily. After Lidenbrock and Axel return to Hamburg, Germany, the geologist resumes his scientific research and Axel marries Graüben.

Analysis

Although Verne's career as a writer had begun in 1850, his works enjoyed little popular success before the publication of *Journey to the Center of the Earth* in November, 1864. The novel sold so well that his Parisian publisher, Jules Hetzel, offered Verne a 50 percent increase in payments for all future novels. Hetzel had no qualms about paying three thousand French francs per novel because he believed that Verne's future novels also would sell well. This significant increase in his earnings enabled Verne to resign his job as a stockbroker. He spent the remaining years of his life as a full-time writer of science-fiction novels. His work remained popular both in France and around the world.

Verne's publisher at first thought that *Journey to the Center of the Earth* and Verne's many other science-fiction novels describing fantastic voyages would appeal almost exclusively to young children. Adult readers, however, also discovered much of interest in Verne's writings, and sales of Verne's books were higher than expected.

A superficial reading of *Journey to the Center of the Earth* or other, equally popular novels by Verne such as *From the Earth to the Moon* (1865) and *Twenty Thousand Leagues Under the Sea* (1870) might make them appear to be little more than highly fanciful but almost unbelievable descriptions of trips to distant places in outer space, under the water, or under Earth's crust. The novels, however, also reveal profound psychological insights into the effects of these mysterious voyages on their characters. *Journey to the Center of the Earth* is not an objective third-person narrative that describes an unsuccessful effort to find the center of the earth but rather a first-person narrative. This form helps Verne to show how a terrifying trip transformed the narrator, Axel, from an immature young man into a thoughtful and psychologically stable adult.

Axel's entrance into the Mount Sneffels volcano constitutes the beginning of his voyage of self-discovery. He is forced to face his fear of dying, his alienation from his obsessive Uncle Otto, and his doubts about the depth of his feelings for his girlfriend, Graüben. Several times during the voyage, Axel is separated from his companions. This solitude gives him the opportunity to reflect seriously on the meaning of his existence. Unlike his blindly optimistic uncle, Axel is not at all certain that he will not lose his life in this dangerous effort to prove the validity of Saknussemm's double hypothesis that Earth is hollow and that, therefore, people can travel to its center. Axel comes to realize that this voyage into a volcano represents a voyage into the unknown, of which he is afraid.

By means of this fictional voyage, Verne helps readers to deal with the hidden and mysterious elements in their own personalities and psyches. The title of William Butcher's *Verne's Journey to the Centre of the Self* (1990) suggests the profound psychological voyage of selfdiscovery that Axel undertook. Readers can experience such self-discovery for themselves when they appreciate the many levels of meaning in Verne's novel.

—*Edmund J. Campion*

The King of Elfland's Daughter

> The Lord of Erl sends his son Alveric on a quest to marry the King of Elfland's daughter and bring magic back to Erl

Author: Lord Dunsany (Edward John Morton Drax Plunkett, 1878-1957)
Genre: Fantasy—heroic fantasy
Type of work: Novel
Time of plot: Indeterminate
Location: Erl, a village in Elfland
First published: 1924

The Story

A poet, novelist, and playwright (he worked with William Butler Yeats at the Abbey Theatre), Lord Dunsany draws upon Irish fable and myth to situate the story of *The King of Elfland's Daughter*. The novel opens with the Parliament of Erl asking for a "magic lord" to rule them because for seven hundred years there has been "no new thing." To accommodate them, their present Lord asks his son Alveric to "pass the fields we know" into Elfland in order to marry Lirazel, the king's daughter. Alveric's father gives him his ancient battle sword for his journey, but Alveric knows that only a magical sword can prevail against the King of Elfland. He visits the witch Ziroonderel, who fashions a new enchanted sword from thunderbolts.

Traveling east to the Elfin Mountains along the border of Elfland, Alveric stops at an old leatherworker's cottage to obtain a scabbard for his magical sword. The old man makes the scabbard but refuses to discuss matters pertaining to Elfland. Alveric thanks him for his hospitality and strides away. Once inside Elfland, Alveric succeeds in fighting Lirazel's guards. Lirazel falls in love with Alveric's powerful grace and chivalry, and she elopes with him back to Erl. Unfortunately, Lirazel cannot easily adjust to the vastly different customs of Alveric's people or to Earth's passage of time. She never quite fits into Erl's community. When their child Orion is born, the witch Ziroonderel becomes his nurse and protects him with her magic.

The King of Elfland, recognizing that his daughter will age and eventually die on Earth, writes a powerful spell in order to call her back to Elfland. He hands it to the troll Lurulu and orders him to cross the border and give the rune scroll to the princess. Lirazel takes the scroll and locks it in a casket; she resists reading it, instinctively knowing that its enormous power can reach beyond the confines of Elfland and draw her back. Nevertheless, when Alveric forces her to worship "Christom things," she intuits that she can never be happy in Erl and finally reads the scroll. A wind from Elfland releases her from the materiality of Earth and blows her back to Elfland, away from "the fields we know."

Lord Dunsany. (Library of Congress)

Although the quest clearly is futile, Alveric remains determined to reclaim his elfish bride and the magic he has lost. He embarks on a quest for the Elfin Mountains and leaves Orion in the care of Ziroonderel. His magic sword, having once crossed the border, now gives away his presence. The King of Elfland makes the Elfin border ebb so that Alveric, obsessed with the retrieval of Lirazel, is doomed to wander without hope of success, his sword's magic warning the king of his approach.

Orion, as his name suggests, becomes a hunter and eventually leads Erl. Orion's magical nature ultimately asserts itself when he recruits Lurulu and other Elfland trolls in hunting unicorns near the border. The Parliament of Erl, once solicitous of magic, begins to realize that Orion's nature draws magical creatures across the border. Afraid of "overmuch magic," they plead with Ziroonderel to give them a spell against the increasing presence of witchery. When she refuses, they go the Christian friar (Freer) to curse the magic Orion attracts and protect them from its influence.

Lirazel, though secure once again in Elfland, still longs for the earthly things she has abandoned, particularly her husband and her son. She pleads with her father for the last great rune that will call them across the border and into her safekeeping. Although reluctant to give up his greatest weapon against the passage of time and the power of material things, he relents. With the last of his runes, the king calls Orion and Alveric back to Lirazel and extends the boundary of Elfland into Erl until Erl passes beyond "the fields we know" and "out of all remembrance of men." Only the holy place of the Freer and his garden remain untouched by the king's rune.

Analysis

Dunsany's novel illustrates the problematic nature of crossing borders. Once intermingled, Elfland and Earth influence each other in uncontrollable and unpredictable ways. Orion's mixed heritage dissolves the boundaries between Earth and Elfland, collapsing the traditional distinctions between the pragmatics of everyday life and the magical tug of the imagination. When the Parliament of Erl arrogantly wishes to incorporate magic within Earth's border, its members fail to foresee that by its very nature magic cannot be easily tamed or relinquished. Nor, perhaps, should it be. Ziroonderel explains to the members of Parliament who fear "overmuch magic" that magic is the "spice and essence of life, its ornament and its splendor." Erl's citizens rightly desire change through magic; they wrongly fear it. They also face the danger of the powerful draw of Elfland's enchantments. The King of Elfland recognizes this danger and warns Lirazel that Elfland will have no measures left against the ruthless march of Earth's material things and of men like the Freer who hate the spice and splendor of Elfland. Because of his love for his daughter, he brings forth the great rune, but he fears the consequences.

The story, far from having a happy, fairy-tale ending, concludes ambiguously. Erl has been colonized by Elfland and has passed out of historical memory. The interplay between Earth and Elfland, represented in the creation of Orion, cannot ever be truly balanced. Overpowered for now, Earth abides for other Alverics, other questers to enter Elfland and perhaps destroy it.

—Jeffrey Cass

The Land of Laughs

Thomas Abbey and Saxony Gardner travel to a small Missouri town to write a biography of Marshall France, a dead but still famous children's book author, and find that France had the power to write his characters into life

Author: Jonathan Carroll (1949-   )
Genre: Fantasy—Magical Realism
Type of work: Novel
Time of plot: The 1970's
Location: Galen, Missouri
First published: 1980

The Story

The Land of Laughs was Jonathan Carroll's first published novel. When it first appeared, it was misleadingly packaged as a juvenile book, most likely because one of the main characters is a writer of children's stories. It was not until a paperback edition of *The Land of Laughs* appeared in 1983 that the book began to earn more critical attention, and it has since become something of a cult classic.

Thomas Abbey, a man in his mid-thirties who teaches English at a boys' prep school, is trying to deal with being the son of a famous actor who died in a plane crash. He leads a solitary life, wrapped up in his hobbies of collecting masks and the written works of Marshall France, a dead but still famous children's book author who captured the imagination of both children and adults with his vivid imagery and poetic prose.

Abbey meets Saxony Gardner, a woman who shares his enthusiasm for France's work. With her encouragement, he decides to write a biography of France. Together they travel to Galen, Missouri, the small town where France spent the later years of his life. After obtaining permission from Anna France, the writer's daughter, to begin their research, Abbey and Gardner rent rooms in the town and begin to explore Galen and meet its inhabitants.

Gradually, they realize there is something odd about the little town. Abbey witnesses a boy getting hit by a car and is shocked that the townspeople are far less concerned about the boy's life than about the identity of the car's driver. Stranger and stranger things happen, until one day Abbey hears a dog talking in its sleep. He confronts Anna, who confesses that her father wrote an unfinished work detailing the lives of every resident of Galen through the year 3014. All the townspeople except Anna and a man named Richard Lee are France's creations rather than normal people. Abbey also learns that France died unexpectedly of a heart attack, and the events chronicled in his journals are no longer happening precisely as they should—for example, the boy was supposed to be hit by a car and die, but the wrong person hit

him. Anna believes that if Abbey can write a biography of France that truly catches the man's spirit, Abbey will be able to continue the future history of Galen and ensure that the townspeople live on as France envisioned.

Caught up in the unbelievable events happening all around him, Abbey plunges into writing the biography and begins an affair with Anna behind Gardner's back. Gardner, hurt by Abbey's infidelity, leaves town to think things over but comes back as Abbey finishes the chapter detailing France's arrival in Galen by train years earlier. The townspeople plan a party at the train station, supposedly to celebrate Abbey's progress on the biography. As Abbey leaves the rented house to join them, the house explodes and Gardner is killed. Abbey realizes that Galen's inhabitants planted the bomb. They no longer need Abbey and Gardner, because Abbey has written Marshall France back into being. The party at the train station actually was a welcoming celebration for the re-created France. Mourning Gardner's death, Abbey flees to Europe, where he eventually uses his newly discovered talent to write his father's biography, bringing him back to life to make peace with him.

Analysis

Since the beginning of his career, Carroll has baffled readers and literary critics, who are unsure whether to classify his work as fantasy or mainstream. The term "Magical Realism," which became more prevalent after Carroll began publishing, seems to suit his work best, as his novels all have in common a seemingly normal world in which the main character begins discovering magical and often dark secrets. Using the techniques of Magical Realism, Carroll, along with other writers such as John Crowley, has been successful in blurring the distinction between mainstream and fantasy to create a unique niche in fantastic literature.

Following *The Land of Laughs*, Carroll published several novels, as well as a collection of short stories, in a similar vein. He has earned a small but dedicated following of readers.

In many ways, *The Land of Laughs* is a typical example of Carroll's writing. He employs devices and themes that are developed further in his later novels, such as talking animals (especially dogs), characters trying to deal with the burden of having famous parents or of being famous themselves, and complicated love triangles.

It is obvious that *The Land of Laughs* is one of Carroll's early efforts. Although the people of Galen hide a secret that is revealed to be somewhat sinister, Carroll's later books address even darker issues, such as abortion, death, and disfigurement, as well as such larger concerns as religion and humanity's place in the world. It is also typical of Carroll's work that, unlike in popular fiction, the reader cannot assume that the main characters will survive unharmed. Carroll is quite willing to kill a major character if it suits his purpose.

The Land of Laughs provides a bit of insight into Carroll's personal life. Galen is based on a small Missouri town called Times Beach, where Carroll lived for a year before moving overseas to Vienna, Austria, the setting of several of his later novels. This tendency to use reality as a basis for his fiction, along with his ability to invoke a sense of whimsy, has helped Carroll create effective works of Magical Realism.

—Amy Sisson

Last and First Men

> A history of the human race from the twentieth century to the death of the Sun

Author: (William) Olaf Stapledon (1886-1950)
Genre: Science fiction—future history
Type of work: Novel
Time of plot: 1918 to two billion years in the future
Location: Earth, Venus, and Neptune
First published: 1930

The Story

Last and First Men is not technically a novel; it has no formal plot or conventional character development. Instead, it describes the evolution of the entire human race from shortly after World War I until the death of humanity on Neptune, two billion years later.

Olaf Stapledon numbers the races and species of humanity as they succeed one another, from the First Men (his generation) through the Eighteenth, a race of superbeings. The First Men collapse as a result of an energy crisis and germ warfare. After a long dark age, a Patagonian civilization develops, but it succumbs to a vast industrial accident. Eventually, the Second Men evolve. They are very intelligent but are exhausted by an ages-long struggle with Martians. The Third Men have a passion for genetics, which they develop into a religious art and use to create the Fourth Men, huge, immobile, telepathic brains. Cold and amoral, the Great Brains destroy their own makers and create the Fifth Men, who are telepathic superbeings. This race is the pinnacle of humanity on Earth.

The Fifth Men create an economic and scientific utopia lasting thousands of millennia. They begin the telepathic exploration of time and discover that the past still exists; in a sense, nothing ever perishes. This realization causes a racial depression, because the anguish of the past is never finished. Discovering that the Moon will crash into Earth, they develop spaceflight and settle Venus. The indigenous Venusians are exterminated, inducing in the Fifth Men a spiritual schizophrenia of guilt.

On Venus, there emerges a winged species, the Seventh Men. Pursued and persecuted by nonfliers, they commit mass suicide. Their successors, the Eighth Men, discover that the sun will flare into a minor nova. They design the Ninth Men to survive them by colonizing Neptune. Humanity endures on Neptune through ten species and one billion years. There the Eighteenth Men are created as the ultimate development of the human race.

Their spacefaring utopian civilization is described briefly, including their attempt to increase the intelligence of the species through establishment of sexually and telepathically linked groups of ninety-six members. Occasionally these group minds link and awake to a single race consciousness. The Eighteenth Men hope that, above the race mind, a universal soul will awake, a godlike mind whose understanding of ultimate purpose will redeem the universe from tragic futility.

The Eighteenth Men discover that a nearby star will become a supernova, finally extinguishing the human race. They undertake a project to seed the galaxy with life, in the hope that something of humanity will be preserved.

Analysis

Stapledon is sometimes considered to be H. G. Wells's successor in the British science-fiction tradition. When *Last and First Men* appeared, science fiction as a formal genre was only a few years old. Stapledon was unfamiliar with it and was not interested in writing a science-fiction novel. *Last and First Men* is an extended philosophical meditation combined with wild and entertaining flights of the imagination.

Stapledon is not concerned with technological advance, a point that may seem odd in the context of a century fixated on technology and within a novel projecting the future for billions of years. As far as Stapledon is concerned, technology and civilization are only marginally connected. Each civilization Stapledon describes is fundamentally concerned with spiritual or philosophical values, and their supreme crises are those of the spirit.

The book's emphasis on spiritual growth focuses on detachment, learning to appreciate one's place against the immensity of space and time, and coming to accept that place rather than railing against it. For example, there is the speech of the Divine Boy, the last great prophet of the First Men, who tells his listeners to see life as a game, an aesthetic experience. Games, he says, are played to win, but players come to care more for the game itself than for victory in it.

Making the same point and drawing out the philosophic thread that binds the book, the final pages are devoted to the words of the last-born of the Eighteenth Men. A nearby sun is becoming a nova, dooming the human race, but the youngest living human, like the Divine Boy, achieves full awareness of the spirit, the end to which all of human history has been directed. He does not curse his fate. The forces of nature and fate that are consuming the human race will somehow make use of humanity's destruction.

Entire species of humanity have struggled to compass these insights throughout the book, but none, not even the Eighteenth Men, completely succeeds. Their race mind sees the universe full of "extreme subtlety and extreme beauty. At the same time we often have of it an impression of unspeakable horror." The attempt to affirm both aspects is the book's ultimate theme.

—*George E. Nicholas*

The Left Hand of Darkness

A prophetic look at gender differences on a planet populated by hermaphrodites

Author: Ursula K. Le Guin (1929-   )
Genre: Science fiction—alien civilization
Type of work: Novel
Time of plot: The distant future
Location: Karhide and Orgoreyn, competing countries on the planet
  Gethen, also known as Winter because of its ice age
First published: 1969

The Story

The Left Hand of Darkness is a report from representative Genly Ai to the Ekumen of Known Worlds, an organization of about eighty planets clearly analogous to the United Nations. Ai has been sent to enlist the two hostile countries of the planet Gethen, Karhide and Orgoreyn, to join the Ekumen. He needs a formal guarantee of welcome for his orbiting spaceship and the Ekumen representatives therein. This requirement is complicated for the ill-at-ease Ai by the dislike between Karhide and Orgoreyn, by their unsettled internal political states, and especially by the sexual ambiguity of the people of this world. They are hermaphroditic, combining both female and male sexual characteristics and playing one or the other sexual role at different points in their lives, depending on complex psychohormonal circumstances.

The Gethenians' competing governments are a challenge for Ai. His Terran reliance on sexual identity as a basis for forming relations of trust with another human offers no guidance on Gethen, only confusion and distrust. Estraven, the head minister to the king of Karhide, is banished, ending Ai's hopes of a friendly reception. The Terran envoy feels little for the exiled ally on whom he had pinned his hopes. Seers known as "Foretellers" predict that Gethen will join the Ekumen within five years. Hopeful of a better reception elsewhere, Ai moves from the medieval-flavored monarchy of Karhide to the bureaucratic country of Orgoreyn, a seemingly orderly and thoroughly organized nation-state reminiscent of both ancient Egypt in its monolithic building style and the Soviet Union in its centralized systems and icebound prison camps for freethinkers.

Ai fails there as well, even though he has the support of Estraven, who has been granted an uncertain refugee status. Ai sides with the Open Trade Faction, a losing political movement, and is sent to a frozen labor camp similar to Soviet Siberia. Estraven rescues him, and both begin an arduous and hazardous trek across the Gobrin Ice that is the contested land between the two countries. Estraven's know-how and Gethenian cold-weather gear make for a successful crossing.

Finally, Ai can call in his spaceship, for the Orgoreyn leaders have trapped themselves in a lie by reporting Ai's "accidental" death. Karhide's king can gain an advantage on Orgoreyn by welcoming Ekumen. Lord Tibe of Karhide has Estraven killed because he had been exiled under sentence of death. Ai's mission therefore is successful, but at the sacrifice of his new friend. The book ends

Ursula K. Le Guin. (Margaret Chodos)

with Ai meeting Estraven's parent (Gethenians do not mate for life) and child, both androgynous, and telling them of his friendship with Estraven on the ice. The implication is that Ai has come to accept the humanity of people without clear gender.

Analysis

The prophetic insight of *The Left Hand of Darkness* lies in its exploration of what came to be called gender issues. As Ursula Le Guin herself has said, in 1969 the feminist movement was only beginning, and even gender bias in language—she uses "he" throughout for the hermaphroditic Gethenians—had not been investigated. The real difference between men and women, however, was an elemental question for Le Guin and other feminist thinkers of that time. Her "thought experiment" of having a hapless Terran male adrift in a world with no gender markers was inspired.

Ai's discomfort at having no clues to guide his relationships is fascinating and instructive. He suffers far greater unease than he would have if confronted with a conventionally alien life-form. The book captures the common human process of perceiving a new acquaintance: The sexual shell often disappears and, over time, the inner, sexless personality emerges. To confront the personality without the matrix of gender, as Ai does, can be frightening. Ai's accommodation to this new perspective is truly humane: To Ai, Estraven becomes familiar yet alien, reassuring yet finally mysterious, like another human. Le Guin thus makes her point about gender differences.

The novel involves far more than gender twisting. The two societies of Karhide and Orgoreyn are wonderfully conceived, evocative of familiar societies while retaining their distinct alien identity. Karhide is medieval and monarchical, a traditional society still youthful in the stiff, independent rectitude of its citizens, a country vaguely reminiscent of Eastern Europe. In perfect contrast is Orgoreyn. Its people have chosen the completely different route of overorganization into bureaucratic apparatus, and the initially benign appearance of the society turns out to be a cover for secret police and prison camps. The two societies inevitably suggest the contrast of the disorderly individualism and frontier ethic of the United States in juxtaposition with the collectivism and group consciousness of the former Soviet Union, with its Potemkin villages and gulags in the snow.

Religions also are contrasted. Handdara, the faith practiced in Karhide, is an Eastern type of religion stressing a yin and yang opposition: "Light is the left hand of darkness/ and darkness the right hand of light." Yomesh, found mainly in Orgoreyn, is more in the Western tradition of a revealed faith based on a prophet, with truth capable of being distinguished from illusion. The contrast in the two religions parallels the sexual and political contrasts in the book, with the suggestion that experience of both viewpoints is necessary for a full and humane understanding.

If science fiction is to be judged not only for the validity and interest of its ideas but also for the integrity and believability of the fictional worlds it creates, *The Left Hand of Darkness* succeeds brilliantly on every count. In its exploration of gender and of the never-resolved differences of East and West, the novel is an excellent primer for the problems that bedevil Earth, yet Gethen is as complete a world as one could wish for, detailed and utterly convincing. Le Guin shows the value of seeing through the eyes of the Other as well as the enormous difficulty in perceiving what is complementary in the initially alien.

—*Andrew Macdonald*

Life During Wartime

An American soldier in Central America finds that the war there is really an extension of an old battle between two families of psychics

Author: Lucius Shepard (1947-   )
Genre: Science fiction—future war
Type of work: Novel
Time of plot: The early twenty-first century
Location: Guatemala and Panama
First published: 1987

The Story

Life During Wartime is an episodic novel made up of novellas, two of which, "R & R" and "Fire Zone Emerald," previously were published separately. "R & R" won a Nebula Award in 1986.

David Mingolla is an American soldier involved in a Vietnam-type war in Central America. During a period of rest and recreation (R & R), he meets Debora, a woman he finds himself drawn to even though he suspects that she is an enemy agent. He witnesses one of his companions being killed after running amok on drugs, and his other companion deserts for Panama. Mingolla is aware that he has latent psychic ability. After considering deserting, he decides instead to volunteer for Psicorps.

Mingolla trains on a Caribbean island with Tully and the mysterious Dr. Izaguirre. His training involves heavy use of drugs and unleashes a rage in him that can lead him to acts of cruelty. It turns out that he is an amazingly strong psychic. As a final test, he is sent to kill an enemy psychic, de Zedegui, who is hiding out in a prison settlement. De Zedegui seems almost eager to die, but before he does he reveals that the war is actually a continuation of a four-centuries-old feud between two families of psychics, the Madradonas and the Sotomayors.

Mingolla's next mission is to kill Debora, who is also an enemy psychic. After first being captured by a rogue platoon of American deserters, he finds her deep in the jungle. They become lovers and find their psychic abilities strengthened as a result. They desert and set out to find the cause of the war. Along the way, they meet up with Tully once more and are joined by Ruy, whose lust for Debora puts him at odds with Mingolla. Their journey is hazardous, including tests put in their way by Izaguirre, who turns out to be the leader of the Sotomayors. Ruy also is a Sotomayor.

In Panama, they find that the two families are trying to negotiate peace. Debora becomes an enthusiastic supporter of this process, but Mingolla is suspicious, especially when he finds himself trying to alleviate the condition of people who have been permanently brain damaged by the psychic experiments of the two families. Peace is declared, but it is short-lived, a ruse to allow one family to attack the other. Mingolla and Debora flee to the Panamanian hinterland.

Analysis

This remarkable and powerful novel is, in one sense, an obvious response to Vietnam. It tells of Americans trapped in a meaningless foreign war, fighting in dense jungle, with the men turning to drugs both for recreation and for fighting spirit. It is more than that, however, for it sets up a dichotomy between two ways of seeing the world. Lucius Shepard explains it succinctly early in the novel when he talks of the Central American people "trapped between the poles of magic and reason, their lives governed by the politics of the ultrareal, their spirits ruled by myths and legends, with the rectangular, computerized bulk of North America above and the conch-shell-shaped continental mystery of South America below."

This conflict is graphically represented in the novel by a clash of genres. Science fiction is represented by the technology of war: Helicopter pilots encase their heads in high-tech helmets that, they believe, confer invincibility and almost godlike omniscience; and soldiers on leave indulge in drug-induced gladiatorial combats. Against this is ranged Magical Realism: Mingolla's assailant is killed by a horde of butterflies, and the war between the Madradonas and the Sotomayors first appears as an episode in a work of fiction. The focus of the novel turns gradually, the earlier sections being more science-fictional and the latter more Magical Realism, but the clash of cultures is always there. It is perhaps at its most vivid in the crashed helicopter whose on-board computer has cannibalized spare parts and now imagines itself to be an incarnation of God.

In a series of vivid and often disturbing incidents, Shepard makes a point not about the madness of war but about the madness of warriors. None of those caught up in the fighting is sane; madness is the only way they can survive. They concoct senseless rituals, commit casual brutalities, and find their humanity swamped by the inhumanity in which they must live. This is shown most sharply in the character of Mingolla, a masterfully drawn portrait that starts with a naïve youth lost when the silly rituals by which he conducts his R & R are suddenly destroyed by circumstances. As he grows wise in the ways of the war, his helplessness emphasized by his Psicorps training, he becomes a creature of violent anger given to acts of casual cruelty. Even after his growing psychic power and his love for Debora have fostered a renewed humanity, this rage will still break through. When he happens upon a ruined village with walls that have become the canvas for a nameless painter who transforms war into art, the only response he can make is to destroy the pictures.

Shepard is a widely traveled writer whose familiarity with tropical settings is apparent in many of his stories. The latter-day Vietnam in Central America is featured in other stories. His work has earned not unreasonable comparison with that of Joseph Conrad and Graham Greene. Certainly this novel is one of his finest works, particularly because of the effective way he blends the traditions of science fiction with those of other imaginative literature to produce an effect that is unique.

—*Paul Kincaid*

Lincoln's Dreams

As a woman dreams of the Civil War, her companion struggles to interpret what the dreams mean for her

Author: Connie Willis (1945-   )
Genre: Science fiction—time travel
Type of work: Novel
Time of plot: The present
Location: Virginia and Washington, D.C.
First published: 1987

The Story

Jeff Johnson, a historical researcher for a Civil War novelist named Broun, meets a mysterious woman named Annie at a publication party for his author's latest novel. Annie is in the company of a sleep disorder specialist, Dr. Richard Madison, who was Jeff's college roommate. Broun wants to consult Madison about the meaning of the dreams Abraham Lincoln had before his assassination.

Jeff discovers that Annie has been dreaming of events during the Civil War. He agrees to take Annie to Arlington House, formerly a home of Robert E. Lee and now the site of Arlington National Cemetery. Annie recognizes the house as part of her dreams. She leaves Madison, who she discovers has been drugging her without her knowledge to prevent her dreams. She asks Jeff to help her discover the meaning of her dreams. Jeff agrees, and while Broun is on the West Coast doing further research on Lincoln's dreams, Jeff and Annie travel to Fredericksburg, Virginia, site of one of the worst battles of the Civil War. They conduct research and proofread Broun's latest novel.

In Fredericksburg, Jeff discovers that Annie's dreams match events and people in the life of Robert E. Lee, leader of the Confederate forces in the Civil War. Jeff also seems to be taking on the characteristics of Traveller, Lee's devoted horse throughout the Civil War period. As Annie's dreams grow worse, they try to decipher the meaning of the dreams and decide if they apply to the past or to the present. Broun's novel, about an ordinary soldier's experiences, becomes an important part of the story line, adding detail about the war to the atmosphere created by Annie's increasingly vivid dreams.

At first, Annie seems to be moving through the war in chronological order, and there is hope that there will be an end to the dreams. This hope is shattered, however, when the dreams begin to move back in time as well. Annie begins to believe that she is dreaming the dreams to allow the spirit of Robert E. Lee to find peace at last. Jeff goes short on sleep as a result of Annie's sleepwalking and because of the increasingly frantic messages from Madison on his answering machine, warning of a dangerous heart condition Annie might have. He decides that Lee is reaching out from the grave to save Annie because he was unable to save his own daughter Annie, who died during the war.

Jeff returns to Washington with Annie and tries to persuade her to meet with Madison and seek treatment for her heart condition. She refuses the treatment, afraid that it might affect her ability to dream for Lee. Jeff gives Annie all of his money and drives her to the subway station. He never sees her again. His life, mirroring that of Traveller after the death of Lee, is greatly diminished by Annie's loss and his lack of knowledge about her fate.

Analysis

Connie Willis's literary career prior to the publication of *Lincoln's Dreams* consisted primarily of short stories, including the award-winning "Fire Watch" (1982), title story of her first short-story collection, published in 1985. She also coauthored two novels, *Water Witch* (1982) and *Light Raid* (1989), with Cynthia Felice.

Willis's work ranges from the deadly serious to comedy. She works equally well in the short-story and novel formats. "At the Rialto," a comedy about a quantum physics convention in Hollywood, shows Willis's comedic touch, as does "Even the Queen," a story about women's issues. Her dramatic fiction is represented by the short stories "Chance" and "Jack," the latter of which takes place during World War II, and the novel *Doomsday Book* (1992), set during the plague years in England. *Lincoln's Dreams* was her first solo novel and won the John W. Campbell Memorial Award in 1988.

Willis has won numerous awards, for both short and long fiction. These include the Hugo and Nebula Awards for best novelette with "Fire Watch," the Hugo and Nebula Awards for best novella with "Last of the Winnebagos," and the 1990 Nebula Award for best novelette with "At the Rialto." *Doomsday Book* won the Nebula Award for best novel in 1992 and tied with Vernor Vinge's *A Fire upon the Deep* for the 1993 Hugo Award for best novel.

Time travel, on both the psychic and physical levels, is a reoccurring motif in Willis's work. The short story "Fire Watch" and the novel *Doomsday Book* deal with physical time travel, via a machine, while *Lincoln's Dreams* deals with the subject by having the traveler experience the past on a psychic level, through her dreams. Willis believes in the interconnectedness of time and in people's ability to be influenced by the past. People ignore that influence at their own peril.

Another major theme in Willis's serious work is the connection between love and duty. Jeff's love for Annie does not override his promise to help her find the meaning of her dreams, even if it means losing her forever. Annie, devoted to Lee, whose anguish she senses night after brutal night, keeps her promise to help him through her dreams, even though it means the loss of everything—her job, her health, her family, and perhaps even her life if she has misinterpreted what the dreams really mean.

Willis's use of language is understated, recounting extraordinary events in a normal, everyday manner of speech. By the end of her book, readers care deeply about the lives of her characters, not because of any flashy plot devices but through the force of her writing. This depth of characterization is a hallmark of Willis's work.

This first novel showed a promising future for Willis, which she fulfilled with works such as *Doomsday Book* and her second collection of short stories, *Impossible Things* (1994). She became a major force in modern science fiction.

—*Catherine Doyle*

Little, Big

The tale of the Drinkwater family, including both the human saga of their loves and struggles and the underlying story of their destined interactions with the fairy realm

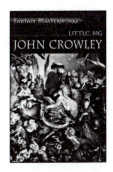

Author: John Crowley (1942-   )
Genre: Fantasy—Magical Realism
Type of work: Novel
Time of plot: The 1880's to the near future
Location: The Edgewood estate in upstate New York and New York City
First published: 1981

The Story

The novel begins in the middle of what the characters self-consciously call the Tale. Smoky Barnable, a shy and old-fashioned bachelor from New York City (called only "the City"), journeys to the idiosyncratically built and literally magical estate, Edgewood, to marry his love, Alice Dale Drinkwater (nicknamed Daily Alice). The story unfolds both backward and forward, from the founding of the clan by architect John Drinkwater and his fey wife Violet Bramble (daughter of a spiritualist reverend) to the tale's culmination, in which Daily Alice's generation and their offspring permanently populate and renew the fading realm of the fairies.

The Drinkwaters all know that they share some secret destiny, although the women more gracefully play their parts and the men tend toward confusion or even irritation. The gifts of the fairies are not all benevolent, as Violet and John's son August discovers. His wish that all women love him leads to his supposed death and actual metamorphosis into Grandfather Trout, giver of ambiguous advice. Violet's illegitimate son Auberon is hurt by lack of contact with "them" and the secret from which he feels excluded. John Storm "Doc" Drinkwater, Daily Alice's father, benefits from his ability to understand animals talking, becoming a successful writer of children's books.

A tarotlike deck is handed down from Violet to her daughter Nora, from her to Doc's wife Aunt Sophie, and finally to Daily Alice's sister Sophie, from whom the cards are stolen. Smoky has an affair with

Sophie, and she and Daily Alice learn to share his love, but Sophie's illegitimate child by cousin George Mouse is taken by the fairies and trained as a messenger, with a horrific changeling left in its place. Smoky and Daily Alice's three daughters, like the Fates, calmly do their needlework and know everything. Edgewood crumbles, but Smoky revives it by repairing a perpetual motion orrery; however, he dies shortly before his crossover to fairyland. Daily Alice becomes the spirit, almost goddess, of that limitless microcosm.

Most of the novel's action is at Edgewood, but not all of it. George Mouse establishes an improbable farm in a block of ruined Manhattan buildings. There, Smoky and Alice's son, Auberon, loves and loses Sylvie (and her twin brother, Bruno). Eventually, after Auberon experiences life as a homeless bum and then as a television writer, he and Sylvie reunite as king and queen of fairyland. Ariel Hawksquill, a magician who teaches Auberon the Art of Memory, introduces the only events in the story of national scale. She realizes that politician Russel Eigenblick (eventually elected president of the United States) is actually Holy Roman Emperor Frederick Barbarossa, returned from centuries of waiting until needed. The depictions of life in "the City," though rarely supernatural, are as awesome and odd as the more fantasy-based events centered at Edgewood or concerning Ariel Hawksquill.

Analysis

Little, Big is a virtuoso blending of fantasy, mythic significance, and realistic (if impressionistic) depictions of compelling characters and places. The novel is metafictive without becoming distanced or ironic. The reader, like the Drinkwaters, can accept the events as the plot of a Tale, directed from outside itself—by the author, by the fairies—and also as incidents enacted with full passion and consequence. Literary references are plentiful, from John Keats (in a City bar, Auberon drunkenly proclaims, "Trooty is booth, booth trooty") to the Mother West Wind Where stories by early twentieth century children's author Thornton W. Burgess. One major influence is Lewis Carroll, as shown by characters named Alice, Sylvie, and Bruno. The major text behind the text is the story of the fairies—particularly the court of Oberon and Titania—as seen in Carroll's *Sylvie and Bruno* (1889), in William Shakespeare's *A Midsummer Night's Dream* (pr. c. 1595-1596), and throughout both literature and folklore. Figures from children's folklore, such as Mother Goose, are presented in new ways. The text is also enriched by references to Renaissance thought, something John Crowley returns to in *Aegypt* (1987) and *Love and Sleep* (1994), and to classical myth.

This mythical dimension is conveyed without losing the foibles, feelings, and quirky interior worlds of the human characters. The novel oddly lacks real-world detail, so that even the Latino neighborhoods and subway-dwelling homeless of New York City become abstract and mythic. The panoply of individual characters and the leisurely narrative style are somehow Victorian and mimetic, no more fantasy, though no less, than the work of Charles Dickens. Along with literary references, Crowley uses the icons of popular culture, from designer psychedelic drugs to soap operas, although like other elements these are given new meanings through their use in context. The Drinkwaters believe that they live in a world centered on them—in a way it is—and the novel reflects that. The novel uses the tiny focus on Edgewood to enter a world of infinite possibility.

The world of the novel is also eternal and cyclical. The repetition among the generations of names and even events helps reinforce this idea, as does the hint that the Drinkwaters will eventually follow their fairy predecessors to whatever new realm comes next. The novel ends with both an invitation to the reader to enter fading Edgewood and the denial of that possibility. The novel implies that although an individual tale may end, tale telling never does, and when the elements are reused, the whole still resides in each part. In both fiction and fairyland, everything finally changes and in that way endures.

—*Bernadette Lynn Bosky*

The Little Prince

The narrator crashes his plane in the desert and meets a young boy,
a visitor from another planet, who teaches him lessons about life

Author: Antoine de Saint-Exupéry (1900-1944)
Genre: Fantasy—cosmic voyage
Type of work: Novel
Time of plot: About 1943
Location: Earth and various asteroids and planets
First published: *Le Petit Prince* (1943; English translation, 1943)

The Story

The Little Prince begins with the famous pair of drawings with which the
narrator, Saint-Exupéry himself, tests the understanding of adults. The
first is of a boa constrictor that has swallowed an elephant. Most adults
see only a hat shape; they cannot see beyond the exterior. For them, he
draws another boa constrictor, this time in cross-section, so they can see
the elephant inside.

After years of loneliness in the world of grown-ups, Saint-Exupéry
crashes his plane in the desert. While he is trying to repair his plane, the
Little Prince appears and asks Saint-Exupéry to draw a sheep for him.
Saint-Exupéry first presents him with the drawing that opens the story,
and the Little Prince protests that he does not want an elephant in a boa
constrictor. The Little Prince rejects several of Saint-Exupéry's attempts to
draw a sheep before accepting a drawing of a box inside which he can
imagine a sheep. This event marks the beginning of the friendship between the Little Prince and Saint-Exupéry, who learns that his visitor
comes from a tiny asteroid and that he is sad. The cause of the Little
Prince's melancholy turns out to be the beautiful Rose, who so tormented
him with her moods that he left his planet.

The Little Prince tells the story of how he escaped from his planet with
the help of a flock of migratory birds. He visited a number of planets, each
inhabited by a solitary figure who represented some foible of the grown-
up world, which has lost its innocence.

When the Little Prince reaches Earth, he finds a garden filled with
roses. He is bitterly disappointed, as he had believed his Rose was unique.
He meets the Fox, who consoles the Little Prince and teaches him wis-

dom. Before they can be friends, the Fox says, the Little Prince must "tame" him. Then they will need each other and be unique to each other. The Little Prince understands that his Rose has tamed him: It is the time he has spent on her that makes her so important.

When the Little Prince asks Saint-Exupéry to draw a muzzle on the sheep to protect his Rose, Saint-Exupéry knows he intends to return home. The Little Prince gives Saint-Exupéry a parting gift: As all the stars flower for the Little Prince because of his Rose, so will the stars ring with laughter for Saint-Exupéry because of the Little Prince's laughter.

The Little Prince asks the Serpent to help him return to his planet by biting him. He tells Saint-Exupéry not to grieve over his body, as it will be simply an empty shell. The Serpent bites the Little Prince, and he falls dead. At daybreak, however, Saint-Exupéry cannot find his body. Years later, Saint-Exupéry hears the laughter of the stars but is disturbed by the fact that he forgot to add a fastening to the sheep's muzzle, so he always wonders if the Rose is safe.

Analysis

The theme of the story is established in the first pair of drawings: Adults have lost true perception, and only those who keep the child alive within them can see through the outward appearance of objects to the invisible essence within. The Little Prince passes Saint-Exupéry's test of understanding when he correctly identifies his drawing of an elephant inside a boa constrictor. The message is repeated in the Little Prince's rejection of each of Saint-Exupéry's sheep until he accepts a drawing of a box in which he can imagine a sheep.

The Little Prince comes to realize that it is the invisible essence bestowed on the Rose by his devotion that makes her unique. Her truth, too, is hidden: Only when the Little Prince leaves his planet does the Rose admit that she loves him. The Little Prince reflects that he should have judged her on her acts, not her words, and guessed the affection beyond her wiles.

Such invisible truths are set against the so-called serious things with which grown-ups are preoccupied. When the Little Prince says that he fears that his sheep may eat the Rose, Saint-Exupéry dismisses the boy's questions, saying that he is concerned with "serious things"—his plane repair and diminishing water supply. The Little Prince is furious with Saint-Exupéry, whom he accuses of talking like a grown-up. The Little Prince delivers a passionate declamation about what is truly important: that his Rose is unique, and that a little sheep could unwittingly destroy her in an instant.

The Little Prince passes on something of the Fox's teaching when he tells Saint-Exupéry that what makes a house, the desert, or the stars beautiful is invisible. Saint-Exupéry recalls his childhood home, made more precious by the legend of a treasure hidden within it. The desert is beautiful because somewhere it hides a well. For the Little Prince, when he is away from his planet, all the visible stars flower because of one invisible Rose. Thanks to the Little Prince's gift of wisdom, for Saint-Exupéry all the stars will forever ring with laughter because of the laughter of the Little Prince, who has long departed.

Saint-Exupéry's failure to find the Little Prince's body may imply a Christlike resurrection. If so, the message is in keeping with the rest of the story. Of all the so-called serious things of the grown-up world, death is the most serious. Death, as the Little Prince teaches, however, is no more real than the serious things that preoccupy the red-faced businessman who incessantly counts the stars he believes he owns. Like the seeming hat that is really an elephant in a snake, and like the vain wiles of the Rose that conceal her love, death is simply another deceptive appearance.

—*Claire Robinson*

The Lord of the Rings

An epic recounting the combat between the free peoples of Middle-earth and the forces of Sauron, the Dark Lord

Author: J(ohn) R(onald) R(euel) Tolkien (1892-1973)
Genre: Fantasy—heroic fantasy
Type of work: Novel
Time of plot: The Third Age, an undefined time in the remote past
Location: Middle-earth, a feudal world populated by men, dwarves, wizards, and other fantastic beings
First published: 1968; previously published as *The Fellowship of the Ring* (1954), *The Two Towers* (1954), and *The Return of the King* (1955)

The Story

The Lord of the Rings, the seminal work of modern fantasy, was first published in sections only as a concession to its length; the division of the work into the three volumes familiar to most readers bears no relation to the development of the story. J. R. R. Tolkien himself divided the work into six numbered but untitled books, two of which appear in each volume. Although *The Lord of the Rings* was begun as a sequel to Tolkien's popular 1937 children's book *The Hobbit*, it so dwarfs the earlier volume in both seriousness and scope as to have reversed the relationship. *The Hobbit*, though successful in its own right, is now considered primarily as a "prequel" to the longer work.

The length and complexity of *The Lord of the Rings* are such as to defy brief plot summary. The main action concerns Frodo Baggins, a hobbit, a member of a diminutive, rural, peace-loving race that lives in the northern land of the Shire. From his Uncle Bilbo, the hero of *The Hobbit*, Frodo inherits a magic ring that confers invisibility on the wearer.

Frodo learns, however, that his heirloom is far more than a toy: The wizard Gandalf explains that it is in fact the Master Ring created by the malevolent Dark Lord, Sauron, ages before. Sauron, a powerful spirit who presides over the hellish kingdom of Mordor in the far east of Middle-earth, invested the Ring with much of his original power, and he has been hunting it since it was taken from him in battle ages before. Should Sauron recover the Ring, Gandalf warns, he would become sufficiently powerful to overwhelm Middle-earth, plunging it into an age of darkness.

Frodo and three hobbit companions, Sam, Merry, and Pippin, set
out for Rivendell, a distant haven
protected by Elrond, a wise and
mighty elf king. Gandalf has been
called away on urgent business, and
Frodo and his friends must begin
the long journey through the wilderness alone. They are pursued by
the Ringwraiths, terrifying, ghost-
like servants of Sauron who are
drawn by the Ring itself. Along the
way, the hobbits receive the aid of
Strider, a man expert in the ways of
the wild. The party reaches Rivendell just ahead of the Ringwraiths,
who wound Frodo and attempt to
possess his spirit.

At Rivendell, Frodo is healed by
Elrond, and a council of representatives of the free peoples (hobbits,
men, elves, and dwarves) debates the fate of the Ring. Some advocate using its power to defeat Sauron, whose armies of orcs and trolls threaten
to overrun Middle-earth. Gandalf, though, explains that the Ring cannot
be used for such a purpose without causing the wielder to set himself up
as a new Dark Lord; the Ring's colossal power inevitably corrupts.
Moreover, the Ring cannot be destroyed by conventional means: Only
the volcanic fires of Mordor's Mount Doom, where the Ring was forged,
can unmake it. Frodo volunteers to undertake the seemingly hopeless
quest of carrying the Ring to the fire in the heart of the enemy's realm,
and the council agrees, detecting the hand of fate in Frodo's selection.

Frodo and eight companions, including Sam, Merry, Pippin, Gandalf,
and Strider—who has been revealed to be Aragorn, heir to the ancient
kings of Middle-earth—set out on the quest. Also in the company are
Legolas, an elf; Gimli, a dwarf; and Boromir, a man from the southern
kingdom of Gondor, the principal bulwark against Sauron's forces.

The company journeys south in the middle of winter. Unable to cross
a mountain range, they attempt to pass through Moria, a subterranean
realm created by dwarves but long since taken over by evil creatures. In
Moria, the company is nearly captured by hosts of orcs and trolls. In
guarding their flight, Gandalf is pulled into an abyss while fighting a
Balrog, a powerful demon.

Escaping to the elven realm of Lothlórien, the company is equipped with boats, in which they travel down the River Anduin. Frodo comes to the decision that he cannot allow his friends to accompany him on the harrowing trip into Mordor, and he steals away from the others; Sam, however, catches up with him. At the same time, the other members of the company are attacked by orcs. Boromir is killed, and Merry and Pippin are captured. Choosing to follow the hostages, Aragorn and the others pursue the orcs, leaving Frodo and Sam to continue the quest alone.

The action then diverges into two principal story lines. Aragorn's party is reunited with Gandalf, who has survived his ordeal and returned with renewed wizardly power. Merry and Pippin escape the orcs and meet the Ents, powerful, ancient, treelike beings who care for the forests. With the assistance of the men of Rohan, they defeat the forces of the treacherous wizard Saruman, who had hoped to rival Sauron. Gandalf and the others then go to Gondor, where they organize resistance to Sauron's invading forces. In a huge battle, Sauron's advance troops are routed, but the defenders of the West remain hopelessly outnumbered. Concluding that their only chance is to distract Sauron's attention so that Frodo and Sam can reach their goal, the allied forces advance toward Mordor.

Meanwhile, Frodo and Sam attempt to approach Mordor through the Dead Marshes, a noxious maze of swamps. There they capture Gollum, a twisted, hobbitlike creature who once possessed the Ring and who has been following Frodo in the hope of reclaiming it.

Intimidated by the power of the Ring, Gollum reluctantly agrees to guide the hobbits into Mordor. He brings them safely through a dangerous mountain pass only to betray them by leading them into the lair of Shelob, a colossal spider. Frodo, stung by Shelob, appears to be dead; Sam fights off the spider and reluctantly takes the Ring. He leaves to continue the quest, and orcs capture Frodo, who recovers from the effects of the spider's poison. Sam realizes his error and returns to liberate Frodo. Dogged by Gollum and hiding from orcs, they continue their journey through the desolate landscape of Mordor.

The climactic scene takes place on Mount Doom. Gollum assaults the hobbits as they struggle up the mountainside, but Sam fends him off as Frodo goes on. Gollum evades Sam and catches Frodo as he stands over the cracks leading to the mountain's fiery interior. Frodo, overcome at last by the evil power of the Ring, refuses to destroy it; instead, he puts it on his finger and claims it for his own. At the same moment, Gollum attacks Frodo and bites the Ring—and a finger—from his hand. Gollum loses his balance and falls into the abyss, destroying both himself and the Ring, and the mountain erupts.

The beleaguered troops of the West are on the verge of being over-come. With the destruction of the Ring, however, everything created with its power is also destroyed. Mordor's gates and fortresses crumble, and the orcs and trolls are driven to madness. As the reinvigorated allied troops complete the rout, Gandalf flies to Mount Doom on the back of an enormous eagle, rescuing Frodo and Sam from certain death. The hob-bits are returned to Gondor, where they witness the coronation of Ara-gorn. They then return to the Shire, which in their absence has fallen un-der the sway of petty evil, to set things to rights in their homeland.

Analysis

It is hard to overstate the importance of *The Lord of the Rings* to the devel-opment of modern fantasy. The work, the subject of cultish ardor in the first years following publication, rocketed to worldwide popularity in the mid-1960's. Counterculture readers embraced its exaltation of na-ture and simple living above progress and the will to power; fans of ad-venture stories were captivated by its headlong pace; and scholars be-gan to appreciate the extraordinary craft with which Tolkien, over a period of decades, had constructed his imagined world. It is not too much to say that virtually every subsequent fantasy writer owes Tolkien a substantial debt, either directly as inspiration (dozens of lesser works are clearly modeled on Tolkien's) or indirectly for having vastly ex-panded the audience—and market—for adult fantasy.

The Lord of the Rings has accumulated a substantial body of scholar-ship, from the appreciative work of such early enthusiasts as W. H. Auden through more recent formalist approaches. The book has also generated a popular companion literature in the form of reference works, illustrative texts, glossaries, and assorted "guides." *The Silmarillion*, Tol-kien's own lengthy mythology of Middle-earth, was published in 1977 but failed to attract a large readership.

Interpretation of so massive a work is a daunting task. Tolkien took pains to refute the popular early views that the Ring was meant to sug-gest the atomic bomb and that the East-West struggles of Middle-earth were modeled on the political order of either World War II or the Cold War. He noted that he had begun the story decades in advance of such developments and added that he "cordially" disliked such allegory. He further denied that *The Lord of the Rings* had an intended "meaning," as-serting that in writing it he had wished primarily to tell a riveting story that would enthrall readers. The prolonged popularity and enduring in-fluence of his masterwork attest his success.

—*Robert McClenaghan*

Lud-in-the-Mist

Master Nathaniel Chanticleer journeys to Fairyland in order to rescue Ranulph, his son, from the magical attractions of "things fairy"

Author: Hope Mirrlees (1887-1978)
Genre: Fantasy—high fantasy
Type of work: Novel
Time of plot: Indeterminate
Location: Lud-in-the-Mist, the capital of Dorimare
First published: 1926

The Story

Bordered on the West by the Debatable Hills and Fairyland, Lud-in-the-Mist is governed by Master Nathaniel Chanticleer, the High Seneschal. Although he is outwardly pleasant and kind, Nathaniel is inwardly unhappy. His unhappiness began several years earlier, when he and some of his friends dressed up for a party as ghosts of their ancestors. An amateur musician, he seized the opportunity to play his lute. Plucking one of the strings rather harshly, Nathaniel heard "the Note," a dissonant pitch that menaced the harmonious, predictable, and prosaic nature of his life. He now frequently feels discontented and longs to hear the Note again, but he is afraid that it will reawaken his youthful restlessness.

Historically, Lud-in-the-Mist rooted out all magic and adventure when it ousted the last of its "noble" rulers, Duke Aubrey. After a battle that lasted three days, Lud's citizens killed all the nobles and drove Aubrey from Lud-in-the-Mist into Fairyland. Because of its connection to the artistic and political caprice of Duke Aubrey, fairy fruit became taboo after the revolution. Eating it makes one delusional, desiring only to flee Lud and escape into Fairyland. Welcoming the new laws, Lud's citizens embraced the "science of jurisprudence." Law now directs Lud-in-the-Mist, and Nathaniel's duty is to uphold it.

Ironically, trouble begins for Lud's citizens in the house of Chanticleer itself. There, while Nathaniel cuts a famous Moongrass cheese for a party, his son Ranulph cries out for him to stop, claiming that if he proceeds, "all the flowers will wither in Fairyland." This violation of taboo shocks the party guests and forces Nathaniel to face his worst fear: His son may have eaten fairy fruit. By his own admission, Ranulph wants only to escape, to get away from Lud-in-the-Mist. Nathaniel calls the town physician, Endymion Leer, and urges him to find a cure. Leer suggests some time away from Lud on the widow Gibberty's farm. Taking Leer's advice, Nathaniel sends Ranulph, accompanied by Nurse Hempen's nephew Luke, to the farm.

Soon after Ranulph's departure, the "Crabapple Blossoms," young ladies at Miss Primrose Crabapple's Academy, disappear into Fairyland. Among them is Nathaniel's daughter Prunella. Although Captain Mumchance fails to discover any forbidden fruit, Miss Primrose is nevertheless blamed for the disappearances and is taken into custody. Miss Primrose admits to Dame Marigold, Nathaniel's wife, that fairy fruit had been smuggled into Lud. Marigold believes that Leer may be involved and urges Nathaniel to investigate. In his research, Nathaniel comes across the case of Diggory Carp, a laborer accused of the murder of Jeremiah Gibberty, the widow Gibberty's former husband. During the trial, Carp had accused the widow of poisoning her own husband because of her affair with Christopher Pugwalker, an herbalist much like Leer. She was not convicted, but Nathaniel begins to suspect her guilt. Moreover, he believes that the young Pugwalker is, in fact, Endymion Leer.

Riding out to the farm, Nathaniel meets Portunus, a mysterious fiddler who tells him to "dig, dig." When Nathaniel arrives at the farm, the widow's granddaughter, Hazel, assists him in digging beneath a stone bust in her orchard. They discover Jeremiah Gibberty's last note, accusing the widow of his murder and of her affair with Christopher Pugwalker. The note becomes substantial evidence for the arrest and conviction of the widow and Endymion Leer. Unfortunately, Nathaniel also finds that his son, with the assistance of the widow, has run off to Fairyland. Compelled not by fairy fruit but by the love of his son, Nathaniel blindly follows him into Fairyland. There he meets the spirit of Duke Aubrey, who ultimately releases Ranulph and the Crabapple Blossoms. Aubrey also hints that one day Nathaniel may again hear the Note. Master Ambrose, Nathaniel's best friend and a powerful speaker in the senate, convinces the citizens that fairy fruit should no longer be forbidden but should be reintegrated into the city's commerce and culture.

Analysis

Little is known about Hope Mirrlees, a minor novelist of the 1920's, whose other books *The Counterplot* (1924) and *Madeleine* (1919) are seldom reprinted or discussed. *Lud-in-the Mist* was retrieved from obscurity by Lin Carter, who republished the fantasy novel in the 1970's.

Mirrlees contrasts the "pastoral sobriety" of Dorimare with the "distinctly exotic" country to the West. The citizens of Lud-in-the-Mist have successfully eliminated variability in and unpredictability from their lives. In doing so, however, they have traded the lively "magic" that lies in art, music, dancing, and singing for the stolid and static world of commerce and law.

The illegal smuggling of fairy fruit threatens Lud's security. For Nathaniel Chanticleer, the insanity that results from eating fairy fruit resembles the lifelong struggle he has had in maintaining a veneer of sanity and respect. The Note he initially hears from his lute represents this struggle, and it also signifies his capacity to accept and comprehend the danger to his son and daughter and to the community at large. His response to Ranulph and Prunella's actions is not one of censure, but one of love. His devotion to the rule of law uncovers the duplicitous actions of Clementina Gibberty and Endymion Leer and preserves the sanity and structure of Lud's government; however, it is his "insane" devotion to his family and his willingness to make a hopeless journey to Fairyland to save his children that prove decisive in the survival of Lud-in-the-Mist.

Allowing fairy fruit back into Lud signifies the necessary balance that must exist between fairy and fact, poetry and prose, stability and change. Even the dead from Fairyland (such as Duke Aubrey, one of the "Silent Ones") call out, asking not only to be remembered but also that their memory not be tarnished by lack of use. The dead represent a stimulus for healthy growth and creative change.

—*Jeffrey Cass*

Make Room! Make Room!

Andy Rusch attempts to locate the murderer of a wealthy black marketer in a decaying and overpopulated New York City of 1999

Author: Harry Harrison (1925-   )
Genre: Science fiction—cautionary
Type of work: Novel
Time of plot: 1999
Location: New York City
First published: 1966

The Story

Andy Rusch, a New York City detective, is summoned from his apartment—shared with aged pragmatist Sol Kahn—to provide security for a protest march by outraged "Eldsters," whose ability to survive on their reduced government stipends has reached the breaking point. The march deteriorates into violent chaos when a nearby appliance store is overrun by desperate mobs and riot control police are called in. With this opening, Harry Harrison introduces the true central character of his story: the imploding remains of twentieth century Western civilization, an edifice collapsing under its own weight of numbers, greed, and uncontrolled consumption of the planet's resources.

One of the victims of this pervasive decline is Billy Chung, a son of Taiwanese immigrants who have all been consigned to a claustrophobic existence in Shiptown, a collection of mothballed military transports anchored off Manhattan in the Hudson River. Desperate for food, money, and security, young Billy graduates from petty thievery to manslaughter when a wealthy black marketer discovers the adolescent rifling through his luxurious and heavily fortified apartment. Billy flees empty-handed, fearing pursuit by the law.

The New York City police force is so overburdened that ordinarily a single murder without strong leads would simply be filed as an unsolved and unsolvable crime. Billy's victim, Big Mike O'Brien, was a kingpin of the New York underworld. The ruler of that underworld, Mr. Briggs, fears that O'Brien's death was the opening move in a gambit being orchestrated by a rival crime syndicate. In order to determine whether this is true, Briggs pulls strings in the police department to ensure that a detective is assigned to the investigation on a full-time basis. Andy Rusch is given the job.

Visiting the crime scene, Andy meets Shirl Greene, O'Brien's mistress. Unwilling to have her evicted, the detective arranges for her to remain temporarily in the apartment. A romance develops quickly between Andy and Shirl, who is essentially honest and kind. The investigation goes slowly until Andy learns that Billy Chung had visited O'Brien's apartment on a previous occasion, as a delivery boy.

Andy's attempt to apprehend the wary and petrified Billy at his Shiptown abode fails, turning the murder investigation into a prolonged manhunt. As the search continues, Shirl is forced to move out of her apartment and into the already cramped quarters shared by Andy and Sol. Sol's technical ingenuity helps make their combined lives more bearable.

As the summer heat wave mounts and water shortages and civil unrest increase, their day-to-day existence becomes increasingly difficult. In October, the murderous heat becomes unseasonably bitter cold. The change is part of a meteorological seesaw that causes widespread crop failures. Rumors of coming famine and more water shortages put additional strains on Andy and Shirl's already deteriorating relationship. Things get worse when Sol dies of pneumonia, unable to get medical attention at the overcrowded city hospitals.

Billy, who had found a summer haven with a millennialist hermit named Peter, eventually moves back into the city, taking up lodging in an abandoned Buick that was left to rust where it ran out of gasoline. The intense cold eventually compels him to move back to his home in Shiptown, where, he hopes, the police have ceased to search for him. Andy returns to Shiptown, discovers Billy at his mother's apartment, and, in a confused scuffle, shoots and kills the young fugitive.

Returning home from this debacle, which ultimately will cost him his position as detective, Andy discovers that the obnoxious behavior of his new apartment-mates—the large and revolting Belicher family—have caused Shirl to pack up and leave. Weeks later, on New Year's Eve, he sees her in the street, being escorted—and apparently financially supported—by a group of wealthy individuals. As the New Year celebration in Times Square attains a quality of manic desperation, Peter arrives, hoping to witness the commencement of Armageddon. He is shocked, and his spirit is broken when the accumulated miseries of the world are not purged by holy fire. Andy, now a beat cop, helps the miserable hermit to disappear into the crowd as the electric ticker tape scrolls out wishes for a Happy New Year.

Analysis

The main character in *Make Room! Make Room!* is neither Andy, nor Billy, nor Shirl, but the city of New York and the broader world condition that it implies. Descriptions of ruin and decline receive more description and exploration than do the humans in the story, who move like ghosts through the dying streets.

Harrison's narrative, written in 1966, certainly is dated in its specifics, but its basic proposition that uncontrolled consumption, population growth, and urban expansion will eventually transform cities into concrete hells still retains much of its original validity. Sol's charmingly homespun discourses on the causes of the current disaster have a distinctly pedagogic tenor, a didactic quality that surfaces at various points in the text. This tone is characteristic of many other cautionary dystopian tales that attempt to predict social outcomes and instruct readers. Most early editions of *Make Room! Make Room!* include a three-page bibliography of nonfiction texts that deal with environmental, population, and resource-depletion issues. Readers interested in other novels that focus on these concerns and that were written during roughly the same period may wish to compare Harrison's book with John Brunner's influential *Stand on Zanzibar* (1968).

The film version of *Make Room! Make Room!*, titled *Soylent Green* (1973), departs from the story in the novel in a number of significant ways. Students and instructors cannot rely on it to give them knowledge of the plot or central themes of the book.

—*Charles Gannon*